Gay Su Pinnell
Irene C. Fountas

Literacy Beginnings

A Prekindergarten Handbook

HEINEMANN
Portsmouth, NH

Heinemann
361 Hanover St.
Portsmouth, NH 03801-3912
www.heinemann.com

Offices and agents throughout the world.

Grateful acknowledgment to the following schools for generously allowing Heinemann to photograph their Prekindergarten classrooms: Madeline English School, Everett, MA; Salem State University Preschool, Salem, MA; Malcolm L. Bell School (Lower Bell), Marblehead, MA; and Bentley Elementary School, Salem, MA.

The authors and publisher wish to thank those who have generously given permission to reprint borrowed material:

Pages 16–17, "O" and "P," from *An Alphabet Salad: Fruits and Vegetables from A to Z* by Sarah L. Schuette. Copyright © 2003 by Capstone Press. All rights reserved. Reproduced by permission of Capstone Press.

Illustrations for "Qq" and "Rr" from *A Child's Day: An Alphabet of Play* by Ida Pearle. Copyright © 2008 by Ida Pearle. Reproduced by permission of Houghton Mifflin Harcourt Publishing Company. This material may not be reproduced in any form or by any means without the prior written permission of the publisher.

Pages 4–5 from *Cock-a-Doodle Quack! Quack!* by Ivor Baddiel and Sophie Jubb, illustrated by Ailie Busby. Text copyright © 2007 by Ivor Baddiel and Sophie Jubb, illustrations copyright © 2007 by Ailie Busby. Published by David Fickling Books, an imprint of Random House Children's Books, a division of Random House, Inc. Used by permission of Random House Children's Books, a division of Random House, Inc.

"Ee" from *Creature ABC* by Andrew Zuckerman. Copyright © 2009 by Andrew Zuckerman. Published by Chronicle Books. First published in Creature by Andrew Zuckerman, © 2007, Chronicle Books. Reproduced by permission of the publisher.

Pages 7–8, "Garbage Truck," from *Dig Dig Digging* by Margaret Mayo, illustrated by Alex Ayliffe. Text copyright © 2001 by Margaret Mayo. Illustrations copyright © 2001 by Alex Ayliffe. Reprinted by arrangement with Henry Holt and Company, LLC.

Pages 4–5 from *A Friend Like You* by Tanja Askani. Scholastic Inc./Scholastic Press. Text copyright © 2009 by Scholastic Inc., photograph copyright © 2009 by Fishing4. Reprinted by permission.

Cover and interior photography: Steve Jacob
Color insert classroom photography: Lisa Fowler

Literacy Beginnings: A Prekindergarten Handbook

ISBN 10: 0-325-02876-1
ISBN 13: 978-0-325-02876-7

5 6 7 8 ML 16 15 14

We dedicate this book to the memory of Marie Clay who helped us all look with new eyes at the emerging literacy learning of young children.

ACKNOWLEDGMENTS

In writing this book we have revisited an exciting place—the prekindergarten classroom which is very different from the time we began our own teaching. We have been inspired by gifted teachers and bright, inquiring, eager children. What young children are learning about the world of literacy at three and four years old is truly amazing.

The work on this book began with the creation of *The Continuum of Literacy learning, Pre-K–8: A Guide for Teaching* (2nd Edition, 2011). Changes in the culture within which young children grow prompted changes in prekindergarten, so, we expanded *The Continuum of Literacy learning, K–8* to include a look at emergent literacy learning and from there this book grew. We have been assisted throughout this process by a remarkable group of colleagues and it is our pleasure to thank them.

Most of all, we acknowledge the contributions of teachers and families who have provided the exciting examples of learning that appear in this book. We thank Barbara Summers, Cora Summers, Tiffany Clark, Elizabeth Ward, Kathy Ha, Kris Pelletier, Diane Powell and Sarah Bishins. We'd also like to thank those teachers who generously opened their classrooms to us: Ashley Preston, Peggy Cole, and Kathy Anibal. We especially thank every child named in this book for their wonderful writing and reading examples.

Our work is continually supported by our wonderful, generous colleagues at OSU and Lesley University and we thank them, especially Cynthia Downend, Diane Powell, Kathy Ha, Andrea McCarrier, and Tina Henry who have special interest in the learning of young children. Their expertise and grounded work with teachers in schools inspired our work.

This book could not have been produced without the talented team at Heinemann who work with us on all of our efforts. With are especially appreciative of Mary Lou Mackin for her gifted management, her leadership, and her knowledgeable decision making about every aspect of our work. We are grateful to Zoe Ryder White for her wonderful editing contributions, to Betsy Sawyer-Melodia for her analytic eye and graciousness in all her contributions, to Alan Huisman for all his attention to precision in words, and to Alison Buraczenski and Elizabeth Ward for reading the manuscript and giving their insightful feedback based on their experiences with young children. We also thank Jan Rossi for her timely assistance in the production process. Making this publication readable and beautiful in every detail is the result of the persistent excellence of our dedicated production editor, Michael Cirone, and the never-ending talents of Lisa Fowler. And, as always, we are grateful for the extraordinary vision and leadership of Lesa Scott, President.

Finally, Gay would like to thank Shirley Wahlman and Jackie Harmon who were so giving and generous in helping her as she learned to teach young children. And, we thank Ron Melhado and Ron Heath for their continual support in all our professional work.

Gay and Irene

TABLE OF CONTENTS

Living and Learning in the Prekindergarten Classroom

Strong, literacy-rich prekindergartens are joyful, busy places where children, through play, develop relationships, explore, negotiate, and learn. In our increasingly complex world, prekindergarten teachers face new challenges in creating classrooms that remain play-based yet also prepare students for the literacy-rich world in which they live. This section begins by capturing a typical day in the prekindergarten classroom of three-year-old Jamal and four-year-old Rachel. We then describe several ways to develop a warm, stimulating, and respectful community in a prekindergarten classroom. We also discuss how to promote constructive learning through inquiry. The section concludes with a description of the organized and engaged learning environment in which Jamal and Rachel are flourishing. We suggest a general framework for a literacy-rich prekindergarten, including sample schedules and ideas for infusing the prekindergarteners' day with literacy.

A Day in the Life of Two Prekindergarten Children

It's a February morning in Jamal and Rachel's school, where they spend about three hours a day. Jamal's class has twelve children, and Rachel's has fourteen. Each of their classrooms includes children who represent a variety of native languages and cultures, and most of whom are learning English as a second language.

Jamal

Jamal, three-years-old

*T*hree-year-old Jamal loves coming to school, and is seen dragging his dad down the hall toward the classroom most mornings! Jamal had been in a daycare program for a year before entering prekindergarten in September, but this has been his first year of formal schooling. Jamal is a rambunctious and energetic boy who loves to build in the block area and run outside with his friends. He has learned to control the volume of his voice and his movements to be appropriate for the activity he is participating in. Early in the year, Jamal's teacher worked with him on negotiating social situations with his peers in a calm and kind way. Jamal has recently been passionate about the block center and has been incorporating small plastic dinosaurs and cars into his imaginative play there.

Let's follow Jamal through his prekindergarten day.

TRANSITION: *Entry, Attendance, Table Time*

Jamal heads into the classroom with his dad in tow and quickly hangs his jacket in the cubby with his name on it.

ATTENDANCE After dad says goodbye, Jamal waits while Isaac finds his name in the basket before sifting through for his own. He sticks it on the name chart that says "Who is here today?" and then looks at the other names on the chart. He touches the little pictures that his teacher has attached to each child's name card.

TABLE TIME For morning table time, the tables have materials for children to explore after they unpack and put their names on the felt board. One table has crayons and paper, one has a basket of favorite picture books, and one has a container of magnetic letters. Jamal has recently become very curious about the magnetic letters and heads over to join Catalina and Isaac at that table.

Jamal pulls a few letters out of the basket, one of which is a J—he holds that one for a moment and says "My J" and puts it on his small whiteboard.

Once all twelve students have arrived, Jamal's teacher rings a small bell. The children know this means they have a few more minutes to play before cleaning up. When five minutes have passed, the teacher starts singing the cleanup song ("Clean up, clean up, everybody everywhere, clean up, clean up, everybody do your share"). The children join in and begin putting away their activities. Supplies are stored in bins at the center of the table, labeled with both pictures and words. With a small amount of negotiation, children are able to clean up independently and then find their spots on the rug quickly for the morning community meeting.

Circle Time

COMMUNITY MEETING Once everyone is seated on the rug, the teacher leads the hello song, quickly greeting each child. As they greet Jamal, the children all sing together (to the tune of "Frère Jacques"), "Hello, Jamal. Hello, Jamal. How are you? How are you? We are glad to see you, we are glad to see you. Hello, Jamal."

Jamal participates in circle time

WEATHER, CALENDAR, SHARING After each child has been greeted, Jamal's teacher directs everyone's attention to a job chart on the wall. A quick review of the chart indicates that it is Jamal's turn to help with the calendar and weather chart. He is thrilled to join the teacher next to the calendar, and with her help, he proudly announces, "It is Tuesday, February 16." He selects a picture of the sun and puts it on the 2/16 square on the calendar and tells his classmates, "It is sunny outside today."

Next, the teacher asks if anyone has anything interesting to share. Several children raise their hands and share stories or objects from home. Isaac is excited to talk about the tooth his older sister lost yesterday, enthusiastically trying to wiggle his own teeth back and forth. Jaden tells the class that she helped her mom make baked apples last night: "They were sticky!" After a few more children share stories, the teacher asks the class whether anyone wants to share what they remember about the trip to the market they took last week. The children have already done some drawing and writing about the experience, and the class has started a large, colorful mural showing different parts of a small supermarket. "I went there with my mommy yesterday," says Jamal, "and we bought milk and tomatoes!"

SHARED READING The teacher then directs the children's attention to the poem "To Market, to Market" which is written on large chart paper. The poem was familiar to many of the children before the teacher started using it for shared reading. Now, after reading it for several days, all of the children are able to join in and say the words as the teacher points below them. "I see "To"! shouts Jamal. The teacher invites him up to point to it on the chart.

PHONICS/ORAL GAMES Before leaving the meeting, the teacher engages the children in a quick oral rhyming game in which they clap when they hear rhyming words in the nursery rhyme "Peter, Peter, Pumpkin-Eater."

Projects

While the children are still on their rug spots, the teacher explains the market-related explorations that will be available to them during the block of time set aside for projects for the next few days. Five tables are set up with different projects for inquiry or exploration. The children are very excited after their field trip to a local market, and a visit to the classroom by a grocer.

Jamal and a classmate sort fruits and vegetables

At the apple table, there are three apples, cut in half, each in a separate bowl. Children count the seeds in each apple and record their findings by drawing the apples and (with the help of the teacher's assistant) tallying the number of seeds underneath each drawing. Later, they will share what they have found. One child bangs on the back of an apple half to try to get the seeds out until his teacher shows him how to gently pick them out with his fingers.

At the sorting table, children, including Jamal, sort a variety of fruits and vegetables in a variety of ways—from biggest to smallest; in color categories; and fruits from vegetables. Each child makes a drawing with circles to show how the food has been sorted.

At the poster table, children look through colorful cut out pictures of fruits and vegetables. They then glue the pictures on poster board, the top half of the poster showing the fruits and the bottom half the vegetables. This poster will be displayed in the pretend market.

At the library table, children browse through baskets of books about the market and about fruits and vegetables. At the bookmaking table, the children draw pictures of fruits and vegetables in blank books to make their own books.

TRANSITION: *Clean Up, Sharing, Snack, Library, Bathroom*

CLEAN UP As the block of time for projects is about to end, the teacher uses a patterned handclap (two claps followed by three rapid claps—over and over) to get everyone's attention. The children stop what they are doing, repeat the clap, and look up at her. She compliments them on their hard work and then tells them what they need to do to clean up. (At other times she might sing the first line of a song they have learned, and they join in immediately as they start the cleanup.)

The children begin cleaning up, with some reminders from the teacher and the teacher's assistant about what needs to be done. Jamal and the other children who have been working at the sorting table return all of their drawing supplies to spaces on the shelves, which are labeled with pictures.

SHARING Once their areas are clean, the children meet back on the rug, where Mohammed shares the book he made during project time. The teacher encourages

Jamal participates in sharing time

6

him to tell the class about the colors he used. "It's red," he tells his friends, describing the apple he drew. "Red is my favorite!"

SNACK The children then line up at two sinks and, two at a time, quickly wash their hands in preparation for having a snack. They all sit at their designated spot at a table (each child has made a placemat with her name on it, which has been laminated). The two snack helpers—today it's Richard and Kira—pass out napkins, cups, and small pitchers of water. A teacher's assistant places baskets of pretzels and plates of cut fruit and toothpicks on the tables, and the children help themselves.

After he has finished eating, Jamal, after a quiet reminder from a teacher's assistant, throws away his toothpicks, which he has been using as little stick figures hopping over his melon bites.

LIBRARY After they finish and clean up their snacks, the children know that it is time to make their way to the rug to look at books from the classroom library. Jamal goes right to the "Cars and Trucks" basket and takes out one of his favorites, a board book about tractors that has real wheels on it. He zooms it back and forth for a moment, then starts poring over the pages. "This has a plow," he says to himself.

Jamal chooses a book

BATHROOM As the children look at their books, small groups are called to use the bathroom before outdoor playtime. Once all the children have had a chance to use the bathroom and wash their hands, the teacher starts the cleanup song again, which reminds the children to put the books back in the baskets where they found them, and the class gets ready to go outside.

Outdoor Play

With some help from each other and from the teacher and teacher's assistant, the children bundle up and get in line, holding hands with their line partners as they walk out to the playground. Outside, Jamal runs in circles around the climbing structure with Henry, making dinosaur noises. When it is time to go inside, they line back up, return to their classroom, and remove and hang up their jackets and sweaters.

Choice Time

After outdoor play, Jamal's teacher describes the activities or areas that will be "open" for the children to visit today. In general, she limits the number of activities or areas available during choice time to five or six. As she points to the list of icons (simple pictures that represent each option [see Appendix K for choice time icons.]), she quickly reminds them of the choices: play corner (currently set up as a market), blocks (where street signs are being used for the pretend roads), library (with familiar books, including some about fruits, vegetables, and other foods sold at a market), sand table, and art where children will be painting pictures of fruits

Jamal and his friends at the sand table

and vegetables. Early in the school year, the teacher chose the area that each child went to, but now the children choose for themselves. The maximum number of children allowed in an area is usually four, but some areas, like computer and listening, may only have space for one or two children at a time.

After the children choose their areas (Jamal puts the clothespin with his name next to the sand table icon on the chart), Jamal makes a beeline for the sand table and begins burying plastic dinosaurs under piles of sand. His friend Braden uses a shovel to dig them up.

TRANSITION: *Clean Up, Songs, Chants, Marches, Oral Games*

CLEAN UP The teacher begins singing the cleanup song, and Jamal and his friends quickly clean up the toys and other materials in the sand table and then offer to help others.

CHOICE TIME

Braden
Jamal
Isaac

Luis

Robert
Marisol
Kira

Richard
Mohammed
Catalina

Henry
Jaden

The children make their choices

SONGS The class comes together for songs. They sing "Apples and Bananas" and "Apple Tree."

ORAL GAMES Next, the teacher engages the children in chanting aloud the rhymes "Pease Porridge Hot" and "Jack and Jill," emphasizing the rhyming words in each.

Reading Time

INTERACTIVE READ-ALOUD After the children have a quick stretch, Jamal's teacher tells them about the book she will be reading aloud to them. She has chosen to read a book that is new to the class, *To Market, To Market* (Miranda, 2001). The children are familiar with the nursery rhyme, "To Market, to Market," from circle time, and are thoroughly delighted by the funny twists this version takes. Jamal's teacher asks the children to predict what the woman will do with all of the animals when she gets home. "Play with them!" Jamal offers.

SHARED READING Following the read-aloud, the teacher leads the children in shared reading of several pieces of the interactive writing they have been doing about their field trip to the market. "We saw lots of apples," they chant together. They also read some pages of another big book, *Eating the Alphabet* (Ehlert, 1994).

Choice Time (Literacy)

Before choice time begins, Jamal's teacher reminds the children of some of the ongoing choices that will be available to them as shown on the choice time list. This time, all of the choices support literacy learning. In addition to letter work with the magnetic letters, and computer, children can go to bookmaking to work on making their own books. Bookmaking might be one of the activities children can engage in at the writing table or it might be featured as an independent choice time activity. Other activities children might engage in at the writing table include making greeting cards,

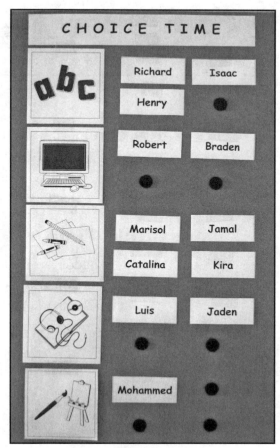

Jamal chooses bookmaking

Jamal works on his book

menus, thank-you notes, lists, observations, posters, signs, and letters. At the art table, one option is for children to create their own market-scene collages using colored paper, markers, and crayons. The listening area is also open for children to listen to a recording of their teacher reading *An Alphabet Salad: Fruits and Vegetables from A to Z* (Schuette, 2003) as they follow along with the pictures in the book.

Jamal chooses to go to bookmaking. As he joins his friends there, some children begin making pictures of things they've read or heard about. Some children are drawing representationally, and others are just beginning to do so. Jamal has decided to draw a picture of a truck and a house from one of his favorite stories.

TRANSITION: *Clean Up*

CLEAN UP The teacher claps her hands to signal that it's time to clean up. The children put away the materials they've been using for choice time. When the room is clean, the teacher asks the children to put on their outdoor clothing and sit on the rug next to their take-home bags.

Circle Time

When the children are settled, the good-bye helper passes out completed artwork, reading aloud the name written on the back of each page. Once everyone is ready, the children sing a good-bye song together ("Good-bye, Jamal, see you later, alligator, in a while, crocodile, good-bye for now") and are sent off to their waiting caregivers. Jamal gives his dad a bear hug, puts on his jacket (with his dad's help), and then drags his dad back out the classroom door.

Rachel, a four-year-old

Rachel

*F*our-year-old Rachel already knows a lot about school.
She has been going to school five days a week since she was three and she knows that it is a place where she can play, make friends, talk, build, pretend, find out interesting things, hear stories, tell her stories, paint— and, of course, read and write. Her teacher writes and Rachel writes; her teacher reads and Rachel reads. Her favorite activity is bookmaking. She already knows that you can do different kinds of reading and writing for different purposes. She knows that sometimes people make lists of things they need to do and that sometimes people write stories about things that happened to them. She knows that people read to get information—her class is studying rocks, and her teacher has been reading the class lots of books that tell about them. She knows that people read signs to figure out where things are.

Let's follow Rachel through her prekindergarten day.

TRANSITION: *Entry, Attendance, Table Time*

Rachel zooms into her classroom, talking a mile a minute. She quickly takes off her sweater, which she hangs on the hook by the label with her name.

ATTENDANCE Rachel sifts through a basket of cards labeled with children's names to find her own and sticks it on a felt board titled "Who is here today?"

"Hawa's not here yet," she notices, after seeing her friend's name card still in the basket.

TABLE TIME Rachel is very much at ease as she walks around the classroom, inspecting the activities her teacher has laid out on the tables. She briefly leans against the first table, where she sees her friends Henry and Josiah sorting magnetic letters. After watching for a moment, Rachel heads to the next table, and types some letters on the computer.

Looking over at the third table, Rachel spots her friends Sophia and Andrew playing a game of Zingo™ and she runs over to join them. "Walking, please," smiles her teacher from across the room. Rachel grins and slows down.

When all of the children have unpacked and had a chance to work at the tables for a few minutes, the teacher claps a pattern (clap…clap… clap/clap/clap) which the children clap back. They know to look up at her and wait for instructions. She tells them to clean up the materials at their tables and come to the rug for community meeting. The children are well-practiced cleaners at this point in the year and take great pride in putting materials away by themselves. Occasionally Rachel's teacher helps children negotiate small conflicts that arise as they put things away, but most often, they work together smoothly.

Rachel watches her classmates sort magnetic letters

Rachel at the computer

Rachel participates in circle time

Circle Time

COMMUNITY MEETING Rachel and her classmates have learned by now that each child sits on her or his own spot on the meeting-area rug (designated by a small carpet sample or a design on the rug). They are (for the most part) able to keep their bodies still and their attention focused on the teacher.

WEATHER, CALENDAR, SHARING After Thomas reports on the weather and Lucy (with the teacher's assistance) tells the class today's date and adds that number to the classroom calendar, Rachel's teacher invites children to share some news from home. She keeps track of who has had a chance to share so that eventually everyone has a chance. Usually she limits the conversation to three or four children sharing, in the interest of time and the children's focus. As Lucas tells the class about how his new gerbil likes to bury itself in the cedar shavings in its cage, Rachel and her classmates turn their heads to look at him, as their teacher has helped them practice.

SHARED READING The teacher then presents a new poem to the class for a shared reading. Since "I Like Red" is a new poem, the teacher reads it aloud first. Rachel and her classmates are familiar with the routine of shared reading, but the teacher reminds them that she will be reading the poem aloud to them first before asking them what they notice. When she asks them to talk about what

Shared reading of poem "I Like Red"

they noticed, the children talk about the color red and refer to a book they previously read with pictures of red fruits and vegetables. Then the teacher invites the class to read the poem with her, pointing to themselves and then to another person on the last line.

PHONICS/ORAL GAMES On the second reading of the poem, the teacher asks children to clap when they say the two words that rhyme. She points out the word *red* at the beginning of the first three lines, reminds children that the *R* is also in Rachel's, Richard's, and Romeo's names, and makes a quick teaching point on hearing sounds in words, listening to the first sound in each. Rachel comes up and finds the word *red* with a little *r* in the last line. Romeo notices the question mark at the end. The teacher asks the children to name some other red foods that they know. "Tomatoes!" says Andrew.

Projects

After circle time, it is project time—a time that the children all look forward to. Rachel's class is in the midst of an inquiry study about rocks. They went rock collecting and had a visit from Lucas' father who is a geologist and studies rocks. During this project period, and for a few days, children are able to work at tables exploring rocks in a variety of ways. One table contains rocks and materials for recording their observations with words or with drawings. Another table has a small scale on it and various sizes of rocks so that children can experiment with trying to balance the scale. A bookmaking table has supplies for making books about rocks—small blank booklets made of folded, stapled pieces of paper, drawing and writing materials, and several simple nonfiction books about rocks. Rachel is working at this table. She spends some time looking through the books and then begins writing her own, talking softly to herself as she works.

TRANSITION: *Clean Up, Sharing, Snack, Library, Bathroom*

CLEAN UP When it is time to stop projects, Rachel's teacher claps a pattern to get the children's attention, and then begins singing the cleanup song: "Clean up, clean up, everybody everywhere, clean up, clean up, everybody do your share." The children join in with the song as they begin cleaning up their tables.

SHARING Once their areas are clean, the children meet back on the rug. Henry shares a drawing that he has done during project time of a particular rock and says, "It has shiny pieces in it."

SNACK When they are finished with sharing, the children wash their hands and go to their table spots for snack. The children talk animatedly as they eat. "I actually ATE a lemon one time," Rachel tells Hawa, crunching on a cracker. (*Actually* is a new word that Rachel has recently acquired and likes to use all the time.) Hawa says, "That's too sour!" The children eat and talk together, and when they finish their snack, they clean up their spots and place their trash in the garbage pail. Rachel tosses out her napkin and walks to the rug with Hawa.

Rachel enjoying snack time

Rachel looks at a book

LIBRARY After snack each day, the children browse through bins and baskets of books the teacher has placed in the meeting area. Rachel starts looking through a selection of books that have been read aloud to the class. Looking carefully at the pictures, she tells the story of *Goodnight Moon* (Brown, 2005) to Billy, who is sitting near her. Rachel especially likes stories with mice in them, so she next picks out *Noisy Nora* (Wells, 1999), a book that her teacher has read a couple of times, and uses the pictures to "read" the story to Billy. They talk happily about Nora's naughtiness and why she's acting the way she is. Next, they look at *Lily's Purple Plastic Purse* (Henkes, 1996).

BATHROOM After the children have all been reading quietly for a while, the teacher calls on pairs of children to use the bathroom.

Outdoor Play

The children get their jackets and sweaters from the closet. In the school yard, Rachel and her friends run and laugh. Rachel, Hawa, and Ishai pretend to be baby mice hiding in their "nest" under the climbing structure.

Choice Time (Literacy)

Before choice time begins, Rachel's teacher reminds the children of some of the ongoing literacy choices that will be available to them. In general, she limits the number of choices to four or five. In addition to library time, letter work (where children are working with the teacher's assistant to sort picture cards by first letter), and play corner, the listening area is also open for children to listen to a recording of their

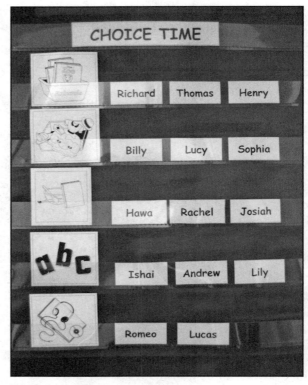

Rachel chooses book activities

teacher reading *Stone Soup* (Muth, 2003) as they follow along with the book. The book activity area (Response to Literature) is also open, where children are encouraged to respond to books that have been read aloud with their own pictures (and, if relevant, words).

Rachel is excited to go to the book activity area. She knows that she can draw and write in response to a book she has heard her teacher read aloud, or that she can choose another activity. Rachel goes back to the *Noisy Nora* book she loves for inspiration. Her drawing (see picture above) is full of action and represents the story. "This is the lamp she knocked down," Rachel says. "This shows it standing up, then it tipped down. This is the lamp that fell down; she's pulling it. I'm going to write a word, too." The lamp is shown falling over three times; to the right the little naughty mouse is pulling it over. Rachel has written part of her name in conventional capital letters. She also writes a long scribble to represent her "word."

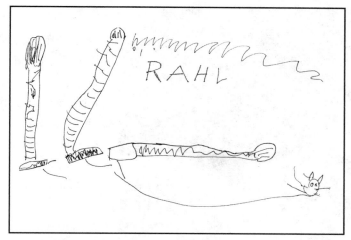

Rachel's drawing based on *Noisy Nora*

> **TRANSITION:** *Clean Up, Songs, Chants, Marches, Oral Games*

The teacher uses her sequence of claps to get the children's attention and then provides them with specific directions about how to clean up. The class meets back on the rug and the teacher leads a quick round of the game Simon Says before asking the children to sit on their rug spots and get their bodies ready for read-aloud.

Reading Time

INTERACTIVE READ-ALOUD After the children are settled and ready, their teacher reads aloud *A Good Day*, by Kevin Henkes (2007), which has large, bold print. The children have heard this simple story before; they know that each animal starts out having a bad day that changes to a good day. Rachel chants along with the "but then" on page 11, anticipating the turn of events. And all the children join in on the last page: "Mama! What a good day!"

Rachel drawing

Choice Time

In addition to blocks, the play corner (which is currently stocked with items found in a veterinarian's office along with some stuffed dogs and cats), water table, art, and music, Rachel's teacher also tells them about the science table, which contains lemons and oranges for children to touch, smell, and draw. After explaining the choices and activities, the teacher invites children to choose the area they'd like to go to first. (Sometimes the teacher allows the children to choose which area they'd like to go to, and sometimes she chooses for them.)

The choice time chart has simple pictures (attached with Velcro) identifying the available areas for the day. Each child has a name card that can be attached to the chart below the area the child chooses. The chart also indicates how many students can fit in each area—usually a maximum of four. When it is her turn to choose, Rachel puts her name in the science box, along with Romeo's and Sophia's. After the children are sent off to their areas (one area at a time), Rachel and her friends busily start touching and smelling the lemons and oranges at the table. Some have been cut into pieces, and some are whole. Rachel knows that part of the science activity is showing her discoveries on paper, so after she spends some time touching and examining the fruit, she takes a piece of paper and begins to draw. Her teacher passes by and asks Rachel what she noticed about the fruit. "They both have bumps," says Rachel, who is drawing exaggerated bumps on her picture. "I wonder if you might want to write that, the word *bumps*," muses her teacher, and when Rachel agrees, she helps her listen for and record the *B* for *bumps* on her paper.

Rachel chooses science

Children going out the door

TRANSITION: *Clean Up*

CLEAN UP Following the same procedure as they did when cleaning up from the earlier choice time, the children put their materials away or stack them in the center of their tables.

Circle Time

The class meets together on the rug for a good-bye song, "Good-bye, so long, farewell, my friend. Good-bye, so long, farewell!" Rachel's teacher opens the classroom door to let the children's caregivers in. Rachel sees her babysitter and meets her at her coat hook. She is already talking about her day as she pulls the zipper up on her pink sweater.

What we can learn from these vignettes

These vignettes reveal that Jamal and Rachel have opportunities to learn many important things. For example:

- School is a place where people work, talk, and play together.
- You can learn many new things about your world at school.
- You help others at school.

- You do your part to keep the classroom clean.

- You learn how to care for classroom materials

- At school, you discover more about the things you encounter in your life.

- You learn how to take turns.

- You learn how to talk nicely to others.

- You learn how to share with others.

- You can tell your stories, and your classmates can tell their stories.

- Stories are told the same way again and again.

- Print is different from pictures; it represents language that you can say.

- You can tell your own stories by drawing and writing.

- You can make books to share your ideas.

- You can draw to show your thinking.

- You can talk to show your thinking.

- There are letters in your name and you can write them.

- Some words sound alike; you can say and hear the sounds in words.

- You can read all together by pointing at the words (a beginning understanding that one spoken word matches one written word).

The classroom offers every child a richness and a social environment that promotes confidence, respect, and curiosity.

Nurturing Young Learners

Three- and four-year-old children discover the world through play. They are active and curious, constantly exploring and solving problems and, in the process, are using language to share their thinking. The language used by these young children reflects the most amazing accomplishments of their early years of life. In addition to all the cognitive and motor learning—walking, manipulating objects, learning what the world is all about—they have also learned language. They have progressed from simple babbling to constructing meaningful statements and questions, using appropriate and interesting intonation, and entering into the give-and-take of conversation. Even more important, they have *learned ways to learn* more about language and how it works.

All of this learning has happened without conscious or direct teaching. Meaningful interactions with their families have provided the support and input they needed to put it all together. Children all over the world go through this language-learning process within their homes and communities. There are some differences, but so many children go through the same process that scientists have concluded that human beings have a natural tendency to learn language (Lindfors, 1999).

Language learning is so important! As we learn language, we learn many ways to use it. Language and play are the child's major tools for learning everything about the world. Language and play are also the most important tools for early literacy learning.

You may think it surprising to be talking about children this young learning to read and write. However, the knowledge that forms the *foundation* for reading and writing is built throughout early childhood through play, language, and literary experiences. A good starting point for each child is his own talk—the sounds, words, and sentence structure.

While they listen to and talk about stories and react to every new and interesting thing they find in the world, children are also learning to understand. As they interact with others, they are learning the structure or "grammar" of language that will be a great resource for learning how to read and write. As they enter into dramatic play with others, they are learning about dialogue and characters.

Taking turns

Through their experiences, they add daily to their oral vocabularies—words they know as they speak and listen. As they play with other children and talk with adults, they learn the "rules" of conversation—how to listen and respond appropriately, how to "get a turn" without interrupting, and how to talk about (and attend to) the same topic for at least a few minutes. As they talk, they begin to see how ideas are related to each other and learn how to sustain attention and curiosity.

Every child arrives at school with a different set of understandings and has developed in a unique way. No single child can be described by any single box or row in a chart, but you can see some patterns in the many aspects of physical, social, and instructional growth over time (see the developmental chart in Appendix F). A child may develop more quickly in some areas than others. Keep in mind that a child can enter a program for three-year-olds having just turned three or may turn four during the year. A child in a program for four-year-olds may have just turned four or may turn five during the year. We hope the patterns will help you grasp a perspective on trends while honoring the uniqueness of each child.

Entry to Literacy

This book chronicles the exciting adventure of introducing young children to reading and writing. Think about how young children see the world: everything they meet is new and wonderful and interesting. They play with these new objects, words, and ideas and discover more and more of them each day. Think about a three-year-old such as Jamal finding out how tall he can build a block tower or sorting his cereal into color groups. The same three-year-old might notice the *J* for *Jamal* in magnetic letters on the refrigerator door or in a note from his grandmother, and might delight in finding all the *J*s in a collec-

Children playing market

tion of magnetic letters. As a three-year-old, Jamal might draw his family and label everyone with a J, one of the only letters he recognizes and writes. As a four-year-old, Jamal might write a "message" that has a number of *J*s, *A*s, *M*s, and *L*s in it, all representing his meaning although not phonetically representing words. He might take a memo pad and marker and go around to family members "taking orders" for dinner. He might draw a picture of his family with one-letter labels for every member and even write his own name with all the letters. During these years, children do not distinguish between playing, reading, and writing. It all involves curiosity, learning, discovery, and excitement. We want to carry that excitement into the prekindergarten classroom!

In this book, we describe the language and literacy learning of prekindergarten children in detail. We present a continuum of literacy learning in six categories and describe many examples of effective teaching. The appendices include songs, rhymes, poems, fingerplays, projects, and lists of books, as well as thirty-five lessons for helping prekindergarten children enter the world of literacy in joyful, engaging ways. We've also included a color photo insert showing several examples of literacy-rich PreK classrooms and specific classroom areas; and examples of children's early writing efforts. This book is intended to support the teachers of young children in prekindergarten and learning centers. It may also be of help to families who want to support their prekindergarteners at home.

Growing Up Literate:

Prekindergartens for the Future Generation

*"If we teach today, as we taught yesterday,
we rob children of tomorrow."*

—John Dewey

Today's prekindergarten classroom is different from yesterday's. Formerly, prekindergarten curriculum consisted mainly of play, snack, manners, story time, and rest period, with music and art added. All of these continue to be important, but today, rich literacy experiences are woven throughout, providing many opportunities for learning through play. For example, children may "read" books or newspapers in the house corner, use menus in pretend restaurants, observe and even create signs in pretend stores. The playtime and social training of traditional prekindergartens has not been replaced but rather infused with literacy.

Children's play reflects the world around them—a world that teems with print. Three- and four-year-olds naturally begin to absorb and recognize the print they see every day. They notice symbols and signs for their favorite restaurants, point out letters in street signs, connect pictures and print on menus, find the cereal they like in the supermarket. All of these actions are signs of children's growing literacy development (Burns and Griffin, 1999).

In today's prekindergarten, teachers work to be intentional as they read aloud, inviting children to discuss stories and share their thinking. They encourage children to label their drawings and paintings and compose and make their own books even before they can write conventionally. They plan sequences of activities that encourage *inquiry*—talking, observing, wondering, and exploring focused topics of interest. All of these changes mean greater opportunities for expanding thinking and language as children grow up literate in our schools.

Long before entering school, most children encounter a great deal of meaningful print in their homes and communities. Many families regularly read stories aloud to their young children and encourage them to use magnetic letters or write to accompany their drawings. Environmental print is everywhere. Television, computers, smartphones, videos, and DVDs introduce new experiences and ideas. Many young children have an amazing degree of tech savvy, beyond that of some adults!

Children are curious about literacy and will naturally engage with reading and writing in a playful way if it is presented not as hard work but as an interesting part of their physical and social world. Enjoyable real-life experiences with literacy are part of high-quality prekindergarten classrooms. For those children who have not had many opportunities with language or print in the home, the prekindergarten classroom can level the playing field by creating those opportunities in school.

The Emergent Reader and Writer

In preschool, children are helped to make meaning and comprehend their world. Their experiences provide a foundation for language and literacy development that will continue throughout the grades.

Clay (2001) described how young children develop systems to process "nonvisual information" prior to schooling. At home with their family and in their community, they learn how to use the system of oral language. They also learn how to understand stories,

build their background knowledge, know what many words mean, and recognize many objects and places that are foundations for learning more. In order to engage with print, children learn how to interpret symbols ("visual information") and build a literacy processing system. By linking their oral language system to the symbols that represent the language, prekindergarten teachers can help children build on their existing systems and add new ones by providing a variety of opportunities to interact with print.

The Developmentally Appropriate Prekindergarten Classroom

While acknowledging that prekindergarteners live in a far different world today, we also want to take care that the language and literacy experiences we provide at school are appropriate for the young children we are teaching. Many years ago, some assumed that prekindergarteners were not "ready" for literacy. This "readiness" view assumed that until children were physically and neurologically mature enough, exposure to reading and writing was time wasted and could even be harmful. We now know that exposure to rich literacy experiences throughout early childhood has a tremendous positive effect on young children, and delaying these kinds of experiences until children are of school age can severely limit ultimate achievement (National Association for the Education of Young Children, 1998).

Developmentally based early childhood programs place the learning of the child at the center. This view contrasts with a fixed curriculum, which provides a sequential list of language or literacy skills through which each child will pass. Forcing young children to sit through meaningless drill would indeed be harmful. Instead, children need to explore. In place of a rigid, developmentally inappropriate curriculum, we need to provide a truly child-centered, literacy-rich prekindergarten experience. The foundation of our teaching is our understanding of the unique development of each child, as we bring our instruction to the cutting edge of that child's development. We provide opportunities for growth while carefully observing children's language, reading, and writing behaviors.

Finding Each Child's Learning Zone

The Russian psychologist Vygotsky (1978, 1986) showed how teaching can lead development forward. He helped us understand that we can identify and intervene at a child's "zone of proximal development" (ZPD) to help her develop new literacy competencies. Examine the following diagram:

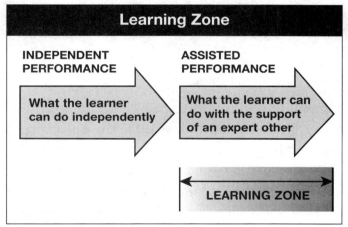

Figure 1.1 Learning zone

The lower boundary, independent level, shows what a child can do alone. The ZPD has an upper boundary, assisted performance, which shows what a child can do in cooperation with a more knowledgeable other, the teacher. This is called the *learning zone* because it is where the teacher targets instruction and assessment. Learning takes place as the child links what is known to new information and skills, and development moves forward. It happens every day—all day!

Prekindergarteners come to school with various backgrounds, personalities, and experiences—so the children in every class represent a variety of learning

zones. Your challenge (and we hope great pleasure) is to observe each child's development and provide opportunities that lead learning forward and result in each child's unique pattern of growth. Parents naturally do this all the time without realizing it. A child learning to dress herself, for example, is not presented with a shirt and shorts and expected to struggle into them alone. Her mother might instead hand her the shirt with the sleeves positioned in such a way to make it easier for her to slide her arms in on her own. "That's right," she might say, "push those arms through!" As the child takes in the mother's instruction, she becomes more able to do the task alone. The support given is not so much that the mother has taken over the task but not so little that the child is frustrated. This balance is what we aim for in teaching young children.

A joint position statement of the International Reading Association and the National Association for the Education of Young Children, adopted in May 1998, provides this rationale for providing instruction in prekindergarten classrooms:

> The ability to read and write does not develop naturally, without careful planning and instruction. Children need regular and active interactions with print. Specific abilities required for reading and writing come from immediate experiences with oral and written language. Experiences in these early years begin to define the assumptions and expectations about becoming literate and give children the motivation to work toward learning to read and write. From these experiences children learn that reading and writing are valuable tools that will help them do many things in life. (3)

In the position statement, these two professional organizations recommend:

- Reading aloud to children and setting up a rich classroom library.

- Creating an environment that includes many signs and labels.

Figure 1.2 Play corner

- Enhancing children's exposure to and concepts about print through the use of big books.

- Helping children learn the alphabetic principle (the fundamental insight that there is a relationship between letters and sounds) by providing opportunities for them to explore letters and sounds in many ways.

- Helping children learn about the sounds in words (phonemic awareness) through language play, games, rhymes, and rhythmic activities.

- Giving children regular opportunities to express themselves on paper (drawing and writing) without demanding "correct" spelling and proper handwriting.

The Continuum of Literacy Learning, PreK in Section 7 comprises many lists of basic understandings that we can expect young children to develop by the time they enter kindergarten if they have strong adult support. These understandings bridge curriculum areas. The categories include: Interactive Read-Aloud; Shared and Performance Reading; Writing About

Reading; Writing; Oral, Visual, and Technological Communication; and Phonics, Spelling, and Word Study. The continuum is designed to guide planning and teaching. The resources in the appendices of this book also include a wonderful list of poems, rhymes, and songs (Appendix A), a list of read-aloud text sets to use throughout the year for three- and four-year-olds (Appendix B), starting points for several engaging, age-appropriate inquiry projects (Appendix C), and thirty-five simple lessons to help get you started with shared reading, interactive writing, and other literacy activities (Appendix D). Some of these lessons can be used over and over with different materials.

The Essential Role of Play in Learning

As we've already said, the rich literacy experience that we advocate in prekindergarten classrooms does not mean teaching children discrete prereading skills by drilling them in meaningless words or having them fill in worksheets. Nor should standardized tests be the basis for making decisions about young children's education. We do not recommend eliminating or even reducing play.

Children, especially very young children, learn through play. Play enhances language and literacy learning. Unfortunately, children in some classrooms now spend far more time being taught and tested on literacy and math skills than they do learning through play and exploration, exercising their bodies, and using their imaginations (Miller and Almon, 2009). Miller and Almon claim that the need for raising test scores, accelerated by Reading First in the last decade, pushed play out of kindergarten. They argue for the many benefits of play in kindergarten and also warn against prekindergarten following the "no-play" trend.

Play has a critical role in supporting the child's social, emotional, and intellectual development. It is the basic activity of early childhood and is essential for development and learning. Language and literacy, as well as science, social studies, mathematics, and the arts, support and enrich the young child's play. When young children play, they are self-motivated and actively engaged. They often engage in pretend play, or play that fosters symbolic development through fantasy. Play is the fuel for their growth, so the prekindergarten program is rooted in play to

"lead development forward" (Vygotsky, 1978, 1986). Through play, critical understandings are gained. Play is an absolutely necessary component of any excellent preschool classroom.

A prekindergarten curriculum that values play needs to achieve an important balance between teacher-initiated and teacher-guided (structured) play and child-initiated and child-directed (free) play. Both are essential. Choice and ample time to complete activities are critical for young children. Teachers need to design play activities that support language and literacy learning and are balanced by free play that emerges from children's interests.

Some children, especially if they have not had many literacy experiences prior to entering prekindergarten, need extra support in early childhood programs. They need a solid introduction to books so that they understand why written language is important. They need to engage in conversation and storytelling to expand their oral language. Songs and rhymes increase their awareness of the sounds in words. Above all, they need the opportunity to use language. All children need these opportunities, and it is possible to provide them within a rich and joyful prekindergarten environment in which reading, writing, and talking are part of play and often *become* play.

Key Understandings to Think About

✳ In today's world, prekindergarteners are surrounded by print to read and real reasons to write.

✳ Today's preschools reflect the world children experience.

✳ Prekindergarten experiences must be developmentally appropriate for children, enjoyable, and promote learning.

✳ The child's "learning zone" shows what she can do with the teacher's help.

✳ Teaching is most effective when it supports children who are working in the "learning zone."

✳ Play has a very important role in young children's learning of language and literacy.

✳ Helping young children develop a foundation for literacy often requires skillful teaching.

Notes

Building a Community of Learners

"Children learn and develop best when they are part of a community of learners—a community in which all participants consider and contribute to one another's well being and learning."

—Carol Copple and Sue Bredekamp

Prekindergarten is the first time most children are expected to interact and learn with others outside their families or extended communities. Some have had few opportunities to be part of a larger group of children; many have been the center of attention in their homes. Many are away from their parents or caregivers for the first time. The separation can be difficult and will require support and attention during the school year. This may be the first time a child has to learn to respond to limits and respect the authority of someone (the teacher) other than the primary caregiver. Children come to school with unique personalities and different strengths, abilities, interests, and temperaments. They have different styles of interaction. Some are timid and watchful, spending time at the edges of activities before feeling comfortable jumping in. Some dive in immediately, holding court in the block area, talking a mile a minute! Your challenge is to create a community in which all of these wonderfully different personalities learn to cooperate, share materials, and demonstrate appropriate group behavior.

Communication is basic to success in school and throughout life. The Continuum of Literacy Learning, PreK (Section 7) lists specific goals in the Oral, Visual, and Technological Communication section. But young children also use language to learn in all areas of the continuum.

A high-quality prekindergarten experience is invaluable in preparing children to thrive in future years of school. They not only stretch their cognitive abilities, expand their language abilities, add to their content knowledge, and learn a great deal about reading and writing, but also learn how to be part of a learning community, and that is no small accomplishment. The communication skills they learn and practice in prekindergarten will also serve them well throughout their entire lives.

Prekindergarteners learn to:

- Listen and talk to others.
- Gradually expand their ability to talk to a group.
- Play alongside and eventually with others.
- Participate in whole-group and small-group activities.
- Appreciate the accomplishments of others.
- Take turns.
- Help others work or play.
- Follow simple routines.
- Read, sing, and chant in unison with a group.
- Feel proud as their work is displayed and appreciated by others.

Supporting Social Skills

With positive modeling and attention, all prekindergarteners can learn how to take turns, listen to each other quietly without interrupting, and manage disappointment. When you are teaching children how to take turns in conversation, passing a soft physical object such as a beanbag to hold when it is their turn to talk can be an effective and concrete reminder for young children who are often very literal-minded.

Children can learn to respect the tools, materials, and toys in the classroom, respect and enjoy the work of their classmates, and speak kindly. When these structures and expectations are in place, the children will be happier, you will be happier, and your room will develop into a warm community of learners.

Early in the school year, create structures for interactions like sharing materials or taking turns that assure success. Many young children have very little experience being part of a group, waiting in line to wash their hands, regulating their bodies as they move about the room, or taking turns with a basket of crayons. You can teach them positive routines for doing things they have never done before. For example, you can make simple charts with picture clues to remind children of the steps to follow when they come into the room in the morning, or what to try when they have a conflict with a friend. Children will be empowered to use these kinds of classroom tools independently and will even, as the year progresses, remind each other to use them ("Sammy, your backpack is still on! Don't forget to look at the morning chart!"). The clearer and more organized you can be about presenting routines and social expectations, the more readily your students will respond.

Creating Community

Creating a learning community is a major goal of prekindergarten teaching and a crucial one for early literacy. Reading and writing are based on (and also create) community. We all belong to the global community of literate people. Writers intend to send messages to readers. Readers are brought together by discussing books. A published writer might find satisfaction and self-awareness in his own writing, but he also sends messages to his readers. Readers take in those messages and filter them through their own understandings, experiences, beliefs, and values, and build more understanding when they talk about their thinking with others. Writers and readers may never meet, but communication takes place and community is formed.

A similar process can take place in a vibrant, literacy-infused prekindergarten classroom. The young child draws for his own satisfaction—whether representing his world and experiences or just loving the marks on paper—and because he is in a community, he learns how to share and talk about his work with others. He notices and appreciates the work of others as well. Over time, these interactions contribute to a feeling of trust, comfort, and the feeling of a supportive family.

The classroom environment supports authentic social interactions and discussions as children work side by side and in groups. They build on the knowledge and reactions of one another and the adults with whom they work. Young children need to feel safe and comfortable in the predictable (yet endlessly interesting) environment of the classroom. One way you support your students' ability to participate positively in your learning community is by establishing routines and a predictable daily structure. Children also benefit from a clear organization of space and materials, consistency and clarity in expectations, proactive discipline, and continuous positive reinforcement.

Getting the Community Started

Your classroom community takes time to develop. We recommend spending the first several weeks of prekindergarten demonstrating, prompting, and reinforcing positive social interactions and conventions. When you take the time to focus on these critical elements, the rest of the school year will be far more productive and enjoyable. Don't feel as though you are "wasting time" by keeping those beginning weeks simple. It is perfectly reasonable to teach the same lesson—about capping the markers until you hear the click, or waiting until you are called on to speak, or saving your jumping for outside play—several times. You can prevent many potential difficulties by ensuring that all of

your students have internalized classroom expectations early on.

A critical element of learning is self-regulation. Instead of continually saying "no" or correcting inappropriate behavior, consider modeling appropriate responses:

- Show children how to stop and think about their behavior.
- State the behavior you are expecting before the child begins.
- Use a quiet, firm tone that recognizes how the child feels (*I can see . . .*).
- State positively what you want the child to do ("Wait for your turn.").
- Give the child some choices that are positive behaviors. ("You can wait for a turn or try the blocks for now.") (Knoff, 2001).

When you read aloud *My Preschool* (Rockwell, 2008), you have a wonderful way to introduce young students to life in prekindergarten and have a great jumping-off place for engaging discussions. Rockwell does an excellent job of showing what children do in preschool and how problems are handled (see Figure 2.1).

One of the most effective ways to build community and foster positive classroom behavior is to involve the children in making decisions. Many teachers ask their students to help create classroom "rules," guidelines, or agreements of how we will work together. When children have a say in the way things go in the classroom, they often feel more invested in following classroom guidelines. If you are creating guidelines with your class, focus on describing the behavior you want—not on a list of "don'ts." "Walking feet inside" instead of "Don't run." This process not only helps the classroom feel like *everyone's* community but also provides great opportunities for shared and interactive writing! (The next chapter describes the importance of social, active, and meaningful learning experiences.)

Figure 2.1 Page layout of *My Preschool*

When we were building with blocks, Will got mad and knocked all my blocks down. I don't know why.
    Miss Andrews had a private talk with him, and he said he was sorry.

Using Circle Games to Build Community

Circle games—an endless variety of language games, action songs, and sharing activities—are a wonderful way to build community and strengthen relationships. In three-year-old Michael's classroom the children begin their community meeting with a clapping chant. Each child's name is used in turn, showing that every member of the community is valued. The children respond glee-fully; they enjoy hearing their own names in the mouths of their classmates and learn their classmates' names in the process. Michael is often so excited to hear his name that he dances in his seat as the chant is said!

Welcome Chant

Michael's here today.

Michael's here today.

We all clap for Michael.

Michael's at school today!

We suggest twenty-five different ways to use circle games to create community (see Figure 2.2 and Chenfeld, 2002, 130–31). Consider using them in the nooks and crannies of the day.

The Benefits of Creating Community

Creating a genuine community of learners has several positive outcomes. Classroom management is easier. An orderly classroom makes it possible for children to attend better and learn more, to participate in the learning experiences you provide without distraction and anxiety. They also come to understand and enjoy one another's quirks and differences. But even more important, children learning within a strong commu-nity will be building skills in collaboration and respect that they will use all their lives.

Twenty-Five Ways to Use Circle Games to Create Community

1. Sit in a circle and roll a ball to each child in turn. The child who receives the ball answers a question like, "What is your favorite food?"

2. Pass a soft ball or other object around the circle. Each child says his own name and/or the name of the person he passes the ball to.

3. Give each child his own place in the circle for a week. Children return to this spot every time they sit in a circle to hear a story or sing. After they know their spots, play "mix-up": have the children walk around and at a sign go quickly back "home" and sit down.

4. Stand in a circle and move from a "tall circle" (stretching high) to a "short circle" (crouching down low) and back again.

5. Walk in tight to make a small circle; then walk slowly backward to make the circle big (repeat).

6. Have children walk around in a circle. Call out commands such as "tiptoe circle," "marching circle," "hopping circle." (Teach one action at a time.)

7. Sit in a circle to sing and enact finger plays, chants, songs, and poems (see Appendix A).

8. Play music and have children move in time with it—marching around, marching in place, putting feet in and out, turning around.

9. Act out songs like "The Hokey Pokey" or "Teddy Bear, Teddy Bear."

10. Take a phrase or expression (such as "you're welcome" or "good morning") and move around the circle having children say it in turn in different ways—soft, loud, mad, like a mouse.

11. Have children hold hands and walk slowly around in a circle, getting faster and faster and then slower and slower until they stop.

12. If children know a word or phrase in two or more languages (such as *hello, my name is, thank you,* or *good-bye*), go around the circle with each child saying the word or phrase, alternating languages. (You can do the same with words in one language that are opposites or that mean the same.)

13. Choose one child to be the leader. Children sit or stand in the circle and do what the leader does.

14. Pretend to be different plants or animals—train engines, trees, flowers, fish, rabbits.

15. Engage in many different actions while sitting in a circle—clapping hands, shaking hands with the person next to you, slapping thighs, touching your nose, making a funny or mean face, blinking eyes, etc.

16. Pass an imaginary object around the circle as each child thinks about how the object looks and feels.

17. After hearing a favorite story read aloud, children pass the book around the circle, telling something they liked about the book (allow children to pass if they can't think of something to say at the time).

18. Go around the circle, asking children to name an item in a category (for example, food, parts of the body, things that grow, things that go fast). Allow children to repeat words others have said.

19. Tell or read a story appropriate for hand movements (for example, *Going on a Bear Hunt*). Have children listen and move while in a circle.

20. Place one child in the center while the others, holding hands, walk around in a circle. At a signal (such as a bell or clap), the child in the center does something.

    All the other children stop and imitate the child in the center. Then the child in the center chooses someone to take his place.

21. Make a circle inside a circle, some children in the inner circle, some in the outer. At a signal they turn to face the child opposite them, shake (or clap) hands, and then turn their backs to each other (repeat).

22. Have a "circle without words." Use sign language or think up friendly gestures for words and phrases like *hello, thank you, you're welcome, I'm happy, come with me, let's read a book, let's make a picture,* or any familiar activity like running or playing ball.

23. Have children sing the alphabet song while you point to the letters on a chart.

24. Have children hold individual cards with letters of the alphabet. (You can limit the letters to just a few with duplicates.) When the name of the letter is called, the child or children holding it bring it to a pocket chart. (Be sure they are correctly placed directionally.) When all the letters have been placed in the pocket chart, say, "James, go and get an A." Repeat until all of the children have a letter again.

25. Invite children to think of new ways to play in the circle.

Figure 2.2 Ways to use circle games to create community

Key Understandings to Think About

* For most young children (especially three-year-olds), working and playing with others in a group requires new learning.

* The preschool experience can be highly supportive in helping children learn what it means to be part of a learning community.

* Many important behaviors need to be taught to most young children (for example, taking turns).

* Creating a learning community is a major goal for the prekindergarten teacher.

* Routines and games help children learn how to be part of a learning community.

* Children who know how to work and play well with others will benefit from these understandings all their lives.

Notes

CHAPTER

3

Promoting Constructive Learning:
Engaging Children in Inquiry

"Ask real questions, questions you yourself wonder about—
what I call acts of inquiry."

—JUDITH WELLS LINDFORS

Walking into the stimulating, busy community of a literacy-rich prekindergarten classroom, you will not see teachers simply sitting and telling children new facts and ideas. You will see children throughout the room engaged in a variety of activities, each designed to allow children to construct meaning for themselves. Learning is not a simple process of transferring knowledge from one person to another. Of course, children do gain knowledge from conversation with adults, but they also put many understandings together for themselves, and this *construction* is the heart of meaningful learning. At age four, Elizabeth, in a signed drawing (see Figure 3.1), put together pieces of a memory—a picnic with a beautiful sun. She has constructed a memory and is communicating her thinking.

Constructive learning is very important at any grade level, but perhaps especially so in prekindergarten classrooms since they are paving the way for children's future school experiences. We do not want children to see school as a place where they simply "take in" facts (although of course they do that in the process of learning). We want them to develop very powerful ways of "learning *how* to learn" and to see

Figure 3.1 Elizabeth's drawing "Orange Sun Picnic"

school as a place for exploration and discovery. As children develop the processes of learning constructively, much more is going on than the simple accumulation of facts. The brain is actually expanding its capability.

The behaviors and understandings described in the Continuum of Literacy Learning, PreK (Section 7) are the result of exploration and discovery. Young children represent their understandings through talk, drawing, and even emergent writing. As you observe young children learn, you will notice many of the competencies listed in the continuum.

Engaging the Learner in Constructing Knowledge

Language is the best example of constructive learning. No one directly "teaches" children to talk, yet they typically learn language by about age five! Before the age of three, they understand connected language all around them. Toddlers learning to speak start with one-word utterances, like *dog* or *no*, and quickly begin to put

words together in short phrases. Without any explicit teaching, simply by listening to the talk all around them, they internalize the rules of language and how learning works. Typical statements like *more cookie, more milk, more nana (banana)* are not just random. They mean that the child has learned a language "rule" and is using it to his advantage. In this stage of language acquisition, he is experimenting and finding out if the listener has understood his meaning. Marie Clay, a distinguished New Zealand child psychologist, has stated that every utterance a child makes represents a hypothesis about how language works that is being tested through conversation.

We can see examples of this in the mistakes that adults delight in hearing. When a young child makes statements like *I falled* or *I holded it*, it means that she has internalized the "rule" for signaling past tense. Later, the irregular uses of the past tense verb will be understood. The child has not heard any adult say *falled* or *holded*; yet she has applied a rule she is learning because she is constantly constructing knowledge of the language. At ages three and four, she continues to encounter and use new language at home and at prekindergarten. Language is a self-extending system; that is, it allows the learner to learn more simply by using it. It is the first self-extending system a child builds. Literacy will be next.

Creating a Program to Support Constructive Learning

Every element of the prekindergarten instructional program can support constructive learning. When children play with blocks, they are constructing understandings about spatial relationships that will eventually help them learn about how buildings and bridges are constructed. *No, put the big blocks on the bottom!* a child might say. As they pour sand or water, they construct understandings about how materials behave. *Look, all the drops are back together again!* As they draw, they develop important understandings about how to place marks on pages to represent their ideas. As they hear stories, they construct understandings of how narrative stories "work"—beginning, problem, series of events, ending. As they work with their names using magnetic letters or cards, they construct their understanding of what a word is—it looks the same everywhere you see it and the order of letters makes a difference! *There's my name—Marta! And over there, by the line-up spots! And there it is again, by my hook!*

The Process of Inquiry

You can support constructive learning through engaging prekindergarteners in the process of inquiry (see Figure 3.2). Inquiry is the kind of *focused* play you do when pursuing a topic of interest. If, for example, you are looking into your family's history, you may use resources like the Internet or visit particular places with stores of information. You may

read historical accounts of relevant time periods or biographies of people your family members might have known. You might engage in a similar process as you plan a garden or do some research on a place you plan to visit. You seek information and wonder more, trying to understand, yet keeping new possibilities open. Scholars of all kinds engage in inquiry as part of their work, and they often report enjoying their work as much as play.

In later schooling, students will be expected to gather and organize information around a topic and sometimes present it in reports and multimedia presentations. So what does this look like in prekindergarten? It may seem that the inquiry process is much too complicated for three- and four-year-olds, but in fact, their natural curiosity has prompted them to explore, discover, and gather information for several years. They have observed, touched—even tasted, whether appropriate or not—the materials in their environment, and they have used language to begin to talk about what they have learned. Through classroom inquiry projects you set the scene for a focused study and guide them in the process, but they do the thinking!

Inquiry Process

1. Identify real questions, problems, or topics of interest.

2. Make a plan for finding out and take action.

3. Gather resources or engage in a variety of experiences to learn more about the question, problem, or topic.

4. Analyze, summarize, and sometimes record the information (talk, write, draw).

5. Draw conclusions and share findings.

(Lindfors, 1999)

Figure 3.2 The Inquiry Process

Two Types of Inquiry

There are two kinds of inquiry: information seeking and wondering (Lindfors, 1999). In information seeking, we engage others or use artifacts and other resources to figure something out or build new understandings. We problem solve, pose real questions, interact with others, and are motivated to find out. We ask questions that can be answered or identify a problem, make a plan and take action, gather resources, analyze and summarize our information, and draw conclusions or report our findings. We reflect on the process. Acquiring and developing knowledge are active, mentally and physically constructive, and satisfying actions.

Figure 3.3 Jamal and his classmates engage in inquiry

We make choices and learn from them. Information seeking usually results in a *product*, an *answer* (or a group of them), and *closure.*

Wondering, the other kind of inquiry, is more open. We seek questions and examine alternative factors. When you and a friend discuss a recently read book or a film you've seen, you often share your thoughts about why a character acted as he did or why an actor played the character a certain way. You might never know the "right" answer. The goal is often the pleasure of the process itself—speculating, asking more questions, sharing insights that are only possibilities. Using open-ended questions is important with prekindergarteners. Using thoughtful language as we teach is crucial to helping stimulate children's thinking.

Both wondering and information seeking are acts of inquiry. One may lead to another. Both are satisfying and essential for human learning.

The children in Jamal's and Rachel's classrooms (see "A Day in the Life of Two Prekindergarten Children" at the beginning of this book) were both wondering and

seeking information throughout their school day (see Figure 3.3). They were examining and counting seeds in apples and making comparisons (*Look at the little star inside the apple!*), sorting fruits and vegetables into categories, making decisions about healthy foods, and engaging in other forms of inquiry or finding out.

When your teaching is inquiry-oriented, you enable the young child to *learn how to* learn, investigate and discover new understandings, and pose wonderings about the possibilities. They learn about choice, how to work in groups, and most of all, how to direct their energies to active engagement that stimulates the intellect.

It is essential for children to learn how to explain and seek information (Resnick and Snow, 2008). They need to be able to "describe physical characteristics of objects, self, and others" (p. 51) and to do so in terms of location. Often young children add gestures and sounds when they do not have the precise words. A three-year-old, for example, excited by his block construction, might leap to his feet and stretch upward to show how tall it is. They almost always act out processes; they can explain cause and effect; and the whole communication reflects the process of inquiry. For the young child, using language in particular ways is the *result* of active exploration.

Inquiry projects in prekindergarten are characterized by great variety. They always involve talking, listening, discovering, touching, experimenting, and finding out. They can involve cooking (see Appendix D, Lesson 3 for a lesson on using recipes), building, looking closely, drawing, painting, writing, and reading. The searching for information is especially rich when children go on field trips or have special visitors they can interview. We provide several descriptions of inquiry projects based on topics such as baby animals, shapes, and moods and feelings (Appendix C), and a general lesson for inquiry learning to help you plan a sequence of experiences to support children in genuine exploration of their world (Appendix D, Lesson 35).

As a summary, the chart in Figure 3.4 may help you think about four simple steps to guide your teaching. It shows a general movement from noticing and wondering about things to asking questions, exploring, and coming to conclusions. In fact, it is cyclic because new questions often result from the

conclusions. Throughout the process, the learner is assisted by talking with others and using (as needed) all the senses—touch, smell, taste, hearing, and sight. The result is an exciting, meaningful expansion of knowledge that continues throughout life.

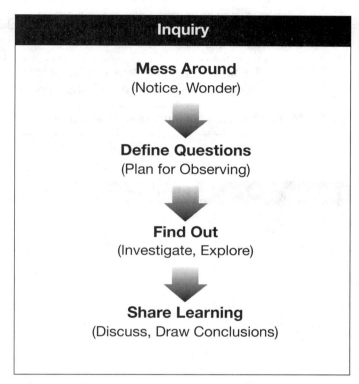

Figure 3.4 Understanding the inquiry process

Key Understandings to Think About

✳ "Constructive learning" means that with the support of adults, children create many of their understandings within their own brains.

✳ Constructive learning is important because children are "learning how to learn."

✳ Every element of the prekindergarten instructional program can support constructive learning.

✳ The ability to engage in constructive learning is built through the process of inquiry (questioning, planning, engaging in discovery, drawing, and sharing conclusions).

✳ Prekindergarten teachers play an important role when they engage children in inquiry.

Notes

An Organized, Engaging Environment for Learning

"Foster a learning environment that encourages exploration, initiative, positive peer interaction, and cognitive growth."

—HEATHER BIGGAR TOMLINSON

A high-quality prekindergarten environment creates an active learning culture that engages children's thinking and supports an enormous amount of learning. Children learn to inquire or search for information, regulate their own behavior, work with and appreciate others, build curiosity about the world and others, and expand language to new and more complex levels. They develop positive attitudes toward the acceptance and celebration of differences among people and cultures. Aspects of the physical environment and accessories for play reflect the diversity of cultures. At the same time the children become aware of the many uses of print in their world as they engage with a literacy-rich environment.

Figure 4.1 Classroom areas

Classroom Areas

The preschool classroom has designated physical spaces where the children engage in specific activities. Some areas are more permanent while others may change according to activity and schedule. Not all areas of the classroom are available for use at a given time. Each has a purpose, and different areas are open at different times. Furniture and many objects in each area are labeled with both words and pictures. The materials for some areas are simply stored on shelves and put on tables or brought out to the meeting area when in use. (See Appendix O for a suggested list of classroom materials.)

Avoid clutter! A key to the management of the classroom's physical space is that *only* those materials that are truly used are stored in the classroom. Eliminating clutter and unnecessary items helps students focus and remember routines. Special materials that are used for only a week or so a year are stored on high shelves or in another area. Get rid of materials that are never used, or store them elsewhere in the school.

Children will enjoy a well-stocked library area and a separate writing area. McGee's research suggests that the number of books available to children at any point in time should be about five times the number of children in the class! So plenty are needed. The writing area needs to be well stocked with all the tools a writer needs—crayons, pens, paper, blank books, stapler, and the like.

The materials in the different classroom areas change throughout the year; with each change, the teacher introduces the materials and shows the children the routines for using them. Each material has a specific purpose, and children learn to use materials appropriately. All materials are stored in clear plastic containers that are labeled—and only one kind of material is in each container. Each is placed on a shelf, which is also labeled with pictures and words. It is easy to see why children can quickly learn how to replace materials at clean-up time.

Organizing Your Classroom

A well-organized, pleasant environment contributes to joyful learning. You may want to begin by creating a simple plan that will support the range of important learning activities. (See Figure 4.2 for an example.)

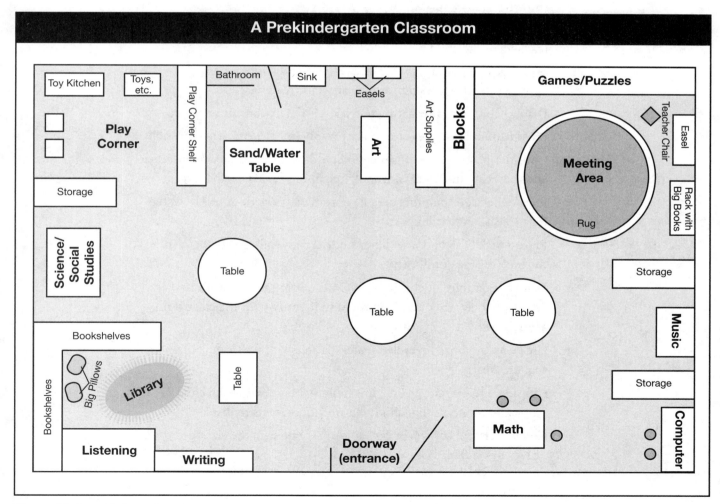

Figure 4.2 A prekindergarten classroom

Tips

- Use low shelving and furniture to define and separate learning areas and to create storage opportunities.

- Arrange furniture to create traffic patterns that discourage running and promote safe movement, but that allow for easy access to emergency exits at all times.

- Be sure that all furniture used by children is appropriate to their size/height and is child-accessible.

- Try to group quieter work areas near each other (library, writing) and noisier areas together (play corner, sand and water table).

- Involve children in the naming of the different classroom areas.

- Organize shelves so they are uncluttered and materials are easy to find. Label all shelves and containers with picture and word labels showing what is on each shelf.

- Avoid clutter by storing or disposing of anything not being used by teachers or the children.

- Add rugs and pillows, small tables, chairs, and lamps where appropriate to create comfortable areas for reading.

- Display children's work at their eye level so they can appreciate it.

- Provide multiple copies of popular toys and other items when possible.

- Consider posting a parent bulletin board near the classroom entrance with news about the class, school, upcoming events, birthdays, etc.

- Locate the art or painting area near a sink to provide access to water for projects and cleanup.

- Place a rack of big books where children can easily access them (near the meeting area or library).

- Display examples of children's art and writing on the walls to celebrate their work and help them to identify with the classroom as their own.

- Create an organized recycled materials area with uniform containers that are clearly labeled.

- Consider creating space on a low bulletin board with each child's name and photo so that children can choose items to display.

- Collect colorful baskets or bins to display books in the classroom library or on tabletops.

Physical Characteristics of a Literacy-Rich Prekindergarten Classroom

Let's step into a literacy-infused prekindergarten classroom and see how the physical space and its contents promote an active learning culture. Of course the classroom setup and focus will vary depending on whether the classes are for three-year-olds or four-year-olds or both. We have also included a color photo insert in this book that shows several examples of literacy-rich PreK classrooms and specific classroom areas. These pictures are intended to illustrate various ways that teachers have integrated play-based activities with literacy learning in colorful, engaging ways.

MEETING AREA As you walk into the room, a cozy, carpeted meeting area is immediately visible. Many teachers have children sit in a group on the carpet for a community meeting. The carpet may have a design that helps children sit

Figure 4.3 Meeting area

in an orderly way (for example, squares or a circle). Some teachers use separate carpet squares for each child. Movement and music activities take place here. There is a low teacher's chair, sometimes a rocking chair, and a display of books the teacher has read aloud to children. Near the calendar is an easel for reading big books and poems; the easel is magnetic so it can also be used for letter and word activities.

Figure 4.4 Library and listening area

LIBRARY Books are everywhere in the classroom, but a very important area is the class library with many picture books in colorful tubs and a variety of baskets, with books stored facing out so children can browse them easily. Books stored on shelves are also displayed so that the front of the book is visible. Books are organized by topics of interest to the children, by author, or by type (rhyming books, pop-up books, etc.). There are simple books with one or two lines per page, as well as alphabet books, counting books, books about colors and shapes, predictable books, and informational books. There are a couple of big, comfy pillows and a few book-related toys, as well as stuffed animals the children can read to. There are big books that the children read in a shared way with the teacher, and there are some little books that match the big books. Big books are displayed on a stand. Books are also displayed in other areas of the classroom, such as in the play corner or on the science table.

LISTENING As part of the library, a listening area has books, two chairs, and a little table with recordings, an audio player, and sets of headphones. The listening area is usually big enough for two to four children. A computer or child's tape player can also be used. Sometimes headphones are not necessary; a small group can listen if the volume is not too loud. Children will enjoy listening to recordings of favorite books you've read aloud as well as recordings of books you've made together as a class. It can be fun to make the recordings yourself, or to ask family volunteers to record themselves reading books aloud.

Figure 4.5 Play corner

PLAY CORNER The play corner contains props that encourage children's imagination and discovery. This area is more carefully planned than the "house corner" of the past and always includes theme-related books and writing tools and other materials that encourage the integration of writing and reading.

Throughout the school year, there may be themes such as restaurant, post office, doctor's office, or market. To encourage understanding of diversity, the play corner might include chopsticks, rice bowls, a tortilla press, or a yogurt maker (Horn et al., 2003). This area might include a range of artifacts that support not only the home but other themes as well: a stove, sink, refrigerator, tables, cupboard, doll bed, dishes, food containers, telephone, and a number of puppets. The area is transformed as different projects develop; it may become a bakery, a bank, a farm stand, a puppet theater, a beauty or barber shop, flower shop, pizza shop, or other things your children are interested in. The play corner always includes dress-up clothes to support the current theme. (Appendix D, Lesson 20 describes how to introduce students to the play corner environment.)

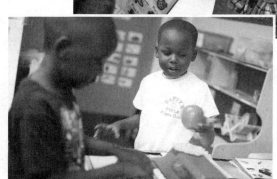

Figure 4.6 Play corner

Figure 4.7 Art

ART An art area offers children a chance to represent their ideas using drawing, painting, collage, or other media. Materials, including recycled materials that children have helped collect, are organized in bins labeled with both pictures and words. Crayons, paints, and paper provide lots of options for skin tones and hair colors. Markers and a variety of other writing tools are available so that children can integrate writing into their art if they wish. Early in the year you may want to begin with very few choices in this area. You can introduce new materials and show children how to use and take care of them gradually throughout the year. You may also want to rotate materials in and out of the art area if you want children to practice working with a certain type of material.

WRITING CENTER The writing center has all the materials children need for making books, including prestapled blank books, a variety of colored and textured paper for covers, crayons and washable markers, white correction tape, scissors and glue, and a tub of favorite books to help stimulate ideas. It includes tools for writing as well: different writing implements, letter stamps and pads, letter tiles, letter sponges, whiteboards, notebooks, note pads, traceable letters, sandpaper letters, stencils, an alphabet chart, and a variety of paper. As with the art area, it will be helpful to

Figure 4.8 Writing center

present a very simple version of the writing center when you introduce it to your class at the beginning of the school year. Label and trace the containers (to place a colored shape on the shelf) so children return them to the same spot. As you add materials, introduce them to the class first so they know what will be in the area and how to use and take care of it. The writing center can include bookmaking as an activity, or once children understand the process you may choose to do bookmaking in a separate, established area.

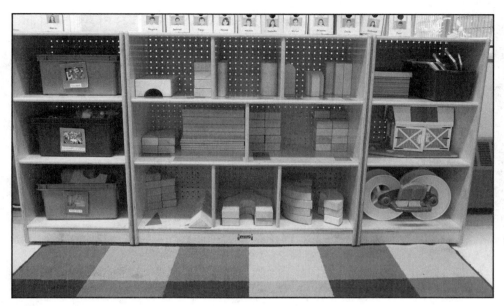

Figure 4.9 Blocks

BLOCKS A block area with various types and sizes of blocks encourages building and exploration of different shapes and materials. Since it tends to become messy, this area is located on a carpet at one end of the classroom. Blocks are organized on shelves, each block's shape taped with a label on the shelf where that type of block is stored. Other toys such as signs, vehicles, Legos, and a dollhouse with furniture and people are included as well. Many teachers include books about topics such as buildings or bridges, a small basket with paper, writing materials, and tape so that children can make their own signs and labels for the block area. As with other areas, it is helpful to introduce new materials gradually.

PUZZLES AND GAMES Another play area holds puzzles and all kinds of manipulatives and games, including letter and word puzzles and magnetic letters. While you will want to maintain a core group of materials—things like simple puzzles, magnetic letters, pattern blocks, and Unifix cubes, other materials in this area can be rotated to support various aspects of your curriculum throughout the year.

Figure 4.10 Puzzles and games

Figure 4.11 Sand and water play

SAND AND WATER PLAY Sand and water tables offer rich opportunity for discovering concepts about volume and capacity as well as how these materials behave when poured. Both tables have cups and other containers of various sizes. Both have clear containers and opaque containers as well, and both have a couple of plastic funnels. The sand table may also contain plastic animals and people, and the water table may have plastic sea creatures and boats, and a bucket of objects that children can use to test the concepts of sinking and floating.

MUSIC This area has simple instruments to help children explore rhythm (for example, small drums, tambourines, and shakers). It may also include a few instruments the children have made themselves, such as shakers made with paper towel tubes and beans, or guitars made with boxes and rubber bands. Making these instruments can also be an area-related activity, with an adult to guide and support the children's work. You may also want to have an MP3 player or other audio device and headsets so that children can listen to, play along with, and remember favorite songs; this helps them internalize language, get the feel for rhyme, and expand vocabulary.

Figure 4.12 Music

SCIENCE/SOCIAL STUDIES An area for science and social studies offers the opportunity for focused inquiry using concrete materials. It has some simple science equipment such as magnifying glasses, and a range of natural materials gathered from outside of school, both by the teachers and by students and their families. This area also contains writing tools and paper and wonderful nonfiction picture books with colorful photographs or drawings

Figure 4.13 Science

on subjects like animals, foods, families, and community. As with other areas, the materials here will be rotated to support inquiry work going on in the classroom. If your class is studying rocks, for example, the table will have baskets of rocks for examining, sorting, and drawing.

MATH An area for math has a range of manipulatives for counting and comparing. You'll see things like pattern blocks, rods, and coins. You may see other manipulatives such as Legos™, counting bears, Unifix cubes, and colored plastic disks, as well as rulers, rods, and games. Numerals are printed on cards, and there are simple counting tasks to match numerals. You may want to restrict what materials children have access to at certain points if you want to support them with practice using a certain material.

Figure 4.14 Math

COMPUTER One or more simple computers are available for children to use under adult guidance. You will want to ensure that children have access only to those programs that support their learning. There are a range of simple, engaging computer games designed for children of prekindergarten age that support literacy and math learning, and that involve looking closely at visuals, letters, and numbers.

Figure 4.15 Computer

Figure 4.16 Name poem

PRINT IN THE CLASSROOM The walls of the prekindergarten classroom are filled with print! Children's names are everywhere— on a name chart, on an attendance record with pictures, on their finished art, in class-written stories. There are signs that reflect the environment. You also see many pieces of group writing that children have produced together. There are poems and songs on charts, and several alphabet charts. Everywhere, there is evidence of the inquiry projects in which children have been involved—charts reflecting their observations and conclusions.

Figure 4.19 Attendance chart   **Figure 4.20** Children's art

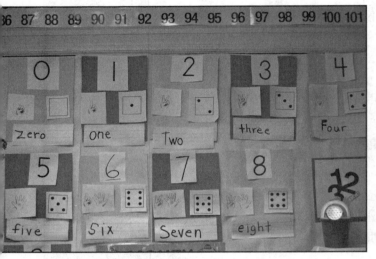

Figure 4.17 Numbers

Figure 4.21 Observing nature

Figure 4.18 Animals on a farm and at the zoo

High-Quality Play

Play is essential in prekindergarten. The introduction of play corner materials and props can suggest possible roles that children might play. It is important for children to make some decisions about their play, so plan for plenty of "free play." Adults are present to guide children's play and provide opportunities for extended conversations. They also model ways of playing, talking, and including literacy activities (writing pretend prescriptions in the doctor's office, jotting grocery lists, looking at a menu, etc.). We provide a variety of suggestions for prop box themes for the play corner that can be used on a temporary basis (see Figure 4.21).

Theme Suggestions for the Play Corner			
Prop Box Theme	**Materials**	**Prop Box Theme**	**Materials**
Pet Shop	Toy animals Boxes for animal homes (cages, aquariums) Computer Receipts Play money "Certificates" of health Materials to make collars, food, pet toys Name tags or aprons for workers	*Shoe Store*	Collection of shoes Shoe boxes Shoehorn Stockings to try on shoes Telephone Credit cards (home-made) or play money Shelves for display Name tags for workers Dressy clothes for customers
Bakery	Play dough Cookie sheets Paper to make cookies, cakes, bread loaves, pies Macaroni and other materials to "decorate" items Play oven or box to make an oven Labels for prices Computer and play money Cookbooks Aprons and bakers' hats	*Gas Station*	Tricycles or toy cars and SUVs Large boxes for pumps Plastic hose Window washing supplies (spray bottles) Large box for car wash Jumpsuits for attendants

Figure 4.21 Theme suggestions for the play corner

continues

Theme Suggestions for the Play Corner, *continued*

Prop Box Theme	Materials	Prop Box Theme	Materials
Camping	Tent or suggestion of one made with brown paper Sleeping bags Rocks for pretend campfire Paper to imitate fire and camp food Camp cookware Flashlight Stories to read Backpacks, bandannas, camping clothes	*Restaurant*	Tables and chairs (1 or 2 sets) Paper plates of different sizes Paper cups Soft plastic silverware Aprons Chef's hat Big pieces of paper to make menus Play food Chalkboard or whiteboard for "specials" Order pads and pencils Computer and play money Telephone
Doctor's Office	Toy medical tools—stethoscope, blood pressure cuff, syringe, bandages White coats or blue "scrubs" Plastic gloves Clipboards for charts Play computer Box for X-ray machine Telephone or cell phone	*Fruit and Vegetable Market*	Paper to make fruits and vegetables or plastic ones Boxes or crates Tables for display Paper bags Play money and box Sign for prices Cash register Play food Aprons for workers

Figure 4.21 Theme suggestions for the play corner, *continued*

As prekindergarteners play, they often keep up a steady stream of conversation—much of it to themselves! About forty percent of the talk of younger children is directed toward themselves rather than other children (Resnick and Snow, 2009). This "private speech" helps them practice language. They talk as they "work," learning to regulate their own actions. Watching Noah playing with the building he's just finished in the block area, for example, you might hear his running commentary, "The car goes up the elevator and the brontosaurus comes, smash!" This kind of practice is important, but interactions with other children and with adults are also critical for expanding children's language and helping them learn the conventions of conversation. We provide a simple lesson on using dramatic play in the classroom in Appendix D, Lesson 20.

Management

Looking around the classroom, it should be evident that management and order are important—not to stifle children but to help them learn self-regulation. The teacher has taught them how to play with others in different areas of the classroom, how to use materials, and routines for engaging in different kinds of activities. They know that sometimes they meet as a whole class, sometimes in a small group, and sometimes with partners or as individuals. Different behavior (and voice level) is needed for each situation. There is opportunity to initiate action but also the expectation to listen to and be guided by the teacher.

Children know that they need to check the classroom schedule to see if the area they want to go to is open. They're able to tell by looking at the icons for each area, and the spaces available. If there is a space open, they put their own name in that space before going to the new area. This is a great way to help children regulate their own movement in the classroom instead of just moving around from place to place. When the children intentionally place their name in a new area, it helps them commit to engaging in the work of that area as well.

The activity of the classroom is *organized* and children are learning how to *sustain behavior and attention* and *regulate* their own behavior. In their book *Tools of the Mind*, Bodrova and Leong (1995) write:

> In our experience, we have found that both extremely chaotic classrooms and extremely teacher-directed classrooms are counterproductive to developing self-regulation and other underlying skills in children. Classrooms where children flit from activity to activity support reactive behavior. But when all the instruction is whole-group, students become too teacher-regulated.

Prekindergarteners need a playful classroom with focused learning opportunities (Ray and Glover, 2009). Reading, writing, and play are seamless parts of a meaningful whole. Children know that they are expected to engage in organized action. Authentic writing and reading *become* play—part of the tools of exploration along with concrete objects. We discuss the many opportunities for playful reading and writing in the next chapter.

Key Understandings to Think About

❋ An organized, engaging learning environment is essential for a highly effective prekindergarten program.

❋ The learning environment is organized to promote active learning on the part of prekindergarteners.

❋ Print is a meaningful part of the preschool environment.

❋ Different areas of the prekindergarten classroom are used at different times and for different purposes.

❋ Management and order are important to help children learn self-regulation.

❋ The whole environment should "make sense" to the children who are working, playing, and learning within it.

Notes

Using a Framework for Language and Literacy Teaching

"Both child-guided and teacher-guided experiences are vital to children's development and learning."

—NAEYC

During the school day, three- and four-year-old prekindergarteners need activities that engage their intellect, curiosity, and imagination. There are many ways you can organize the school day, depending on how much time you have with the children. We have not attempted to describe every instructional context you might use in a prekindergarten classroom. There are many excellent resources to help you design and manage different areas; interact with children around play; and teach them math, science, and social studies.

All of these activities, as well as rich and varied experiences with art and music, are important parts of the child's learning. Our purpose in this book, however, is to describe how you can support three- and four-year-olds in early literacy development. Nevertheless, in this chapter, we present an overall framework for instruction so that you can see an example of how activities fit together and to provide some options for how you might plan your days. Vary the selection of elements, time allotments, and sequence to fit your needs.

Adjusting Instruction for the Age of Your Students

It is important to remember that there will be some basic differences in how your day unfolds depending on the age and development of your students (see introduction, and see Appendix F for a detailed developmental chart).

Three-Year-Olds

Your three-year-old students may find themselves in school for the first time. So separation from their caregivers and learning to function in a group setting will likely be focuses for the beginning months. You may need to slowly introduce them to the classroom routines and help them adjust over time. In addition, three-year-old children require more structure and time for transitions. They need clear directions provided both verbally and visually, and they do best with predictable routines that repeat daily. Posting a daily schedule in the classroom with words and matching pictures will help three-year-olds in particular establish a routine that they can then reference using the pictures on the schedule. Three-year-olds also require more opportunities to move around physically and need more adult help navigating all activities. Keep these issues in mind and consider the three-year-old's abilities in all areas of development (cognitive skills, fine motor skills, gross motor skills, speech and language skills, social/emotional skills) as you plan your class schedule for the day. (See Appendix F.)

Four-Year-Olds

In contrast, many of your four-year-old students will already be familiar with preschool. They will be more independent in navigating their day and better able to sit and focus for periods of time, and they will have more fully developed skills to draw upon as they engage with all that your classroom offers. Your plans for each day can be more flexible and your expectations of your four-year-old students will be higher as you prepare them for entry into kindergarten.

Essential Learning Experiences

Every day will include some essential learning activities and routines, including morning community meeting, snack time, bathroom, and outdoor play; in addition, each day should include some literacy opportunities. Choose from the options to create a predictable schedule that fits your day and time segments. You will also, of course, keep your particular students and their developmental levels in mind as you select activities.

Some activities, like choice time and reading, will occur daily. Others you will need to allocate over the week or alternate. If you have only a half day with your children, you will adjust your schedule to fit that time frame. However, often an activity can accommodate more than one learning area simultaneously, for example:

- Texts you read aloud to children may be related to inquiry projects you are undertaking and may serve as a springboard for writing.

- Texts you produce during interactive writing can be related to inquiry projects or to children's individual writing/drawing time.

- Read-aloud can build science knowledge and link to cooking.

- Once children understand the process, book-making can be an established area and can be related to inquiry.

- Inquiry is almost always the way children learn about science, social studies, and literature. Inquiry activities can also become temporary physical areas of the classroom.

Essential Prekindergarten Learning Experiences	
Activity	**Description**
Circle Time	Guided by the teacher, the children meet together as a community to greet one another, share experiences, and plan or culminate the day. They review the calendar or weather, and engage in oral phonics games or shared reading.
Projects	Through inquiry, children explore their physical or social world; for example, nature, foods, animals, weather. They notice comparisons and the process of change and growth. They explore and develop concepts such as numbers, size, and shapes through inquiry activities. Inquiry-based projects build knowledge in math, science, social studies, art, music, cooking, and drama.
Outdoor Play	Outdoor play, weather permitting, is also important; children need the fresh air and exercise, as well as the opportunities for gross motor movement. Children need to run, jump, climb, play outdoor games, and enjoy physical activities.
Choice Time	Children choose or are assigned to one of several play areas. Some areas are permanent (such as blocks), other areas change throughout the year (such as play corner supplies). The choices include play corner, blocks, music, library, puzzles and games, sand and water play, science, social studies, bookmaking, computer, listening, math, and art. All of the activities listed above have central elements of play in that children are actively exploring and making discoveries.
Choice Time (literacy)	One choice time activity is usually literacy-focused and preceded by the teacher's introduction and demonstration. Choice time is followed by a brief sharing period in which the children talk about what they have discovered. Literacy activities might include computer, listening, play corner, bookmaking, book activities, and writing.
Reading Time	Interactive Read-Aloud: The teacher reads one or two selected texts aloud to the class. (See Chapter 11.) Shared Reading: The teacher and children read together from a shared text. (See Chapter 12.) These reading experiences often lead to book activities.
Book Activity	Children respond to a text that has been read aloud to them, that they have read in a shared way, or that they have written together through interactive writing. Activities might include drama, cooking, drawing, art, interactive writing, independent writing, bookmaking, or music. (See Chapter 16.)
Writing Time	Interactive Writing: The teacher and children work together to create a shared text that is based on experiences the class has had. It can be related to science, math, or social studies and is often a response to books that have been read aloud. It becomes a text for shared reading. (See Chapter 16.) Independent Writing: Children tell their stories in pairs and to the group. They write for a variety of purposes. They make lists, cards, books, and posters for many different audiences. The writing may be linked to inquiry projects or read-aloud books.
Library Time	Children have the opportunity to choose books from the classroom library. They look at the books and tell the story or talk about them.
Phonemic Awareness, Letters, and Phonics	Children learn something about sounds, letters, and how words work. Usually this involves a poem, rhyme, or demonstration. For four-year-olds it might be a very short lesson followed by a hands-on activity that may be part of choice time. (See Chapters 19, 20, and 21.) Activities may include oral games, fingerplays, or circle time activities.

Figure 5.1 Essential prekindergarten learning experiences

Managing Activities

It may seem daunting to coordinate these many activities. Remember, you won't be doing all of them every day, and they won't all be happening simultaneously! There are several things that will help you both plan and carry out your day's activities.

Reading Activities

The reading activities you use do not necessarily have to follow each other or be in the same block of time. The sequence of events in your classroom will depend on your observations of your children and the demands on your schedule. Some teachers find that it works best to intersperse reading activities with other kinds of work/play, and some teachers find that children are able to stay engaged with a sequence of reading activities. Later in this book we will discuss in detail how writing and reading are connected. But for this discussion, we list suggestions for managing three essential literacy activities: interactive read-aloud and shared reading, library time, and book activities.

Interactive Read-Aloud and Shared Reading

In *interactive read-aloud* you select appropriate texts and read them to the children as you think and talk together about the text. They have a chance to talk with you and one another and to interact around the text. Choose books with very few words on a page, or books with pictures and words that children can easily identify from the pictures, or books with actions (i.e., "Here is the baby's nose," point to own nose). Being read to is a familiar activity for most prekindergarten children and a beloved one for all. Interactive read-aloud brings your community of children together, develops a shared repertoire of familiar stories, and provides wonderful opportunities for deepening thinking through discussion. For three-year-olds,

select simple short stories and read favorites over and over. They love rhyme and repetition. As children grow in experience, they can understand more complex stories but still need familiar themes and topics. Simple animal fantasy is popular with all children. (See Appendix D, Lesson 2 for a simple lesson on interactive read-aloud.)

During *shared reading* you and the children read in unison from an enlarged text. (Big book or enlarged print chart of a song or poem.) This gives children the opportunity to learn early reading behaviors such as moving across the page from left to right and matching voice to print. Shared reading is by nature inclusive, encouraging all children to participate as "readers," whether they are able to recognize letters and sounds or simply enjoy the rhythm of the words. For three-year-olds, you may want to point to and "read" labels or names. As they become more experienced they can read one line of print with your support. Often teachers spend time with younger children just teaching them to say and enjoy simple action poems and songs. Later they can be introduced to a print version or partial version of the poem or song. (See Appendix D, Lesson 1 for a simple lesson on shared reading.)

Here are some suggestions to make reading time enjoyable and effective.

- Have children sit on their assigned spots on the rug (for example, a taped-out square, carpet squares, small mats).

- Sit on a low chair and be sure that all children can see and hear.

- Reread favorite stories, songs, or poems.

- Select new texts based on your ongoing observations of the group's interests and responses.

- Over time, include a variety of genres, topics, and formats.

Library Time

The literacy-rich prekindergarten classroom has a clearly designated library of colorful books that have been selected for their appeal and value to prekindergarteners. (See Appendix B for a list of preschool text sets organized by theme, and Appendix E for recommended PreK picture books.) Children can look at books on the rug or at a table.

- Have books in labeled tubs or baskets by category—topic, author, illustrator, type (rhymes, silly books, ABC books). Colored dots on books and tubs will help children put books away.

- Teach routines for getting books and putting them back. Children place books face out in the tub or on the shelves at a signal (like a favorite song or chant).

- Include books that have been read to the group. You may want to have a "books we have shared" section.

- Have a basket of books by the classroom authors for all to enjoy.

Book Activities

Children respond to literature through *drawing* and *writing* after hearing a book read aloud, as well as talking about the book, engaging in dramatic activities, creating art, or participating in a cooking project. It might be a whole group or a small-group activity that makes a book experience memorable.

Children may incorporate some of the features of the texts in their drawings, and in their writing may use some "temporary" spellings (not conventional) as they learn more about print. Children will respond differently depending on their level of development. Children who are just learning to control their crayons may find representational drawing difficult; others may produce recognizable drawings. Some may be ready to put down letters representing the sounds they hear in words. You

can expect to see a wide range of writing (pictures, letters, words, scribbles) depending on the developmental stage of the child. Because development is uneven, you may see a child with weaker fine motor skills expressing more complex ideas in a less refined way.

- Children draw (and often write) about what they have just read or heard read.

- Children discuss, retell, or reread (in response to pictures) books with a partner.

- Children engage in art projects related to stories, including collage, puppets, painting, etc.

- Children engage in dramatic play such as playing with puppets, cooking a pot of stone soup, or baking gingerbread.

Writing Activities

Just as with reading, you may choose to place writing activities back to back; for example, you may use interactive writing or interactive drawing (Horn and Giacobbe, 2007) as a quick lesson right before children write and draw on their own. But it's also fine to place them at different points in the day if you feel your children benefit from having these activities spread out.

Shared and Interactive Writing

During *shared writing* you compose and then write a message or story on a large chart. You act as the scribe, but the children participate in every aspect of the writing process. You usually write in large print on chart paper on an easel so that everyone can see. You can adjust shared writing to meet the needs of three- and four-year-olds. For example, for younger children you might just label a picture or object or write a very short sentence about one of the children. As children learn more, gradually increase complexity.

Interactive writing is the same as shared writing except that you sometimes "share the pen." You occasionally select a helpful and appropriate point for an individual child to come up to the easel and contribute a letter or punctuation mark. Some three-year-olds may not be able to contribute to the writing at all, but they may be able to point to the letter or word that the teacher wrote. Before they can handle a writing tool, they can still point out the features of the writing with the teacher's support. (See Appendix D, Lesson 5 for a simple lesson on interactive writing.) When implementing interactive writing:

- Use the meeting area.
- Keep the session moving along quickly and don't take too long.
- Seat all children so they can easily see the easel.
- Write with dark marker on white or cream paper so that the print is very visible.
- Teach children to come up to the easel quickly and sit down quickly (interactive writing).
- Have the name chart, alphabet chart, and other resources handy as reference tools.
- Have children say what they are going to be writing several times.
- Reread the text often using a pointer.
- Keep interactive writing texts to reread later and to revisit for letter or word study.

Independent Writing, Drawing, and Bookmaking

Writing time is structured; it is important for children to learn the routines. It begins with a tip that will help them as writers. Then children draw, tell stories, or write while you circulate and confer with individuals or work with a small group. Often children are making books. Writing time ends with a sharing session. Adjust the length of work time to meet the needs of younger and older children.

- Provide a short demonstration or lesson on any aspect of writing. In preschool, think about a brief talk or tip about what writers or

illustrators do. At first, your lesson will be on routines (how to choose paper, where to get the blank books, etc.). Later, you may demonstrate labeling drawings or saying words slowly as you write down a letter for a sound you hear. Some lessons may help the children think about craft, such as where writers get ideas or how they put titles.

- As you *circulate and confer*, you have brief conversations with individuals, inviting them to think of what they want to draw, talk about their drawings, tell or "read" their stories, and/or write letters for words. Alternatively, you might sit with a small group and support them.

- In a *sharing session*, children talk about their drawing and writing with others. Sometimes they share with the whole group and sometimes with a partner.

Below are some suggestions for a successful writing time in your classroom:

- Teach children routines for taking, using, and putting away materials. Bring out more choices in paper and other materials bit by bit as they learn "how we do our drawing and writing." For the first part of the school year, the mini-lessons will all focus on "how we do our writing time."

- It's a good idea to have a writing area with bookmaking supplies. If the children are doing a writing activity such as making cards or menus, or if they are making books, they will have all they need in one place.

- Observe students carefully as you have individual conferences; compare their current behaviors and understandings to the Continuum of Literacy Learning, PreK (see Section 7) and look for what most children can *nearly* do as writers or illustrators; then create short lessons based on that information.

- Have short conferences with individuals or small groups; invite children to tell their stories and "read" or talk about their writing and drawing; draw them out by talking about what you see or what the drawing makes you think about. Their drawings or marks on the paper represent their thinking.

- Differentiate instruction to meet the needs of a wide range of children.

- Demonstrate how to share and talk about drawing, writing, and books.

- Invite a few children to share with the whole group, or have them share their writing or books with a partner or group of three. (See Appendix D, Lessons 9 and 11 for simple lessons on bookmaking.)

Specific curriculum goals for writing are included in the Continuum of Literacy Learning, PreK found in Section 7.

Phonemic Awareness, Phonics, and Word Study

It is appropriate for prekindergarten children to start learning about the sounds in words through enjoying songs, fingerplays, or rhymes. They also become acquainted with alphabet letters and begin to notice them through play and through making their names. A complex body of understanding is built over time, and for most children this learning begins even before they enter prekindergarten. Section 5 of this book includes several chapters that provide suggestions to help children learn about letters, sounds, and words in enjoyable ways. (See also Appendix D, Lessons 14 and 15 for lessons on oral games and phonemes, and picture sorting.) Areas of learning include:

- *Phonemic awareness.* Drawing children's attention to the individual sounds in the words of *oral language.* It begins with general phonological awareness of rhymes and word parts like syllables.

- *Letter work.* Helping children notice the *distinctive features* of letters (what makes one different from all the rest) and learn their names.

- *Phonics.* Helping children learn the relationship between the letters and sounds.

Much of the work in prekindergarten will be focused on awareness of sounds and of letters rather than formal phonics lessons. To increase phonemic awareness and letter awareness, you may want to:

- Play oral games (e.g., rhyming).

- Provide quick and active lessons on phonemic awareness/phonics/letter work.

- Incorporate songs, poems, rhymes, and finger plays to help children hear the sounds in words.

- Help children explore letter features by using magnetic letters they can manipulate.

- Connect sounds and letters to children's own names.

- Explicitly demonstrate sorting magnetic letters by features (tails, tall sticks, circles, etc.). (See Appendix D, Lesson 28.)

- Explicitly demonstrate making words (including names) with magnetic letters.

You can link these activities to work children do later in a letter and word center. (See Chapter 15 for more information regarding phonemic awareness in the PreK classroom.) Some suggestions that may be helpful:

- Put chalk boards, magnetic letters, letter puzzles on tables or in centers.

- Use alphabet and letter puzzles.

- Place ABC books in a special place for children to look at.

- Provide games (e.g., picture lotto with letter sounds or rhymes or concepts) and teach children to play them.

- Provide magnetic letters they can manipulate.

- Provide paper, blank books, and writing utensils.

Areas for Choice Time

Certain areas of the classroom that you use during choice time may be permanent—bookmaking, cooking, writing, library, blocks, play corner, a table with manipulatives (e.g., puzzles, beading, Legos), an art table and easels for working on and displaying art, the sensory play area (e.g., sand table/water table/shaving cream). Or areas may be temporary and focus on a topic of inquiry such as plants, shapes, or food.

All activities have an element of play, but some are more focused on inquiry or literacy. Other areas, such as blocks or play corner, support motor skills or the imagination. These areas, too, can play a major role in inquiry; for example, the play corner can become a market, or children can be encouraged to design and build a restaurant in the block area.

Managing play areas can be tricky, since several activities are happening simultaneously. Here are some tips:

- Quickly review the day's choices right before children start to work in a specific area.
- Teach children routines for taking, using, and putting away writing and drawing materials. Bring out more choices in paper and other materials bit by bit as they learn "how we do writing" and are able to incorporate and manage the area's materials.
- Give a detailed explanation, including demonstration as needed, of only one new area each day.
- If there are specific activities that you would like every child to experience, plan to switch these once a week. You can ensure that all children experience the specific activities over the course of the week (they work in other areas when they have completed the required activity).
- Use "noisier" areas during indoor play time.
- Use literacy-oriented areas to extend children's learning of phonemic awareness, letters, stories, and bookmaking.

Circle Time

The meeting area for circle time is the hearth of your community, so it is important to create a space that feels cozy and inviting yet is spacious enough for children to sit comfortably. Often teachers use a brightly colored rug with prominent patterns or designs. Each child needs a spot to sit, whether it is in a taped-out square or on a piece of carpet or mat. Think carefully about how you arrange your children's spots. You know them well, so you know which children need to sit closer to you or to other teachers in the room, which children need a bit of extra space around them, which children are able to sit in spots near books without becoming distracted, etc. The children should be spread out enough so that they do not touch one another, and everyone should be able to see your chair or stool.

Some important supplies to have prominently displayed in your meeting area are:

- A Velcro (or some other type) attendance chart with all children's names or names/photos.
- A large, clear calendar depicting the current month with Velcro or pocket-chart number cards. (Be sure to have a birthday list for days that will need special attention.)
- A large, clear weather chart with either Velcro or pocket-chart weather icons (e.g., sun, clouds, snow, rain, wind).
- A simple job chart or birthday chart with photos or name cards for each child.

As children arrive in the morning, it will take them some time to take off their coats and find their places. Ease this transition by making available a few simple table activities they can participate in immediately—small manipulatives, baskets of crayons and paper, other easily tidied-up items. You might also have a basket of children's literature books or individual (stapled) writing books that they draw and write in each morning. At the appropriate time, signal that it is time for them to come together for morning meeting.

- Use a favorite song or signal to tell the children to assemble as a group. (For example, "Hello children. Hello children. How are you? I am glad to see you!" to the tune of Frère Jacques.)

- Teach children routines for sitting on their bottoms together but not so close that they touch someone else. They can sit in a circle or on a particular spot looking at you.

- Invite children to help you take attendance. Hold up each child's name card in turn and ask the students whether that child is present or absent. This can be modified many ways: the children can be prompted to scan and determine who is absent, or they can take turns leading the attendance.

- Engage children in a brief conversation, for example: "Who has something important to share?"

- Keep your work with the calendar quick and practical rather than teaching a long lesson. Simply say, for example, "It is the month of January and today is January 5." Children can take turns placing the number for the date onto the calendar.

- Keep the weather chart work short and sweet as well—say something like, "The season is winter. The weather is snowy." You might invite them to give the short weather sentence when they can take it over. Another job for the week might be placing the appropriate weather symbol (cloud, rain, snow, sun) on the weather chart.

- Post the job chart prominently in the meeting area. At the beginning of the week, each child will be assigned to a weeklong job (e.g., line leader, hand out cups/napkins for snack, wipe tables for snack, calendar helper, celebrate birthdays). Use the chart to keep track of who is doing what job each week. On a separate checklist of your own, keep track of how many times children have done each job to ensure that everyone has a turn at each job.

- Be sure the meeting is short and efficient.

You will, of course, arrange your schedule in the way that best fits your time blocks and your students. It is always important to vary more active times with less active times and structured times with free choice. Most of all it is important to observe and get to know your children and to provide them with engaging and interesting experiences throughout the day.

Sample Framework For Teaching and Learning: Three-Hour and Six-Hour Day

We've provided two sample schedules and two sample instructional frameworks, each providing an example of a day. Figures 5.2 and 5.4 show a three-hour day and Figures 5.3 and 5.5 show a six-hour day. It is important to set a schedule and stick to it so that young children will experience a predictable environment and take responsibility for working together to achieve their goals. Children are more comfortable, relaxed, and empowered when they know what to expect each day. Adjust your schedule to fit your particular students and the amount of time you have with them. If you are working with three-year-olds, plan more transitions and play time. With four-year-olds, you can gradually lengthen work activities.

Communicating with Families

Communicating the richness of children's learning with families is important. Family members can talk about the new learning children are experiencing in school and build on it at home. Parents and caregivers are your partners in supporting children's development. The more you help them understand, the more they can support the child in helpful ways. Family members may not realize how much children are

Suggested Schedule for a Three-Hour Day	
Approximate Time	**Activity**
5 minutes	Transition: Entry, attendance, table time
15 minutes	**Circle Time**
30 minutes	**Projects**
15 minutes	Transition: Clean up, sharing, snack, library, bathroom
20 minutes	**Outdoor Play**
30 minutes	**Choice Time**
5 minutes	Transition: Clean up, songs, chants, marches, oral games
15 minutes	**Reading/Writing Time** (alternate)
30 minutes	**Choice Time** (literacy)
5 minutes	Transition: Clean up
10 minutes	**Circle Time**

Figure 5.2 Suggested schedule for a three-hour day

Suggested Schedule for a Six-Hour Day	
Approximate Time	**Activity**
10 minutes	Transition: Entry, attendance, table time
20 minutes	**Circle Time**
5 minutes	Transition: Songs, marches, movement, oral games
20 minutes	**Reading Time**
30 minutes	**Book Activity**
20 minutes	Transition: Clean up, sharing, snack, library, bathroom
20 minutes	**Outdoor Play**
40 minutes	**Projects**
30 minutes	**Lunch**
45 minutes	**Choice Time**
5 minutes	Transition: Clean up, songs, chants, marches, oral games
45 minutes	**Writing Time**
10 minutes	**Shared Reading**
45 minutes	**Choice Time** (literacy)
5 minutes	Transition: Clean up
10 minutes	**Circle Time**

Figure 5.3 Suggested schedule for a six-hour day

Suggested Framework for Teaching and Learning (3 Hours)		
Approximate Time	**Activity**	**Sample Activities**
5 minutes	Transition	Entry, attendance, table time
15 minutes	**Circle Time**	• community meeting • calendar, birthdays, helpers • weather • sharing • storytelling • shared reading (songs, poems) • phonics/oral games (letter and word games) • songs, marches, movement, fingerplays, circle games
30 minutes	**Projects**	Inquiry-based activities: science, math, social studies, cooking, art, drama, music
15 minutes	Transition	Clean up, sharing, snack, library, bathroom
20 minutes	**Outdoor Play**	
30 minutes	**Choice Time**	• play corner • blocks • music • library • puzzles and games • sand/water table • art • special table (inquiry projects, etc.)
5 minutes	Transition	Clean up, songs, chants, marches, oral games

15 minutes	**Reading/Writing Time** (alternate)	Reading:
		   • interactive read-aloud
		   • shared reading
		   • library time
		Writing:
		   • interactive writing/shared writing
		   • independent writing/drawing
		   • bookmaking

30 minutes	**Choice Time** (literacy)	• computer • listening • play corner • bookmaking • letter/word activities • book activity • writing
5 minutes	Transition	Clean up
10 minutes	**Circle Time**	• songs, marches, movement, oral games • sharing • home preparation • dismissal

Figure 5.4 Suggested framework for teaching and learning (3 hours)

Suggested Framework for Teaching and Learning (6 Hours)		
Approximate Time	**Activity**	**Sample Activities**
10 minutes	Transition	Entry, attendance, table time
20 minutes	**Circle Time**	• community meeting • calendar, birthdays, helpers • weather • sharing • shared reading (songs, poems) • phonics/oral games (letter and word games) • songs, marches, movement
5 minutes	Transition	Songs, marches, movement, oral games
20 minutes	**Reading Time**	• interactive read-aloud • shared reading • library time
30 minutes	**Book Activity**	• play corner • art • cooking • writing
20 minutes	Transition	Clean up, sharing, snack, library, bathroom
20 minutes	**Outdoor Play**	
40 minutes	**Projects**	Inquiry-based activities: science, math, social studies, cooking, art, drama, music
30 minutes	**Lunch**	
45 minutes	**Choice Time**	• play corner • blocks • music • library • puzzles and games • sand/water table • art • special table (inquiry projects, etc.)
5 minutes	Transition	Clean up, songs, chants, marches, oral games
45 minutes	**Writing Time**	• interactive writing/shared writing • independent writing/drawing • bookmaking
10 minutes	**Shared Reading**	• big books • charts
45 minutes	**Choice Time** (literacy)	• computer • listening • play corner • bookmaking • letter/word activities • book activity • writing
5 minutes	Transition	Clean up
10 minutes	**Circle Time**	• songs, marches, movement, oral games • sharing • home preparation • dismissal

Figure 5.5 Suggested framework for teaching and learning (6 hours)

learning about literacy even before they can read for themselves or make more than a few marks on paper. Or family members may see only perfect letter or word recognition or writing as valuable. The more you can help them understand how children are emerging as comprehenders, readers, and writers, the better support their families can provide.

Getting the Conversation Started

Communicating with the families of the children who will be in your class even before school begins welcomes them and invites them to be active in their children's lives at school. You may want to send a letter or a postcard to the child and his family. You can imagine the joy and excitement they will share when they read it together. This is also a good time to ask about stories, interests, hobbies, work, or cultural traditions they may want to share as valued visitors to the classroom. You might also send out a call for recyclable materials such as toilet paper rolls, cans, boxes, gift wrap, and magazines that can be used to create art.

Using Weekly Newsletters

Weekly newsletters (sent home by email and/or as printed copies) are a powerful means of communicating. In the example in Figure 5.6, notice how Debi and Anna encourage families to think about their children's learning. It would be impossible to tell everything that happens in a prekindergartener's week! But you can communicate highlights that you think are important. Family members will enjoy talking with their children about the week's experiences and will appreciate knowing what is happening. They can reinforce the learning at home and can also ask children to retell stories they have heard or sing songs they have learned in school.

The following outline will help you put together a newsletter:

1. Begin with a general comment about the progress of the class over the week. You can mention some general growth, such as the ability to listen to stories for a longer time or tell stories while looking at picture books. You can mention an exciting new area of learning or a new theme for playing in the play corner (such as setting it up as a restaurant).

2. Briefly describe any special events or happenings—special visitors or speakers or field trips.

3. Thank parents or others who may have visited to help out. A parent or grandparent may have come for a morning to read stories to children or help on a field trip.

4. Mention some special activities children have enjoyed—planting seeds or cooking soup, for example. Be specific about what children are learning from the activity (how to notice growth and change or observe how heat changes food).

5. Discuss specific areas of inquiry in which children have participated. You may be exploring a theme (for example, water and containers, rocks, food, or leaves) that you can describe. It is important to let family members know that when the children are observing, talking, and exploring, they are actively thinking.

6. Provide helpful lists. For example, if family members know the books children have been hearing read aloud, they may be able to get them from the library. They will also appreciate lists of songs children are learning and copies of favorite poems.

7. Provide any necessary practical reminders (safety rules, upcoming events, required permission forms).

You may not have time to make all the points listed above, so be selective. Just be sure that the communication going home is highly positive as well as informative. This special kind of communication helps to make parents partners in their child's education.

Dear Parents,

As you are aware, the children are changing and developing in so many ways. We are seeing a growing sense of confidence in each child. While we have many individual goals for each child and for the group, this growth in confidence and in understanding of the classroom community is a goal we have for all of the children.

Last week, we read some stories that inspired a lot of discussion about snow. One of the stories was *The Biggest, Best Snowman* by Margery Cuyler. In this story, the main character, Little Nell, is told by her sisters and mother that she is too little to do anything. But she and her animal friends make the biggest and best snowman. We used this story as the basis for an art project. We gave the children materials to represent snow and snowmen and let them know they could make whatever scenes they wanted. The scenes they made are very beautiful and are now hanging on our class bulletin board. They will be there for a bit, so please come in and take a look! We also read *A Penguin Story*, by Antoinette Portis, which is about Edna, a penguin who lives at the South Pole.

We have been discussing the cold weather and how things freeze. One day we brought ice cubes from the school freezer to our water table. The children thought it would be fun to pretend that the ice cubes were Ice Age glaciers, and they asked for the sea animals and dinosaurs to play with. They colored the ice cubes blue using eye-droppers and liquid watercolor. We also filled buckets with water, left them outside, and predicted what would happen to the water. Later, we brought them in and discovered that the water in the buckets appeared frozen. When we poured the buckets into our water table, we saw that they had only two inches of ice on the surface and the water below was not frozen. That was an interesting discovery to the children and they discussed why this might have happened.

Here are some books we have read recently:

All About Alfie, by Shirley Hughes (a series of four stories that can be purchased individually)

A Visitor for Bear, by Bonny Becker

The Great Paper Caper, by Oliver Jeffers

A Penguin Story, by Antoinette Portis

The Biggest, Best Snowman, by Margery Cuyler

The Mitten, by Jan Brett

We had a special speaker this week who taught the children about recycling. He brought lots of examples that the children could touch. They had a good time learning about what can and cannot be recycled.

The children really enjoy working together and making interesting discoveries. They are learning so much about their world. All of our play in the classroom brought us even closer as a community, and we are learning about caring, empathy, trust, collaboration, and connecting. As we see the children develop confidence and a caring perspective, we begin to see them emerge and truly engage with the world. We are all having a great time playing and learning.

Have a great weekend,

Debi and Anna

Figure 5.6 Example of a Weekly Newsletter

Key Understandings to Think About

✳ Prekindergarteners need an organization of activities that engage their intellect, curiosity, and imagination.

✳ The prekindergarten child's day should be characterized by organization and predictability in terms of activity (but always incorporating new and interesting content).

✳ Core literacy activities are important (including visiting the library, phonemic awareness/phonics lessons, reading and response to literature, inquiry, and science, math and social studies explorations).

✳ It is helpful to establish a framework for language and literacy learning and to teach children routines related to the framework.

✳ Consistent, meaningful communication with families about children's literacy learning is very important.

Notes

SECTION

2

Language:
The Foundation for Learning

In this section, we discuss the important role of language in all of children's learning. We talk about language learning as developing a strong oral vocabulary of known words and learning the structure (grammar). But we also look at other aspects of language such as the way words are put together in meaningful ways and how children learn to hear the sounds in words. We take a special look at literacy learning for children who are English language learners.

The Critical Role
of Language in Learning:
Using Language to Learn

*"Inviting children to talk about themselves and about what they
know honors them for who they are."*

—MARTHA HORN AND MARY ELLEN GIACOBBE

Prekindergarten plays a very important role in supporting language growth and development. Talking is the way prekindergarteners process all the new information they are gathering as they use their senses (look, hear, feel, touch, and taste). Language is the most important cognitive tool for interpreting and explaining the information they pick up as they explore and learn.

As we've discussed, play is the basis for so much of the learning that prekindergarteners do. There are three essential contexts for play: (1) cognitive—exploring, asking questions, and thinking; (2) emotional—expressing feelings within the social context; and (3) creative—putting together new learning. Through play, children can be responsible for their own learning and they can use language not just to know but to show they know something. "Talk is the root of literacy" (Kempton, 2007, 47).

Quality talking and listening support memory and enhance understanding. The kinds of talk that children engage in as they play (and in other contexts as well) foster risk taking, support and demonstrate comprehension, and strengthen community.

The New Standards Project (Resnick and Snow, 2008) convened a group of researchers to describe the learning we can typically expect from three- and four-year-old children who participate in prekindergarten. They described how children should be able to use language to guide their own learning, enter into conversation, make plans, and play with words and sentences.

Resnick and Snow (2008) described four kinds of talk: narrative, explaining and seeking information, oral performances, and giving and understanding directions. All are essential. They also addressed the conventions of language and the expectations for grammar, word choice, and taking turns that grow over time. We briefly describe each of these kinds of talk below and also introduce the important area of vocabulary development.

The Oral Language continuum (see Section 7) contains detailed descriptions of the understandings about literacy that young children acquire through their use of language. Language is key to learning across all areas of the preschool curriculum.

Narrative Talk

A narrative is a story, and we all know that children are natural storytellers. We've all been followed around by a small child who is determined to tell us all about her trip to the zoo with her grandma, or the new toothbrush he got at the dentist. "And then, guess what, do you know what happened? Did you know that the dentist gave me a toothbrush? For free?!" Prekindergarteners tell stories about their personal memories as well as imaginary stories. They may blend the stories of movies or television shows with other adventures they imagine or with their personal experiences. They may also retell stories they have heard read, or they may respond to the pages of wordless picture books by creating a story in their own words. Young children often tell long stories connecting many details. "Guess what? We went to the aquarium, and we saw the shark there, and then the shark went swimming over us in the tank, and then we saw its teeth, and then, did you know sharks have lots of rows of teeth? And then we eated our lunch, and then . . . and then. . . ." You get the idea!

As teachers we usually think of stories in a traditional European way: a beginning, revelation of the story problem, a series of events, the problem resolution, and the ending. Narratives following this structure may be simple or complex, but they are predictable. There are many different kinds of story structures (Resnick and Snow, 2008). Some cultures string together a series of seemingly unrelated events that ultimately build an overall meaning or make a point. Others include many characters that are not necessary to the main theme but represent family values and community. Still others tell traditional stories that have an element of fantasy yet reveal underlying meanings about their own lives. Some families tell traditional stories that have been passed down through centuries; some tell stories about the lives of their own family members; still others tell funny stories from their own lives.

Children come to prekindergarten with their own familial and cultural backgrounds, and they may understand stories and story structure in different ways. As teachers we need to appreciate the unique ways children tell stories and help them expand their understanding of what a story is and how a story goes. We can support prekindergarteners' understanding by using story boards, drawings, dolls, and stuffed animals as props that support children in using oral language in a narrative way. (See Appendix D, Lessons 18 and 19 for lessons on storytelling and puppet making.) As we model and as children absorb what they are hearing and seeing, they will be able to tell longer stories from their own experiences. Using a shared experience like a neighborhood walk, a trip to the library, or any number of other lively and memorable moments in the life of a prekindergarten classroom (when the mouse ran across the bookshelf during morning meeting, when the water table sprang a leak and made a puddle on the floor, etc.) as the basis for a narrative that is told and retold can be a wonderful way to model various forms of storytelling.

Retelling familiar tales is a beloved form of story-telling in many prekindergarten classrooms. Four-and-a-half-year-old Kenny heard the story *The Lion and the Mouse* many times and can now go through any picture book version of the tale and "read" by using the pictures and what he knows of the way the story goes to tell what happens. Take a look at Kenny's words and sound effects (Figure 6.1) as prompted by a wonderful new almost wordless version by Jerry Pinkney (2009).

> **Once upon a time there was a little mouse. He was scared. Whooo. Whooo. Screech.**
>
> **He ran to a lion and he caught him. Grr.**
>
> **The big lion let the little mouse go and he went home to his children. Squeak, squeak, squeak.**
>
> **And then the big lion was in trouble. Roar, roar.**
>
> **And the little mouse chewed and chewed and got him free.**
>
> **And they were happy and they were friends.**

Figure 6.1 Kenny's retelling of *The Lion and the Mouse*

All prekindergarteners benefit from the opportunity to tell and retell their stories. The best way to help children absorb and understand the story structure on which much of English literature is built is to read aloud to them often. Children who have numerous opportunities to hear simple stories like *The Three Little Pigs* can look at the pages of just about any picture book version and tell the story, complete with "I'll huff and I'll puff. . . ." Simply hearing stories read aloud with enthusiasm, delight, and expression helps children learn about many story elements, including how they are organized.

Explaining and Seeking Information

School is all about seeking information and communicating it to others, which prepares students not only for future job performance but also for the sheer enjoyment of learning in one's personal life. If the investigations or inquiry projects they undertake as prekindergarteners are interesting and authentic, children will be more motivated to work for deeper understanding and to report it in a way that will be understandable to others (not just "for the teacher"). Prekindergarteners love to report what they have observed: "We seed the elephant baby." "We growed flowers."

They start with simple stories about what they may have seen or done. By the end of prekindergarten, children are able to describe their knowledge with detail.

Four-year-old Elliott made a collection of leaves and then produced a "long" book about them (some pages are shown in Figure 6.2). Notice that he knows informational books have both pictures and print. His first page has his name (spelled accurately) and the word *leaf* (spelled *lɛi*). While Elliott was busily working on the book, his mom remarked that she could hear an *f* at the end of *leaf.* So Elliott added an *f* to the first page.

Figure 6.2 Elliott's leaf book

Construction of the twelve-page book involved a large amount of productive talk. Elliott first collected the leaves and compared them with one another. He then placed a variety of leaves on each page and added marks, letterlike forms, and some letters. When the book was finished, he had an artifact that he could share with others—a guide for telling and retelling what he had observed and concluded. While the end product is wonderful and was very special to Elliott, the talk involved in its creation was even more valuable to his learning. As Elliott glued leaves and made marks, chatting the whole time about what he was thinking and doing, he was learning how to construct and report information.

You might organize children's learning by themes—rocks, trees, magnets, and growing plants, for example (Resnick and Snow, 2008) can become valuable inquiry projects. Guided by the teacher, children explore a topic in depth over some time—a week or several weeks—so that they are able to connect ideas, practice asking questions, and summarize learning. Teachers guide learning by planning experiences and modeling the kind of language they want to help students use. This kind of intense study builds content knowledge and vocabulary and provides wonderful opportunities for children to practice the kind of language involved in explaining and seeking information.

Performance and Response to Performance

In prekindergarten, young children learn to communicate with an audience outside the family. This experience stretches their language abilities, because it generally takes more effort to communicate clearly with people outside the family sphere. Children will also learn to respond to the performances of others by listening actively and thinking. Eventually, performance and response to performance will become very sophisticated, as students are expected to discuss and even critique performance. In the New Standards document referred to earlier (Resnick and Snow, 2008), performance includes anything that is addressed to an audience—speeches; storytelling; recitation of songs, rhymes, and poems; movement; action rhymes and songs; dramatizations; reading aloud in chorus; making reports, etc. All require active listening on the part of the audience, and all require an awareness of the audience when communicating.

Every time you read aloud or tell stories to prekindergarteners, you help them become active listeners. It's important to select texts that are understandable for children in those age groups—texts with content and language that will engage children. Prekindergarten children love stories in which they can participate through movement and sound, like *We're Going on a Bear Hunt* (Rosen, 2009) or *I Went Walking* (Williams, 1990). They like to hear their favorite stories read over and over and learn to join in gleefully on refrains. Reading favorite stories again and again is not time wasted, because children are learning new language structures by participating, using new vocabulary words, and learning how to listen and respond. We have provided an extensive list of read-aloud selections appropriate for three- and four-year-olds in Appendix E.

Prekindergarteners can also give simple performances themselves. When they join in on a shared reading of a text, they are doing just that—making their voices reflect the meaning of the text. They learn to say rhymes, tell stories, or participate in brief dramatizations, using voices that can be heard by others.

Giving and Understanding Directions

Prekindergarteners learn to follow and eventually to communicate directions using words and drawings. They learn the kind of language that supports learning and action—asking questions, following directions, and solving problems. A simple process like making a peanut butter* and jelly sandwich can be a concrete activity leading to the creation of a simple set of directions that includes pictures. The ability to use words to support action is a foundation for all of the more advanced work they will do in school and in their lives. When three-year-olds enter prekindergarten, they naturally talk to themselves to guide their actions ("Car goes up the ramp, zoom! Down again!"), and as you teach you can model the kind of valuable language that will help them cooperate with others and get help with what they want to do.

Let's look at an example (Figure 6.3). The children are in a circle. The teacher is showing them a shelf with tubs of books, covers facing out. Notice how the teacher explicitly expands the children's language.

Conventions of Language

The earlier sections focused on the uses of language, which are very closely tied to thinking. As children find the need to use language to communicate increasingly more complex ideas, they begin to take on new conventions. They use the forms to communicate what they need to do. Form follows function. Skillful users of language have a tool at their disposal, and the more clearly it is used, the more successful the user is. Language is a social tool, and there are important understandings that children need to develop over time. Prekindergarteners can begin to learn rules of conversation:

- Taking turns.
- Looking at the speaker.
- Responding to the topic of the speaker or signaling a change of topic.

---

* Check the children for allergies first.

Example of Teacher Language

TEACHER: We have some beautiful books in our room. Today we are going to learn how to take them out and put them away. This basket has books about Goldilocks and the three bears. Watch while I take the book out. I hold it with both hands and look at the cover. (Demonstrates.) I can read the book or tell the story of the book by turning the pages and telling about them. (Demonstrates.) When I come to the end of the book, I take it with both hands and put it back in the same basket with the cover facing out. (Demonstrates.) Can anyone tell me how that helps our friends in our classroom?

TONY: You can see it.

TEACHER: That's right, it helps to have the cover facing out so the next person who wants to look at the book can see what the book is.

The teacher has two children demonstrate, both taking a book from the same basket.

Then the children work as partners to perform the task.

TEACHER: So, when we have reading time, you can take a book from the basket and look at every page and tell the story. Then you can put it back in the basket with the cover facing out so we can all see it.

Figure 6.3 Example of teacher language

- Getting a turn in a polite way.
- Using particular phrases such as "thank you" and "you're welcome."
- Addressing people by name.
- Knowing where and when it is appropriate to talk.
- Adjusting tone of voice to fit the setting (classroom, playground, large group, small group).

- Building on others' comments.
- Asking questions to support dialogue.
- Choosing topics that expand vocabulary and show new learning.
- Clarifying meaning.
- Having a point when speaking.
- Informing others and being informed.
- Negotiating responsibilities.
- Expressing opinions and feelings.

All of the skills listed above may be very new to three-year-olds, but they can begin to take them on. No one expects perfect skilled conversational behavior from preschoolers, but it is amazing how much they can learn in just two years. It takes a long time to learn and automatically use these social conventions, and they are dependent on the social customs of the home and community as well. If children have daily opportunities, they will become aware of the kinds of talk that are expected in school. Instead of grabbing a marker from another child as he may have done earlier in the year, Tomas might say, "Sofie, can I have the red marker when you're done?" And Sofie, instead of ignoring Tomas as she might have done earlier in the year, might reply, "Okay, when I'm done making my balloon."

Vocabulary Development

Vocabulary is a vital part of a learner's knowledge of language. An extensive oral vocabulary makes a huge difference in prekindergarteners' learning. Before they begin school, children have had conversations with others in their homes and communities, but the words used in these contexts are less varied than the vocabulary they will encounter in school. Prekindergarten opens up the world of language for young children.

Think about the way children have learned their vocabulary up to now. Parents did not teach their children words like *drink, apple juice, kiss,* or *bye-bye* as single words. They used them in meaningful conversations with their children: *Sweetheart, say bye-bye to Auntie Sue. Bye-bye, Sue! See you soon!* Or: *You look so thirsty. Let's go back to the stroller and get you a drink of water.* Children heard the words again and again in sentences with examples they could see, touch, and feel. They connected nonverbal gestures with words. We take a similar approach in the prekindergarten classroom. We don't aim to teach words in isolation but within the context of meaningful conversation.

You can expand children's oral vocabulary in almost every context. Reading aloud to children is a wonderful foundation; however, you also want to engage them in talk about texts. (See Appendix D, Lesson 13 for a simple lesson on using book boxes, which engages children in talk about texts.) You will find our section on oral language (in the continuum and in Chapter 7) useful for identifying what the child can already do and what he needs to learn how to do to demonstrate effective language behaviors by the end of the prekindergarten program for four-year-olds. We also provide several lessons that are particularly useful for developing oral language. (See Appendix D.)

Key Understandings to Think About

✳ Language plays an extremely important role in young children's learning.

✳ Children learn to use language in different ways: narrative, explaining and seeking information, oral performances, and giving and understanding directions.

✳ Children's language expands as they interact with a wider variety of people. They learn different ways of responding.

✳ Children learn more about how to use language conventionally (the "rules" of conversation, for example) as they find the need to do so.

✳ Vocabulary refers to the words that children use and understand in oral language.

✳ You can expand children's vocabulary through conversation, particularly about texts that you read aloud to them.

Notes

Developing Strong Oral Vocabularies in Prekindergarten

"Knowledgeable teachers recognize the value of expanding children's vocabulary in the course of studying topics of interest, and by reading aloud high-quality books with rich vocabulary."

—Heather Biggar Tomlinson and Marilou Hyson

Vocabulary instruction has often been "neglected" in prekindergartens (Neuman, 2009), but now teachers are giving more attention to this important area of learning (Neuman and Dwyer, 2009).

When we think about vocabulary for PreK, we mean speaking and listening vocabularies—the words children understand and use in oral language. But as teachers we also think about the body of words children can read/write—their reading and writing vocabularies. For PreK children, the most important goal is to increase oral vocabulary, but it is also important to

notice the words they first learn to read and write. They may be emotionally important words, such as their own names, *love, mom,* and *dad.* Some may be words they simply see very often, such as *the.* Many children enter kindergarten able to read and write a few words. Those who do not will benefit from having rich oral vocabularies and early understandings of print and how it works.

Vocabulary contributes significantly to reading comprehension. In fact, speaking, listening, reading, and writing vocabularies are essential for success in just about every area of study in school. The ability to express oneself throughout life is related to the words we understand.

Vocabulary is more than just knowing words. It involves understanding concepts, connecting networks of information, and developing categories and bodies of knowledge. It drives reading and oral language comprehension. Further, vocabulary understandings are cumulative. The more words we know, the easier it is to make the connections that help us learn more:

"Vocabulary instruction . . . must be more than merely identifying or labeling words. Rather, it should be about helping children to build word meaning and the ideas that these words represent. By understanding words and their connections to concepts and facts, children develop skills that will help in comprehending text." (Neuman and Dwyer, 2009, 385)

Prekindergarteners come to school knowing many words that have been useful in their homes, but they may not have been exposed to the kind of academic language that is useful in school settings. They may not have heard people talk about or even identify the title or author of a book. They may not realize that books are written and illustrated by people and that they are like the stories people tell. Many children lack labels for objects in the environment that they have not seen or experienced in a meaningful way. It is never too soon to help children get excited about learning new words, and many develop a habit of it. Some young children astonish us by using a particular word that has caught their attention. At the age of four, Rachel suddenly began to sprinkle her comments with the word *actually*:

Actually, I want milk.

Actually, it's my computer.

Actually, no.

Her parents did not teach her the word and could not remember using the word very much themselves. But somehow she had picked up an interesting word from listening to adult conversation, television, or other children.

Intentional Vocabulary Instruction

Intentional vocabulary instruction can help prekindergarteners rapidly expand not only their knowledge base but the words that describe it. Vocabulary teaching should be systematic and explicit. By this we do not mean drilling children on words in isolation. We know of no research that supports the "word of the day" approach. Children learn new words when they have opportunities to develop new understandings and concepts through in-depth study.

As concepts are developed you can intentionally use the new vocabulary and help children, over time, take it on themselves. You can encourage them to use the new words as they engage in inquiry projects around a topic over several days. For example, children studying rocks will have the opportunity to be exposed to (and then to take on for themselves) words like *smooth, hard, bumpy,* and *rough.* (See Appendix D, Lesson 22 for a lesson on using descriptive words.) As they engage in inquiry, they have a chance to build on the previous days' learning, gradually incorporating new words into their vocabulary banks: *That bumpy one is funny! It looks like a crocodile!* Children must use a word in a meaningful way several times before it becomes part of their personal repertoire. Even after the particular topic has been exhausted, it is helpful to revisit it in book activities or discussion so that the new words can be practiced again and again: multiple encounters with words in meaningful contexts will mean making them their own.

The Contribution of Reading Aloud to Vocabulary Expansion

Reading aloud to your children and discussing stories is a wonderful way to build vocabulary. As we've mentioned, it is of utmost importance to choose your read-aloud books carefully and with intention and to prepare for discussions with your class about the books you've chosen. When choosing your read-alouds, keep an eye out for a few new words that you'll want to highlight and explain as you read.

Every read-aloud text offers opportunities for children to learn a few new words. Mo Willems' *Knuffle Bunny* (2004) is an engaging and much-loved story appropriate for three-year-olds. In the story, a young child named Trixie goes with her daddy to the Laundromat; she is carrying her favorite stuffed animal, Knuffle Bunny. Trixie is only babbling, but her dad acts like she is saying words. As the story goes on, Knuffle Bunny is lost at the Laundromat and Trixie becomes very upset. After frantic searching, they find the toy and Trixie says her first words, "Knuffle Bunny." This story reflects an experience common to most young children, but look at some of the sophisticated vocabulary used:

> But a block or so later . . . Trixie realized something.
>
> Trixie turned to her daddy and said, "Aggle, flaggle klabble!"
>
> "That's right," replied her daddy. "We're going home."
> (11–14)

Children can identify with Trixie's frustration at her inability to communicate, but after a few readings, they will also become familiar with (at least in listening vocabulary) with words like *realized* and *replied*, which appear much more often in written language than in ordinary oral discourse with children.

A beloved book appropriate for four-year-olds is *Lilly's Purple Plastic Purse*, by Kevin Henkes (1996). Lilly loves school and wants to be a teacher just like her teacher, Mr. Slinger. One day she brings her new purple plastic purse to school and plays with it so much that it is taken away for the day. She takes out her anger by drawing a mean picture of Mr. Slinger, but the issue is resolved by the next day. Children love Lilly's antics, and also encounter some vocabulary that stretches them, for example:

> "Let's be considerate of our classmates."
>
> Lilly had a hard time being considerate.
> (10)

The glasses were so glittery. The quarters were so shiny, and the purse played such nice music, not to mention how excellent it was for storing school supplies. (11)

Each time you read a story to a group of young children, you give them examples of new words within a meaningful context. As you select books to read aloud, you need to consider children's current vocabularies. A book should have some but not too many new words, and it's helpful if the concepts they label are concrete and understandable and the pictures provide information in a very clear way.

The kinds of texts mentioned above invite revisiting, both rereading them to children and having children look at the pictures and tell the stories. If they are familiar with the language, they are very likely to use the new words in the context of sentences. Rhyme and rhythm greatly enhance the appeal of the text and children's ability to remember and use some of the language. You may even want to keep copies of the week's interactive read-aloud books along with audio recordings in the listening center so that children can listen to them again and again.

The Interactive Read-Aloud and Literature Discussion continuum (Section 7) lists vocabulary as a factor in selecting texts to read to children and specifies the curriculum goal of helping children acquire new words from those texts. Without interrupting children's appreciation of the meaning and language of a story, we can bring new vocabulary to conscious attention through repetition and discussion.

Using Poetry to Expand Vocabulary

You can also use poems, songs, and rhymes on charts (with simple supporting pictures) to engage children in shared reading (see the list of poems, rhymes, and songs in Appendix A). Once they become familiar with the text, they will be able to "read" it for themselves, chanting along with the whole group or even with a partner. Memory is operating here but not in a rote way. The language is pleasurable and familiar; children enjoy the patterns and rhymes again and again and in the process they learn new vocabulary words but also more complex language patterns and grammatical structures.

Think about the potential learning in Figure 7.1. The fingerplay "Where Is Thumbkin," is simpler but still involves words like *where, very, today,* and *thank you.* At first, three-year-olds may join in only with the hand gestures (hiding the thumbs, bringing them out, having them bow, and then hiding them again), but they will gradually become familiar with the rhyme and join in on the words as well. This rhyme has the additional value of practicing questions and answers. In "Twinkle, Twinkle, Little Star," children encounter words like *twinkle, world,* and *wonder.* They also have the opportunity to hear words

that rhyme, which supports awareness of the sounds in words. Name poems also provide engaging opportunities for children to learn new words. We have included many examples of rhyming poems in Appendix A.

Increasing Children's Awareness of Words

As children learn more about vocabulary and develop a sense of the listening audience, they choose to use the interesting new words that they have learned through conversation, hearing books read aloud, and the shared reading of poetry. They become conscious of making word choices that capture their meaning. This learning may be evident in their talk about their drawings or even their attempts at spelling interesting words.

Where Is Thumbkin?

Where is Thumbkin?

Where is Thumbkin?

Here I am.

Here I am.

How are you today, sir?

Very well, I thank you.

Run away.

Run away.

Twinkle, Twinkle, Little Star

Twinkle, twinkle, little star,

How I wonder what you are!

Up above the world so high,

Like a diamond in the sky.

Twinkle, twinkle, little star,

How I wonder what you are!

Figure 7.1 Rhyming poems

Hawa made a book and her teacher wrote her language on stick-on notes that she placed on the back of each page (Figure 7.2). Notice how Hawa's language in the book she made reflects her experiences and awareness of vocabulary. She drew pictures on each page of her book, telling about swimming in her grandma's

pool, then picking apples and getting an ice cream. Finally, she tells about going home.

Children need to "own" the words; they need to understand and use them in everyday talk. The words need to resonate with meaning gained through personal experiences or encounters. (See Appendix D, Lesson 16

Figure 7.2 Hawa's book

for a simple lesson on "Me" boxes.) For some words, once or twice is enough. For more complex words, it may take dozens of encounters in a meaningful context, which is why vocabulary drills are the least effective way for prekindergarteners and kindergarten-to-third-grade students to learn new words.

Be careful to embed intentional vocabulary instruction in meaningful conversation about topics of interest and stories that have made an impact. Labeling objects in your room with pictures and words is another opportunity to expose children to new words and to support their developing awareness of print in the world.

I picked apples in the park.

I got ice cream and it fell down.

Then we went home.

Figure 7.2 Hawa's book, *continued*

Key Understandings to Think About

✳ Expanding vocabulary involves much more than learning words.

✳ Intentional vocabulary instruction can help prekindergarteners more rapidly expand their knowledge base and the words that describe it.

✳ Reading aloud is an effective way to build vocabulary. The reading should be accompanied by conversation about the text.

✳ Shared reading of poetry can also contribute to vocabulary expansion.

✳ Children should be adding five to ten new words to their working vocabularies every day.

✳ Vocabulary instruction should be embedded in meaningful conversation.

Notes

CHAPTER

8

Phonemic Awareness and Phonics:
The Sounds of Language

*"Phonemic awareness is necessary for success
in learning to read and write."*

—Marie Clay

At the same time they are beginning to understand the role of print in their world, children are developing phonological awareness. In the oral language system, single sounds, or phonemes, are strung together in streams that are heard as meaningful words by the speakers of a language. Children need to learn to hear these individual sounds in words. This is no small feat for several reasons, not least of which is that speakers do not separate words into sounds. There are no real spaces between the sounds in words. To make it even trickier, the phonemes in words influence one

another to produce different sounds in different words: *bun/burn,* for example.

Young children start to become generally aware of the sounds of language as they enjoy listening to or saying rhymes and songs. Language play is very appealing to children and has always been a significant element of childhood from infancy. As children learn to say rhymes themselves (helped along by the rhythm), they begin to hear that some words sound alike at the end. Some chants use alliteration (all or many words starting with the same sound, like "Peter Piper picked a peck of pickled peppers"), which can help children become aware of the sound of a particular phoneme.

This general awareness becomes more finely tuned as children have more experiences in shared reading and writing. Children might next begin to notice parts of words that are similar in sound (beginning, ending). Prekindergarteners can often suggest the first sound and letter of a word or hear the sound of the ending letter. Interactive writing, coupled with individual writing, is the most effective tool we have found for helping children hear sounds in words and to start to represent them with letters. Some teachers find that a simple class word wall can also be useful for highlighting sounds in words with prekindergarteners. Often teachers label many objects in the classroom (door, books, blocks, chair), and children gradually begin to connect oral vocabulary with print. You can also display print from the environment, for example, a stop sign.

Our continuum (Section 7) includes detailed goals for the preschool curriculum in phonics, spelling, and word study. It lists the understandings children will need *as they enter kindergarten.* We want to make clear that children are not expected to know the entire alphabet or how to spell words before entering kindergarten. Rather, the continuum identifies foundational understandings such as the ideas that letters have different shapes, that words have sounds in them, and that there is a relationship between letters and sounds. Of course, some children will learn a few or even many written words that have great meaning (*Granny, love, Mom*).

Understanding Phonemic Awareness

There are several key terms associated with children's early understandings of the sounds of language. It can be easy to confuse them, and they are all important! Let's review the common ones:

- *Phonemes*—the individual sounds you can hear in words. For example, *cat* and *like* both have three sounds. You can hear them in sequence if you say the word slowly.
- *Phonemic awareness*—the ability to hear the individual phonemes (sounds) in words.
- *Phonological awareness*—the ability to hear syllables, rhymes, and individual sounds. Phonemic awareness is part of phonological awareness.
- *Alphabetic principle*—understanding that letters in written words represent sounds in oral language.
- *Phonics*—knowing letter-sound relationships, or the sounds represented by the symbols.
- *Onset and rime*—these terms refer to parts of words. The onset is the opening or the first part of a word of one syllable (<u>bl</u>ack, <u>c</u>ar, <u>p</u>at, <u>c</u>ake). The rime is the rest of the word (bl<u>ack</u>, c<u>ar</u>, p<u>at</u>, c<u>ake</u>).

There are a few others that may be useful as you think about using oral games with children:

- *Blending*—putting together the sounds (*c-a-t/cat, m-ake/make*).
- *Segmenting*—saying the individual sounds or parts that form a word (*c-a-t, m-ake*).
- *Manipulating*—adding or taking away (deleting) a sound in a word (*it/fit, l-ake/ake*).

Your primary goal as you help develop children's phonemic awareness is to help them listen for word parts and sounds by engaging them in reading, writing, and oral language activities. We do not advocate using drills, difficult examples, or nonsense words to help children learn to hear and segment or manipulate the sounds. The entire activity should be playful and enjoyable. Too much specific attention to sounds—as if it is a task to be done "correctly"—not only confuses children but also shuts them down to the delight and enjoyment of learning about language. It is natural for children to play with the sounds of words. Weir's (1962) study of children in their cribs revealed that children "practiced" new words and sounds as they lulled themselves to sleep. You want to build on this natural curiosity and help children play with sounds in words in your classroom with that same spirit of delight in discovery.

Books That Involve Language and Word Play

You can lay a strong foundation for later phonics learning by inviting children to notice the sounds of language. The most enjoyable way to do this is by reading aloud some wonderful books that "play" with language. There are many wonderful alphabet books and rhyming books on our list in Appendix E, including *My Truck Is Stuck* (Lewis, 2002), *Chicken Little* (Emberley and Emberley, 2009), and *Chicka Chicka Boom Boom* (Martin, 2006). Books of poetry such as Martin's *Big Book of Poetry* (2009) are treasure troves of poems that will delight young children with language.

When children enter kindergarten, they will be introduced to phonics in a systematic way that includes a daily phonics minilesson, application of principles (such as noticing the first letter and sound of a word), and sharing. We describe such lessons in *Phonics Lessons, Grades K, 1, 2,* and *Word Study Lessons 3* (Pinnell and Fountas, 2003). We provide some examples of the short, very focused lessons (e.g., name puzzle) that are appropriate to use with four-year-olds in a prekindergarten class. (See Appendix D.)

Songs, Chants, and Rhymes

Rhythmic language provides many opportunities for children to enjoy the sounds of language. Rhymes are easy for children to remember because of the repetition and rhythm. There is an inherent pleasure in saying them. Children notice similarities and differences in sound patterns as they say these chants and rhymes

over and over. Many also involve finger, hand, or body movements that promote coordination and interpretation of the rhyme. Here are some examples (many more are included in Appendix A):

The Rattlesnake
I was walking near the lake
and I met a rattlesnake.
He ate so much of jelly cake
it made his little belly ache.

Itsy Bitsy Spider
The itsy, bitsy spider
Climbed up the waterspout.
Down came the rain
And washed the spider out.
Out came the sun
And dried up all the rain.
And the itsy, bitsy spider
Climbed up the spout again.

I'm a Little Teapot
I'm a little teapot
short and stout.
Here is my handle,
Here is my spout.
When I get all steamed up,
I just shout:
"Tip me over
and pour me out."

At first, young children may only approximate the words and motions, but over time, you will help them develop a repertoire of songs and rhymes that they know well.

You can use these rhymes in many ways:

* To start or end the day.

- To signal cleanup time or a move to the rug.
- While lining up.
- While walking across the yard in a line.
- To sing to another class.
- To illustrate and display in the school corridor, on the sidewalk, or in the bathroom.
- To make class books (one page per line).
- To include and illustrate in personal poetry books (you provide photocopies of the rhymes, and children add their own drawings).

To teach a rhyme or song:

- Say the words or sing them.
- Repeat the words several times, and then have the children join in.
- Talk about the meaning. When the children understand what the words mean, they can remember more easily.
- Demonstrate actions as you sing or say the words.

- Perhaps draw pictures on a chart or hold up a picture (of a spider, for example) to remind the children.
- Vary your voice (high or low, loud or soft).

Clapping Syllables

A basic understanding for children to develop in prekindergarten is that words can have one, two, or more syllables. Children can easily be taught to hear syllable breaks. This ability will be helpful later as they learn to match print with their vocalizations when reading and as they begin to take words apart. In prekindergarten classrooms you might simply tell children that you are going to show them a way to hear the parts in words. Use the word *parts*, as syllable is too technical a word for the prekindergarten age group. In order for children to understand this principle, you will need to use pictures of words with a various number of syllables.

Figure 8.1 Hearing word parts

Here is a suggested process (see Figure 8.1):

- Place three key pictures in the pocket chart or on a chart (for example, *cat, apple, banana*).

- Say *cat* and clap once. Invite the children to clap along with you as you say the word again. Tell them that *cat* has one part.

- Then say *apple* and clap twice to show the syllables.

- Invite children to do it with you, and tell them that *apple* has two parts.

- Repeat the process with *banana*.

- Hold up a picture card and invite children to say and clap the word the picture represents.

- Then have them group the cards with pictures of words with the same number of syllables.

- Repeat the process over several days until children are very good at saying and clapping words.

Provide group support for clapping syllables for some time. Also, be sure that the pictures are meaningful to children and that they can pronounce the words clearly.

Picture Sorting

Picture sorting is an engaging way to develop children's phonemic awareness. The same sets of picture cards can be used to highlight a variety of skills. Start by gathering some simple pictures categorized by their labels' beginning sounds. You can find some good ones by cutting up old phonics workbooks, or you can order the Phonics Lessons Enlarged Picture Card set (Heinemann, 2004). Children can contribute more pictures to the collection by looking through magazines and newspapers at home, but be sure that the name of the object in the picture will be clear to everyone. (More than one object in a picture, for example, adds complexity.) Select the best (and easiest to remember) pictures and glue them onto cards.

The first step is to help children learn to say the name of each picture. Then they can sort the pictures by:

- Beginning sounds.
- Ending sounds.
- Rhyme.
- Number of parts (syllables).

(See Appendix D, Lesson 15 for a lesson on picture sorting.)

Developing Phonological Awareness with Oral Games

You can use oral games to help children learn how to listen for and identify words in sentences, syllables in words, the first part (onset) and the last part (rime) of one-syllable words (e.g., *c-at*), and the individual phonemes in words (*c-a-t*). These games accomplish a lot of work in a very short time and are easy to tuck in throughout the day. See Appendix D, Lesson 14 for a basic lesson on oral word games.

The following oral games can be played as time allows (even less than a minute) to build children's sensitivity to units of sound:

Blending. Have children blend the sounds in words (e.g., you say *c-a-t* and they say *cat*). Or have children blend the onset with the rime (e.g., *c-at, d-og*) or blend syllables (e.g., *ba-na-na, banana, um-brell-a, umbrella*).

Segmenting. Have children segment sounds in words. For example, you say *cat* or show the picture of a cat and they say *c-a-t*. Or they can segment *dog* to *d-og* and *cat* to *c-at*.

Manipulating phonemes. Have children add sounds to the beginning or end of words or change a sound in a word (e.g., *and/band, an/ant, look/took*).

Hearing word parts. Hold up individual picture cards (see Figure 8.2) and have children clap (or shake a noisemaker or beat a drum) on all the beats

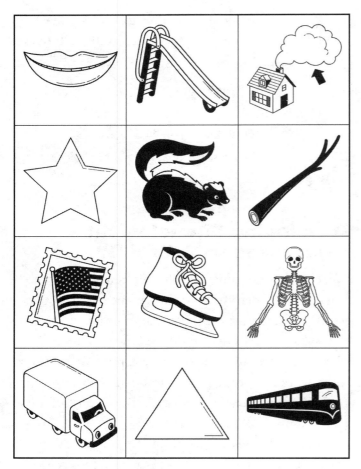

Figure 8.2 Picture card set

(syllables) of the words the cards represent. (Or you might use the children's names. Ask the children to clap and count the syllables of their first and last names together.) You can have the children whisper the word and clap syllables or have the children clap the syllable without saying the word at all.

Listening for Sounds

Young children enjoy playing I Spy. Start by saying, "I spy with my little eye something you are wearing that starts with /sh/ [*shirt*]." Then let each child lead a round of the game. You can also play the game with ending sounds.

Mystery Sounds

Say four words that begin with the same sound such as *basket, ballroom, ball, big*. Have the children tell the first sound. Repeat the same process but include one word with a different first sound (*cake, car, hat, coat*). Ask the children which of the words starts with a different sound. Repeat using four words, one of which has a different end sound (*hot, bed, not, fat*).

Collecting Sound Pictures

Create a poster together of magazine pictures that start with the same sound (e.g., *lamp, light*) or end with the same sound (*hen, pen*).

Connecting Ending Sounds

Say four words such as *stop, mop, hop, top*. Ask the children to tell you the last sound.

Tongue Twisters

Have fun saying tongue twisters like *Peter Piper picked a peck of pickled peppers* or *Susan sipped some strawberry soup*.

Phoneme Fun

Show children a puppet and explain that this puppet has a name (choose the name depending on which sound you want to work on) and that he has a little problem that makes him start everyone's name with the same letter (e.g., if you tell students the puppet's name is Larry, he would call Irene, Ron, and George *Lirene, Lon, Lorge*. If you tell them the puppet's name is Molly, she would call them *Mirene, Mon, Morge*).

Looking for Sounds

Group words by their first sound by finding all items in the classroom that begin with the same sound (*door, doll, desk*).

Matching Sounds

In a pocket chart, display cards that have pictures whose labels start with the same sound except for one. Have the children say the labels and find the one that starts with a different sound.

Concentration

Place a group of picture cards facedown. Children turn over two cards and say the name of the items. If the names start with the same sound, the child who turned them over keeps the pair (*baby/book, cat/car*).

ABC Travel

This popular game can be played while children are standing in line. The destination or mode of transportation can change: picnic, rowboat, beach, etc. For example, "I am going on a picnic and I am going to bring an apple." The next child says, "I am going to bring an apple and a banana." The list keeps expanding as the children add items starting with every letter/sound in the alphabet. (Make the game more fun by taking silly things like an ape and a balloon.) You can also simplify the game by having children think of something that begins with the same sound—*ball, balloon, bear*. Change the sound when they run out of ideas.

Rhyming Words

Say a nursery rhyme the children know (see Appendix A). Leave out the rhyming word and ask the children to fill it in. For example, "Jack and Jill went up the _____."

Letter Names

See related lessons in Appendix D: Making Letters (Lesson 29), Letter Exploration (Lesson 27), Letter Sort (Lesson 28), Alphabet Bookmaking (Lesson 8), Alphabet Hunt (Lesson 23), and Alphabet Linking (Lesson 26).

Alphabet Soup

Place magnetic letters in a bucket. Have children stir the bucket with a wooden or plastic spoon and scoop out one letter. Have them find the letter on the large alphabet linking chart (Appendix G).

Labels

Label the furniture items and other objects in the classroom. Use clear printing. Occasionally stop in front of the items and read the labels, inviting the children to tell the name of the first letter.

Letter Play

Teaching the "letter of the week" slows down student learning (see Fisher, 1996, and Chapter 19 in this book). Different children enter your class knowing different letters. You can, however, celebrate a particular letter on a particular day: create art with things that begin with the letter, read books or play oral games that emphasize the letter, sing songs that include the letter, point out objects in the classroom that begin with the letter, eat a snack that begins with the letter, ask the children to bring in something that begins with the letter. (For example, you might create *p*aintings, sketch with *p*encils, eat *p*retzels, chant "*P*eter *P*iper," read "The Three Little *P*igs," etc.)

Key Understandings to Think About

✳ Children simultaneously develop awareness of the sounds of language and the role of print in their world.

✳ The goal of teaching phonemic awareness is to help children notice and play with the sounds in words.

✳ Reading aloud to children supports their ability to notice the sounds in words.

✳ Songs, chants, and rhymes increase children's awareness of sounds.

✳ You can do some very specific activities such as clapping syllables to increase awareness of sound parts in words.

✳ Oral games can increase children's awareness of sounds in words.

Notes

9

Supporting English Language Learners in the Prekindergarten Classroom

*"The most supportive early literacy environments
for ELLs focus on developing vocabulary, building
oral language, and sharing literacy experiences."*

—Nancy Cloud, Fred Genesee, and Elyse Hamayan

Many young children enter prekindergarten classrooms having learned a first language other than English. We use the word *learned* consciously—whatever language they speak at home has been *learned*. Every child has learned a sound system and a body of meaningful words in their first language. They have learned the "rules" by which words are put together in sentences that are meaningful to speakers of the language. They have learned expressions that make language interesting and colorful. While the structures and systems of languages might vary tremendously, the *process* and even the sequence of learning language are much the same all over the world (Lindfors, 1999).

The Continuum of Literacy Learning, PreK (see Section 7) presents curriculum goals across six areas:

- Interactive Read-Aloud and Literature Discussion
- Shared and Performance Reading
- Writing About Reading
- Writing
- Oral, Visual, and Technological Communication
- Phonics, Spelling, and Word Study

With the exception of understanding some particular word (phonics) structures, these behaviors and understandings are not particular to English. Whatever language children speak, they can build these understandings while engaging with texts written in their own language. English language learners (ELLs) are simultaneously acquiring a new language and building understandings of English as a written language. They are learning new vocabulary words and connecting them to concepts that they already understand as well as making new discoveries. Even more important than vocabulary, they are learning a new "grammar," the rules by which sentences are put together.

In every instructional setting reflected in the PreK Continuum, you can support the expansion of ELLs' knowledge of English. Through hearing texts read aloud and discussing them, learners have the opportunity to try out new language vocabulary and syntax.

Shared and performance reading provides an authentic reason to use the same language structures over and over so that children can internalize them. Writing and oral expression make it possible for students to use what they know about English, and through phonics and word study they are helped to look closely at the features of print and become aware of sounds.

Unless you are providing a bilingual program (which we highly recommend), the children you teach will be learning to speak and eventually to read and write English. But they already know *a process for learning language,* and they are also expanding their home language. Everything you do will support this learning, and young children are incredibly fast language learners. We describe twenty suggestions and then summarize the important principles for working effectively with young English language learners (Figure 9.1).

Suggestions for Working with English Language Learners in Prekindergarten

1. Provide a visual demonstration.
2. Keep language clear and simple.
3. Invite children to act out what they mean.
4. Engage children in conversation, but allow silence until the child becomes comfortable.
5. Check understanding.
6. Invite children to repeat the language of stories.
7. Provide "wait and think" time.
8. Avoid correcting children's attempts at language.
9. Use repeated readings of read-aloud books, shared reading, and poems to give children opportunities to articulate book language again and again.
10. Explain the vocabulary words in texts as necessary.
11. Teach and check for understanding of academic language.
12. Value and encourage drawing and talking about drawing.
13. Have children repeat the messages they are attempting to write.
14. Help children create repetitive written texts so that they can articulate the same English language structures again and again.
15. Use previously written texts as resources.
16. Help children with the pronunciation of words, and teach them to say words slowly and accept approximations.
17. Learn as much as you can about children's home languages and cultures.
18. Provide "hands-on" activities using letters and pictures.
19. Be sure that English language learners are in a position to hear and see everything while you are teaching.
20. Create strong connections with children's homes (language and culture).

Figure 9.1 Suggestions for working with English language learners in prekindergarten

Provide a Visual Demonstration

Do everything you can to *show* in addition to telling. Act out directions and processes. Use real objects whenever possible. Invite children to repeat your actions, sometimes using simple words.

Keep Language Clear and Simple

Say it one clear way and repeat with concrete action. Avoid too much language, which can be confusing and overwhelming.

Invite Children to Act Out Meaning

Often, children understand but lack the words to respond. They can *show* understanding. For example, a child can touch and hold up a favorite book and show a picture. He can draw and point to something in a picture.

Engage Children in Conversation

It is important for all of your prekindergarteners, but especially your English language learners, that you make your instruction highly interactive, with a great deal of oral language surrounding everything that children do (although sometimes it is helpful to provide concrete demonstration with very little oral language). At times, you will want to practice conversation by taking turns speaking.

Inviting children to talk about the texts that you have read aloud to them will help them expand the number of words and phrases they can use in conversation. They will approximate at first, but their ability to use new words correctly will develop

quickly. Joselito, talking about the book *Knuffle Bunny* (Willems, 2005), first said, "Girl. Bun," which became, "Girl, bunny," which became, "Girl want bunny!"

Check Understanding

Make your own oral language as simple and clear as possible. Use gestures or act out processes and then ask children to do so to be sure they understand you. Very often, they can understand more than they can say. If you are giving directions, for example, be sure that the visual support is there and that you repeat the directions as often as needed. You might bring a marker with you to the meeting area, for example, and say, "Push the cap down on the marker until you hear the click," as you demonstrate doing just that, several times. You may ask students to "show the class" what you've done so that you are certain they've understood. Try not to require long sequences of actions; break the steps down into easily managed chunks.

Repeat the Language of Stories

It is often helpful to English language learners to repeat some of the language they hear in books. As you're reading *We're Going on a Bear Hunt* (Rosen, 2009), for example, you might ask children to join you for the refrain, "We can't go over it. We can't go under it. Oh no! We'll have to go through it!" That's why repetitive language in books is so attractive. (And native English speakers can also profit a great deal from this activity. The language in books is often more complicated than any child would use in oral conversation.) The more ELLs expand their knowledge of English syntax by "book talk," the easier it will be for them to comprehend and eventually to read texts.

Provide "Wait and Think" Time

When you are trying to formulate a response in a language you are just learning to speak, you need a little more time to organize your thought into words before you articulate it. Try saying something like, "Let's all think for a minute before we try to answer." Demonstrate to children how you think about what you are going to say or write.

Avoid Correcting Children's Attempts at Language

Research shows that parents seldom correct their young children's "grammar," yet children gradually expand their understanding to take on conventional English syntax. Consider English language learners' attempts as approximations along a path of learning and work to understand them. You can summarize or rephrase children's sentences in a conversational way without correcting them. Correcting can discourage active learning.

Rearticulate Book Language

Shared reading involves children in a great deal of language repetition, often language that is different from or more complex than the language they can currently use in speech. This experience gives English language learners a chance to practice their new language, learn the meaning of words, and use the sentence structures of English. Several repetitions of a new language structure within a meaningful and enjoyable activity will enable a child to add the new structure to her repertoire.

Explain Vocabulary

Examine the texts you plan to read aloud to English language learners. Are there labels that will be unfamiliar to them even though they are common English words? Do

they know the labels in their own language? Mark any words that need explanation or even a concrete example such as a picture or the actual object. If there are too many unknown vocabulary words in the text, choose a simpler one and build labels over time. Direct attention to pictures and use understandable oral language when you introduce texts. Help learners relate new words to words they already know. During and after reading, check with children to be sure they understand vocabulary and concepts. Allow time within the lessons for children to bring up any words they do not know.

Explain Academic Language

English language learners, as well as many other children, might need support to understand concepts like "the beginning" or "the ending" of a story. Many children do not understand the concepts of *first, last, beginning,* and *ending* as they apply to print. For example, they need to understand the concept of "beginning" if they are to respond to the question, "What letter would you expect to find at the beginning of your name?" Teach these concepts through examples and discussion. As you read stories, consciously use the vocabulary and encourage children to use these words in their conversation. In small groups or with individuals, you can play quick games. For example, "Everyone turn to the beginning." "Go to the end." "Show the front cover."

Draw and Talk About Drawing

English language learners can represent their thinking by drawing. Even a little talking about the drawing will be meaningful. Demonstrate by talking about their drawings in clear sentences that you think they can understand. "I see a girl standing next to a house. Is that you? It looks like you because of the pigtails you drew," you might say, pointing to the parts of the drawing as you mention them.

Repeat Messages Children Attempt to Write

During interactive, shared, and independent writing, keep the sentences simple enough that English language learners can say them. Have them repeat the sentence they are going to write several times so that they will be able to remember it. Few, if any, four-year-olds will be able to write sentences independently. If the sentence is difficult for children to remember, you may need to simplify it. Once the sentence is decided, be prepared to act as the child's memory while she is constructing it.

Repeat English Language Structures

A sentence like "Mary likes bread and butter," repeated for children who need this kind of support, will help them learn how to connect nouns using *and*. You can also repeat the verb in the answer to a question: "What do you like? I like apples." Then record children's answers on a chart. (See the example in Figure 9.2.)

Of course, not everything you write will have such built-in repetition, and you don't want writing messages to become tedious, but it's easy to engineer some repetitive texts that will help English language learners internalize language structures.

Use Previously Written Texts as Resources

Once a text has been successfully produced in interactive writing, dictation, or independent writing and children can remember and read it easily, you can use the text as a resource for talking about language—locating specific words, noticing beginning and ending sounds, noticing rhymes, and so on. In the chart in Figure 9.2, for example, you might ask children to find their own names.

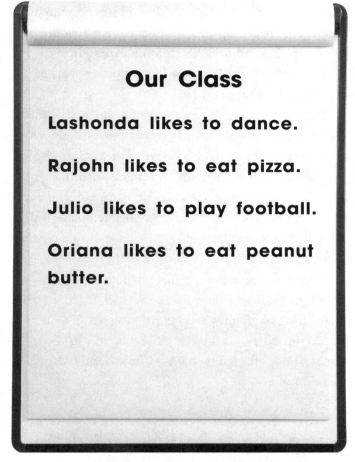

Figure 9.2 Our Class

Pronounce Words and Say Words Slowly

You will need to accept approximated pronunciations of words. Very few non-native speakers achieve standard pronunciation. If you were to speak any language other than English, chances are, you too would have an "accent." Nevertheless, prekindergarteners have the very best chance of matching English phonology exactly, because they are starting so young. They acquire new sound patterns easily because they are so flexible. But it takes time. Avoid using words as examples that are especially hard for a non-native speaker to pronounce. Demonstrate how to say words slowly, providing more individual help and demonstration if needed. Notice how English pronunciation improves as children experience reading and talking. Remember even native speakers display regional variation.

Accept alternative pronunciations of words with the hard-to-say sounds, and present the written form to help learners distinguish between them. Sounds that are like each other, have similar tongue positions, and are easily confused, such as *s* and *z, r* and *l, sh* and *ch, f* and *v*, can be quite difficult for English language learners to differentiate. They also often have difficulty with inflected endings (*s, ed*) because they have not yet achieved control of the language structure. Speak clearly and slowly when working with children on distinguishing phonemes and hearing sounds in words, but do not distort a word so much that it is unrecognizable. Distortion may make a word sound like one they do not know.

Learn About Children's Home Languages and Cultures

Some schools have a preponderance of one language other than English, and that makes it easier to study children's home language. But many schools have forty or fifty language groups, and you may have as many as twenty in your own prekindergarten classroom. Still, it will help if you can learn something about the sound system of every child's first language. That knowledge will give you valuable insights into the way your students "invent" or "approximate" their first spellings. For example, notice whether they are using letter-sound associations from the first language or whether they are actually thinking of a word in the first language and trying to spell it.

In addition, you may want to include labels for objects in your room in several different languages and even include some books read in other languages in your class listening center. Also, be sure that even the English language picture books you provide reflect the cultures in your classroom in every possible way. The more you understand about the children's native cultures, the more you can make meaningful connections.

Provide Hands-On Activities

Give English language learners a chance to manipulate magnetic letters, move pictures around, and work with word and letter cards. Repeat activities that your learners find most beneficial. Build up the speed with which your ELLs recognize a set of clear picture cards. These will form a core vocabulary that children in the group share. Support children in naming the pictures on each card, on the alphabet linking chart, and in a personal *ABC Book*. Be sure the print for all charts is clear and consistent so that children who are working in another language do not also have to deal with varying forms of letters. You'll find examples of good pictures in the Kindergarten *Phonics Lesson CD* (Pinnell and Fountas, 2003) or you can purchase the Phonics Lessons Enlarged Picture Cards set (Heinemann, 2004).

Provide a Good Vantage Point

Make sure that your English language learners are not sitting where it is hard for them to see charts and other visual aids. If they are sitting to the far left or right of a chart, their view will be distorted.

Create Strong Connections with Children's Homes

Even if a child's parents or caregivers do not speak English very well, they are still concerned about their child's education. Make every attempt to communicate with them, just as you are trying to communicate with the

Figure 9.3 A class of English language learners

child. Home visits are extremely beneficial, but if that is impossible, invite your English language learners' family members to come to school and make the invitation informal and friendly. Often, parents meet their children at school in order to walk home with them. Take the opportunity to walk out with the child and say hello or show the parent something the child has produced in drawing or writing. Parents may not realize the significance of their children's attempts to label a picture, for example. Encourage children to talk about their drawing and writing with (or even read an easy sentence to)

a parent or sibling at home, even if that parent or sibling is not yet fluent in English. If children have siblings at school, ask the siblings to read simple stories to the younger children at home.

Working with English language learners, you have the wonderful opportunity to observe them as they absorb their new language. If they participate in a rich language environment, they change every day! These observations will help you learn a great deal about language learning in general and will thus support your effective teaching of all children.

Key Understandings to Think About

✳ Children who from birth have learned a language other than English have already *learned how to learn language.*

✳ In their native languages, English language learners have acquired a vocabulary, are aware of the sounds in words, and have internalized a system of rules for putting together sentences.

✳ The best way to expand learners' knowledge of English is to engage them in conversation.

✳ An interactive read-aloud is also an effective way to expand learners' knowledge of English.

✳ English language learners benefit from creating repetitive texts in interactive writing, and they should revisit these texts often.

✳ Strong connections with children's homes and their home language and native culture will strengthen your ability to teach English language learners.

Notes

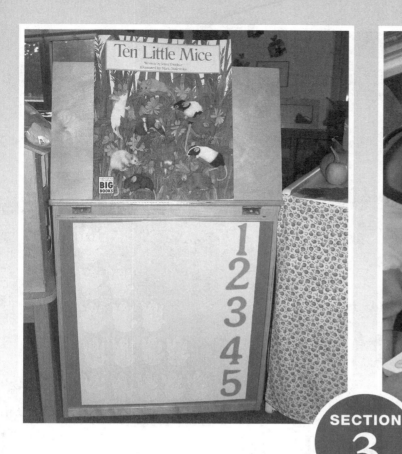

Supporting Emergent Readers

While most children will not leave prekindergarten able to read conventionally, their development as emergent readers can be supported in many ways. A primary goal is to help children see themselves as readers whether they are reading conventionally or not. This section introduces three critical areas of learning in prekindergarten: story awareness, language awareness, and print awareness. We then provide in-depth descriptions of how to use interactive read-aloud and shared reading in the prekindergarten classroom, as well as specifics about how teaching interactions with students in the context of shared and independent reading will help them develop early reading behaviors. Finally, a brief theoretical description of the reading process sheds some light on how the literacy children experience in prekindergarten contributes to their development as readers.

Learning to Read:
Three Critical Areas of Early Learning

*"The first contacts that children have with written language
are complex, involving words, written messages, and storybooks,
and children notice features of written language that adults
would not think to teach them about."*

—Marie Clay

Learning to read is a complex process. The process that now seems such a seamless and fluid act to us as adults involves, for children, just learning, taking on many different bodies of knowledge. Not only do children need to become proficient in each of these bodies of knowledge, but they must also learn to use all this information in a smoothly orchestrated way to read and understand connected print. The Continuum of Literacy Learning, PreK (see Section 7) describes the many understandings young children develop even before they can read and write—gathering information from looking at pictures in books and understanding that they can use pictures to communicate, to name just two. The phonics, spelling, and word study continuum lists specific early literacy concepts. In this chapter we discuss three important areas of literacy learning: story awareness, language awareness, and print awareness.

Story Awareness: Language Structure, Meaning, and Organization

Parents have discovered that even children younger than a one-year-old can "respond" to stories that are read to them. They buy plastic books that can survive the bath or juice spills and read them over and over. Cuddled up on a lap, very young children can pat the pictures and make noises imitating the parent's reading.

Eighteen-month-old Makayla, for example, sits in her father's lap as he reads *Where's Spot?* (Hill, 1980). As he reads each question, she lifts the flap and chirps something that sounds like "No." From time to time, he gently moves her hand off the page so that he can read the print. She assists him in turning the pages, right to left, and looks with him at the left page as he reads the text on that page. Makayla already understands that books hold meaning and that they are read in a certain way.

When two-year-old Brian and three-year-old Jesse listen to their grandmother read *We're Going on a Bear Hunt* (Rosen, 2009), they make hand movements and noises that fit the text and anticipate what comes next. "Look out, the bear's in there!" they gleefully warn the characters. Three-year-old Iris can "read" the *Three Little Pigs* and several other folktales by looking at the pictures. She produces an astonishingly appropriate retelling that matches each page, using much of the language of the story and repeating dialogue with expression. "Not by the hair on my chinny-chin-chin!" she belts out enthusiastically.

We call this behavior "talking like a book" (Clay, 1991). Responses to story reading such as these do not involve attention to print; the children are cued by the pictures and are enjoying the pattern of the story as well as the close personal relationship with a family member. They are, however, internalizing some important early behaviors related to reading, and they

have done so because they have had many story reading experiences.

The ability demonstrated by Brian, Jesse, and Iris is not unique to children who have early access to hearing stories read aloud (although it does give them an advantage in using "school language" to learn literacy). Many children join in while they watch favorite DVDs or TV shows. They chant along with the cheering at football games. Even at very young ages, they sing along with the kind of music their families like. Many can tell stories central to the religion of their family and can repeat often-told family stories. It is all part of the natural desire to be part of the community around them.

These young children are acquiring language syntax and vocabulary, and they are learning the structure of different kinds of texts. Some families simply do not have a tradition of reading stories, especially to children so young. But every child has the natural ability to respond to the language and pictures in books. When children enter prekindergarten, you can quickly establish a love of reading stories by carefully selecting books and making them accessible to everyone by reading them aloud. As children have more experiences with extended texts like stories and very simple informational books, they acquire the most important foundation for reading—language. Language encompasses the structure, the vocabulary, and the meaning of oral and written texts.

One very enjoyable way to help children construct stories themselves is by using wordless books. These books require the "reader" to infer the story from illustrations. Great wordless books capture children's imagination and help them generate language. In *The Treasure Bath* (Andreasen, 2009), a little boy's imagination makes a simple bath an adventure. The same kind of thing occurs in a little girl's imaginary train ride in *Trainstop* (Lehman, 2008). A simple day at the beach comes to life in the wordless book *Wave* (Lee,

2008). In *Welcome to the Zoo* (Jay, 2008), the writer/illustrator provides a rich display of artwork to create a fantasy zoo. This text requires the reader to notice the characteristics of animals and introduces the concept of looking at maps. A more complex story is told in the wordless book *South* (McDonnell, 2008). The book has a few "words" such as *weep* and *ZZZ* for sleeping. In this animal fantasy, a little bird is left behind by his flock. A kindly dog helps him find them again. Books like these provide wonderful opportunities for children to use (and develop) language as they construct a story that fits the pictures.

Language Awareness: Talking Like a Book

Even young children are quite aware that when read aloud, print sounds different from ordinary oral language and that when they "read," they can imitate this written language (Clay, 1991). Four-year-old Mike is very good at this "talking like a book" (see Figure 10.1). Of course, Mike has heard this favorite story read aloud many times. By looking at the pictures, Mike can convey the story, incorporating the patterned language on each page: he never deviates from the phrase, "but he was still hungry." But the process is much more than memorization. Mike is internalizing the grammatical structures that will help him make sense of written language.

The language of stories fascinates children; there is an inherent pleasure in language play. It is amazing how children start to repeat the language they hear in the stories they are exposed to, making it their own after a reading or two. The book *Please, Baby, Please* (Lee and Lee, 2002) uses alternative arrangements of the three words:

> Don't eat the sand, baby, baby, please
>
> Now hold my hand, baby, please, baby.

A book does not have to be in rhyme or have a language pattern for children to absorb and repeat it. Young children are delighted with the familiar language that they hear in *No, David!* (Shannon, 1998):

> No, David!
>
> No, no, no!
>
> Don't play with your food!

The selection ends with "I love you, David!" which children do not forget.

Mike's "Reading" of *The Very Hungry Caterpillar*	
Text: *The Very Hungry Caterpillar*, by Eric Carle	**Mike's "Reading"—Cued by the Pictures**
Page 3 "One Sunday morning the warm sun came up and—pop!—out of the egg came a tiny and very hungry caterpillar."	Page 3 Pop! The tiny caterpillar come out of the egg. He was very hungry.
Page 5 "He started to look for some food."	Page 5 He go to look for food.
Page 6 "On Monday, he ate through one apple. But he was still hungry."	Page 6 On Monday, he eat one apple. But he was still hungry.

Figure 10.1 Mike's "reading" of *The Very Hungry Caterpillar*

While you will be looking for simple stories that are appropriate for prekindergarteners, some of these stories include language that will also stretch children's knowledge of complex sentences, such as those in the text of *Lilly's Purple Plastic Purse* (Henkes, 1996):

> "And, best of all, she had a brand new purple plastic purse that played a jaunty tune when it was opened."

Using interactive read-aloud daily will provide ample opportunity to expand children's knowledge of the structure (syntax) of language. As you are choosing books for your read-aloud, above all, be sure that the story, language, and illustrations are highly engaging to children, as in *Cock-a-Doodle Quack Quack* (Baddiel and Jubb, 2007) and *Dig Dig Digging* (Mayo, 2002) (Figures 10.2 and 10.3).

If children hear several books in a series read aloud and have a chance to look at and talk about them, they get to know an engaging character over time. Children love hearing stories like *Tacky the Penguin* (Lester, 1988), about a little penguin whose imperfections help him save his whole family. *Tacky the Penguin* is a sturdy board book that will stand up to lots of handling by three- and four-year-olds. (Board books are printed on very heavy cardboard with a sturdy binding.) There is a whole series of books about Tacky.

Other engaging books available as board books include *Little Blue Truck* (Schertle, 2008), which features animal noises; *Hurry, Hurry!* (Bunting, 2007), which tells a story with very little print and repeated words; and *Where Is the Green Sheep?* (Fox, 2004), which features object words and opposites. Another wonderful series introduces basic concepts in the context of the adventures of an engaging dog, Bow-Wow. *Bow-Wow: 12 Months Running* (Newgarden and Cash, 2009) shows the months of the year and changing seasons, and *Bow-Wow's Colorful Life* (Newgarden and Cash, 2009) focuses on colors while telling a wordless (except for the color words) story.

Figure 10.2 Pages from *Cock-a-Doodle Quack Quack*

Figure 10.3 Pages from *Dig Dig Digging*

Print Awareness: Letters, Words, and How Print "Works"

As they are learning to enjoy stories even before they can read words, children are learning some basic concepts of print:

- Even though the pictures have important information, you read the print. Children learn to distinguish between print and pictures.

- You start with the cover of the book and turn the pages by taking the right page and turning it over to the left.

- You read the left page before the right page.

- You look at the black marks, and the spaces help you to notice the words.

- You read left to right across the print and sweep back to the left margin to read the next line.

- You read from the top of the page downwards.

- The story is over when you reach the last page (and something important happens).

As they learn more about letters, they begin to understand concepts like these:

- Words are made up of letters. You can identify letters in print.

- There is white space between words.

- There are capital (uppercase) and lowercase letters in print.

- A word always has the same letters in it in order, left to right.

- You match one spoken word with one printed word (cluster of letters with white space on either side).

- The first letter of a word is important.

- You look at the letters in one specific way (as opposed to objects).

- You can notice words that start like your name.

The preceding lists comprise what we call "early reading behaviors," and internalizing them is a very important goal of prekindergarten education.

As children notice more about written language, they begin to find visual signposts—letters or collections of letters they recognize; they may even learn to read some words. Four-year-old Spencer, for example, can notice the letter *s* even when it is embedded in print, because he's so familiar with the *S* in his name. He recog-nizes the word *is* because he has seen it so often and used it in writing. Camilla's book about *The Teacher from the Black Lagoon* (see Figure 10.4) shows her awareness of story and text features. Notice the speech bubble with writing on page 4. She uses real letter forms (including the *i* and *m* from her name) as well as pretend writing on page 5. She signs her name on the last page.

As you work with prekindergarteners, you will observe evidence of new literacy learning every day.

Page 1

Page 2

Page 3

Page 4

Figure 10.4 Pages from Camilla's book about *The Teacher from the Black Lagoon*

Page 5

Page 6

Figure 10.4 Pages from Camilla's book about *The Teacher from the Black Lagoon, continued*

The key is to make their experiences meaningful and memorable. Even though three- or four-year-olds may not develop the full awareness of print itemized in the second list, they should become much more sophisticated as they have experiences with print. These early reading behaviors are the real goal of prekindergarten literacy teaching. They are developed over the prekindergarten and kindergarten years, and they provide a firm foundation for reading instruction in first grade.

Literacy learning for prekindergarteners must be intentionally fostered (Joint Position Statement, NAEYC/IRA). We cannot assume that children will take on literacy behaviors simply because print is all around them, nor will they learn how stories work by hearing just a few. Our intentional acts of teaching will lead them to new understandings. The instructional practices of interactive read-aloud, and shared reading, along with opportunities for interactive writing and independent writing, will help children gain these early understandings.

Key Understandings to Think About

✳ In learning to read, children acquire many different kinds of knowledge. They need to use this variety of information in a smoothly orchestrated way as they process print.

✳ Even very young children begin to learn the way stories are organized.

✳ They start to take on the language of stories—"talking like a book"—as they pretend to read.

✳ As they enjoy stories, they start to learn some basic information about how print works.

✳ Developing early reading behaviors is an important goal for prekindergarten teaching.

Notes

Using Interactive Read-Aloud to Support Emergent Readers

"Reading aloud is the foundation of literacy."

—Don Holdaway

Reading aloud to children is the best way we know to teach them to love books. It exposes them to book language, new vocabulary, exciting new information, and engaging illustrations. Many children who enter prekindergarten have been read bedtime stories for two years or more; others have heard many "lap stories," beginning from the point at which they could look at a book and listen to even part of a story. Others have had less experience in hearing written language read aloud. Luckily, with a rich prekindergarten program, you can help those children "catch up" on their reading! If the activity is engaging and fun, they learn very quickly. In this chapter we explore the important role of conversations with children in connection with

reading aloud to them. (See Appendix D, Lesson 2 for a simple lesson on interactive read-aloud.) In the next chapter we discuss shared reading, which allows even young children to "experience" the act of reading.

Prekindergarteners should be read to at least once a day, two or three times if possible. It is important to plan read-alouds thoughtfully, not just to pick up whatever book is closest. The Interactive Read-Aloud and Literature Discussion continuum (Section 7) recommends a wide range of genres and forms for these young children. They will enjoy simple animal fantasies, realistic stories about children, traditional folktales, simple informational texts, and others. By selecting a wide range of interesting, beautiful books, you provide every child with a rich, shared literacy foundation. (You can also find examples of text sets, organized by theme, for three-year-olds and four-year-olds in Appendix B.)

Selecting Texts to Read Aloud

Choosing texts that fit the developmental level and interests of your young students is extremely important. Prekindergarteners are likely to be either bored or bewildered by books with very complex themes, such as *The Giving Tree* (Silverstein, 1964) or *Love You Forever* (Munsch, 1995), which require understanding symbolism and abstract concepts. They may understand at a literal level but will miss the adult message.

While prekindergarten children are not ready for advanced themes and symbolism, they love stories, and they come to the table with plenty of skills. Most prekindergarteners can follow a series of events, identify simple problems, enjoy characters and talk about what they are like, and ask questions to clarify understanding. There are plenty of age-appropriate books that will intrigue your students and stimulate rich conversation in your classroom. (See Appendix B for text sets, and Appendix E for a comprehensive list of recommended PreK read-aloud books.)

Choose simple stories that are easy to follow with the help of large, clear illustrations. Select poetry, songs, and rhymes. Include wordless books that invite children's thinking. Some texts have print that is large enough for the group to see as you read it. *Here Comes the Big, Mean Dust Bunny!* (Thomas, 2009) tells a humorous rhyming story in speech bubbles. John Lithgow's *I Got Two Dogs* (2008) has enlarged print, rhymes, and tells another funny story. Classic books like *Corduroy* (Freeman, 2008) and *Curious George Rides a Bike* (Rey, 2006) are wonderfully engaging for young children.

Select informational texts that have large, clear pictures and focus on familiar topics that children can understand. You can also find some excellent and

engaging books centered on a specific concept, such as the alphabet, beginning numerals, days of the week, seasons, shapes, or feelings. "How to" books are another favorite. A unique one is *Little Yoga: A Toddler's First Book of Yoga* (Whitford and Selway, 2005).

Some books can be used to spark a discussion about what children know or can do. Two examples are *I Know a Lot of Things* (Rand, 1956, 2009) and *I Can Do It Myself* (Kingsley, 1980). A page in *I Know a Lot of Things* reads, "I know the world is wide, and a star is far away." Children will be thrilled to contribute to a discussion of what they know, and this discussion is an opportunity to foster (and highlight) children's developing independence. You may hear things like, "I know how to cook noodles!" "I know how to jump!" You might also steer the conversation toward things that children are learning to do in school as well.

Children can also talk about friendship after reading a book like *A Friend Like You* (Askani, 2009), which shows photographs of unlikely animal pairs (a piglet and a little Maltese dog, for example). The pairs are real and information is provided about each of them in the back of the book. You can tell the stories of these animals and how they became friends as children look at the pictures. The text of the book is very simple—a two-page spread is shown in Figure 11.1.

Books like *Just How Long Can a Long String Be?!* (Baker, 2009) prompt children to take different perspectives on ordinary things such as a ball of string. The story is tied together by a little bird whose favorite use for string is to help in building a nest. In a similar vein, *Duck! Rabbit!* (Rosenthal and Lichtenheld, 2009) uses the same line drawing and helps the reader view it as both a duck and a rabbit.

Texts can be used to illustrate a sequence of events as well as provide information. In *I'm Your Bus* (Singer, 2009) a personified bus talks about what a school bus does through the day. It also rhymes, which is appealing to children. (See Appendix D, Lesson 4 for a lesson

Figure 11.1 Pages from *A Friend Like You*

on simple story sequencing.) Another rhyming book, *Our Abe Lincoln* (Aylesworth, 2009), presents a song (to the tune of "The Old Gray Mare") about the life of Abraham Lincoln. The purpose is not for children to learn a great deal about Lincoln, but they will enjoy the text and become familiar with some concepts.

Prekindergarteners also love books that play with language. An example is *Chicka Chicka Boom Boom* by Bill Martin. (The book list in Appendix E includes many excellent examples of books of rhymes and poetry.) When children hear poems and rhymes, they start to notice the words that sound alike at the end. Recognizing rhyme is one of the first signs of phonemic awareness. These books will also have rhythm, which is very appealing to children.

The PreK Continuum in Section 7 specifies ten characteristics of engaging texts that are appropriate for prekindergarteners. These characteristics are briefly defined in Figure 11.2. No one of these ten factors alone makes a text appropriate or inappropriate. You make the decision based on thinking about all of the characteristics in relation to texts you are considering.

Interactive Read-Aloud Routines

When reading aloud, make sure that all of the children are seated so that they can hear you and see the pictures. Make sure, as well, that you can see everyone. Most prekindergarten teachers have children seated on their bottoms in a designated place on a carpeted floor. Some use round or square carpet remnants; others have a carpet with a design that incorporates squares depicting various things (letters, numbers, pictures).

Interactive read-aloud is infinitely more productive and fun if you take the time to explicitly teach children the routines early on. You will develop routines that work for your particular students and classroom, but in general you will want your students to know these procedures:

- Sit down on the floor with your legs folded ("criss-cross applesauce").
- Sit up straight with your hands in your lap.
- Look at your teacher.
- Raise a hand or put a thumb up in front of you if you want to say something.
- Listen to and look at the person who is talking.

Text Characteristics to Consider in Selecting Books to Read Aloud		
Characteristic	**Definition**	**Importance for Prekindergarten Children**
Genres/Forms	Genre refers to type of text—for example, poems, traditional tales, animal fantasy, realistic fiction. Each of these genres has characteristic features. A text of a certain genre may be in one of several forms—for example, oral story, picture book, unusual forms such as pop-up books.	Prekindergarteners need to hear simple, straightforward texts that are easy to follow. They respond to fiction genres such as stories of children and families, animal fantasy, traditional tales, and to informational texts about familiar topics.
Text Structure	The structure is the way the text is organized and presented. It may be a story with events in sequence. Or it may be an informational text that is presented in categories. For young children, information is often organized around familiar structures such as days of the week, seasons of the year, the alphabet, and numbers.	PreK children need to experience texts that are organized in many different ways.
Content	The content refers to the subject matter of the text—what it's about. The content of some texts requires that readers have some background knowledge in order to understand it.	PreK children should encounter mostly very familiar content—texts about everyday events and objects, families and neighborhoods, pets, animals, and similar topics.
Themes and Ideas	The themes are the big ideas that are communicated by the writer of a text—friendship, love, overcoming fears, etc.	Themes should be simple ideas that PreK children can understand and that they care about.
Language and Literary Features	Books use language that is different in many ways from spoken language. Writers may use words in a figurative way; they may use vivid description or dialogue. In books for young children, writers often use words that stand for sounds *(pop, moo)*.	Prekindergarteners who have heard many texts read aloud acquire an internal sense of the language writers use. But texts must be understandable. Highly figurative language that is hard to understand may be too difficult.
Sentence Complexity	Sentences vary in length and also in the number of phrases and clauses that are within them. Longer and more complex sentences generally make a text harder.	In general, PreK children need texts with sentences they can follow and understand. There may be some long sentences because the writer is using literary language, but they should be easy for children to understand in phrases.
Vocabulary	Vocabulary has to do with the meaning of the words in the text. Words may have several meanings, and the same word may mean subtly different things within a sentence or paragraph. The more familiar the words are to a reader, the easier a text will be.	Most of the words in texts should be in children's oral vocabularies, but PreK children should also expand their vocabularies through hearing texts read. It is easier to learn new words against a background of known words.

Figure 11.2 Text characteristics to consider in selecting books to read aloud

continues

Text Characteristics to Consider in Selecting Books to Read Aloud, *continued*

Characteristic	Definition	Importance for Prekindergarten Children
Words	This category refers to the characteristics of words such as the length, number of syllables, inflectional endings, and general ease of solving. In interactive read-aloud, however, the teacher solves the words, so this will not be a factor in text selection.	Attention to vocabulary will take into account word complexity. As with vocabulary, most of the words in texts should be in children's oral vocabularies. A few words are new to the children and are of high interest.
Illustrations	The illustrations are the drawings, paintings, or photographs that accompany the text and add meaning and enjoyment. In informational texts, illustrations may include graphic features such as maps.	PreK children need to experience a wide variety of illustrations created through a variety of media. They enjoy large, colorful, or humorous illustrations, but they also can appreciate more delicate and serious work.
Book and Print Features	The book and print features are the physical aspects of the text—what readers cope with in terms of length, size, and layout. Book and print features also include tools like the table of contents, glossary, pronunciation guide, index, and sidebars.	Print features should be considered carefully. Some books have a few words in large print that PreK children can see and notice. They can also become familiar with simple features such as title, author, and illustrator.

Figure 11.2 Text characteristics to consider in selecting books to read aloud, *continued*

- Be thinking of what you can say about the book.
- Just listen to the story the first time through, but join in on refrains when your teacher invites you.
- At the "turn and talk" signal, move your body to face a classmate and take turns talking about the story; at the "turn back" signal, turn to look at your teacher and listen to the story. Make sure to give children plenty of guidance when teaching them to turn and talk. You may want to tell them (and show them how) to each say just one thing. A minute or two is plenty of time.
- Talk about the book after you've heard it read.
- Draw and write about the book after you've heard it read and talked about.

Many children have gone to daycare or been part of play groups, but for some, prekindergarten is their first experience with a group read-aloud. With careful teaching, even young children new to school can follow these simple routines. Again, you will find methods of teaching that fit your class, but here's a general approach that is effective:

1. Demonstrate the behavior yourself. Describe it in words that are simple. Tell children why it is important.
2. Have two or three children demonstrate the behavior while the others watch (maybe in a circle). Have everyone clap when they do it well.
3. Have everyone demonstrate the behavior and clap for themselves.
4. Insist on the behavior every time with gentle reminders and more demonstration as needed. (If you constantly allow deviations, children will become confused about your expectations.)

5. Give specific praise to the children when they demonstrate the expected behavior.

6. Use positive commands whenever possible; tell children *what to do* rather than *what not to do.*

Using Interactive Read-Aloud as a Teaching Approach

You and your students will have productive conversations about books if you follow these steps:

1. Plan opening remarks.

2. Stop to invite quick comments during reading.

3. Discuss the text after reading.

4. Plan an engaging, related activity (book activity) following reading (art, writing, drawing, cooking).

Opening Remarks

The first words you say stimulate and guide children's thinking. There is no one way to introduce any book. It depends on what you know about your students and the prior experiences you have provided in the classroom, as well as your goals for thinking about reading. The behaviors and understandings to notice, teach, and support that are listed in the Interactive Read-Aloud continuum (Section 7) will help you construct your opening remarks. An example is presented in Figure 11.3.

Invite Comments

Ahead of time, identify two or three places where you will stop during the reading of a book. Many teachers mark the places with stick-on notes, then make comments or ask questions like:

"Talk about what you are thinking."

"What do you think will happen?"

"I was wondering why. . . . What do you think?"

"What do you think about [name of character]?"

"Turn and talk about _____."

You can also clarify concepts or promote new thinking during quick stops, but don't overdo it. You can ruin the flow of the read-aloud if you select one so difficult that you have to make explanations after every page.

Kitten's First Full Moon (Henkes, 2004) is a simple and straightforward story, but it does present some challenges. To thoroughly understand it, children need to be aware that a baby animal (like a human baby) might not understand that the moon isn't really a bowl of milk. Further in the story, the kitten climbs a tree to get the moon and then sees the reflection of the moon in the water, which she tries to pounce on, again thinking it is a bowl of milk. Here, children need to understand the concept of reflection on water.

While reading the book, this teacher decided to stop on the page where the kitten was stuck in a tree to ask children how they think the kitten is feeling. She also planned to stop to clarify the concept of reflection. This is not the time to launch into a long, scientific explanation of reflection. Comparing the still lake to a mirror and looking carefully at the illustrations is enough to boost the understanding of those children who may be confused.

Turn and Talk

After children have learned the basic read-aloud routines, you can teach them to turn their bodies toward a partner and talk softly about what they are thinking. This lasts only a minute or so, so teach them to make some quick comments and then let the other person talk. Then, at a "turn back" signal, they stop talking immediately and move into listening position. It's worth taking the time to practice this movement until children know and understand it. Sometimes children can quickly share a few of the things they talked about with the whole group; at other times you will just want to go on with the reading.

In reading *Kitten's First Full Moon*, this teacher planned to "turn and talk" at the point where the kitten returned home and found a great big bowl of milk

Introductory Conversation, *Kitten's First Full Moon*

Remarks	Teacher's Goals
Teacher: We are going to read a book by Kevin Henkes today. Kevin Henkes has written a lot of really good books and we are going to read them this year. The title of this book is *Kitten's First Full Moon.* And there is the little kitten. (Shows the cover.)	• Draw attention to author and signal that the name of the author is important. • Inform children that some people write many books. • Foreshadow future connections (author). • Draw attention to the title. • Demonstrate the importance of the illustrations.
Teacher: You know a kitten is a baby cat and this one is not very old. She has never seen the moon when it is full. Do you know what it means when we say the moon is full? **Carter:** It's big and round. **Angelina:** It shines.	• Call on children to use background knowledge. • Check on a basic understanding.
Teacher: Yes, a full moon is big and round and shiny. Did you know that the moon changes? Sometimes it looks like there is just a little of it and sometimes it looks round like a bowl. In this book, kitten is going to think the moon is a bowl of milk. I'm wondering what a little kitten would want to do with a bowl of milk? *Several children make predictions that the kitten would want to eat it or lick it up. One child says that cats like milk.*	• Provide background knowledge. • Demonstrate predicting and invite children to predict.
Teacher: So think about the moon looking like a bowl of milk. Look at all these moons when I open the book. (Shows end papers and then the title page layout.)	• Reinforce the concept of a full moon. • Draw attention to end papers and illustrations.
Teacher: Let's read to see if the little kitten gets that full moon that looks like a bowl of milk. Do you think that is possible? *Several children say that the kitten cannot really get the moon. One child says that it might happen like a magic story.* **Teacher:** I agree with you. It would have to be make-believe, but the kitten is so little that she doesn't know that. She is going to try a lot of things and maybe she will get in trouble. (Starts reading.)	• Help children think critically about the story. • Start children thinking about what might happen.

Figure 11.3 Introductory conversation, *Kitten's First Full Moon*

on the porch just waiting for her. (Figure 11.3) She simply asked the children to talk about what they were thinking (rather than directing them to guess who might have left the milk or how the kitten feels now), and she got a rich range of responses:

> "Her owner put it there."
>
> "It's a real bowl of milk."
>
> "She is happy now."
>
> "She should have stayed home."

Discussion After Reading

Children should understand that they are expected to talk about a book after it has been read. This discussion does not have to be lengthy, but it will extend children's comprehension as well as their ability to use language (both sentence structure and vocabulary) in more complex ways. Sometimes you can give an open invitation to make comments about the story or informational text. Sometimes you might want to ask them to discuss a particular aspect of the text.

The last words of *Kitten's First Full Moon* are "Lucky kitten," and the illustration shows the kitten sleeping contentedly beside her empty bowl of milk with the full moon in the sky. (Throughout the book, the writer has been saying "poor kitten.") This teacher invited children to talk by saying, "Lucky kitten! Why do you think Kevin Henkes wrote *lucky kitten* on this last page?" The children offered a variety of explanations, including that the kitten was lucky to be back home again and lucky to have a bowl of milk waiting for her!

Book Activities

To make wonderful books memorable, children can respond to them in various ways—role-play, make puppets, paint pictures, cook soup, make clay or play dough objects, etc. We provide a list of suggested whole-group or small-group activities that may be appropriate for your young children, depending on their ability to engage with the demands of the task. (See Figure 11.4.) Most will need teacher support as a choice time activity. As always, use your knowledge of the children to select or vary the suggested activities. We hope this list will help you create others as you read aloud wonderful books. (See Appendix B for preschool text sets for use in book activities.)

Rereading Texts

Rereading and revisiting favorite texts is very beneficial. You may not want to reread every book that you share with children, but well-chosen, engaging books can be read aloud many times as you call attention to different aspects of the writer's craft. Of course you won't use words like *writer's or illustrator's craft* with prekindergarteners; you'll just draw attention to what the author or illustrator did to make this book interesting or help us understand it. (The concept of "author" or "illustrator" can be a new one for young children as well, particularly three-year-olds. You may want to spend some time early on discussing what an author is and what an author does. Always read the names of the authors and illustrators when you are reading aloud to your students.)

When rereading *Kitten's First Full Moon,* you could help children compare how the kitten felt throughout the book when she was trying to get the moon with how she felt at the end when she got home and found milk waiting for her. On one page layout Henkes describes a series of the kitten's actions (going through the garden, for example); the pictures on the opposite page illustrate each action. This sequence is repeated in reverse as the kitten goes home toward the end of the book. It's a great way to help children see how illustrators and writers have different ways of showing readers what happened.

Book Activities

The following is a sampling of activities you can use to engage young children in thinking and responding to books you read aloud or use for shared reading.

- **Character Puppets**
  Engage the children in making finger puppets, stick puppets, or sock puppets and then have them put on a puppet show for each other.

- **Character Paintings**
  Have the children paint a favorite character and then add a speech bubble, inviting the children to dictate while you write what the character is saying. Label the character.

- **Character Creations**
  Have the children make a multimedia character from one of the stories they love. Make available yarn, cotton balls, recycled materials, and a variety of colored papers.

- **Dramatic Retelling**
  After hearing a story several times children can take parts and reenact the dialogue with you as narrator. Select well-known stories such as *Three Little Kittens, Three Little Pigs, The Three Bears, Little Red Riding Hood, The Three Billy Goats Gruff, Henny Penny, The Mitten, There Was an Old Lady Who Swallowed a Fly.*

- **Class Mural**
  Have the children paint the setting and then paint characters or objects to put in it. Add the title of the book and label character names or objects and read them to the children. If you have a group of children who have learned a lot about letters and sounds you may want to use a little interactive writing and invite them to write the first letter of some of the words.

- **Food Links**
  - Make stone soup (cut up vegetables in broth and add a stone!) after reading *Stone Soup.*
  - Make peanut butter (check for allergies) and jelly sandwiches after reading *Peanut Butter and Jelly.*

- Make blueberry muffins after reading *Blueberries for Sal.*
- Bake chocolate chip cookies before or after reading *If You Give a Mouse a Cookie* or *The Doorbell Rang.*
- Make gingerbread people after reading *The Gingerbread Man.*
- Bake some bread after reading *Bread Bread Bread.*
- Bake muffins after reading *If You Give a Moose a Muffin.*

- **Art Links**
  - Decorate and have a hat parade after reading *Hats Hats Hats.*
  - Glue leaves to make a leaf collage after reading *Why Do Leaves Change Colors?*

- **Planting/Cooking Links**
  - Roast or plant pumpkin seeds after reading *It's Pumpkin Time.*
  - Bake apples after reading *Apples and Pumpkins.*
  - Plant a carrot top after reading *The Carrot Seed.*

- **Music Links**
  For many books you can sing the songs together or add body, hand, or finger movements. Consider engaging books such as *Shake My Sillies Out, There Was an Old Lady, Mary Wore Her Red Dress, Bear Went Over the Mountain,* or *I'm a Little Teapot.*

Figure 11.4 Book activities

When rereading, you can also give children an opportunity to try out the language of the text. In *Kitten's First Full Moon,* this sentence is repeated several times: "Still, there was the little bowl of milk, just waiting." It is always placed in the middle of the layout, crossing two pages, clear black print against a white background. The illustrations are black-and-white drawings; the only other pictures in the layout are the little kitten on the left and the full moon in the upper-right-hand corner. Children can remember and "read" this page when they look at the book during library time.

Supporting Independent Use of Read-Aloud Books

Children will be eager to look at and perhaps retell or "reenact" books that you have read to them. This highly beneficial activity helps them internalize the structure of stories, notice features of informational books, and practice the language of books.

In your classroom library, you may want to designate a shelf for books (displayed with covers facing out) for books you have read to the class. When they visit the library, children can choose these books, look at the pictures, and retell the story for themselves. This "pretend reading" is also called *reading reenactment.* It provides support for using book language, or "talking like a book." It is amazing how young children who know very few letters and can't read can reproduce the precise language structure of books they have heard and enjoyed.

Some teachers collect several versions of a familiar fairy tale such as *Goldilocks and the Three Bears* or *The Three Little Pigs* to read to the class over a series of days. Children delight in noticing the similarities and differences between different versions of the same story, both in the illustrations and the text. If you choose to do this, it is important to select familiar stories with simple, repetitive text that will support children in noticing variance between stories. In kindergarten and first grade, children are often asked to compare and contrast different versions of stories on their own or with partners, and this group activity in prekindergarten paves the way for independent work down the road.

After you have read and reread quite a few books to the class, teach children to "read" a book with a partner. They can reenact the book in unison or take turns page by page. This helps them understand that reading a book can be a social act.

Key Understandings to Think About

✳ Reading aloud to prekindergarteners is the best way to teach them the purposes and benefits of reading; it also expands their vocabulary, helps them understand sentence structure, and increases their background knowledge.

✳ It is very important to select appropriate, engaging texts to read to kindergarteners. Breaking characteristics into categories can help you look closely at texts to evaluate them.

✳ Children will find it easier to listen to texts read aloud if they learn some simple routines.

✳ It is important to *plan* interactive read-aloud sessions so that the instruction is powerful.

✳ Book activities make wonderful books more memorable.

Notes

Using Shared Reading
to Support Emergent Readers

"Literacy ought to be one of the most joyful
undertakings ever in a young child's life."

—DON HOLDAWAY

Shared Reading

Shared reading propels young children into approximating the reading process with confidence. It builds on the coziness of the kind of lap reading that is often started at home, where the adult and child interact around a text they can both see and touch. The "lap story" is a warm, positive experience in which children feel secure; these early experiences build a love of books.

While you cannot (much as you might like to) gather your entire class onto your lap as you read, shared reading offers groups of children some aspects of the lap story. All can see the art and the text, which is enlarged, and they benefit from the high support of unison reading. The experience provides a pleasurable model of reading and builds a sense of community. It differs from interactive read-aloud in that children interact with and examine the text as you read instead of just listening to the story and looking at the pictures. (See Appendix D, Lesson 1 for a simple lesson on shared reading.)

You'll choose much shorter, simpler texts for shared reading. Children will want to experience highly engaging big-print poems, rhymes, songs, and stories that lend themselves to many readings. Many songs and poems become favorites, and young children often carry their memories of the language used in these texts into the schoolyard or back to their homes. (For example, Sarah and Nya played a game outdoors during recess in which they performed an elaborate series of hops and jumps while belting out the familiar words from a classroom shared-reading favorite: "Chicka chicka boom boom, will there be enough room?")

In shared reading, you read from an enlarged text with very clear print. You lead the reading, pointing to the words with a long pointer (not your hand or some other tool that blocks the print). Texts can be informational or fictional; animal fantasy is popular. Often these texts involve language and word play—*Truck Goes Rattley-Bumpa* (London, 2005) or *Chicka Chicka Boom Boom* (Martin, 2006), for example. Others, like *Miss Mary Mack: A Hand-Clapping Rhyme* (Hoberman, 2003), invite hand motions. They often use words that imitate the sounds they represent (*onomatopoeia*): *bang, swish-swish,* or *pop,* for example. (You will find a rich array of poems and songs for shared reading in Appendix A.)

Shared reading is an opportunity to demonstrate what reading is really like as children notice various aspects of print and are able to say the words along with you. Children feel like readers even before they can recognize words. In the process, they start to notice visual details of words but, more importantly, they learn how print works by moving through the book page by page and following the print left to right. Three-year-olds need a great deal of language experience and need to hear many texts before they can be expected to notice print. Most children will not be able to follow print left to right until they are in kindergarten. These processes are only approximated for quite a while.

Selecting Texts for Shared Reading

Text characteristics and behaviors to notice, teach, and support are specified in the Shared and Performance Reading continuum (Section 7). You consider the same ten text characteristics you evaluate when you choose interactive read-aloud texts (see Chapter 11) but do so in the context of shared reading's particular needs. For example:

- The print should be very simple and easy to see.
- The print should be large enough for the whole group (or a small group) to see clearly.
- There should be clear spaces between words and between lines.
- There should be a limited number of lines on a page (usually one or two unless the text is a well-known short poem of about four lines). You can sometimes place a small picture at the end of each line to help readers remember the words. We do not recommend using pictures *instead* of words in lines of print. You might put a picture at the beginning of a line or end as a cue, but don't leave out the word.
- There should be simple punctuation marks that children can notice and use.
- Illustrations should be clear and simple and support the meaning of the text.

When in doubt, stick to simpler texts. Many "big books" have very complex sentences and lots of lines of print. Some familiar children's books have been made into big books, but shared reading is not the time to use them, because they are generally too complex. Children may learn to chant along with repetitive elements of a favorite read-aloud story but will be unable to notice features of print if there is too much text. One of the huge advantages of shared reading is that it makes it easy for children to notice visual signposts—a

	Shared Reading Routines
Step 1	Introduce, read, and discuss the book as a read-aloud. Read it again while pointing under the words so children can see the print.
Step 2	Read it again and invite children to join in on the easiest parts (or all of it if the text is very simple).
Step 3	Read it several times until the children are very comfortable joining in.
Step 4	Revisit the text, concentrating on what you want to teach children to do. For example: • Read an exciting or a favorite part with expression. • Read dialogue with expression. • Read the beginning. • Read the ending. • Notice ending punctuation. • Locate the first word in a line. • Notice letters that you know.

Figure 12.1 Shared reading routines

word that starts like a child's name, for example. ("I see a *C*, I see a *C*!" said Charlie, as his class read *Chicka Chicka Boom Boom*.)

Using Shared Reading as a Teaching Approach

Simple routines for using shared reading are listed in Figure 12.1. These steps will usually extend over several days when you are using a new text.

Notice which texts the children most enjoy and return to them again and again. If a text is too hard, put it away (though perhaps you can try it again later in the year). You'll know it's too hard because your

children won't enjoy it as much and won't all be able to join in as you read. Each time children revisit a shared reading text they will notice more, provided they are still enjoying the language, illustrations, and story. When a text is very familiar, children will revisit it independently.

Children can also participate in shared reading using stories or poems that you have written on charts or in class-made big books. Children feel a particular sense of ownership for the messages and stories you compose together using shared and interactive writing, because they have participated in their construction (McCarrier, Pinnell, and Fountas, 2000). These texts are already very familiar because the children have reread the lines many times during the writing.

Poems, songs, and rhymes are wonderful shared reading material as well. Helpful steps are listed in Figure 12.2.

Children love using a bright-color marker (or removable highlighter tape) to emphasize words or letters in the text. Help children understand the concept of *letter* (an individual sign) and *word* (a cluster of letters surrounded by space) as you talk about the text.

We have included numerous rhymes and songs, many with body movements, that will be useful as you work with children in shared reading (Appendix A). In Appendix E we have also included a list of rhyming and poetry books. A simple poem like this one can be used many times:

<u>Rain, Rain</u>
Rain, rain go away,
Come again another day.
Little Johnny wants to play.

You could place it in a pocket chart and have children's pictures or names on cards ready to substitute for "little Johnny." If this poem sounds dated to you, substitute other adjectives such as "big boy," "funny," or "ball player." For rhythm, you need four syllables and many names such as "Marietta" fit well. You can also say the child's full name (for example, "Maura Smith") or say it twice ("Maura, Maura"). After children learn it well, place it on an easel in the library so that children can read it alone or with a partner.

It is easy to make shared reading too complicated. Stick to simple texts, remembering that your goals are that children will begin to join in as you read with accuracy and enjoyment and that they will begin to get the feel of reading themselves. Children can learn and remember longer poems, of course, but sometimes you may want to use shared reading time for only a part of a poem so that you can narrow your focus. A poem (with hand motions) that young children enjoy is shown in Figure 12.3.

Children learn this rhyme easily and enjoy the hand motions. They especially like saying the last line very fast while they make the bunny jump in the hole. But it's hard for them to do these things and simultaneously attend to so many lines of print. So after children know the poem well, you might write the first four lines on a chart, along with pictures of

---

Steps for Shared Reading of Poems

Step 1 Select very simple poems—usually four lines. (You can make a four-line poem into a book by writing one line on each page.)

Step 2 If you want to read a longer poem, work with the first four lines; later, add another four lines on a second page.

Step 3 Teach children the poem, song, or rhyme first (in the absence of print) so that they can say it together.

Step 4 Introduce the poem, song, or rhyme on chart paper and read it to the children while pointing.

Step 5 Read it several times until the children are very comfortable joining in.

Step 6 Revisit the text, concentrating on what you want to teach children to do. For example:

- Read the ending with expression.
- Read dialogue with expression.
- Notice ending punctuation.
- Locate the first word in each line.
- Show where to stop reading.
- Notice the spaces.
- Notice letters that you know.
- Locate a word that starts like your name or that you know.

Figure 12.2 Steps for shared reading of poems

Action Poem "The Bunny"

The Bunny	Hand Motions
Here is a bunny With his ears so funny,	*Make a fist and hold up two fingers to represent ears.*
And here is his hole in the ground.	*Make a fist with the other hand—slightly open to represent the hole. Say it slowly.*
When a noise he hears, He pricks up his ears,	*Twitch the two fingers that represent the ears.*
And jumps in the hole in the ground.	*Take the hand with "ears" and put it in the "hole" made by the other hand. Say it very fast!*

Figure 12.3 Action poem "The Bunny"

the bunny and a hole, attached with Velcro, so they can be part of the action. The children can read the first four lines using the print you have written, then finish saying the rest of the poem without any accompanying print.

There are several shared reading lessons in Appendix D, a basic introductory one (Lesson 1) as well as lessons on text innovations (Lesson 17) and big books (Lessons 10 and 12).

Making Shared Reading Successful

Here are some suggestions for successful shared reading with prekindergarteners:

1. Be sure that all children can clearly see the print.

2. Use black print on a white or cream background.

3. Illustrate the text but do not put print on top of illustrations or mix illustrations with print.

4. Point using a long, thin stick, not your finger, a marker, a ball, or anything else that will obscure the print, because children will not attend to it but will simply chant along. You can highlight the end of the stick with bright paint or a rubber pencil eraser.

5. Start early—as soon as all the children are looking at the print.

6. Keep the momentum going.

7. Point crisply under each word, but at the same time demonstrate some phrasing and good expression.

8. Vary the kinds of texts you use—poems, descriptive sentences, simple stories, repetitive texts, and texts that children have written together using shared/interactive writing.

9. Keep sessions short, gradually lengthening the sessions slightly as children's attention spans increase.

Key Understandings to Think About

✳ Shared reading is a way to help young children experience many aspects of the reading process before they can read or write.

✳ Shared reading is an excellent way to help children gain control of early reading behaviors (see Early Literacy Concepts in the Phonics and Word Study continuum and Shared Reading continuum in Section 7).

✳ Texts for shared reading should be simple and accessible.

✳ Teaching routines will help children participate in and enjoy shared reading.

✳ Shared reading should be as easy as possible for children so that they begin to notice aspects of print.

Notes

Developing Early Reading Behaviors in Shared and Independent Reading

"What a child can do with assistance today she will be able to do by herself tomorrow."

—LEV VYGOTSKY

Even though we would not expect most prekindergarteners to decode words independently, they can all come to understand a great deal about the process of reading. During shared/performance reading (especially of pieces of writing created through shared/interactive writing), you can use some very specific language to help children understand more about the reading process.

Prekindergarten children "read" in many ways. Even very young children learn quickly to start at the front of a book and turn pages right to left all the way to the end. They may also look at a book and, cued by the pictures, retell the story from memory, often using much of the exact language of the text. They may move along a line of print, saying the message with a great deal of accuracy but without truly noticing the details of words. They may start to point to a few interesting words they recognize, like *mom* or *love*. At first, a child might recognize a word using only one feature, such as the *y* in *my*. Every time the child sees a short word with *y*, he thinks it is *my*. He might or might not notice the *y* in longer words. Obviously, this is a highly inefficient way to recognize a word, but it does indicate growing awareness. Once a child has noticed something specific about a word, he is ready to notice more visual features. Some children will begin to "track print" as they imitate the teacher's pointing. (Even though some of them may hop their fingers around randomly, it still reveals a growing familiarity with print.)By about the middle of kindergarten we would expect all of them to be able to track print left to right.

The goal is not to teach children to read individual words or to expect accuracy but to support the constant expansion of children's awareness of language, sounds, and print. It is important that they have many opportunities to explore literacy in the context of meaningful stories and poems. Using supportive language can help with all of these things.

An important concept is the combination of *teach, prompt,* and *reinforce* (see Figure 13.1). As you *teach* you show and demonstrate what to do. A lot of that happens in prekindergarten! Once children understand the concept, you can *prompt* the behavior during shared reading. If they consistently demonstrate the behavior, you can *reinforce* it by stating what they have done. This chapter suggests language you might use in this very specific way to help children to learn these early reading behaviors.

Reading Left to Right/ Returning to Left

As you work with children in shared reading, you may want to comment on the process you are expecting. Here are some examples:

"You start here and read this way." (Teach)

"Now go back here." (Prompt)

"You read all the words across the line." (Reinforce)

Establishing Voice-Print Match

Prekindergarten children may not fully understand matching written words with spoken words but they can all move in that direction. Demonstrations are helpful. Here is some language to use as you demonstrate:

"Look at how I point under the words. I make the words I say match the words on the page." (Teach)

"Watch how I point under each word when I say it. I make it match." (Teach)

"Point under each word as you say it." (Prompt)

"You pointed under each word." (Reinforce)

Teaching Interactions to Support Early Learning Behaviors		
Teach	**Prompt**	**Reinforce**
Demonstrate and describe the specific behavior to help the child learn something new.	Prompt the child to use a new, specific behavior that has been taught.	Praise the new, specific behavior when the child has initiated it.
Examples: "See how I'm holding the book on the edges." (modeling) "Watch how I turn the page." "Look how I point while I read. I make the words I say match the words on the page."	Examples: "You hold the book on the edges." "Turn the page." "Using your pointer, point to each word as you say it."	Examples: "You know how to hold the book on the edges." "You turned the page." "You pointed under each word."

Figure 13.1 Teaching interactions to support early learning behaviors

Monitoring Voice-Print Match

Even in shared reading, children can begin to understand that voice-print match is something important and that you can notice it. You want children to match one spoken word to each group of letters along the line. Here is some language to use:

"If you run out of words, go back and make it match." (Demonstrate by saying each word while touching under the words.) (Teach)

"We ran out of words. Let's go back and make it match." (Teach)

"Let's try that again and make it match." (Teach)

"Did you have enough (too many) words?" (Prompt)

"Did you run out of words?" (Prompt)

"You made it match." (Reinforce)

"You had just enough words." (Reinforce)

Learning How Print Works

Our goal is to help prekindergarteners build basic understandings about how print works—the largely unmeasured understandings that many advantaged children achieve long before they enter school (although this is definitely not true of all middle-class and upper-middle-class children). This body of understanding forms a strong *foundation* for understanding the instruction that takes place in kindergarten and first grade, where the curriculum focuses on various aspects of print. Vulnerable children (who know little else) will focus *only* on those aspects. But sophisticated children (who understand a great deal about print even though they cannot read) take the information and fit it into what they already know. This is a new kind of reading "readiness." When children have an idea of the big picture of reading, all the information they get about print makes more sense.

Key Understandings to Think About

* As children have opportunities to explore print, they will learn more about how it works.

* During shared reading, specific language will help you demonstrate early reading behaviors such as voice-print match (see the Phonics and Word Study continuum, Section 7).

* Once children know a behavior, specific language can be used to demonstrate and prompt them to use it.

* If children display an important behavior indicating an awareness of print, the behavior can be reinforced by stating specifically what they have done.

* The goal with prekindergarteners is to help them build foundational understandings about how print works.

Notes

Learning to Read:
Understanding the Reading Process

*"Wondering is an important way to go beyond
present understanding (of text)."*

—Judith Wells Lindfors

We now turn specifically to the fundamentals of reading. Even though most prekindergarteners are not reading conventionally or are reading only a few words, it is helpful for prekindergarten teachers to understand the reading and writing processes in depth, because every action taken in the classroom contributes to children's success in these areas down the road.

Reading is thinking. The learning goals in the continuum (Section 7) are organized as three ways of thinking—*within* the text, *beyond* the text, and *about* the text; bulleted lists describe actions for

thinking in each of these ways. Reading involves doing a great many complicated things at the same time. And, for most children beyond about grade one, it all happens silently, in the head! We can't see or hear the thinking taking place, but we know it is going on, because the individual is reading the words and understanding the meaning. The mental actions or ways of thinking that take place as we read are broadly defined below.

Readers think within *the text*. We read the words and put together information so that we understand the facts or follow a story. We move smoothly and quickly enough through the words to understand their meaning not just as separate words but as sentences and ideas. If we are reading aloud, we put our words together so that the reading sounds smooth and expressive, revealing the text's meaning. We remember information from earlier parts of our reading as we move through the text. When we are finished reading, we have an understanding of what happened in the text. We can remember some information.

Readers think beyond *the text.* When we read, we do much more than just recognize the words and understand what happens. Reading can stimulate memories of events in our own life or situations in another book we have read. If we are reading a biography, we probably think of everything we have heard or read about that person. If we read an informational book, we think of what we already know and notice new information. As we read, we are always making predictions about what will happen. We think about what characters are like and why they act as they do. We think of ideas that the writer may have implied but that are not actually written on the page. As readers, what is in the head is as important as the print we are reading.

Readers think about *the text.* We also notice things about the text itself. We might notice that the story starts in a surprising way, or we might be critical of the ending. We unconsciously notice how the writer has organized and presented information. We make decisions about whether or not we like the text, whether we think it is true, or whether it would interest others, and we can state reasons for these decisions. We reflect on the text and think about the "turning points" (when something important happens to change things). We are thinking *analytically* and reading *critically.* We stand back from a text and look at it.

What Readers Do

Even though prekindergarten children are at the very beginning of their literate lives, it is important for prekindergarten teachers to understand the processes these children are building. The teaching done in prekindergarten can do a great deal to provide a strong foundation for reading and writing even if the children do not read "for real" (recognize and solve words). Many of the cognitive actions of "real" reading have their roots in children's experiences at ages three and four.

Reading is much more than connecting the sounds of speech to the letters in words. Fluent readers perform a great many actions all at once. We do this in other activities as well. Think about what you do when you are riding a bike. You are moving your legs, holding your body in a position to maintain balance, holding the handles and steering, and picking up information by looking ahead as well as using your peripheral vision. You are well aware of how to slow down, speed up, turn, and stop, and you know how to make corrections if you take a wrong turn, start to lose your balance, or meet an unexpected obstacle. Good bikers do all of this automatically and smoothly, and reading is far more complex than riding a bike. The following summary only partially describes the complex activity of reading. These are not simple actions in and of themselves; they are true, interrelated *systems* of strategic actions that happen simultaneously as we read (see Figure 14.1).

Thinking Within the Text

When we talk about "thinking within the text," we mean everything we do as readers to propel ourselves forward. We:

- *Solve words.* Of course, we need to accurately identify or figure out words. We sometimes think only about using letters and sounds, but there are many ways to

Figure 14.1 Systems of Strategic Actions

solve words. Our students in prekindergarten are just beginning to notice words but in just a few years, there will be a huge amount of learning.

Kaye (2008) studied second-grade readers and found that they could sound out unknown words letter by letter when they needed to but did not often do that. Instead, they tended to use larger parts of words like syllables and endings. They used the *visual information* (the way the letters and words looked) in very efficient ways. They also used the *meaning* as well as the grammar or *structure* of the sentence to help figure out the words. For example, we might be reading something like, "The rose is red and has sharp thorns." If we already know that the story is about a garden, it makes it easier to predict the word *rose* as we look at the letters. And once we've read the word *rose,* it is easier to predict *red* and *thorns.* Also, as speakers of English, we know how sentences are supposed to sound; that's because we know the "rules" of *language structure.* We have an internal sense that lets us narrow the kinds of words that might come next. We wouldn't think that the word after *sharp* would be *the* even though we notice the first two letters. We look through the whole word with lightning speed, but we also have a conscious idea of the words that *could* or *couldn't* make sense there.

Kaye's (2008) proficient readers had more than sixty ways to solve words! But solving a word means more than saying it; the reader needs to know the meaning. Reading is much easier if we already know the meaning of the words in the book, so it is important for readers to have a large oral vocabulary. Teachers can help prekindergarteners become word solvers by expanding the words the children know when they hear them; therefore it makes sense that good classrooms include lots of conversation about many topics, including the books that are read aloud.

- *Monitor and correct.* We use *visual information* or the print to check whether our reading is right; when we make a mistake, we correct ourselves. We might do this by looking more closely at the letters or word

parts, but there are other sources of information as well. Even when we read all the words correctly, we are constantly checking on ourselves to be sure that they make sense and sound right.

Kaye's (2008) second-grade readers used the *meaning* and their sense of how reading should sound, the *language structure,* to check whether their reading was making sense and sounding right. Prekindergarteners are on their way to using meaning and language structure when they utter a complex statement like "I saw a really big horse on the way to my grandma's!"

Hearing stories and other texts read aloud is a wonderful way to help children learn how reading should sound. Often, teachers use large texts and have children "read" together as a whole class or small group—an activity called shared reading. Actually saying the words allows them to internalize how meaningful language should sound. This activity is particularly helpful for English language learners.

- *Search for and use information.* Reading is an active process. We are always searching for and using all kinds of information: *visual information, meaning,* and *language structure.* Those three sources of information are huge bodies of knowledge. (1) We search for and use the *visual information* that represents the language of the text. That means the printed letters and words, of course, but we also notice the way lines are arranged, the punctuation, the size of the print, and features like words in bold or italics. (2) We search for and use the *meaning.* For young children that means following and understanding the story and also getting information from pictures. As adult readers we also often use pictures to help us understand what we are reading, but we can understand and visualize without pictures as well, especially while reading fiction. Young children often "pretend" to read as they look at the pictures of a favorite storybook. They have learned to tell stories as they look at pictures and often use some of the engaging language of the book as they do so. This behavior means that the child is forming a strong foundation for learning to read; he already knows how to search for and use information. (3) We search for and use the *structure* of the language or the syntax. This means we know how words go together and can predict what words might sound right next in the reading of a text. This ability helps us as readers to use language structure effectively as part of the information we use.

- *Summarize.* We are always storing the information we gain from reading. As we read a text, we keep a summary in our heads, which helps us understand the rest of the story and discuss the whole story at the end. As prekindergarteners listen to books read aloud, they are doing exactly the same thing; they listen and remember the important information, using it to understand the story or informational book. As they hear more books read, they get better and better at organizing information in their heads. Afterward, they can tell what the story was about, remembering important details as they look at the pictures.

- *Adjust reading for purpose and type of text.* We read differently for different reasons. Contrast the following kinds of reading: (1) reading a novel right before going to sleep; (2) studying a book for a test; (3) reading a biography of a well-known person; or (4) reading a manual to learn how to operate a new coffeemaker. We read different kinds of texts in different ways. We slow down to look at a word closely and then speed up again; we stop to think or look back in the text. Prekindergarteners may not be reading the words, but in your classroom, they watch as you demonstrate the way a reader adjusts when using different kinds of texts; they also have the opportunity to draw and talk about all kinds of experiences.

- *Maintain fluency.* As we read narrative or informational texts aloud, we make dialogue sound like talking as our voices rise and fall. We put words together in groups to make phrases, and we pause at punctuation. We stress certain words in sentences to make the reading sound meaningful. And we move along

at a reasonable rate—not too fast and not too slow. As adults, we usually read silently, but many of the same actions still apply. For example, when we read a novel, we have a sense of what the characters sound like. Prekindergarteners who hear stories and other kinds of books read aloud daily develop an understanding of how reading is supposed to sound and take on this behavior when they tell a story while looking at the pictures of a known text even before they can read it. You can often see children tell a story fluently while turning the pages of a book.

The above behaviors happen simultaneously as we read. To be an effective, fluent reader, all of the behaviors must be in place. Observing a young child reading aloud, we can see evidence of these systems of strategies, but much of the work is happening in the child's head. The next two categories of thinking are observable in the children's talk about books. As you think about them, remember that prekindergarten children can engage in all of them as you read books aloud and talk about them.

Thinking Beyond the Text

Processing a text not only means reading the words on the page and understanding the author's message; it also means bringing our own thinking to the reading. When we read a story, article, or book, we connect what we are reading with our own experiences. We bring knowledge *to* the text. We think beyond the text when we read something independently but also when we hear a text read aloud—great news for prekindergarten teachers! Well before children can read for themselves, you can help them learn to think beyond the text and to share their thinking with others. They can build up years of experience in deeply understanding texts before grade one. All it takes is establishing storytime routines in the classroom and selecting appropriate texts such as those on the extensive list in Appendix E.

As readers thinking beyond the text, we:

- *Predict.* We are always thinking about what might happen next or what a character might do. Part of the satisfaction of reading is making predictions and confirming or disconfirming them. As adults, we hardly realize we are predicting but we do it constantly. (Possibly we are most aware of the process when reading a mystery.) But prediction is present in different ways in both fiction and nonfiction. Even very young children can anticipate what will happen next.

Cookie's Week (Ward, 1997, 2004) is a simple story that goes through the days of the week with Cookie the cat, who has a new mishap each day. By Wednesday, the children will be predicting a new disaster the next day. The book ends by saying, "Tomorrow is Sunday. Maybe Cookie will rest." The picture shows Cookie asleep in bed but with one eye open. Children readily predict that Cookie will again get into mischief. The "If You Give a Mouse a Cookie" books by Laura Numeroff are other great texts to use when working on prediction—each page is set up as an if-then situation, so children have plenty of opportunities to predict!

Reading favorite stories several times is a good way to help children feel the power of prediction. During the second or third reading, you will find them eager to predict what will come next. You may question whether they are making true predictions, since they already know what will happen; but from the children's point of view they are using prior knowledge to understand and predict the text.

- *Make connections.* We bring background knowledge to every text we experience, whether it's knowledge of the world, personal experience, or connections with other texts. For example, if we are reading a book about the Statue of Liberty, we probably unconsciously recall facts we previously knew that help us identify new information. Our having viewed the statue from a boat or visited it makes a difference in our reading as well. If our relatives were immigrants,

we may have heard family stories involving the statue. Or we may recall texts—both fiction and nonfiction—in which the statue figured prominently.

Even prekindergarteners bring background knowledge to reading and make connections between texts, especially if you carefully select texts to build this kind of strategic action. They can start to recognize books by authors like Kevin Henkes and enjoy hearing several books about a character like Lily. Books like *Over in the Meadow* (Wadsworth, 2003), delight children with rhythm, rhyme, and repetition and allow children to make connections with background knowledge by matching mother animals with their babies. Even if they have never seen a hedgehog, they are gradually able to identify one as they hear books read like *Goodnight Moon* (Wise Brown, 2005), *Olivia* (Falconer, 2000), *Little Fur Family* (Wise Brown, 2003), and *Time for Bed* (Fox, 1997).

Especially at first, children will make very simple connections to the books you read—"I have a red car too!" "I have a brother!" While comments like these may be true, they don't do much to help children create meaning. With some prompting, you can guide children to make connections that move beyond the surface—"My brother takes my toys too! I get mad!" You can help them extend their understandings by asking for examples from several children and talking about what they have in common or asking how they felt.

- *Synthesize information.* We are always acquiring new knowledge and new ways of thinking as we read fiction and informational texts. We may read a biography of a famous person and revise our opinion of the person or gain new inspirations from the new knowledge we gain. Young children are always learning new stories that help them think differently about everyday life or enter into a world of fantasy. A book like *Eric Carle's Opposites* (2007) opens children's perspectives to the meaning of opposites; *Freight Train* (1993), by Donald Crews, draws attention to the cars and characteristics of a train.

- *Infer.* As proficient readers we "read between the lines." We have ideas about what a character is like or why he acts the way he does. We understand more than the writer has said explicitly. Even young children can infer the feelings of distress the owl babies have (*Owl Babies*, Waddell and Benson, 1996) as they wait for their mother to return, and the relief and joy they feel when she swoops down to them. They can feel empathy when Trixie's bunny is lost (*Knuffle Bunny*, Willems, 2004). They can talk about why all the animals live in or near water after hearing *In the Small, Small Pond* (Fleming, 2007).

The kinds of thinking listed above may seem simple and natural—just what happens when you read stories to young children—and that is true. But at the same time, you can demonstrate and invite children to talk in a very intentional way: "I'm thinking about how the owl babies felt when their mother came swooping back. What are you thinking?" You can elicit children's thinking and demonstrate how to go beyond *happy* and *sad*. Through your modeling, children will add to their repertoire of words used to describe feelings. You can also ask students to add to what they are saying; for example, if a child says, "Trixie is sad!" when she realizes her bunny is lost, you might say, "Why is Trixie sad? Say a little bit more about that," prompting the child to explain. "She's sad because her bunny is lost at the Laundromat and her Daddy doesn't even know!" Engaging daily in this kind of thinking and making ideas explicit through language will have great benefit in terms of cognitive development and reading comprehension.

Thinking About the Text

As readers, we also consider the text as a piece of writing. We notice and evaluate what the writer (and illustrator, if appropriate) has done to get the meaning across. If we have a favorite writer, it is probably because we enjoy the writing style, we like the types of plots he or she uses, or we enjoy the setting or ways of revealing characters. That is because we are thinking about the text as an object. We:

- *Analyze.* We learn to think analytically about the texts we read. If we discuss a book in a club, for example, we talk about the meaning we got from the text (thinking beyond the text), but we may also read aloud examples that show the writer's skill at showing what a character is like or foreshadowing the ending. We notice how the writer has organized the text to present information or how the plot unfolds.

Even young children can develop favorite writers and illustrators. They can talk about the similarities between Eric Carle's *The Very Hungry Caterpillar* (1994) and *The Very Quiet Cricket* (1990). They can notice how everything mentioned in the story *Goodnight Moon* matches something in the pictures. After hearing and looking at the pictures of *We're Going on a Bear Hunt* (Rosen, 2009), they can talk about how they know which part is imagination and which part is real. They can talk about how the writer showed that Carl was a good dog in *Good Dog, Carl* (Day, 2010). These discussions are not entered into for the purpose of labeling techniques or talking in literary terms such as *setting* or *plot*, but even young children can begin to understand that books are created by authors and illustrators.

- *Critique.* We also evaluate the texts we read. We think about what is believable or well stated. We think critically about whether the ideas presented are logical and well supported. We identify bias. We do this whenever we read a biography or a news article; it is the mark of a reader who thinks deeply.

Prekindergarteners in general are not ready to critique texts in this way, but they can talk about what they like about a book, author, or illustrator, and they can identify their favorite parts of stories. They can say what they like (or don't like) about illustrations. They can even borrow ideas from books for drawings or stories, which shows that they have noticed and liked aspects of texts.

Helping Children Expand Their Thinking

The above material may seem pretty complicated, and it is. Reading involves complex mental activity. But you do not need to worry about directly teaching each of these ways of thinking when you work with children. In fact, you shouldn't! This would make it tedious. If you think about the texts yourself and then get children into conversations about them, they will begin to think in deeper ways about texts and to use each of these ways of thinking.

In *It's a Secret!* (Burningham, 2009) a little girl wonders about what her cat Malcolm does when he goes out at night. One evening she imagines that she, Malcolm, and Norman (who lives next door) are all dressed in fancy clothes, are cat-size, and go together to an amazing party. The story is quite realistic at the beginning but turns soon to fantasy and then back to realism at the end. The thinking revealed in the conversations about this story (see Figure 14.2) are natural. Children are just expressing their ideas. (The third column is our analysis of what is happening.)

Over two years of prekindergarten, you can have hundreds of conversations with your young students. Each will nudge them to think about texts and express their ideas. To stimulate conversation, use language like:

- "Let's look at this picture to help us think."
- "Listen while I read this part again and tell me what you think."
- "I'm wondering if. . . ."

- "I noticed that. . . . Did you?"
- "What were you wondering when. . .?"
- "What part did you like? Why?"
- "What makes you think that?"
- "What part of the story made you think that?"
- "[Name], what are you thinking about?"

You will think of many more ways to encourage conversation. Some additional suggestions are:

- Wait patiently while children put their words together.
- Listen for opportunities to probe further by asking why.
- Let shy children "pass" rather than force them to speak but make it easy for them to contribute when they are ready.
- Use turn and talk to give all children the chance to talk.
- Try to get children to listen to and respond to one another's comments rather than always making your own comments in between.
- Demonstrate your own thinking and ask for their response.

In many ways, conversations like this are highly intentional—that is, you are actively working to support expansion of comprehension. But in other ways, they are very much like friendly talks you would have with a friend or a family member about a book you have read. They can't really go wrong if they are real conversations!

Discussion During and After Reading *It's a Secret!* Aloud		
Speaker	**Transcript**	**Analysis**
Teacher	We are going to read a wonderful book called *It's a Secret!* by John Burningham. You know sometimes cats go out at night. The little girl in this story, Marie Elaine, wonders what her cat does when he goes out at night. We are going to find out what she thinks he might do.	
(reading)	"One evening in the summer, Marie Elaine came down to the kitchen to get a cold drink from the fridge. There, by the cat door, was Malcolm the cat, and he was all dressed up in fancy clothes and a hat." It's getting exciting, isn't it? What are you thinking?	Stops briefly at a strategic place to draw attention to it and invite comments.
Nathan *Dorrie*	It's a magic cat. He is wearing clothes. Cats don't really do that.	
Teacher	We'll have to see what happens in this story. Maybe Marie Elaine will find out what Malcolm does when he goes out. *Continues to read until she comes to two pages where Malcolm helps Marie Elaine and Norman escape from dogs by climbing a crane. They go up to the rooftops where the party is going on.* They are having a lot of adventures, aren't they?	Confirms children's comments and probes deeper.
Ellie *Kevin*	Where are they going? Maybe they're going to the sky.	Asks a question. Makes a prediction.
Teacher	Let's read and see. "Finally they arrived at the place on the rooftops where the party was about to start." You know on the top of some big buildings, the roof is flat and cats could walk around and play games on them. *[Turns the page.]* Wow! Look how dressed up all the cats are. *She reads the next two pages.* Are you thinking about how Marie Elaine and Norman are feeling?	Provides background knowledge. Builds anticipation. Invites comments.

Figure 14.2 Discussion during and after reading *It's a Secret!* aloud

continues

	Discussion During and After Reading *It's a Secret!* Aloud, *continued*	
Speaker	**Transcript**	**Analysis**
Margaret	They're dancing and they're having fun.	Makes an observation.
Roman	It's like a dream.	Makes an inference based on the observation.
Kevin	Yeah, maybe she dreamed it.	Agrees with the inference.
Teacher	It could be that. We'll finish the book and maybe we'll find out.	Creates anticipation.
	Without interrupting the flow of the story, the teacher encourages a few short discussions and comments during the reading. These opportunities to notice and talk contribute to the discussion after reading, below.	
Teacher	What are you thinking about the story?	Opens the conversation.
	Several children comment that they liked the story.	Listens attentively.
Teacher	That's good. What did you like most about it, Ellie?	Confirms children's comments and probes deeper.
Ellie	When they got little and all dressed up.	Expresses opinion based on specific memory.
Marcus	I liked it when they were dancing.	Expresses opinion based on specific memory.
Michael	And when they saw the queen.	Expresses opinion based on specific memory.
Teacher	I liked those parts too. What about the ending?	Confirms comments. Probes further.
Ellie	She was happy because she knew the secret.	Make inferences about the feelings of character and reasons for those feelings.
Marcus	It wasn't really the secret but she thinks it is.	
Ellie	Because she dreamed it.	
Kevin	Or maybe she just made it up.	
Roman	She couldn't get little like that in real life.	

Figure 14.2 Discussion during and after reading *It's a Secret!* aloud, *continued*

continues

Discussion During and After Reading *It's a Secret!* Aloud, *continued*

Speaker	Transcript	Analysis
Teacher	What do some of the rest of you think? Was she dreaming it or imagining it?	Asks for evaluation.
	Children are uncertain and offer several opinions.	
Teacher	We don't really know, do we? But it was a good story. When did you know it was going to be something like a dream or imagination?	
Roman **Kevin** **Ellie**	When she got tiny and dressed up. No, when they got away from the dogs. When they danced.	Notice aspects of the story.
Teacher	All those things told us that it was going to be a make-believe story like a dream or imagination. You are good noticers. Let's look at this page *[shows the first picture of the cat dressed up].*	Confirms significance of children's comments. Draws attention to a turning point in the story.
Kevin	That's when the cat got to be like magic.	Notices turning point.
Teacher	And I noticed something at the end. *[Turns to the last page.]*	Draws attention to another turning point.
Roman **Ellie**	He's just a cat again. But she knows the secret.	

Figure 14.2 Discussion during and after reading *It's a Secret!* aloud, *continued*

Key Understandings to Think About

* Reading is thinking.

* Reading is a very complex process.

* There is much more to reading than saying the words.

* Readers think in many different ways as they process texts.

* Readers think within, beyond, and about the texts they read.

* Conversation during and after reading supports children's thinking.

Notes

Supporting Emergent Writers

Prekindergarteners can come to see themselves as writers long before they are able to write conventionally. Preschool children engage in drawing and writing to tell their stories, imitate adults, play with writing materials, send messages, or explore. In this section we explain early writing behaviors and then discuss specific ways to help students create stories and begin to "write" messages. We discuss how to use shared and interactive writing in the classroom and go into detail about how teaching interactions can lead students forward as writers. Through many opportunities for storytelling, and rich and playful writing experiences, young children quickly learn to see themselves as writers and to love the process.

15

Learning to Write:
Understanding Early Writing Behaviors

"The fastest way to teach a child to read
is to teach him to write."

—MEM FOX

Today's children are born into a world full of print. The degree to which literacy is evident in homes varies, but almost all children see adults being literate every day—if not reading novels and informational texts, then making lists, writing notes, reading newspapers or magazines, reading directions or recipes, filling out forms, using email and text messaging, reading labels on food packaging, and doing countless other tasks that require literacy. In a way, children start becoming literate almost from the day they are born, as they notice elements of the world, which are bound to include literacy.

Early Writing Behaviors

Early attempts to approximate writing are valuable experiences for young children. Through approximation and demonstration, they gradually acquire complex understandings about communicating in writing. In 1975, Marie Clay brought this important idea to our attention with a little book called *What Did I Write?* A central concept is that young children frequently scribble or write strings of letters and then ask a parent to read it! Think what that question—"What did I write?"—means. The child knows that marks on paper represent meaningful language, and he wants to try it for himself. Clay suggests that children are not inherently frustrated by the writing task but, rather, are intrigued by it, especially if we respond to their efforts with enthusiasm. "Observations and examples of work suggest that while the child is discovering letter forms and creating his early messages the task seems to have its own attraction if his efforts have been responded to with appreciation" (Clay, 1975, 3).

Clay's research on the writing of five-year-olds has great relevance for prekindergarten teaching. For example, she suggests that the *gross approximation* of letter forms that appears in early drawing and scribbling develops into later writing behavior. Interestingly, these approximations are not just random lines but often have some specificity; that is, a child learns details such as a particular letter or how to write her name and reproduces them many times. Three-year-old Matthew makes great use of the letters in his name (see Figure 15.1). His approximations (notice the extra lines on the *E*) will later be refined and added to as he is exposed to more text and as he spends more time drawing and writing. In a classroom of three-year-olds, you might expect to see a portion of the class with very little ability to hold a writing implement or to produce anything

Figure 15.1 Matthew's approximations of the letters in his name

more than a scribble. A portion of the class might be able to make lines, circles, and scribbles, and still others might be able to produce writing like Matthew's.

". . . the child is reaching out towards the principles of written language and any instruction should encourage him to continue to do this" (Clay, 1975, 15). This suggests that it is important for even young children to have many opportunities to draw and write.

Clay (1975) identified some important principles that apply to prekindergarteners:

- *The recurring principle.* Children repeat what they know over and over. We find this concept in their drawing and also in writing that seems almost like self-imposed practice of the known letter. Three-year-old Elizabeth has learned particular letters and numbers and takes the opportunity to "practice" a pattern over and over (see Figure 15.2). Her choice of letters and numbers most definitely has something to do with the fact that she lives in Ohio and her parents went to Ohio State University!

- *The directional principle.* The convention of writing in English requires that words be written left to right across each line and from top to bottom on the page. This is a purely arbitrary convention that the child must learn. Other languages have different conventions. There is nothing "natural" or ingrained about it. If a child writes or scribbles from left to right, this is a sure sign that she is beginning to internalize this convention. As a child works out the rules of directionality, the starting position is often critical. Four-year-old Anthony is working in a very flexible way as he tests the limits of this rule (see Figure 15.3). He has written his name as *ha*. He started on the left margin and wrote his name left to right. Then, apparently using the right page edge as a starting point, he wrote it again, *ah*. Eventually, he will learn to always use the left edge as a starting point. Many children will reverse letters and words through this age.

Figure 15.2 Elizabeth's writing

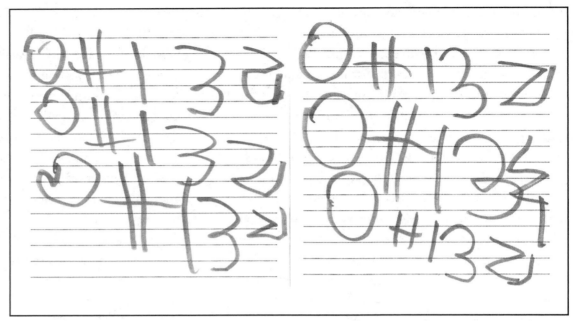

Figure 15.3 Anthony's drawing and name

- *The inventory principle.* Children often systematically produce a collection of everything that they know about writing—all the letters or even all the words. In the example in Figure 15.4, four-year-old Ashley has produced all the words she knows how to write "right." *Mom, Dad, Grandma, Nana, Papa,* and her sister *Ellie* are a rich resource for Ashley. She also includes short easy words that she knows, like *the, hi, go,* and *no.* There is also some evidence that she is making connections between words: *cat, cap, car.*

- *The contrastive principle.* Establishing opposites is a special kind of thinking. Sometimes children compare things that are similar and at the same time different. It may be that there is an intriguing tension in comparison and contrast or it may be that this is just one of the ways we learn about our world. Ashley, who will turn five in a couple of months, made a book (from prestapled blank paper) about many things she likes (two pages are shown in Figure 15.5). Each page has a single topic with a relevant picture and Ashley's attempt to write a label. This is a sophisticated example. You'll find younger children just contrasting shapes or size.

M & Ms are shown on the left page, Skittles on the right page. She has included the feature that distinguishes these two similar candies.

Clay (1975) also found that young children attend to and reflect on the signs they see—letters and even punctuation. They may make up some of their own signs. Two-year-olds may be satisfied just to make marks on paper, "but somewhere between three and five years most children become aware that people make marks on paper purposefully, and in imitation they, the children, may produce similar marks" (Clay, 1975, 48). The written exchange between three-year-old Matthew and his mother in Figure 15.6 shows that he is learning to respond to writing with a connected message.

Figure 15.4 All the words Ashley knows

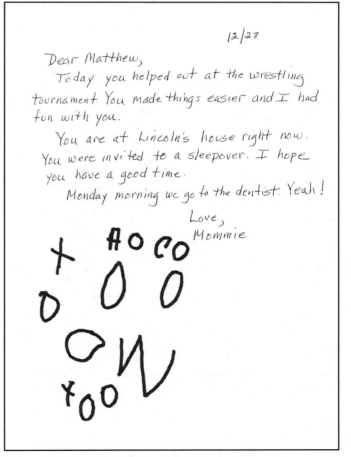

Figure 15.5 Ashley's M & Ms and Skittles pages

Figure 15.6 Matthew's response to his mother's note

Purposeful Writing

An active prekindergarten writing program fosters the link between meaning and written signs. In some of the examples presented in this chapter, children seem to be experimenting with writing for their own enjoyment. But others have real-life purposes. Young children observe people all around them who are using writing for a purpose, and they easily internalize this aspect if they have the opportunity. They make grocery lists, write notes (see Elliott's "thank-you" note in Figure 15.7), label their drawings, and make signs. They play at writing just as they play at cooking, building, housekeeping, or other things. The more you can create these opportunities in the prekindergarten classroom, the more the children will learn about *both* writing and reading.

Much of children's early writing represents an attempt to communicate. Four-year-old Iris is quite concerned that the Tooth Fairy will not reward her (see Figure 15.8). Her note of apology, in which she uses conventional letter forms and makes very good attempts at spelling, says, "Dear Tooth Fairy, I am sorry I swallowed my tooth. Love, Iris." She draws and labels her drawings. Every attempt that a young child makes to write tells us more about what he knows about literacy. In this book we have also provided a color photo collection which includes examples of children's early writing efforts. These are organized in a way that illustrates a progression in their writing as they internalize the principles described here.

Figure 15.7 Elliott's thank-you note

Figure 15.8 Iris' note to the Tooth Fairy

Key Understandings to Think About

✳ Early attempts at writing reveal what young children are learning about literacy.

✳ Early attempts to approximate writing are valuable experiences for young children.

✳ We can see patterns in children's early attempts at writing.

✳ We want to encourage writing attempts in preschool classrooms to help children make the link between meaning and written signs.

Notes

Using Shared and Interactive Writing to Develop Emergent Writers

*"Writing in preschool is not about teaching writing,
it's about nurturing writers."*

—KATIE WOOD RAY AND MATT GLOVER

It seems unbelievable to think of children writing in prekindergarten, but most prekindergarteners will be able to do many of the things on the lists below before they enter kindergarten. For example, children:

- Draw and write about their experiences.
- Draw foods (and other things) they like and label them.
- Make up stories and draw to represent the events (in sequence).
- Use aspects of print such as speech bubbles, punctuation, titles.

- Construct menus, receipts, signs, and other functional items.
- Write notes and letters to others.
- Draw, label, and invent writing to tell about their observations and discoveries through inquiry.

Prekindergarteners can also write about their reading. They can:

- Draw pictures (or make paintings or a collage) about what they have learned about a topic.
- Label pictures or talk about them and tell the teacher the labels.

- Retell stories with a series of pictures.

- Draw speech bubbles to represent talking in the stories.

- Write a simple sentence showing the exciting part of a story or the ending.

- Write a simple sentence telling about something (an interesting fact or question).

- Make a book that reflects a story or informational text that they have heard read.

How do young children learn to see themselves as writers? They learn from demonstration and participation and by trying things out for themselves. Shared and interactive writing, usually with the whole class or a small group, allow young children to participate in the writing process with a high level of support. Shared and interactive writing are *collaborative* processes. All aspects of writing can be demonstrated through shared and interactive writing; as children experience more of it, they will start wanting to write for themselves.

Prekindergarteners can be given time to write at various points during the day (see the sample frameworks in Chapter 5, Figures 5.4 and 5.5). Many teachers begin by having children draw and then encourage them to add writing to their drawings. This "writing" may be curly squiggles at the bottom of the page for one child, partial or invented letters for another, and strings of letters for yet another. Children can write about reading after read-aloud or shared reading or when writing independently. In your classroom, you could set aside time during which children know they are expected to respond in some way to the book or poem that has just been read and discussed. They can talk or "read" (retell) with a partner. They can draw and/or write. During this time you can interact with and assist a small group or individual students. This will be infinitely more successful if you take the time to teach children routines for using materials and putting them away.

The continuum (Section 7) contains two continua important for emergent writers: (1) Writing About Reading (any writing young children do in response to books and stories) and (2) Writing. The Writing About Reading continuum identifies possible types and forms of writing, as well as goals for extending thinking about texts. These goals are categorized as evidence of thinking within, beyond, and about the text—just as the continua related to reading are (see Section 3)—because writing about reading extends thinking and provides evidence of the thinking that readers (listeners, in the case of most prekindergarteners) do. The Writing continuum codifies the process in which children choose topics that are important to them and draw/write what they think and have experienced. Children can draw and write texts that tell stories, provide information, express feelings or images (are poetic), or perform some other function. The goals for children's progress are sorted into:

- Craft (the quality of the text)

- Conventions (the degree to which the writing reflects awareness of how print looks and works in writing)

- Process (the creation of writing from getting an idea to finishing and sharing the piece)

Prekindergarteners can make progress toward all these goals. Of course, we do not expect them all to develop in the same way, nor do we expect them to be writing words conventionally or even necessarily writing letter forms or letters with letter-sound correspondence. Just as with reading, our aim is to lay a foundation on which children can begin to build their identities as writers who make meaningful marks on paper to communicate information.

Writing Time

Many prekindergarten teachers set aside a time for writing, drawing, or bookmaking. This almost always means art and writing on topics the children choose. Two basic types of writing are useful.

Shared and Interactive Writing

In shared and interactive writing, you and the children compose and write a text together that is then available as reading material. (For detailed descriptions of interactive writing and its uses, see McCarrier, Pinnell, and Fountas, 2000). The children love to go back to these illustrated pieces and read them again. The two processes are similar in that you are composing a message together as a class. In shared writing, you are the only one using the pen. In interactive writing, you "share the pen," occasionally inviting a student in the class to come up to the easel or chart to:

- Write a known letter (sometimes the first letter of the child's name).
- Place a hand on the chart to "hold" a space while the next word is being written.
- Write a letter that is connected to a sound children heard in the word.
- Write a known word.
- Sign his or her name.

Be selective about when you have children come to the easel, because you don't want it to take too long. Select just a few places in the text where individual contributions will be appropriate and have value for learning. See Appendix D for lessons on both interactive writing (Lesson 5) and interactive drawing (Lesson 6).

Mrs. P and her class have made a very simple book about things the children like to do (Figure 16.1). Children first drew pictures to represent something they enjoy doing. After the class discussed the pictures, Mrs. P wrote something on a sentence strip for each child. (On the page "Elizabeth Plays," the teacher invited Elizabeth to write the *E* for *Elizabeth*, a letter she knows well because of her name, and the *p* for *plays*, and Mrs. P wrote the rest.) Finally, the words were glued onto the paper. The result is an enlarged text that the children can use for shared reading.

Figure 16.1 Pages of class big book, interactive writing

In the example in Figure 16.2, four-year-olds are writing about their self-portraits. Each time, with the teacher's support, they have written "I see [name]." (The children have written what they can and the teacher has filled in the rest.) Manuel wrote *I* and the *M* and *A* of his name. Esther wrote the entire message for her portrait. The spelling is conventional, because this piece will be used for shared reading. When children write independently, they use letter-like forms, letters, and approximated spellings according to their current knowledge. Three-year-olds will need more support with the concept of self-portraits—possibly using mirrors or photographs—and many will not add words or letters, although they frequently add scribbles or pretend writing.

The general components (rather than steps, because you will keep cycling back and forth) in shared and interactive writing are discussed below.

Tapping into experience: provide background and engage children's interest. Shared/interactive writing can be used for just about any purpose but it is *not writing just to write.* It is rooted in experience, thinking, and conversation. It often will emerge from and even guide inquiry into topics of interest. For example, a prekindergarten class is learning about plants. They have several growing plants in the room to examine. They have plant specimens to look at with a magnifying glass. They have drawn plants in various stages of growth. They have walked around the school yard to identify and compare plants. Literacy is integrated into this study as the teacher reads aloud books related to plants. *In the Tall, Tall Grass* (Fleming, 1995) prompts a discussion of the relationship between plants and animals. "They're all mixed up together!" Simone says. Retelling the story *Stone Soup* (Brown, 2010) they talk about plants we eat. "I eat tomatoes from a tomato plant. I wouldn't eat a stone though," says Raoul. The teacher also reads *The Great Big Enormous Turnip* (Tolstoy, 2000), which has a lot of action that the children take turns acting out. All of this experience provides the thinking and language base for writing and writing helps to extend the thinking and language.

Talking: determine a text's purpose. During the investigation, the teacher says, "We are going to plant some bean seeds so that we can watch them grow into plants. Let's make a list of what we are going to need." Also, "How do you think we can keep a record of how our bean plant looks as it grows?" Children suggest drawing or writing a bit about the plant every few days. The writing, then, will take the form of a descriptive record. After reading *The Great Big Enormous Turnip*, the teacher says, "Would you like to do your own story about the turnip?" Another option might be, "How can we show and write about what happened at the end of the story?" After a

Figure 16.2 Pages of big book, "I See"

discussion like this, you and the children decide on the type of writing and drawing that will be needed. Keep this process very simple. Of course you will need to do a great deal of demonstrating and guiding, but it is important for children to be involved.

Composing: decide what to write. After general discussion and planning, you and the children decide the precise message. You will be using very simple sentences or labels with prekindergarteners, so it will not take long. Even though you've established a general plan, compose one sentence or label at a time. Have the children repeat it so that they can remember it, but don't be afraid to be their "memory." Each time you complete a sentence or label, reread the whole piece to help the group come up with what to write next: "Okay, now it says, 'The turnip was as big as our school.' What should we say next about the turnip?"

Constructing: write the message. Once the message (or a meaningful part of it) has been composed, start to write it down—word by word and letter by letter. The wonderful thing about writing is that it makes language "stand still." Having written a word, children are free to reread the sentences to help them remember the next word. It "slows down" processing and makes it easier to focus on the details. Have children say words slowly, thinking about the sounds and making whatever connections with the letters they can. Select only words that have easy-to-hear sounds. Say the word slowly in order to teach children the process; then tell the letter yourself, sometimes connecting it with the name of one of the children: "*Turnip*, that's *T* like in *Tyrone*." Quickly write harder words yourself so the lesson will not be too long. While constructing the message, invite children to come up to the chart to contribute a letter or word or place their hand on it to hold a space while you begin a new word. Be selective, again, to keep the process moving.

Rereading: check the writing. Rereading what they have just written (or written yesterday) is what writers do when they are thinking of what to write next. Interac-

tive writing is an excellent context in which to model this process, and your students will soon be doing the same thing when they are writing independently. Reread to:

- Check whether the message sounds right.
- Check whether it says what you mean to say.
- Judge the use of spaces and other simple conventions as appropriate to children developing understanding.
- Decide the kind of illustrations that will be needed.

Summarizing: focus on what was learned. At the end of a shared/interactive writing session, help children remember what they learned. For example, you might say, "Today we wrote about the exciting part of the story. You learned to say the words slowly to hear the sounds. What helped us think about the first letter of words?" Children might respond, "Our names" or "The name chart." "That's right. So when you are writing words you can say them slowly and think of any letters you might know."

Revisiting: notice the details of the text. Keep the shared/interactive writing pieces that you and your students have created together on display. They are ideal material for shared reading and will help children remember what they have learned or books they have heard read aloud. Over time, the walls of your classroom will be filled with beautiful art and meaningful writing. The shared/interactive writing text can be revisited at any time for word study. You can demonstrate noticing features of words and eventually ask children to do it themselves:

- "Find a place where you used good spacing to divide the words."
- "Find the word ____."
- "Find a little word."
- "Find a big word."
- "Find the letter ____."
- "What word begins like your name?"

Extending: help children understand the uses of writing. Completed pieces of shared/interactive writing displayed in the classroom become valuable resources. Children often refer to them to help them write a letter or a word. When you are reading aloud, you can refer to a chart based on literature to help children make connections between stories. You can reread a piece with science or social studies content to help remember information. You can refer to a list (a list of supplies necessary for a project or a grocery list, for example) to check whether you have everything or to help you start a new list.

Shared writing and interactive writing give very young children an opportunity to use writing and reading in authentic and practical ways—just as adults do. In the process, they are learning a great deal about letters and sounds and how print works.

Independent Writing and Drawing

Parents and teachers have long recognized art's benefit in young children's learning. And we know that children tell stories with their drawings and use them to represent their world. A child's drawing or marks on a page represent his thinking. We have no trouble understanding Conner's picture of Spiderman (see Figure 16.3). Look at the action! His friend Elizabeth liked it so much that she put a sticker on it and her name.

Tomas' "Big Bad Bullybug" (Figure 16.4) has plenty of personality and clearly reflects his interpretation of a beloved book, Ed Emberly's *Bye-Bye, Big Bad Bullybug!* (2007).

Figure 16.3 Conner's picture of Spiderman

Figure 16.4 Tomas' picture of "Big Bad Bullybug"

Figure 16.5 Matthew's swimming party

Matthew's picture of a swimming party (Figure 16.5) also has some action. His mom has written his story using his words.

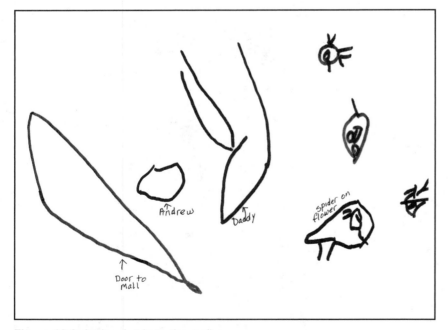

Figure 16.6 Andrew's trip to the mall

Matthew's younger brother Andrew drew a picture of a trip with Dad to the mall (Figure 16.6). Notice how everything is arranged in the space to the right of the door. He has also provided language to describe a detail that captured his attention—a spider.

Children can also use drawing to reflect what they have done or something they have learned. Figure 16.7 is Matthew's record of the apples he tasted. He liked the yellow one.

Just a step from drawing is experimenting with all kinds of writing. In Figure 16.8, Matthew used both letters and letter-like forms to create a longer message. And in Figure 16.9 he experimented with both print and scribbling, while writing his name almost conventionally at the bottom.

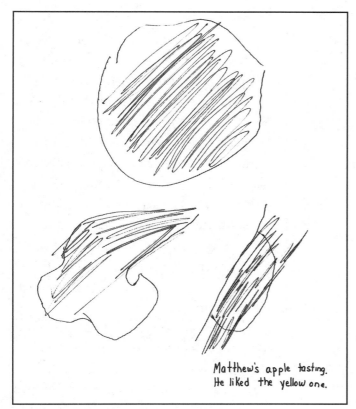

Figure 16.7 Matthew's apple tasting

Figure 16.8 Matthew's letters and letter-like forms

Figure 16.9 Matthew's print and scribbling

Figure 16.10 Matthew's "I Love You" message

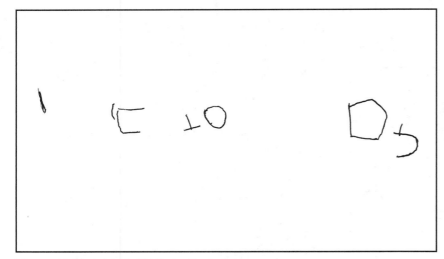

Figure 16.11 Ashley's "I Like to Dance" message

At about the same age, Matthew showed that he could copy his mother's writing, but he was still flexible in his approach to writing (see Figure 16.10).

Four-year-old Ashley provided a clear message in the writing shown in Figure 16.11. If at first glance the marks seem meaningless, take another look. The message is "I like to dance." A lowercase *i* is there followed by a space. The next word is represented by a form that looks very much like an upside-down *L*, and again there is a space. A primitive but accurate *to* is followed by a space, and we can see a *D*-like form and a backward *c*.

Almost any subject can call for some writing, as shown in the outline of Ashley's foot shown in Figure 16.12, a page from a book she made about "things I like." Notice that she is hearing sounds in words.

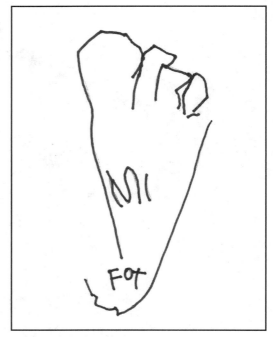

Figure 16.12 Ashley's "My Foot"

Bookmaking

Writing *for* prekindergarten children shows them that what they can say can be written. Over time, they become more aware that their words are being written down. They form sentences more clearly and often stop courteously so that the writer can catch up. Vivian Gussin Paley (1987) has written about her enriching methods of taking dictation of children's own stories, which are then dramatized by the class. Though it may be helpful for the adult to occasionally write the child's talk as a label or record of the story told in his pictures, dictation is not the only experience children need. According to Ray and Glover (2008), using a great deal of dictation may interfere with the child's learning to transcribe for himself. A balance is needed.

For the young child, writing for oneself is an opportunity to solve problems; adult support can help them learn a great deal and also feel the power of writing. It is possible for four-year-olds to think of themselves as writers and illustrators; Katie Wood Ray and Dan Glover (2008) recommend many kinds of writing, including list making, writing as part of exploration and inquiry, and literacy as part of dramatic play (notes, lists, signs), among others. They also believe bookmaking has great potential for helping children become writers: "Children who make picture books are engaging in complex thinking about writing as a process" (Ray and Glover, 2008, 107). (See Appendix D, Lesson 11 for a lesson on bookmaking.) As you read aloud many books, you provide models of how a writer and an illustrator "made a book" using several pages.

You can demonstrate bookmaking to the group through shared/interactive writing, after which children need to attempt it independently. Ray and Glover (2008) suggest that the word *make* is very important, because it signals that the child is going to work for a real purpose. In other words, children may not see themselves as ready to *write* a book but *making* one sounds doable. When making a little book, children:

- Talk with others about the kinds of illustrations the book needs.
- Compose even before they can write.
- Convey meaning over several pages.
- Communicate meaning through illustrations.
- Work at a project for a time, building stamina as writers.
- Create an enjoyable and lasting product to be used in the classroom or at home.

All of the above benefits are there even if the book is composed almost entirely of pictures, as in Figure 16.13. As you can see, Sam's book communicates a story—a series of events with a satisfying ending.

Here is what Sam had to say about the story:

"There are two bad robots and they're attacking this city. He's destroying it with his claw and this one pulled the roof off the house. Then they fly away in their spaceship. He thinks they won. And then the spaceship blows up."

When children add words to their books, they:

- Begin to understand that there is a relationship between the pictures and the words.
- Learn how to connect pictures and writing.
- Learn how to place pictures and print on a page.
- Hold a message in the mind while performing the somewhat laborious task of encoding it.
- Begin to use left-to-right directionality and spacing.
- Start to say words slowly and make a connection between sounds and letters.
- Practice the manual skills that they will need for writing.

Figure 16.13 Sam's book
The Robot Attack

In addition to all these benefits, bookmaking is social. Knowing they can share their books with others increases children's motivation. It is also fun: "Instead of writing *as part* of other play and exploration, writing *becomes* the play and exploration in which children engage" (Ray and Glover, 2008, 109).

In *My Family* (Figure 16.14), Kayla stuck to a single topic and communicated a different idea on each page. Her ideas change either by the activity or the family member. Notice she is able to represent whole sentences in temporary spellings.

Through bookmaking, children have the opportunity to experience writing in all its complexity. Here are some suggestions for implementing bookmaking in the prekindergarten classroom:

1. Demonstrate making a larger book using shared/ interactive writing. The book can be about animals, plants, insects, or anything else children have been studying. It can also retell a favorite story. Sometimes teachers make a smaller version to place in the library or in a tub in the library or bookmaking area. You can also make a few small books yourself to give children as models.

2. After demonstrating how to do it, make bookmaking an activity during choice time or include it as a book activity in the framework for teaching and learning. Bookmaking is also part of writing time.

Figure 16.14 Kayla's book, *My Family*

"My Family"

"I love my family. My family likes to play with me."

"My dad is fun. My brother is cute."

Figure 16.15 Eleani's book, *Rocket Ship*

3. Set up a specific location for writing materials, including materials for bookmaking (a table with supplies stored in tubs kept on the table or on nearby shelves). Include stapled blank books of various shapes and sizes. Show children the area and put up a sign with a picture. (This could be the same place as the writing center if you don't have a lot of space!)

4. Make simple supplies available (prestapled blank books of various sizes with three or four pages, crayons, pencils, washable markers, art supplies) and show children how to use them.

5. Place an alphabet chart and name chart nearby and, through shared/interactive writing, show children how to use them as resources. You can also use these charts during phonemic awareness/phonics lessons.

6. Place some familiar books (from read-alouds) on the bookmaking table. Show children how writers sometimes look at books to get ideas.

7. Observe children while they work and occasionally offer support (see Section 6 of this book).

8. Ask individual children to "read" their books to you by telling what the pictures mean on each page. It is not necessary to write down all their words. When children use language to tell the story or share information, they are learning how to produce the same text orally again and again. This

A Conversation About Eleani's Book, *Rocket Ship*	
Teacher	**Eleani**
• "Tell me about the pictures in your story."	• "It's a rocket and it's going zoom up to the sky. I made the rocket ship and the fire going up.'
• "Are these the stars?" [pointing to circles and dots]	• "The stars and the moon [pointing]. It is going up to the moon. That's what it says."
• "Tell me about the last page."	• "It's really small and it's going way up to the moon far away. And I made my name."
• "That's an exciting story! You can share your book at sharing time."	

Figure 16.16 A conversation about Eleani's book, *Rocket Ship*

kind of articulation is different from just talking. The speaker/writer is reenacting the same set of information over and over. Demonstrate this kind of reading and also help children read and point to any real words they have placed on the page.

9. At the end of choice time or writing time, have children share their books by "reading" them to a partner, or ask several children to "read" their books to the class. Demonstrate this process when children are learning how to do it.

The goal of bookmaking is to help children think as writers. You want them to work with *intention* so that they are purposefully moving forward. Through bookmaking they will learn much about planning, and teaching is the key. Ray and Glover (2008) advise "side by side" teaching. While children are writing, you can move around the room observing and occasionally sitting beside a child and interacting for a few minutes. A sample conversation about Eleani's book (Figure 16.15) is presented in Figure 16.16.

As a teacher, you "pose problems, ask questions, and make comments and suggestions that stimulate children's thinking and extend their learning" (NAEYC, 1997, 12). Often, you will need to draw children out. For example, a child who asks you what her picture is or what she wrote is enjoying putting marks on paper but probably is not yet taking on the purpose of bookmaking. You can support chidren with prompts like these:

- "You know a lot about _____. Would you like to make a book about it?"
- "What did you do when you went _____? Let's plan a book about that."
- "That was a good story you told this morning. Can you remember parts of it for the pages of your book?"
- "You were making up a play in the play [puppets, store, house] corner. Do you want to write a book about that?"
- "This looks like _____. Is that right?"
- "I see that you have some blue and yellow and red."
- "I noticed that you were drawing a _____ like in [book that has been read aloud].'"
- "Is that like in [book that has been read aloud]?"
- "Where did you get your idea?"
- "What are you going to do on the first page?"
- "What are you thinking about for the next page?"
- "That will be a good story. Let's plan what to do on each page."
- "Why did you decide to make the flower so tall?"

- "When did you start this book? How long have you been working on it?"
- "Do you want to add some writing to your book?"
- "Watch me point to the words you wrote while I read it."
- "I like your story. Let me show you how to read your book."
- "I like what you did on this page. You made it interesting."

This sort of teaching is responsive. You cannot plan exactly what you will say when you have a conference with a young writer. The Writing continuum in Section 7 includes more suggestions for the behaviors and understandings you will want to nurture in your young writers.

The Process

The Writing continuum addresses the writing process specifically for prekindergarteners; these young children can engage in every part of it:

- *Rehearsing and planning.* We have just described how bookmaking supports planning. Prekindergarteners can draw and write for specific purposes, engage in planning, choose topics, choose paper and other materials, and adjust their writing and drawing according to purposes. They can tell stories orally, placing events in chronological order. Through inquiry, they can understand that a group of ideas is related and they can reflect that in their drawing and writing. They are beginning to understand that writers get their ideas from their own experiences and from what they have learned. They also can become aware of an audience for their writing as they share with others.

- *Drafting and revising.* Even young children can use their conferences with you to support their writing and drawing. They learn that they can make changes by adding or deleting materials

or by reorganizing. They learn that there are some tools they can use as writers; for example, they can add pages to a book or use sticky notes to add information to drawings or writing. Through experience, they gain confidence that they can produce a piece of writing that consists of a continuous message.

- *Editing and proofreading.* For prekindergarteners, editing and proofreading are not intended to "correct" the product and make it conventional. Your purpose is to help children understand that writers try to make their writing and drawings interesting and easy to read. You can demonstrate editing and proofreading when you put the final touches on a piece of interactive writing, which is spelled conventionally because it is a joint teacher/student project and is intended to be read by everyone in the class. Point out clear letter formation in the pieces as well as good spacing. As you notice children including letters and words in their own writing, you can point out use of space or well-formed letters: "The way you made that letter makes it easy to read."

- *Publishing.* Prekindergarteners publish all the time as they produce group writing with illustrations. Sharing their own pieces of writing with the class is another form of publication at this level.

- *Sketching and drawing.* For most prekindergarteners, drawing is the beginning way to represent ideas; it assists them in planning.

- *Viewing themselves as writers.* Prekindergarteners can approximate writing on their own, working without teacher help. They can make attempts to solve problems, and develop the habit of thinking of ideas to write about. (Once you start thinking like a writer—or bookmaker—you are always seeing topics and opportunities.) They can try out techniques they see others using. After producing many pieces, they can select their favorites.

Key Understandings to Think About

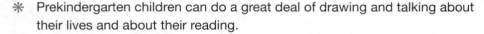

✳ Prekindergarten children can do a great deal of drawing and talking about their lives and about their reading.

✳ As they learn more about written language, they will add marks that look like writing to their drawings.

✳ Shared and interactive writing can provide powerful demonstrations of how the writing process works.

✳ After they experience shared and interactive writing, children will begin to write for themselves if they are encouraged and have time and materials.

✳ Children's early writing is approximated, but in it we see much evidence of their growing knowledge of symbols.

✳ Bookmaking is an important activity for young writers.

✳ Specific teacher language is highly supportive of young writers as they expand their knowledge.

Notes

Developing Early Writing Behaviors Through Teaching Interactions

"A class environment which creates the assumption that children will write will have writers."

—MARIE CLAY

In all the writing contexts described in Section 4, you work alongside young writers. Language interactions around writing are a very powerful support for learning. As discussed in Chapter 13 in relation to developing early reading behaviors, you can also *teach*, *prompt*, and *reinforce* important early writing behaviors through language interactions (see Figure 17.1). These kinds of interactions are far more effective than saying something

a child has done is "good" or drawing happy or frowning faces on papers. Prekindergarteners are looking for clear directions that will help them grow in their ability to express meaning in drawings and words. The suggestions in this chapter are mostly intended for working with four-year-olds who have established a good understanding of how writing "works" (although they cannot necessarily read or write more than a word or two).

Using Language to Support Early Writing Behaviors		
Teach	**Prompt**	**Reinforce**
Demonstrate and describe the specific behavior to help the child learn something new.	Prompt the child to use a specific behavior that has been taught.	Praise the new specific behavior when the child has initiated it.
Examples: "I can write your name on your picture." "I will leave some space before I start the next word." (Demonstrate using your finger or your hand.)	Examples: "Try some of the letters to make your name." "Leave some space before you start the next word."	Examples: "You wrote the *J* for your name." "You left a good space before you started your next word."

Figure 17.1 Using language to support early writing behaviors

Composing Sentences

Conversation is a great way to help children extend their ideas through talk. Examples of language that will help include:

> "You can talk about what you are thinking about that." (Teach)
>
> "This is one way to say it." (Teach)
>
> "Talk more about that." (Prompt)
>
> "What can you tell about that?" (Prompt)
>
> "Tell more about your thinking." (Prompt)
>
> "What happens first? [next?] [last?] (Prompt)
>
> "That is an interesting way to tell about that." (Reinforce)
>
> "That sounds exciting." (Reinforce)

Once the child has decided on a sentence, you may want to have him say it a couple of times and point on the page to where the words (a label, pretend writing, a message using temporary spellings) will go.

Placing Words on the Page

If children participate in shared/interactive writing, independent drawing and writing, or bookmaking every day, they will learn a great deal about placing words on the page. Even when children are producing scribbles to represent writing, they usually separate them from the picture. Language you can use to help children place words on the page includes:

> "Start here [*point to the left margin*]." (Teach)
>
> "Write here [*point, leaving a space*] next." (Teach)
>
> "When you get to the end, start here again [*point to the left margin*]." (Teach)
>
> "Show where you are going to start writing." (Prompt)
>
> "Feel the space with your finger." (Prompt)
>
> "Show a place where you left good space." (Prompt)
>
> "You started on this edge of the paper." (Reinforce)

"You put your writing under the picture." (Reinforce)

"You put your writing in a line." (Reinforce)

"Look at all the good spaces." (Reinforce)

Each piece of drawing and writing a child produces is an opportunity to explore placing print on paper, and the wonderful thing is that the product can be saved and revisited through conversation. Your goal is not perfect products. Instead, the young child's approximations become more conventional over time; experience is the key.

Forming Letters

Be consistent when you demonstrate how to form letters. Describing the directional movements aloud is also helpful. For example, as you make an *h*, you can say, "Pull down, up, over, and down." Prekindergarteners can initially make the letters in the air using large movements. This enjoyable activity is a wonderful way for them to move their bodies and learn letter formation simultaneously. They also love the tactile experience of creating letters out of clay or playdough.

Language you can use when children are learning to write letters includes:

"Listen to how I say the words to help me. Say the words to help you make letters. *Pull down* when you start to make an *h*." (Teach)

"You know how to start it." (Prompt)

"Think about how to write it." (Prompt)

"You knew how to start it." (Reinforce)

"You knew how to write it." (Reinforce)

Language describing the formation of lowercase and uppercase letters (the "verbal path") is provided in Appendix H, along with a suggested lesson (Appendix D, Lesson 7) for introducing this language, which children pick up easily.

Using Sound Analysis to Construct Words

As you write words during shared/interactive writing, demonstrate saying the words slowly, listening for the sounds in sequence, and writing the letters that represent them. Even though you will be writing very simple messages with prekindergarteners, don't sound out every word; select one or two that have particular instructional value. For example:

Words that have easy-to-hear sounds.

Words that start like children's names.

Words that are very familiar to children and that they use often in oral language.

Easy one-syllable words.

Use your own judgment about how many sounds to ask children to listen for. For example, for the word *lost*, you could ask children to say it and think of the first sound, perhaps connecting it to someone's name. Then, quickly write the *o* and *s* and ask children to say the word again and think how to end the word. If they can say the sound, that is excellent. You can always say something like, "You are saying the sound. The letter that goes with that sound is *t*." You can have a child locate *t* on the alphabet linking chart or point it out yourself.

Once you have shown children how saying the words can help them, they will start to use this technique as they write independently. Language to use includes:

"You can say the word slowly and listen for the sounds." (Teach)

"You can say the word slowly and listen for the first [last] sound." (Teach)

"Say the word aloud. Say it slowly." (Prompt)

"Listen for the sounds you hear in the first [last] part." (Prompt)

"It sounds like [*another word they know*]." (Prompt)

"It starts like [*a known word*]." (Prompt)

"You said that word slowly." (Reinforce)

"You heard those sounds." (Reinforce)

"You heard the sound and wrote the letter." (Reinforce)

Using Visual Analysis to Construct Words

Writing words means more than listening for the sounds and connecting them to letters. Good spellers also use visual patterns. While prekindergarteners are not expected to use conventional spelling, they will often learn the details of a word that they use a lot or that means something very important—*the* or *love*, for example. Language that draws children's attention to visual features of words includes:

"Add this to make it look right." (Teach)

"You know this word." (Teach)

"Watch me write this word fast." (Teach)

"It starts like [ends like] _____. (Prompt)

"How do you think it would start [end]? (Prompt)

"Think carefully before you start." (Prompt)

"Do you know a word that starts like that?" (Prompt)

"You made it look right." (Reinforce)

"You wrote it like you know it." (Reinforce)

"You wrote it without stopping." (Reinforce)

Monitoring and Correcting Words

Prekindergarteners should not be expected to "correct" their spelling, nor will it help them if you correct it for them (although you may want to make a quick note of the intended language at the bottom of the page or on the back or on a sticky note, as a reminder to yourself and family members). They can, however, notice significant accomplishments in their drawing and writing

and whether they want to add or change something. Demonstrate this behavior during shared/interactive writing, thereby developing the habit of carefully examining writing while it is being constructed and after it is finished. If you are working with four-year-olds who have strong control in how to write words, you can teach, prompt, and reinforce self-monitoring using language like this:

"Let me show you how to check if all the sounds are there. [*Run a finger under the word, left to right, while saying the word slowly.*]" (Teach)

" "What did you notice [*after a hesitation or stop*]?" (Prompt)

"What's wrong? Why did you stop?" (Prompt)

"Do you think it looks like [*say another word*]. (Prompt)

"Check to see if all the sounds are there." (Prompt)

"Look closely at it and check it." (Prompt)

"You made it look right." (Reinforce)

"You worked that out all by yourself." (Reinforce)

"You tried to work that out all by yourself." (Reinforce)

"You checked it carefully." (Reinforce)

Revisiting Text

Any simple, conventionally spelled text that children have written can be revisited to learn more about letters, sounds, and words. A text produced through shared/interactive writing is ideal, because children have a strong sense of ownership. First, demonstrate the action yourself. After children understand it, have them perform it on their own. Here are some possibilities:

"Find a place where we used good spacing."

"Find [*known word*]".

"Find a word that starts (ends) like your name."

"Find a word that starts like [*a classmate's name*]."

"Find a word that starts with [*letter*]."

"Find a little word."

"Find a big word."

"Find the letter _____."

"Find a word that ends like _____."

"Find a word that ends with _____." [*letter*]

Using Mentor Texts to Help Children Draw and Write

In Chapter 11 we discussed using interactive read-aloud to help children think and talk about texts. The same books that you read aloud to children are very valuable as models for writing. All writers take ideas from their own reading, and three- and four-year-olds will do the same. Through shared and interactive writing, model making your own books on the same topic or using the same kind of structure as favorite books that you have read to the children. Anne Rockwell's *My Preschool* (2008) tells what happens during a little boy's day in preschool. The simple language and clear, colorful illustrations describe familiar everyday events. It is the perfect springboard for writing your own enlarged text with children about their school experiences. And four-year-olds toward the end of the year will enjoy hearing *A Place Called Kindergarten* (Harper, 2006). In this story the animals on a farm miss Tommy, who gets on a bus and goes to kindergarten for the first time. The text includes the beginning letters of the alphabet (with related objects), as well as a wonderful short poem.

I Eat Fruit (Tofts, 2007) is an informational flap book that appeals to very young children. It's extremely simple and helps build vocabulary. Each two-page spread has a clear, simple picture of a kind of fruit (a bunch of grapes, for example) and the single word that represents it in print large enough for a group to see. Opening the right flap, you see the fruit broken down into smaller, labeled, pieces. Children will love making their own flap books about foods they love. *The Vegetables We Eat* (Gibbons, 2007), can be used in sections during an inquiry project on vegetables and how they grow. *A Cool Drink of Water* (Kerley, 2002) is more complex but still accessible. Reading and discussing texts like these help children see everyday objects and activities from different perspectives.

Children like books about important experiences in their everyday lives. *I'm Getting a Checkup* (Singer, 2009) focuses on a trip to the clinic or doctor's office, which can be stressful for a young child. *What Should I Make?* (Nayar, 2006, 2009) shows a little boy, Neeraj, making chapatti (Indian flat bread) with his mother. First, he plays with the dough and then makes the bread. The text ends with a "how to" section on making chapatti. *The Tushy Book* (Manushkin, 2009) is a rhyming book about that important part of a child's body.

As you read books like these, suggest to children that they can make their own books about topics they know and care about. Many children think stories exist only on television or in books. Once they realize they can tell stories, draw, and write about anything they think is important, the door to productivity will open. They also understand that they can learn how to write from other authors. Beautiful picture books become their personal mentors.

Key Understandings to Think About

✳ Children learn a great deal about literacy through early writing.

✳ The ability to expand writing grows over an extended period during which children talk, draw, and write every day.

✳ Working alongside young writers helps them expand their use of language, drawing, and beginning writing.

✳ Specific language interactions help children extend their ideas, place words on a page, form letters, use sound and visual analysis to construct words, and monitor and correct writing.

✳ Books that you read aloud to children serve as good examples for children as authors of their own books.

Notes

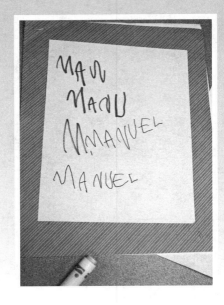

The Reading-Writing Connection

"Writing can contribute to the building of almost every kind of inner control of literacy learning that is needed by the successful reader."

—MARIE CLAY

Writing and reading are intimately connected processes. Readers recognize letters and words and reconstruct the language and meaning that the writer intended (while adding their own interpretations). Writers compose ideas and then map them out in written language to make their meanings clear to readers. For young children, learning in one area helps learning in the other (Clay, 2001). Compared with reading, writing is a "slowed down" process that allows young children to closely examine aspects of print as they write the simple messages they want to express. And, in writing or telling stories, young children often draw on the books they have heard read aloud.

When they have frequent opportunities to use drawing/writing tools and materials and they are exposed to many models of print, children learn very rapidly. Working with young writers, you see almost daily growth! They are constantly making discoveries about how written language works. Their behaviors become increasingly complex. So much is involved in moving from having an idea to finding the language that represents that idea and then actually getting the message down on the page.

We have written about this process for kindergarteners and first graders elsewhere (Pinnell and Fountas, 2009), but even prekindergarteners can begin to communicate messages. Most three-year-olds are developmentally ready to draw a picture (even in a primitive way) and then verbalize what the picture represents. From there, they go on to more planning and the ability to tell and represent stories. You can demonstrate every step of this process using shared or interactive writing with a whole group or small groups (see Chapter 16 and McCarrier et al., 1999).

When planning your teaching, it helps to think about the things writers need to know and do in order to move from an idea to a written message that can be read by others. A simple way to describe this is:

- What you think, you can talk about.
- What you say, you can write.
- What you write, you can read or someone else can read.

But that description is not enough. You need to break down the process so that you can support children every step of the way. The list below goes into more detail about what children need to know about writing. Not all prekindergarteners will develop proficiency in each of these elements! You will be exposing them to these elements of writing rather than expecting them to internalize them and use them as they write.

1. *You use language to tell your message.* As they grow in understanding, young writers formulate thoughts about a topic and make a decision about the message they want to convey. They put their thoughts into language by putting words together, or "composing" the message. As a teacher you help small groups or individuals compose. In the process of composing, your writers often represent their thinking through drawing. They draw and talk

about their drawings. As described in Chapter 16, an especially helpful technique is "bookmaking" (Ray and Glover, 2008; Horn and Giacobbe, 2007), which supports children's ability to tell their stories over several pages. Often, after producing a book that is all drawing, the writer can learn to "read" the book by using the same language every time. Four-year-old Henry, for example, knows that one way he can share what he did on his trip to the beach with his family is to put it into a book. He knows that on each page, he can draw a picture of one thing he did on his trip.

2. *You can hear the individual words in a sentence.* Young children have developed an oral language system. As they talk, they produce a speech stream, putting their words together in a way that does not make space between each word evident. To begin to think about segmenting the speech stream into individual words, children first need to be able to hear the boundaries of each word. Sentences like "I like pizza" become three separate sound units rather than one continuous stream of sound. Three-year-olds often use a few letters or letterlike forms along with a picture to represent messages. Four-year-olds may demonstrate some understanding of the relationship between letters and sounds, such as making a letter for each word in a message. Children vary greatly in the degree to which they can or want to represent their stories with letters, but with support and encouragement they will become increasingly interested in print. Explicitly demonstrating the process of writing words during shared and interactive writing is a powerful instructional tool. Four-year-old Henry, at the end of prekindergarten, is sometimes able to write down a letter to represent a word in the sentences he adds to his books. When he "reads" his books, he remembers what sentence goes with which picture, and says each word in the sentence.

3. *You use white space to show readers each word in your sentence.* Once children are able to listen for the individual words that make up a sentence, you show

them how to place each cluster of symbols on the page so there is some white space between each word. Readers know where a word starts and ends because of white space on each side. During shared reading, you can highlight the spaces by pointing to the printed words as you read them. In bookmaking, children place one picture on each page to tell a story or tell about something. Many teachers give children who are working on using white space something concrete—a popsicle stick, a bingo chip etc.—to use as a placeholder when they create their white space. Henry has been experimenting with white space, sometimes leaving spaces between his letters that are larger than the letters themselves! This is fine—he is beginning to understand that words are discrete entities surrounded by space.

4. *You place letters and words on a page in a particular way that shows the kind of writing it is (e.g., list, letter, story).* Writers use space on the page in different ways. Stories are usually written in paragraphs with continuous sentences. A list places one word or phrase under the previous one. A letter has an opening, sentences below it and a closing phrase at the end. You show young writers how to think about where they will place the print (or even scribbles) so readers will understand whether it is a list, letter, or story. You can demonstrate this process in shared/interactive writing. In their own writing, prekindergarteners are not likely to produce formal examples, but they do use writing for different purposes. We sometimes see the emergence of forms such as notes to people, lists, and stories—shown by placement of print or scribbles. Henry tends to make books that tell stories, and each page has a picture with letters below it representing words.

5. *You can say words slowly to hear each sound.* To be able to record the symbols (letters) as a writer does, young children need to listen for the sounds in words. To hear them, the writer first learns to slow speech down. The word *make* becomes /m/-/ay/-/k/ as the child says the word very slowly to hear each of the three sounds.

(Blend the three sounds rather than segmenting them sharply.) You may want to have children watch your mouth as you say the word slowly and then have them say it slowly with you. The final step is for the child to slowly say the word independently. When children say a word slowly, they can listen for the individual sounds, or *phonemes.* They can take the sounds they hear and connect them to the letters that represent them. As you demonstrate this process in shared/interactive writing, be sure children say the words slowly with you and also without you. They may begin to say the words slowly and write a few letters while they are working independently. Henry says to himself as he writes, "B-eeee-ch. B-ee-ch." Then he writes a *b* on his paper to represent the word *beach.*

6. *You can listen for the order of the sounds in each word.* As children say words slowly and listen for the individual sounds, they need to learn how to notice the order of the sounds in words. Each word is made up of a precise sequence of sounds. Some are easy to identify and connected to letters; others are more difficult. *You will not want to turn this into a tedious process, but present it in a fun and engaging way.* At this point Henry is hearing and writing only the first letter (or sometimes the last letter) in words when he makes his books, but as he develops across kindergarten, it's important for him to listen for the sequence of sounds and write them in order. This may be something he learns to do independently in kindergarten. During shared writing, Henry observes his teacher writing the sounds of words in order as she says them slowly.

7. *You think about the letter or letters that represent each sound.* As writers listen for the sounds, they begin to think about how to represent the sounds with symbols. For some sounds there is one letter and for others there are several. For example, *make* has four letters and three sounds, *ate* has three letters and two sounds, and *eight* has five letters and two sounds. Invite your prekindergarteners to say words slowly during shared and interactive writing and write the letters in the words for them. They will begin to

notice some letter-sound relationships, especially those they can connect with their names. Henry loves to come to the easel and add letters he knows when his class does interactive writing. He has recently started doing this independently as well, adding a letter to represent a word in books he makes on his own. He knows that letters correspond to sounds, and he is making more connections between which symbol (letter) represents which sound all the time.

8. *You think about what the letter that represents each sound looks like.* Once writers know the sounds they want to write and the letters that represent them, they think about the written symbol and its features. For example the sound of /b/ is represented by a symbol that looks like a long stick with a circle attached at the bottom. Working with their names is a good way to help young children attend to the distinctive features of letters. Henry was delighted to be able to write an *H* to represent the hat he drew in his book about going to the beach.

9. *You use what you know about how the letters look to make their forms on paper.* When writers are able to perceive the letter form, they can then use their motor skills to construct it. Children who know what a *b* looks like now need to form it efficiently. Sometimes you will want to use language that temporarily assists writers in making these motions correctly—for example, "pull down, up and around" for the letter *b*. You can use this kind of verbal path when making letters in shared or interactive writing (as long as it does not detract from the meaning of the message). Young children will also enjoy making letters in the air with large movements using the same verbal path. Henry and his classmates love to practice making letters together this way. This activity can be tucked in between other projects and is a great way to inject some physical activity into a transition!

10. *You can write some words you know quickly.* Some words occur frequently in the language (e.g., *the, to, we*). Teach children to write these frequently used words quickly, from beginning to end. Then they will be able to slow down and attend to the new words. They can also use what they know about frequently used words to help them write other words. *While you would not want to drill them on isolated words,* once children begin writing they may acquire a few words that they like to write (like *Mom*, their name, *love*). These words will be great resources as they learn more about written language. Henry is able to write his name and has also recently added *mom* and *dad* to his repertoire.

11. *You use what you know about words to write new words.* There are over 600,000 words in the English language, and children could never learn them one at a time. They need to learn many words and then use what they know about those words to help them learn new words. For example, if the child knows how to write *Mom* and wants to write *me*, he can think "*Mom* starts just like *me*." Or if Ivan wants to write the word *I*, he can think "I know *Ivan* and the word *I* starts like my name." They develop a network of knowledge about words that expands as they apply known principles to new words. They need to learn that whatever they know about words can be a resource for writing. Many of their early messages do not phonetically represent words but are made up entirely of the letters in their name.

12. *You have a variety of ways to construct words.* Writers do not rely only on sounds to construct words, but also their knowledge of letter patterns and what they know about other words to construct hundreds of new words. Encourage prekindergarteners to notice everything they can about letters and words; they can often find patterns such as double letters or words that rhyme. Henry, for example, loves to notice patterns like words ending in *y* when his class does shared reading.

These principles summarize a variety of understandings young writers need to learn so they can begin to get their ideas down on paper. This complicated network of knowledge is developed over time. The great thing is that all the time they are learning about writing, they are also learning about reading!

The Contribution of Writing to Reading

Writing contributes to reading in many ways; likewise, reading contributes to writing. As children take on literacy in a playful way, they grow in both areas, as briefly described below.

Meaning and language. When they are writing, young children are working with *meaningful messages.* That process begins even before they write actual letters or words (see Chapters 16 and 17). Often, they use some of the language that they have acquired from the books they have heard read aloud. If you invite them to try some of the simple, often repetitive sentences that you have used in shared/interactive writing (see Chapter 17), many will "borrow" words and language structures but adjust them to their own content. Sometimes children will compose "safe" messages (such as "I like . . ." or "I see . . ." books) for a long time. You would not want them to be stuck there, afraid to invent and try other things, but the security of familiar language is helpful. Bookmaking using drawings (as described in Chapter 16) helps children extend their ideas and language.

Hearing sounds in words. A key factor in learning to use letter-sound relationships is to hear the individual sounds in words. This may sound easy to us as adults, but for young children the ability to isolate sounds and realize that they come in sequence within words is a breakthrough. You can demonstrate how to say words slowly and think about the sounds. When a child hears a sound (any sound—not just the first one) and connects it with a word he knows, he is beginning to be able to identify sounds in words. This information forms a strong foundation for later learning about how to use letters and sounds in reading.

Learning about letters. As they write and make attempts at letters, children look at them more closely. They begin to realize that letters have particular shapes and that it takes precise movements of the fingers to make them. Even before they know the names of letters, they will start to recognize shapes like circles, sticks, tunnels, and dots in the words that they see often and try to write.

Learning about letters and sounds. As children say words slowly, they start to connect them with letters that they can write. Many of the examples in Chapters 15 and 16 contain evidence that children are making connections. Connecting a sound with a letter and then using that letter are evidence that a child is learning the alphabetic principle—that there is a relationship between letters and sounds.

Learning how print works. As they participate in shared/interactive writing and do some of their own writing, children learn more about placing words on a page and making lines of print. That information directly benefits them as they begin to read. These early reading behaviors, described in Chapter 13, are developed in both writing and reading.

Key Understandings to Think About

 Writing and reading are closely connected processes; what is learned in one area helps learning in the other.

 Writing is a complex process, even for young children.

 As they learn to write, children are also learning about meaning, language, sounds in words, letters, and how to organize print.

Notes

Learning About Letters, Sounds, and Words

Learning about letters, sounds, and words is important to developing young readers and writers. This section provides many practical, easy-to-implement ways to support children in this learning. Through games, songs, and other playful experiences with letters throughout the day, children develop a strong foundation. We describe many ways to use children's names, a powerful and highly engaging resource for literacy learning, as well as games that will help increase children's language and print awareness.

ride

Learning About
Letters and Words

*"To write messages the children must come to terms
with the distinctive features of letters which make
any one letter different from all the others."*

—MARIE CLAY

In the past, letter learning was sometimes thought to be the first step in learning to read. However, overwhelming evidence indicates that initial literacy learning is much more complex than learning the letters of the alphabet, and is hardly a step-by-step process. It is a highly demanding task of visual discrimination that takes place over a long period of time, the goal of which is fast letter recognition.

Letter knowledge is necessary, but it alone is not enough to learn to read and write. Much other learning takes place as young children become literate.

Children will be reading and writing stories long before they can identify all the letters of the alphabet.

Of course, as teachers, we still need to be sure that letter learning takes place. After all, letters represent the sounds in the words we say. In English, the relationship between sounds and letters is not perfect. One letter can represent one sound, as in the word *man,* where you can hear the three sounds represented by the three letters. But a sound can sometimes be represented by more than one letter, as in the word *through.* You hear only three sounds in *through,* but there are more than three letters. Also, a letter can represent more than one sound—the letter *c* in the words *can* and *face*—and letters can also be "silent." Readers and writers work out all these complexities over years as they learn how to look for patterns in written language.

In the past, "letter of the week" was a common practice in kindergarten, and even grade one (and in some prekindergarten classes) but teachers now realize the severe limitations of this practice. When you spend a great deal of time on "letter of the week," many children work on letters they already know, while others see and study letters out of context. Sometimes children forget last week's letter while working on this week's because they are looking at one item at a time.

This practice does not reflect how children learn letters. First, "letter of the week" suggests that letters are learned first (and in sequence) and *then* children learn to read, when in reality all of this learning is taking place at the same time. The more connections children make between the multiple understandings required to read, the faster they learn. Rather than presenting letters sequentially, week by week, a much more effective practice is to help children *engage* with letters, to learn how to look at them, write them, play with them, and put them together to make words. They tend to learn first the letters in their names and in the names of family members or friends. Or they may learn the letter that is at the beginning of the name of a favorite restaurant or store.

Learning a letter is not a simple matter of saying the letter name and singing the alphabet song. Two kindergarten teachers, (Bell and Jarvis, 2002), wrote about "letting go of 'letter of the week'" after they began to discover just how much literacy infused the life of their students before they walk through the classroom door. They found that they could support literacy development through a wide variety of authentic literacy experiences in their classrooms. For example, they could draw (and sometimes add print) to explorations

in inquiry projects and draw and write to tell about real experiences or to represent a favorite story. They could refer to simple recipes while cooking or make menus for a play restaurant. They could also make great use of all the print in the environment. Children see letters in meaningful places every day!

Learning to Look at Letters

Readers see letters as different from one another, but to young children, they may look pretty much alike—a lot of black sticks and curves. The child must learn to notice the *distinctive features* of a letter: what makes it different from every other letter. Look how little difference there is between these letters: *h, n, r, u*. Orientation also makes a difference—distinguishing between *d* and *b*, for example. If three- and four-year-olds make mistakes in using these letters, it does not necessarily mean that they are "seeing" the letters wrong, just that they do not yet see the importance of direction. It takes quite a bit of time to learn every detail of letter features.

Letter Learning

Systematic instruction in letter learning means planning a series of short lessons that show children how to look at letters, learn their names, and, over time, connect letters to the sounds in words. A minilesson for the youngest children is a very brief (around two minutes), focused introduction to a particular understanding, usually presented to the whole class. These lessons are conversational, include visual images and manipulatives, and are engaging to children (some examples are provided in Appendix D: Name Puzzles, Name Poems, Name Chart, Tissue Paper Names, Making Letters Using Play Dough, Making Names Using Tactile Materials, Letter Exploration, Letter Sort, Alphabet Hunt, Alphabet Linking, Alphabet Nature Walk, and Alphabet Hide-and-Seek). You can

Figure 19.1 Simple letter sort

also use the contexts of shared reading and writing to demonstrate how to look at and use letter forms.

Supporting Children as They Learn About Letters

Quite a bit of letter learning takes place during shared reading and shared/interactive writing, as you help children notice and use letters that are embedded in meaningful text. That is important learning, but young children also enjoy playing with the letters themselves.

Tactile Experiences with Letters

Magnetic and foam letters are wonderful tools for young children. Students can sort and match letters (see Figure 19.1 and Appendix I). They can find the first letter of their names and eventually make their names or other words. They can point to the letters and name them.

Children also enjoy simple, clear letter cards. In the photograph in Figure 19.2, children are matching magnetic letters with letters on cards.

Figure 19.2 Matching letter cards with magnetic letters

Letter Charts

It will help to display some clear, simple alphabet charts in several areas of the classroom. Some of the more elaborate alphabet charts show letters shaped like animals or people or even letters wearing hats, presumably to make letter learning easier and more fun. There is no research to support this practice, however, and these devices can make letter learning harder because the shape of the letter is often obscured. Good sets of simple, plastic, multicolored magnetic letters and some simple alphabet charts with clear, black letters (see Figure 19.3 and Appendix G) work best, because the images are clear and uncluttered.

Once you have introduced the alphabet chart and children start becoming familiar with it, it becomes a resource they can refer to when they are writing. You can also work with the chart in other ways. For example, have students:

* Read the chart letter by letter, saying the key words (*B, b, bear*).
* Read the pictures (*apple, bear, cat*).
* Find a letter or picture quickly.
* Read letters or pictures as you point to them randomly.

One enterprising four-year-old decided to make her own chart (see Figure 19.4). She either copied the words or got help from an adult but constructed some for herself. Notice that she is still flexible in the orientation of her writing. If she starts on the right margin, she writes from right to left.

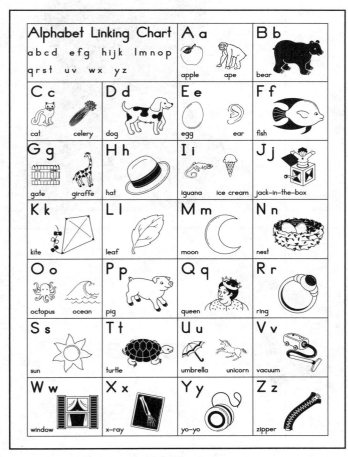

Figure 19.3 Alphabet Linking Chart

Figure 19.4 Alphabet Linking Chart by child

Alphabet Books

Alphabet books are useful and entertaining resources for young children and serve as powerful tools in letter learning. Some are appropriate for reading aloud. You can also provide a variety in the class library. The following examples are particularly appealing to young children, and more are included in the bibliography of children's books in Appendix E:

- *The Bouncing, Dancing, Galloping ABC* (Doyle, 2006) is full of action words and alliteration: "F is for flying as fast as I can" (6).

- *Bruno Munari's ABC* (Munari, 1960) is a classic presentation of simple, bold illustrations and labels.

- *The Zoo I Drew* (Doodler, 2009) presents wonderfully large zoo animals and rhyming text for every letter of the alphabet.

- *Creature ABC* (Zuckerman, 2009) is an engaging puzzle using simple and beautiful wildlife photographs. There are two pages for each letter; each letter is represented by one animal. On the first page for *Ee*, for example, you see the letter (upper- and lowercase) in big print and the foot of an elephant, which fills a whole page. Turn the page and you see the word *elephant* and the elephant's head (Figure 19.5).

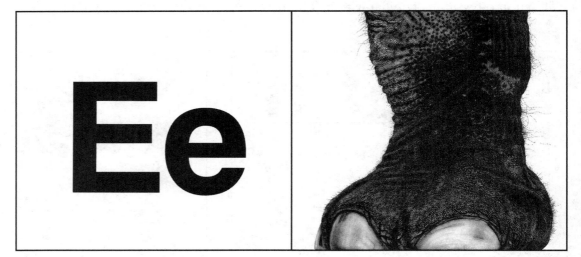

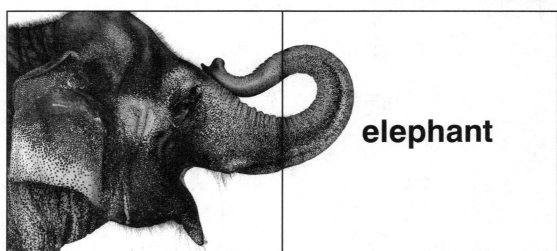

Figure 19.5 Pages from *Creature ABC*

- *A Child's Day: An Alphabet of Play* (Pearle, 2008) consists of examples of ways to play—one for every letter; for example, *Mm, mix; Nn, nap; Qq, quack; Rr, ride.* Each letter has a simple illustration of a child performing the act. (Figure 19.6)

- *An Alphabet Salad: Fruits and Vegetables from A to Z* (Schuette, 2003) is a simple nonfiction book based on fruits and vegetables: "O is for onion. Onions smell strong. Sometimes the smell makes a person's eyes water." Each page has a clear, uncluttered photograph of the fruit or vegetable. (Figure 19.7)

Children can look at these books, enjoying the pictures and reading the names of the letters they recognize. They can also:

- Point to and say letter names.

- Match letter forms in the book with plastic or foam letters.

- Make a class alphabet book. (See Appendix D, Lesson 8 for a lesson on alphabet bookmaking).

- Make individual alphabet books with just the letters they know.

Figure 19.6 Pages from *A Child's Day: An Alphabet of Play*

Figure 19.7 Pages from *An Alphabet Salad: Fruits and Vegetables from A to Z*

Letter Books

As children begin to recognize some letters and learn their names, place some letter books that focus on a single letter in the class library (see Figure 19.8). You will find reproducible letter books in *Guided Reading* (Fountas and Pinnell, 1996) as part of the *Leveled Literacy Intervention System* (Fountas and Pinnell, 2009) Lesson Resources CD, K, and in Phonics Lessons, K.

Figure 19.8 Individual letter books

In these books, a letter appears in clear print on the cover. On each page spread, the letter appears on the left page and there is a simple picture of something that begins with the sound of that letter on the right page. The word is written under the picture. Once they know the names of the pictures, children can "read" these books from cover to cover, turning pages. They are learning by:

- Saying a sequence of words that all have the same sound at the beginning.

- Increasing their awareness of beginning sounds and the letters that represent them.

- Seeing the letter and its visual features a number of times.

- Building a repertoire of examples of words that they can associate with a letter.

As children build up categories of words connected to a particular letter, they may begin to produce products like the collection of words starting with *C* shown in Figure 19.9.

Figure 19.9 Words that start with *C*

Supporting Children as They Learn About Words

Word learning, too, can happen naturally while children are expanding language through stories and learning letters. We do not recommend asking children to work on words in isolation before kindergarten (and very little time should be spent on it even then), because it is a meaningless task. Our goal by the *end* of kindergarten is for children to know between twenty-five and fifty words they can recognize quickly and easily.

Prekindergarteners will often begin to notice words in the environment—a stop sign or the name of a favorite restaurant, for example. Children are naturally curious about print in their environment and love to "read" it. Often, you will find that they do not recognize the word or letter out of the context in which they usually see it. This is typical in development; nevertheless, they are noticing print!

If young children are immersed in literacy and learn how to look at print, they will inevitably begin to take on some new words (see Ashley's list of all the words she can write, Chapter 15, Figure 15.4). They will want to learn their names as words as well as names of family members and friends. They will notice words that appear often in their reading or writing (such as *the, go, can, like*).

You may want to have a simple "word wall" in the classroom—a display of the alphabet with words that

begin with each of the letters (see the example in Figure 19.10). If you decide to use a word wall, don't overdo it. Put the children's names on the wall and then stick to a few words that are very easy and that children use often such as *I* or *the*. Take your cues from your students when deciding which (if any) words beyond their names to include. Some teachers like to create an additional word wall where examples of environmental print can be posted—words from cereal boxes, etc. that children bring into the classroom (Figure 19.11).

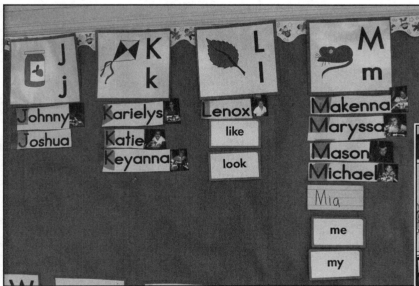

Figure 19.10 Simple word wall

Figure 19.11 Word wall with environmental print

Helping Children Notice Words

When you notice that a group of children in the class knows some high-frequency words, confirm their knowledge and extend it if appropriate. Here are some suggestions:

- Use language that makes it clear you are talking about a *word* (not a letter): "This word is [*word*]." (Some children confuse letters and words and may be focusing on only a *part* of the word.)

- Tell children to look at the beginning of the word, and show them what that means (first letter on the left).

- Read the word to children as you run your finger under the word left to right.

- Help them connect their knowledge of names to words—for example, *I, Iris; and, Andrew; car, Carl.*

Locating Words in Text

As they move closer to kindergarten entry, some children will begin to track print and most will do so by the middle of the kindergarten year when they need to be able to recognize specific words in text. The real challenge to the beginning reader is not memorizing a word in isolation but reading it within continuous text while keeping the meaning in mind. Practice in locating words helps develop this ability, because it

familiarizes children with the visual search needed to recognize the word by its features. Children can locate *known* or *unknown* words. Locating known words helps them recognize the words rapidly and without a great deal of effort while reading. Locating unknown words helps them think about and predict the beginning letter and remember other visual details about a word. Some routines for locating a word are:

1. Suggested language when the children know some beginning sounds: "Say *but*." (Children respond.) "What letter would you expect to see at the beginning of *but*?" (Children respond.) "Find it, run your finger under it, and say it."

2. Suggested language when children are recognizing high-frequency words: "You know the word *the*. Think how it looks." (Show a model on the whiteboard if you think they need it.) "Find *the* on this page and put your finger under it." (Children respond.) "Turn the page and find *the* on the next page and put your finger under it." (Notice how quickly children can locate the word.)

In the prekindergarten classroom, all or most word learning arises out of the natural need to tell stories and write messages. Meaningless drill on word cards will not be helpful to young children.

We have provided suggestions for a variety of word games and activities in Chapter 20 and Chapter 21.

Key Understandings to Think About

✳ Letter and word learning are essential in the process of becoming literate.

✳ Children need a wide variety of direct experiences that help them learn how to look at letters and connect them with the letter names and sounds.

✳ Children need to see letters in many different contexts.

✳ Letter and word learning take place during shared reading and writing.

✳ Children also need specific teaching to learn how to look at letters.

✳ Children will learn a great deal about words as they attempt to read and write.

✳ Children need to learn the *concepts* of *letter* and *word* and how they are different.

✳ Children benefit from some specific instruction on words and from practice in locating words within connected print.

Notes

Names:

A Powerful Resource for Literacy Learning

*"The most powerful and effective way for children
to begin learning the complex process of learning about letters
is by writing their own names."*

—CAROL LYONS

A child's name is a wonderfully engaging place to start learning about the features of print. Children's names are often their most beloved and important words, and names of family members are valuable and interesting to them as well.

Once children learn that their names are words and that they are made with the same letters in the same order each time (see Figure 20.1), they begin to understand the concept of *word*. They may also notice and start to recognize and write words like *yes*

and *no*. They may be motivated to recognize names of family members or words like *love* or *play*. We have known some three- and four-year-olds who recognize and write the name of a home sports team or draw sports figures!

Once children have learned their own names, they start to recognize some of their classmates' names and make connections between names. Three-year-olds may simply start to find "my letter" (the first letter of my name) or learn to write it as a letter

Figure 20.1 Jeremy's name spelled with magnetic letters

to label drawings. But most four-year-olds have learned to recognize their names and can start to use them as a resource. For example, they can:

- Find their own names on charts or in sentences or poems.
- "Read" the name chart.
- Find letters that are alike.
- Name the letters in their names.
- Talk about the *first* letter of their names.
- Talk about the *last* letter of their names.
- Count the letters in their names.
- Select magnetic letters to make their names (in sequence).
- Write their names.
- Notice one of "their" letters in another word.
- "Sign" their drawings and stories with their full names or some of the letters.

In addition to the lesson noted below, see Appendix D, Lesson 30 (Tissue Paper Names), Lesson 32 (Name Poems), Lesson 33 (Name Puzzles), and Lesson 34 (Making Names Using Tactile Materials).

Name Charts

Place several charts with children's names on the walls of the classroom. You can make these charts with the children, so they will immediately be familiar and meaningful (see Appendix D, Lesson 31 for a lesson on name charts). Start with something very simple—just children's first names (see Figure 20.2)—then create

variations such as a lunch chart, attendance chart (see Figure 20.3), or helper's chart (see Figure 20.4). Adding photographs to these charts helps children begin to recognize their classmates' names as well as their own.

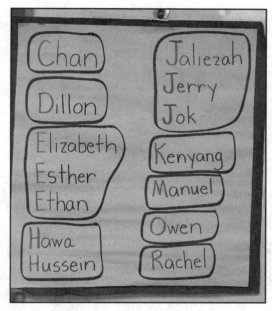

Figure 20.2 Simple name chart

Figure 20.3 Attendance chart

Figure 20.4 Helper's chart

Here is a bit of the conversation that took place as the children were writing about their experience together:

TEACHER: We have decided to write, "We got potatoes." Let's say that together. [Children say the sentence.]

TEACHER: So the first word we want to write is *we*. Say *we*. Someone in our class has a *W* at the beginning of his name. Let's look at our name chart.

CHILDREN: William.

WILLIAM: My name has a *W*.

TEACHER: William has a capital *W* at the beginning of his name. William, can you come to the chart and make a *W* to start our message?

The teacher directed the children to consult the name chart each time a word was added to the story. She did most of the writing but selected just a few places where she invited individual children to contribute a letter and sometimes a known word.

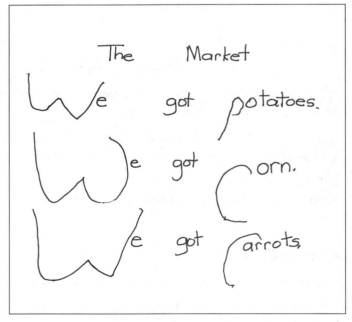

Figure 20.5 A trip to the market

Display the name chart in a prominent place when you are working with children on interactive writing. Any set of names will include models for most of the letters. Teach children how to make connections between the text they are composing and writing and the letters in their names. This helps them pay close visual attention to the features of print. In the example in Figure 20.5, the children and the teacher have written about their trip to the market using interactive writing.

Poems and Children's Names

Many poems lend themselves to inserting children's names (see Appendix D, Lesson 32 for a lesson on name poems). Children enjoy participating over and over again in shared reading of poems like those in Figures 20.6 and 20.7. Many more examples are included in *Sing a Song of Poetry, K* (Pinnell and Fountas, 2004). Revisiting the poems is a good opportunity for children to visually locate names embedded in continuous print. Poems like these can also be made into a simple book that children can illustrate and then read together (see Figure 20.8).

Yum, Yum, Yum

Travis likes pizza.

Yum, yum, yum.

Travis likes pizza.

In his tum.

Figure 20.6 "Yum, Yum, Yum"

Apples

One, two, three

Apples on a tree.

One for John.

One for Debra.

And one for me

Figure 20.7 "Apples"

Apples

One, two, three.

Apples on a tree.

One for Jamal.

One for Layla.

And one for me.

The End

Figure 20.8 "Apples"

Simple Sentences About Children's Lives

Using interactive writing or simple sentences that children dictate to you, make a chart or book about children in the class (see Figure 20.9). Include all the children by creating several short books rather than making one long book with twenty or thirty pages.

Sentences like these can also be displayed in a pocket chart or written on flip charts. You might write one sentence each day and reread all the sentences. After several days, cut the chart into strips so that children can draw a picture on them and take them home, or glue the strips into a book for the library corner.

Our Class

Shana likes to pet her dog.

Sara likes to kick the ball.

Jake likes to play with blocks.

Something Special

Sari has red shoes.

Karina has a ponytail.

George can run fast.

Figure 20.9 Sentences with children's names

Cut-Up Sentences with Children's Names

Once children have created and reread some simple sentences about their lives, you can use them for cut-up sentences (see Figure 20.10). Children will enjoy putting these sentences back together and reading them. Children can then play with the sentences at home or glue them on paper and draw a picture.

Name Puzzles

Name puzzles (see Figure 20.11) help children use their own name to learn about letters. By putting together their names, children learn how to look at letters. They notice the distinguishing features and orientation of letters. They learn that words are made up of letters and that the order of letters is always the same. (See Appendix D, Lesson 33 for a lesson on name puzzles.)

First, cut up a set of letter cards and use the letters to form your students' first names. Store the letters of each name in an envelope on which you have printed the child's name. Keep the envelope in a folder. Arrange children in a circle so they can place their envelopes on the floor in front of them and you'll be able to observe their work. Then tell them that they are going to put together their name puzzles.

- Suggested language: "I'm going to show you how to put together your name puzzles. Take out the letters that are in the envelope in your folder. Lay your envelope flat in front of you.

Figure 20.10
Cut-up
sentence

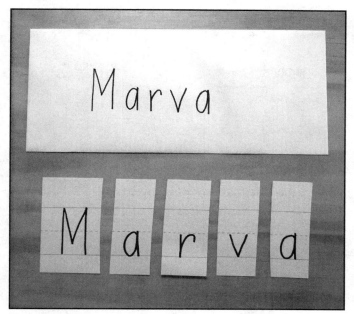

Figure 20.11 Name puzzle

Be sure you can see your name. Use the letter pieces to make your name. Put down the first letter first; then put down the next letter. Be sure the letters match exactly."

- Emphasize that each letter has to look the same as the letters written on the envelope.

- Using a chopstick or other small pointer, point under each letter, demonstrating how to check letter by letter and saying the letters as you go.

- Show how to mix up the letters so they can form the name again.

- Be sure all the children have formed their names at least once.

Repeat the lesson as needed. After children have learned to put together the puzzle for their first names, they can take their name puzzles home and play with them there. You may eventually want to add last names to the puzzles as children near kindergarten entry. At first, this task is a very simple matter of matching letter for letter. You could even try this with three-year-olds after they can recognize and locate their first names. It will be very productive for four-year-olds.

In addition, labeling children's cubbies and coat hooks with their names helps them begin to recognize their names. Some teachers also help children focus on the letters in their names during transitions. For example, you might say, "If your name begins with *M*, stand up and walk over to your spot in line." Using names makes beginning word and letter awareness active, personal, and fun. Through this work, children own an important bit of written language and are motivated to learn more.

Key Understandings to Think About

✳ The most important word to most young children is their first name.

✳ A child usually starts learning the concept of what a word is when he understands that his name is a word made up of letters that are always the same and in the same order.

✳ There are many ways you can use children's names to help them learn about print.

✳ Through conversation, you can connect children's names to the letters and words they see in print that they are reading or writing.

Notes

Using Group Games to Increase Language and Print Awareness

*"Games belong at the heart of childhood,
and they help us remember the child in each of us."*

—David Booth

All the areas of literacy learning mentioned in this book can be enhanced by playing some simple games. Children will enjoy them thoroughly and at the same time deepen and broaden their literacy! Circle games can take place with your whole class or in smaller groups, and the card and board games can be included in various centers. Some teachers set up special "game centers" in several areas of the classroom, each featuring a different game. Games may take place anytime during the prekindergarten day. You can play games during meeting time or use them as transitions. They can be used as "lessons" when you are teaching routines.

Circle Games

As soon as children have learned to sit in and walk around a circle, you can incorporate some literacy learning into your circle games. For example:

- Children sit with their names on cards in front of them. They take turns saying their names, telling one of the letters (first or last letter, for example), and finding another child whose name has the same letter in the same position.

- Each child holds a letter. One child walks around the circle until he finds a matching letter. Then everyone trades letters and another child is given a chance to find a letter that matches hers. As children learn more, they can match their letters with a picture, find a word that begins with that letter, or match upper- and lowercase letters.

- Place letters on the floor in a large circle. Have children walk around the circle. At a signal, they sit down by a letter. They take turns saying the name of the letter in front of them. Vary the game by having them say the key word from the Alphabet Linking Chart (Appendix G) instead of the name of the letter.

Card and Board Games

Children like to play simple card and board games. All of these games can be learned by four-year-olds as they progress towards kindergarten. Once they understand the initial directions, the games can be varied to focus on new skills. You can play the game with a few children at a time. During choice time or while children are having free play, you can sit down with a small group for a few minutes and get them started. A game can be placed in a specific area of the classroom once they know how to play it.

Letter Cards

Children can work with letter cards in many ways. For example:

- One or two players work with a group of letter cards that are turned facedown. Turning the cards over one at a time, they see how many they can name.

- Each child lays out four letter cards in front of him. The children take turns drawing a letter card from another pile. If they can match the letter on the card to one of their four letters, they get to keep it, placing it on top of the matched card. They continue until all the cards are placed. The winner is the one with the most cards. (The same game can be played with picture cards.)

Board Games

The key to using board games successfully is to be sure that children understand how to use them. Here's a process for teaching the rules of a simple game:

- Tell the children they are going to learn to play *[name of game]*.

- Select an extremely simple set of pictures or letter cards that everyone can recognize. (Limit the number of examples.) Make enough sets for half of the children.

- Choose a partner.

- Have children sit in a circle so that everyone can see you and your partner.

- Walk through the steps of the game with everyone watching. Talk about what you are doing—describe it in words—as you are doing it.

- Then have two children walk through the process—again with everyone watching. Talk about each move as they do it. Have everyone clap at the conclusion of the demonstration.

- Have children play the game with a partner. Walk around helping everyone.

- When the games are finished, have children applaud themselves and say the name of the game.

The two simple games below can be played with pictures, letters, or words. They may be more appropriate for four-year-olds, and children are likely to need some support especially when they are just learning how to play.

Follow the Path (see Figure 21.1). By drawing cards with dots or numerals on them (use only quantities or numerals the children know) or using a die (if they're familiar with this device), children move markers along a "path" of squares containing pictures, letters, or words. When a player lands on a square, she says the name of the picture, letter, or word in order to stay there. The player who reaches the end of the path first wins.

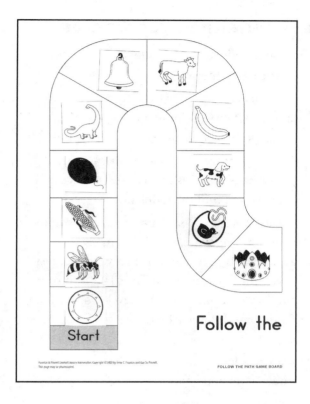

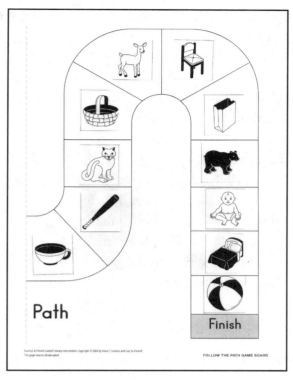

Figure 21.1
Follow the Path

Lotto (see Figure 21.2). Lotto is fun to play and involves visual discrimination. For prekindergarteners, use mainly pictures, though letter or word lotto may be appropriate late in the year for four-year-olds. Children have the opportunity to identify, match, and clearly say the names of familiar objects or animals. Additionally, they learn to take turns, listen, and observe. All of this will come in handy when they enter kindergarten.

The basic game board, which you can make out of card stock, has six squares, three across and two down. (You can also make a smaller board with four squares, two across and two down.) You need enough game boards for the number of children who will participate, typically between two and four players. Randomly write, draw, or paste pictures, letters, or words in the boxes of each game board, perhaps leaving one square blank. The players' boards should all be different from one another. You may want to color-code your boards and make sure each player has a different color.

Figure 21.2 Lotto

Make a set of picture, letter, or word cards that match the pictures, letters, or words shown in the squares on the game board. Also gather a supply of plastic chips or other markers. Place the picture, letter, or word cards and the plastic chips or other markers in the middle of the table. (Many versions of picture lotto can be purchased in colorful sets. You may want to reduce the complexity at first.)

Players take turns drawing a card and saying what it is. All players search their game boards for a corresponding picture, letter, or word. They place a marker in any spaces that correspond. The first player to cover his entire board with markers wins the game. (The game can continue, if desired, until everyone's card is filled.)

Games Using Technology

A wide variety of games using technology—available in handheld form, on special computers, and as computer software—are available. Exercise caution when buying and using them. Some can be played only by one person at a time, can be expensive, are breakable, go out of date quickly, and do not provide the tactile stimulation of magnetic letters, sandpaper letters, and handmade (or commercially printed) cardboard, plastic, and paper materials. But some technological games may be appropriate and engaging options for your play areas. If you can, test them yourself with some young children beforehand to be sure of their durability and to see how long children's interest is sustained.

Some Guidelines for Games

Games have great educational value. Here are some suggestions for using them:

- If you take the trouble to make a game, laminate it or find some other way to make it sturdy so that you can use it over the years.

- Create a storage system for games—labeled plastic bags or boxes that conserve space and allow you to find them quickly.

- Creating games on a computer allows you to print reproducibles, which has many advantages. Be sure to use a very simple, easy-to-see font of appropriate size. (Look at some good early reading books—level A or B in the Fountas and Pinnell Text Level Gradient™—for a model.)

- Stick to a few games that children really understand and enjoy.

- Observe children closely to determine the right length of time to play a game.

- Vary the *content* within the games to keep them from becoming boring.

- Keep directions very easy, using the simplest possible version of a game when you first teach children how to play.

Key Understandings to Think About

✳ Simple, enjoyable games can enhance literacy learning.

✳ The key to successful use of games is to be sure that children understand how to play them.

Notes

Assessment of Literacy Learning

This section presents some simple ways to assess the literacy understandings of young students both to inform current teaching and to pass on to the children's future teachers. We suggest carefully documented, focused observations of individual children as they work both alone and as part of a group. The section includes frameworks for observing children's growth as readers and writers and their letter, sound, and word knowledge.

Observing Reading Behaviors

"Teachers can become astute observers of reading and writing behaviors and skilled at producing responses which advance the child's learning."

—Marie Clay

For prekindergarteners, "reading behavior" means their interest in books that are read aloud and their ability to take on the language of books. For some prekindergarten children it may also mean engaging independently with print. In this chapter we discuss ways to guide your observations. As you work with young children, your best tools are your own eyes and ears. Sit beside a child and watch him working. Observation is the best way to assess their growth in understanding. Assessment (both formal and informal) is often ongoing and comes as a result of your observations of children as you interact with them. Talk with a child and listen to what he says. Let the child read and invite the child to talk more. Teaching interactions improve when you notice how a child is attending to information. This will inform and guide your reading and writing instruction and will help you to adjust or maintain just the right amount of support for the child's zone of proximal development (see Chapter 1).

Use the continuum in Section 7 as a guide for what to look for, remembering that it describes goals just prior to kindergarten entry. Your best evidence will be gathered while children are deeply engaged in literacy-related activities that they love. Value approximations!

Here, we describe some systematic ways to assess understanding as children move through the year prior to kindergarten entry. Each assessment below can be accomplished in about two weeks, systematically observing two or three children each day and taking notes. Each observation only takes a few minutes. Performing these observations three or four times a year gives you a good body of information that will help you plan your instruction and allow you to be very specific in your conferences with parents.

Interactive Read-Aloud

Observe the child during an interactive read-aloud, thinking about the questions in Figure 22.1, which pertain to the understandings you can expect if children have had many experiences with interactive read-alouds when they are three and four years old.

Observing a Child Participating in an Interactive Read-Aloud

(Enlarged Published Texts, Poems, or Texts from Shared/Interactive Writing)

Does the child:

1. Look at the book while you are reading?
2. Respond nonverbally to the meaning?
3. Join in when invited on repetitive parts of the book?
4. Make comments that are appropriate spontaneously or when invited during reading?
5. Make comments after reading that indicate an understanding of the book?
6. Retell the story after several readings by looking at the pictures?
7. Use some of the language of the book?
8. Draw pictures or attempt writing that represents the meaning of the book?

Figure 22.1 Observing a child participating in an interactive read-aloud

Shared Reading

Shared reading is a highly supported activity, but there is still much for a child to learn. Observe the student while keeping in mind the questions in Figure 22.2. Again, you would expect to observe these behaviors after children have had many shared reading experiences. Often the children have internalized the language even though they are not attending to the print. Also, for shared reading you will frequently use texts produced during interactive writing. These texts are excellent ways to hold their attention.

Observing a Child Participating in Shared Reading

(Enlarged Published Texts, Poems, or Texts from Shared/Interactive Writing)

Does the child:

1. Join in on the rereading with some accuracy?
2. Look at the print while reading (rather than just repeating)?
3. Stress words appropriately while reading?
4. Use appropriate intonation while reading?
5. Use some phrasing while reading?
6. Notice some visual signposts (for example, words that start with his name or known words)?
7. Locate a few words in the text (for example, words that start like names)?
8. Revisit the text when working independently and produce an accurate (or almost accurate) "reading"?
9. Move eyes left to right across the print?
10. Go back to the left margin to read the next line (return sweep)?
11. Match the spoken words with the written ones (point under each word while reading)?
12. Talk about the pictures in a meaningful way, noticing details?

Figure 22.2 Observing a child participating in shared reading

Independent Book Experiences

While a few prekindergarteners will begin reading simple texts, you would not expect this performance as a general rule. But you can learn a great deal about children's literacy understandings by observing their behavior as they handle books individually or with a partner (see Figure 22.3).

You can gather all the information you need simply by enjoying a book with a child, but you may want to ask some questions and make a few requests as you read to gather evidence of specific understandings. For example, you could say:

* Point to the title of the book.
* Point to [*any important part of the illustrations*].
* Show me your favorite part of the book. Why is that your favorite part?
* Show me the beginning of the story.
* Show me the end of the story. Tell me about the ending.
* Can you find a word that starts like your name?
* Can you find the word _____ ?
* Find a [*name of letter*].

Your careful observation is critical to your effective teaching of the young child. We have found that a simple sheet of boxes with children's names or index cards taped on a clipboard are handy tools for capturing information on each child.

Observing a Child Interacting with a Book Independently

Does the child:

1. Hold the book right side up and start with the cover?
2. Turn the pages right to left?
3. Look at the pages in order, left to right?
4. Talk about the pictures in a meaningful way, noticing details?
5. Retell the story, covering essential parts?
6. Use some book language appropriate to the book when retelling?
7. Demonstrate sustained attention by looking at the entire book?
8. Notice some visual features of words (such as a first letter or large-size print)?
9. Point to and say the title of the book?
10. Demonstrate ability to draw and talk about the book?

Figure 22.3 Observing a child interacting with a book independently

Key Understandings to Think About

❋ Observing the reading behaviors of three-, four-, and five-year-olds means gathering evidence on how they respond to texts, handle them, and notice aspects of literacy.

❋ You can gather evidence of literacy understandings by asking children to respond, either orally or in a drawing, to texts that are read aloud.

❋ You can gather evidence of literacy understandings by observing children's behaviors during shared reading.

❋ You can interact briefly with individual children in connection with a single text and gather information about their literacy understandings.

Notes

Observing
Writing Behaviors

*"The main assessment question that guides us is,
'What does this piece of writing show me the child
knows about writing?'"*

—KATIE WOOD RAY

This book includes many examples of young children's writing. These products are evidence of their growing ability. Keep a folder with each child's drawings and writings during the year to document change over time in their growth as writers. This folder is a wonderful resource to share with families during conferences, since they give you the opportunity to point out just how much knowledge these pieces of writing represent. (Some families may be under the impression that writing must be correctly spelled to be "good.") If you collect samples over time, you can demonstrate progress in the children's approximations.

Across ages three and four, children will be moving towards the goals listed in the Writing continuum for prekindergarten (Section 7). Entering three-year-olds will vary widely. Most will just be making random marks on paper or producing very simple drawings. But in the two-year span, you will see much evidence that they are learning what the world of literacy is all about. These observations will be helpful from about the middle of the four-year-old year to kindergarten entry.

Shared/Interactive Writing

Shared/interactive writing is a group activity—often involving the whole class—but you can still observe individuals for evidence of understanding (see Figure 23.1).

Observing a Child Participating in Shared/Interactive Writing

Does the child:

1. Show that she knows the routines of shared/interactive writing?
2. Engage actively in conversation to generate ideas for writing?
3. Contribute ideas for sentences?
4. Suggest understandable sentences?
5. Choose among alternative sentences?
6. Listen to the suggestions of others?
7. Look at the print while rereading the message as it is being constructed?
8. Remember the next word when constructing a message?
9. Say words slowly while thinking about the sounds?
10. Identify a sound and predict the first or last letter of a word when constructing it?
11. Use resources such as the name chart or alphabet linking chart to help in linking a sound to a letter?
12. Contribute legible letters or word parts in the construction of a text?
13. Talk about the illustrations that would be appropriate for a text?
14. Reread the text on her own?

Figure 23.1 Observing a child participating in shared/interactive writing

Independent Drawing and Writing

This book includes many examples of young children's drawings. As they begin to produce and talk about their drawings, it is a natural extension to make some marks on the page (and eventually real letters)—to "write." Over the years from three to five, children who have many experiences with drawing and writing can make amazing progress, and you will see the evidence suggested by the questions in Figure 23.2.

Observing a Child Drawing and Writing Independently

Does the child:

1. Appear eager to draw or write?
2. Talk about drawings or writing in understandable language?
3. Generate ideas that can be expressed in language before, during, and after drawing?
4. Experiment with all kinds of marks on the page to represent writing?
5. Use known letters (from his name, for example) to generate pretend messages or labels for drawings?
6. Demonstrate some knowledge of the connection between sounds and letters (the alphabetic principle)?
7. "Read" the story that has been written?
8. Add details to drawings?
9. Add some form of writing to drawings after talking about them?
10. Remember drawn/written products after writing and talking about them?

Figure 23.2 Observing a child drawing and writing independently

Bookmaking

Bookmaking is an example of independent drawing and writing that has enormous value in the young child's view of herself as a writer. Children who have had a great deal of experience hearing books read aloud, looking at books, and making books will demonstrate the understandings suggested by the questions in Figure 23.3 when they make their own books. These expectations describe accomplishments typically made by about the end of prekindergarten and are typical of children who have had a great deal of rich experiences writing books in their prekindergarten classrooms.

Assessment should not mean extra work or take time away from your interactions with children. As we discussed previously, we encourage you to make a habit of carrying a clipboard with the assessment questions you have selected, along with paper divided into boxes, one for each student. Make quick notes about your observations and interactions. Also examine children's writing and the books they make for evidence of learning, being sure to observe the process as well. It is especially important—and very rewarding—to watch young writers produce their early writing attempts. You will notice how they learn from the writers of books you read aloud. Samples of children's writing over time are a visible record of learning that you can share with families.

Assessment (both formal and informal) is often ongoing and is the way teachers will continually be thinking about children as they interact with them. The information gained from assessment will inform and guide what the teacher does in terms of interactions with the children around reading and writing. It allows the teacher to adjust and/or maintain just the right amount of support for the child's zone of proximal development (see Chapter 1).

Observing a Child Make a Book

1. Are the ideas in the book connected in some way?

2. How is the book organized? Is it related to the writer's purpose?

3. How does the writer (illustrator) represent meaning?

4. Is the writer (illustrator) intentional about what is being represented on the pages?

5. What evidence is there of the writer's awareness of the shapes of letters?

6. What evidence is there of the writer's awareness of the sounds in words and their relationship to letters?

7. What does the writer know about layout of print (directionality, spacing)?

8. What does the writer know about layout of illustrations in combination with print?

9. How does the book sound when the child "reads" it (language structure, intonation)?

10. What evidence is there that the child has noticed features of texts (title, page numbers, labels for pictures, for example)?

11. How long did the child remain attentive while working on the book?

12. What problem solving did the child do during the writing?

13. To what extent did the child take risks (attempting to spell words, paying attention to detail, telling a complex story, using new information)?

14. Is there evidence that the writer is aware of an audience (peers, teacher, families)?

15. What new understandings did the child develop in the process of making the book?

Figure 23.3 Observing a child make a book

Key Understandings to Think About

＊ You can gather evidence of children's literacy learning by observing children's behaviors during shared and interactive writing.

＊ You can gather evidence of children's literacy learning by observing and interacting with them as they draw and write.

＊ You can gather evidence of children's understanding of how texts work by observing and interacting with them as they make books.

＊ The products of children's writing can be saved as evidence of their growth in literacy learning over time.

Notes

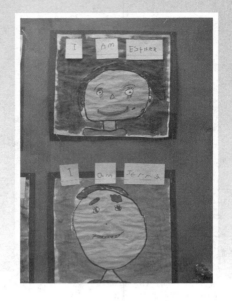

Observing for Evidence of Sound, Letter, and Word Knowledge

"Teachers have to observe closely, holding their own prior assumptions in limbo, and find out where individual children are before embarking on new learning."

—Marie Clay

We do not expect formal and complete knowledge of letters and sounds by the end of prekindergarten. That would be holding these young children to age-inappropriate standards. However, assessing your prekindergarteners' sound, letter, and word knowledge tells you a great deal about their growing literacy and the range of differences in individual children. Some questions you might ask are presented in the lists that follow. For three-year-olds, you will probably want to simply look for evidence of growing awareness as they participate in the activities of the classroom. As four-

year-olds show signs that they are aware of sounds, and can recognize some letters and words, gather more formal assessment data using questions like those presented in this chapter.

Assessing Awareness of Sounds

An important early literacy skill is the ability to hear the individual sounds in words, and a few quick, easy observations (see Figure 24.1) will help you determine

---

Evidence of Sound Awareness

Can the child:

1. Say words slowly?
2. Say any phoneme in the word separately?
3. Identify the first sound of the word (by saying the phoneme or the name of the letter)?
4. Identify the last sound of the word (by saying the phoneme or the name of the letter)?
5. Separate the first sound of the word from the rest of the word (d-og)?
6. Say a sound in response to a letter?

Figure 24.1 Evidence of sound awareness

Evidence of Letter Learning

Can the child:

1. Connect (sort) letters by any visual feature (tails, dots, circles, tall sticks, short sticks, tunnels)?
2. Match letters that are the same?
3. Locate a letter within a group when given an example (a letter card or magnetic letter)?
4. Find the letters in his name?
5. Name the letters on the alphabet linking chart?
6. "Read" the alphabet linking chart?
7. Quickly locate a letter when it is named?

Figure 24.2 Evidence of letter learning

---

how well a child is able to do this. The first task children must master is becoming aware of the individual sounds in a word by saying it slowly—no small feat for a prekindergartener!

Assessing Awareness of Letters

Children must learn how to look at print or how to identify the distinctive features of letters before they can attach a name to the letter or connect it with a sound. The questions in Figure 24.2 will help you observe their understanding of the visual features of print.

Assessing Awareness of Words

Understanding that a word in print is a cluster of letters with white space on either side that can be connected to something meaningful that you say is an enormous accomplishment for prekindergarteners, but they can do so on the basis of very few examples. The idea that a name is a word is an important early concept. Most prekindergarteners will not be able to

read words, but they may exhibit some of the basic understandings suggested in Figure 24.3. You may want to check which of the following understandings your four- and five-year-olds have as they enter kindergarten. Do not be concerned if they cannot do everything on this list. Any strength observed is important for the kindergarten teacher to know.

Evidence of Word Understanding

Can the child:

1. Recognize her name in isolation or on a list?
2. Recognize her name when embedded in print?
3. Make connections between her name and other words?
4. Identify the first word in a line of print?
5. Recognize a high-frequency word (I, a)?
6. Recognize some words that appear frequently in the environment (STOP, UP, etc.)?
7. Demonstrate that she knows the difference between a letter and a word?

Figure 24.3 Evidence of word understanding

Occasionally, you may want to ask questions modeled on those in the preceding lists to check on a particular understanding. You can do this when children are writing, during shared reading, and when you are revisiting any familiar text.

As children get ready to enter kindergarten, you may want to consider giving a few systematic assessments of alphabet and phonics understandings. You can easily find such assessments. Here are three sources:

Clay, M. M. 2006. *An Observation Survey of Early Literacy Achievement*. Portsmouth, NH: Heinemann.

Fountas, I. C., and G. S. Pinnell, 2007. *Benchmark Assessment System 1: Grades K–2, Levels A–N*. Portsmouth, NH: Heinemann. [Optional assessments for alphabet knowledge and phonemic awareness.]

Pinnell, G. S., and I. C. Fountas. 2002. *Phonics Lessons with CD-ROM, Grade K: Letters, Words, and How They Work*. Portsmouth, NH: Heinemann.

In Chapter 25, we also provide four simple systematic assessments you might use to gather specific information.

Key Understandings to Think About

✳ You can assess children's awareness of sounds with a few quick
game-like tasks.

✳ You can observe for evidence of sound awareness while you work with children in writing.

✳ You can ask children questions to assess their knowledge of texts they are revisiting.

Notes

Systematic Assessment:
An End-of-Prekindergarten Checkup

The best way to prepare prekindergarteners for the learning they will encounter in kindergarten is to infuse their days with joyful language and literacy opportunities, as we've described throughout this book. Kindergarten teachers won't be expecting their new students to be reading or writing conventionally! Children who have spent a year or two being read aloud to, participating in shared reading and shared or interactive writing, and having the literacy-rich experiences we have described have been developing the language and literacy skills that will serve them not only as kindergarteners but throughout their literate lives. If children have had satisfying, exciting experiences with literacy as prekindergarteners, they will enter kindergarten joyfully and confidently. If you have provided experiences and support that lead your students' literacy learning forward, they will be poised to continue developing as kindergarteners—and they will continue to be engaged, curious learners.

You may want to use a few simple systematic assessments to help mark your students' growth and to provide their kindergarten teachers with some specific information. Even if children know just a few letters, that's wonderful! It means that they know *how to recognize letters*. The quantity is not as important as the process they are using for letter recognition. The kindergarten teacher will expand on this process, so that all letters are known by year-end. The same is true of hearing sounds in words.

Here are just a few quick optional assessments that can be used to evaluate the learning that has taken place in prekindergarten. We provide four formal assessments that you might use with particular students:

1. Letter Recognition
2. Phonological Awareness
3. Concepts About Print Interview
4. Word Writing

In addition we suggest collecting the child's drawing and writing samples as rich documentation of learning.

We are suggesting that these four assessments only be used at the *end* of prekindergarten; they represent knowledge typically built in the first months of kindergarten. Any strengths or partial understandings noted give the teacher a place to start. Of course, as you observe your students' growth throughout their prekindergarten years, notice not only how they take on language and literacy, but how they develop socially, physically, and emotionally as well. We've summarized other aspects of prekindergarteners' growth and development in Appendix F, the Preschool Developmental Information Chart.

These four assessments will give you a good idea of the print knowledge of children who are about to enter kindergarten. The goals will seem quite far away for the entering three-year-old, and it is extraordinary to see how much progress can be made in just two years of prekindergarten. The concepts about print interview is perhaps the most important because it tells you how much children know about how print works. Children's writing samples are also an excellent assessment of their growing attention to concepts of print, phonological awareness and letter-sound relationships, as well as letter formation and word writing.

Letter Recognition

Children develop a complex variety of knowledge about letters. You may want to use a letter recognition sheet such as that in Figures 25.1a and 25.1b (also available in Appendix L) to determine the child's knowledge of letter names.

To administer the assessment, point to each letter and ask the child, "What's this?" If you get continuous nonresponse, stop the assessment or ask, "Do you see any you know?" Begin with uppercase letters. Notice and count the number of uppercase or lowercase letters known, as well as confusions or substitutions.

Figure 25.1a Uppercase Letter Recognition Sheet

Figure 25.1b Lowercase Letter Recognition Sheet

Phonological Awareness

The young child's sensitivity to the sounds in language will be an important factor in reading development. The first goal is to help the children say words slowly enough to be able to notice the sounds they hear. Then they can attach the sound to a symbol when they engage with print. By the end of prekindergarten, you may want to document the child's ability to hear the first sound in a word and their ability to hear rhymes.

Initial Sounds

Begin the assessment by giving the child four picture cards and telling the names of the pictures. Have the child say the picture name and find another picture that starts the same (e.g., *bear/bird*). (See Figure 25.2a and Figure 25.2b.) We have provided the two sets of cards in Appendix M. Select a few pairs of pictures to use.

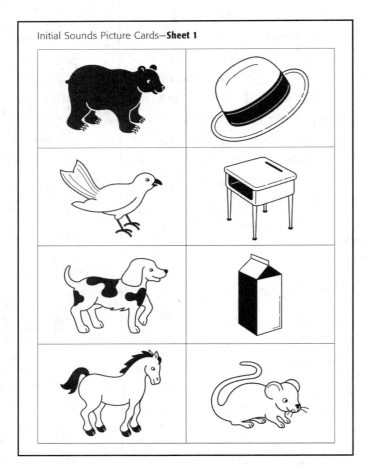

Figure 25.2a Initial Sounds Picture Cards, Sheet 1

Figure 25.2b Initial Sounds Picture Cards, Sheet 2

Rhyming Words

The child's ability to hear the rhymes in words is also important to reading. This sensitivity to ending word parts is developed in the shared reading of songs and poems as well as in oral games.

To begin, show two pictures that rhyme, say the words, and tell the children they sound the same at the end (e.g., *bee/tree*). After reviewing the names of the pictures, have the children find two pictures that rhyme. (See Figure 25.3a and Figure 25.3b.) We have provided two sheets of rhyming pictures cards for your use in Appendix N. Select a few pairs of pictures to use from the set.

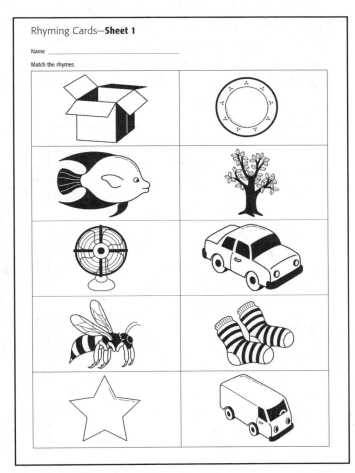

Figure 25.3a Rhyming Cards, Sheet 1

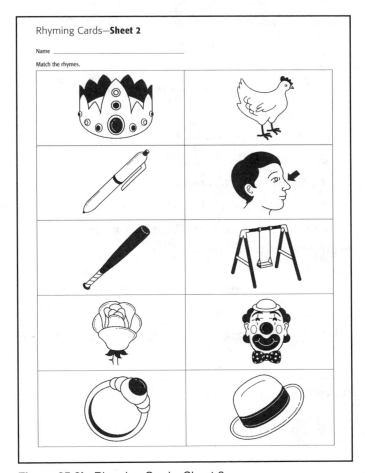

Figure 25.3b Rhyming Cards, Sheet 2

Concepts About Print Interview

The third optional assessment we are providing is designed to help you notice the understandings about print the young child has developed. Write the following sentence (see Figure 25.4) on a strip of paper and include the particular child's name. Be sure to leave a good amount of space between the words. Hold the sentence in front of the child and read it once as you point under each word. Read it a second time. Use the following questions to gather information:

1. Show me your name.
2. Show me the first letter in your name.
3. Show me the last letter in your name.
4. Show me *I*.
5. Show me the letter *s*.
6. Show me the word *can*.
7. Where do I start reading?
8. What is this? (Point to a period.)

This will give you good information on the child's beginning attention to print.

> (child's name) **and I can see the sun.**

Figure 25.4 Sentence strip

Word Writing

The final optional assessment we suggest is word writing. It may be useful if you have particular students who are producing letter-like forms. Begin by having the child write his name. Then ask the child to write any words he knows. You may want to prompt the child to write any other names he knows or suggest some simple familiar words like *cat, mom, doll, cup,* or *feet*. Notice the child's approximations and categories of words that are meaningful to him. As he writes you might ask, "What did you write there?"

Notice that Elliott has written the names of his parents (Mom, Dad) and grandparents (Oma, Papa)

Figure 25.5a Elliott's word writing sample

(Figure 25.5a), as well as family members (Nana, Bea, Ips) and started writing his sister's name, Mallory, and the labels for zoo (on his toy), and Wii that he has noticed in his home (Figure 25.5b). When his mom doesn't want the dog to hear the word *walk*, she spells it: W-A-L-K. Since he watches football games with his family, he often hears the fans say O-H-I-O (Figure 25.5b). Finally, he writes *R* for his last name, *BB* for his pacifier, and the word *cat*. Then he writes the letters of the alphabet in order (Figure 25.5c).

In just one word writing sample, think about the rich information about letters, sounds, words, and left to right, top to bottom direction he has controlled by the end of preschool.

Figure 25.5c Elliott's word writing sample

Writing Samples

In addition to these short formal assessments, collect and date each child's drawing and writing attempts to document the child's increasing knowledge about letters, sounds, images, and how print works. A child's writing samples reveal the best evidence of what aspects of print he is attending to and show writing development over time.

Figure 25.5b Elliott's word writing sample

Key Understandings to Think About

✳ Observational assessment is the most useful in documenting growth in the prekindergarten child.

✳ A few simple systematic assessments used with particular students at the end of prekindergarten can provide useful information.

✳ Writing and drawing samples document the child's attention to print.

✳ A few systematic assessments that you conduct at the end of prekindergarten with particular children who seem to be noticing print may provide the children's kindergarten teacher with helpful information.

✳ When using this kind of systematic assessment with four-year-olds, it is important to note their strengths as well as their needs.

Notes

The following photos show examples of literacy-rich PreK classroom areas. They illustrate some of the ways that teachers have integrated play-based activities with literacy learning. While the physical space of individual classrooms may differ, the prekindergarten classroom should always be well-organized, warm, colorful, inviting, and engaging to children, and be full of books and print.

Whole Classroom

There is an abundance of print on display throughout the classroom—on charts, labels, books, posters, bulletin boards, and children's artwork. Notice the way tables and shelves have been placed to make cozy areas for meeting, reading, writing, and other activities. There are no high barriers; the teacher can see across the entire room, but areas are defined, each with its purpose.

The reading area has shelves with books attractively displayed, along with several places where children can look at the books they select.

Whole Classroom

All furniture is child-size, comfortable, and brightly colored. This rug provides a comfortable place for children to sit and has identifiable animals they can place themselves on to gather in a group. Print is displayed on charts throughout the room.

Some areas are theme-based and may include props, books, and activities related to a single inquiry. Notice the simple homemade fire engine complete with hose. The blocks are organized, ready to use with other props.

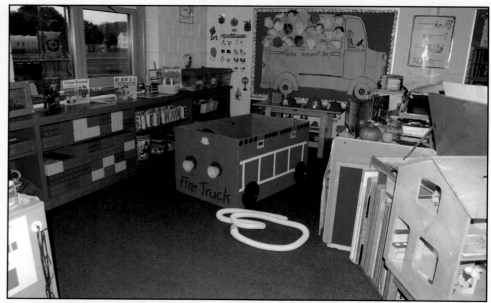

Children's art work and writing are on display throughout the classroom. Notice the cozy corner table for two with a book displayed. Here children can look at books or draw and write.

Meeting Area

The meeting area always includes a comfortable rug for sitting on during circle time and an easel for shared reading. It may also include teaching aids such as name charts, a calendar, and job and weather charts.

In the meeting area, children's names are clearly printed on a chart at eye level. Other print is displayed on charts, and a pocket chart is handy.

Library

A wide assortment of colorful, appealing picture books are arranged on labeled shelves or in baskets with book covers facing out. Labels include both pictures and words. The books in these bins are organized by topic (for example **Animals**) which is signaled by print and also by a picture.

Library

The reading area is a comfortable, quiet place with good lighting. In this reading area books are displayed face out, which lets young children quickly find their favorites or discover interesting new books.

This reading area has a variety of books shown facing out. There are also pillows, bean bag chairs, and child-size chairs on the carpet.

Listening Area

A part of the library, this listening area also has books, a small table and chairs, a CD (or tape) player, and headphones.

Play Corner

This play corner has the usual home props for dramatic play. It can represent many environments besides the home–for example, a restaurant or store. The menu on the wall adds meaningful print, and related books are also displayed.

A variety of theme-based props and writing fill the play corner. Some materials are permanent, others rotate throughout the year according to changing themes.

The materials and props in this play corner encourage imaginative play.

Art

Materials are stored in labeled bins below the easels so that children can access them easily.

Writing

As with art, a variety of materials are provided for writing, including pens, pencils, markers, different papers, blank books, and stamps.

The writing center is labeled. Each kind of material is placed in its own bin (there are some multiple bins that children can take to individual tables). Each bin is labeled and its place on the shelf is similarly labeled. Children can easily take out materials such as crayons and put them back in the right place.

Blocks

Various types and sizes of blocks encourage building as well as exploring different shapes and materials. Notice the construction-related children's books that encourage building.

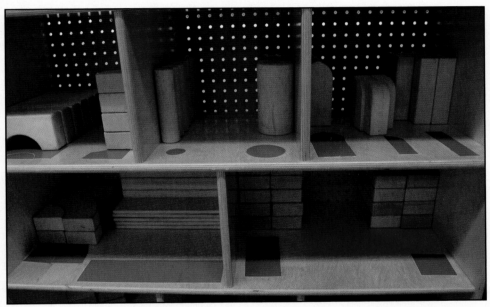

These blocks are neatly organized on shelves with labels and precise shapes to show children where each kind of block goes. Taking them out and putting them away helps children become aware of shapes.

Toys such as signs, vehicles, and dollhouses may be included in the block area to encourage imagination.

Puzzles and Games

A core group of simple puzzles, magnetic letters, pattern blocks, and Unifix cubes can be supplemented with other games and manipulatives throughout the year.

Sand/Water Table

Children explore the concepts of volume and capacity as they play with cups and containers of various shapes and sizes, as well as small plastic toys and other objects.

Music

The music center is labeled with print and pictures. Simple instruments are available.

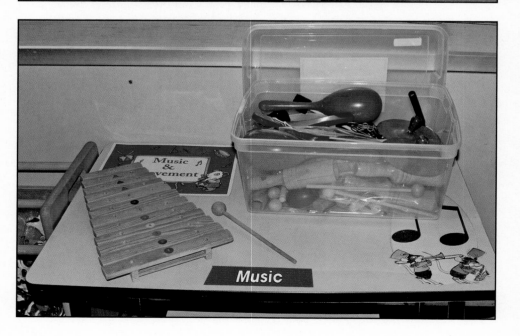

Music

Some instruments can be child–made. Notice the labeling on this crate of percussion instruments. Experimentation in music helps children develop a sense of rhythm and melody.

Science, Math, Social Studies

Simple science equipment and a range of natural objects and nonfiction books support inquiry and exploration.

Science, Math, Social Studies

Labeled bins of manipulatives enhance the math area and can be easily pulled out for exploration.

Inquiry is supported by interesting things to explore. Here a hermit crab is finding a new shell. The crab is there to see, along with engaging print and a book.

Theme-based science and social studies projects might include an exploration of natural objects, foods, and related books. Some might be related to a theme such as fall.

Science, Math, Social Studies

Some objects are related to inquiry projects that continue for a specific time. Other objects might stay in the center all year.

Children love objects to look at, touch, and smell. This table provides ample opportunity to look at the textures of nature. Books are included too.

Growing plants is an inquiry project that helps children learn to observe change over time. Inquiry projects lend themselves to interactive writing.

Science, Math, Social Studies

Simple manipulatives help children explore mathematical concepts.

Computer

One or more simple computers are available for children to use under adult guidance.

OWEN

Owen used circles to create his picture of himself, which is accompanied by letterlike forms to represent "writing." He is familiar with the O at the beginning of his name but also knows that some writing has sticks.

JOCK

Jock told his story **"I ate soup"** through his picture of himself and a big bowl of soup. Notice the detail in the pupils of his eyes and the steam rising from the soup!

ELIZABETH 1

In all of the drawings included here, Elizabeth told a story through a picture. She told the story of her new dress through her picture of herself all dressed up. Notice the use of color and the big smile. She said, **"I pick out my dress at the store."**

ELIZABETH 2

Talking about this picture, Elizabeth said **"I eat cake at a birthday party."** She told the story with a picture of the colorful cake. Notice the five candles!

ELIZABETH 3

Elizabeth told the story of this picture by saying **"I wear my dress at the party."** She may have represented the five candles again.

ELIZABETH 4

Elizabeth described this picture as **"My sister and I put on makeup."** She has learned that your picture has to match your story. Here you see two girls, Elizabeth and her sister.

ELIZABETH 5

This picture has a lot of action. Notice the detail of hair, mouth, eyes, feet, and clothing of the larger figure. You will understand the head peeping behind from Elizabeth's description: **"My sister gave me a piggyback ride."**

ANNA

Anna drew a picture of a tree and then provided her own description in writing below. Notice that she used real letters in two rows. Her writing has no phonetic relationship to words, but she has learned how writing looks.

M

ESTHER

1

Esther wrote her own name on the paper and then wrote the names of her parents, Eddy and Adalos. She drew her mom and dad below the writing.

ESTHER

2

Esther drew two more friends and wrote their names.

IRIS

Iris wrote her name and drew a picture of herself and her friend with a taller figure who might be one of their mothers. She wrote: **"I am having a play date with Clara."** Iris wrote left to right using all capital letters. Notice how many of the sounds in words she was able to represent with a letter. She wrote the single-letter words **I** and **a**. At this point, she was not using spaces to separate words.

Jesse produced a colorful book about African animals that showed how much he had learned about the characteristics of each, including body shapes and markings. All of the drawings are recognizable once you know the category. Jesse has obviously looked at and heard read books about these animals. He knows that all of them belong in the same category and are appropriate for a book with this title. His book has design and clear organization. He placed one animal on each page with a one-word label; this layout imitates nonfiction books. Jesse wrote in capital letters; most spellings are attempts that show he can represent almost all of the sounds with letters. **Lion** and **gorilla** are spelled accurately, and Jesse has also noticed that some words have double letters, or he may have heard two **l**'s in **elephant** and two **r**'s in **giraffe** as he said the words slowly and broke them into syllables. He was starting to use some lowercase letters.

JESSE

1

African Animals

JESSE

2

Zebra

JESSE

3

Lion

Jesse made a seven-page book about a gerbil who lived in the desert. He stuck to the topic and provided some interesting information. The composition of his book was meaningful and logical. Notice that he could spell some high-frequency words with accuracy (**the**, **is**, **hot**, **had**, **a**, **some**, **do**, **end**). For other words, he could produce a representation with consonants and vowels closely related to the sounds. In fact, he represented almost all of the sounds in each word. His illustrations closely matched the words and also show his knowledge that the desert features sun and cacti. One page of the story is entirely print. Jesse was still using all capital letters and left little space between words, but he has learned that print goes left to right in lines across a page. His story has a title page and an ending page, indicating that he has learned how a book is organized as well as some print features.

JESSE **4**

The gerbil lives in the desert.

HE GRBUL
ILVS IN
+EDASRT

JESSE **5**

The gerbil had a family.

THEGRBUL
HAD A FAML

JESSE **6**

The gerbils don't hibernate. Some desert animals do.

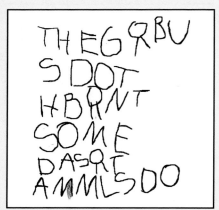

THEGRBU
S DOT
HBRNT
SOME
DASRT
AMMLSDO

JESSE **7**

The End

THE
END

MARISOL **1**

FALL
ThELEVZ FALL FROM
The TREZ WEGET
EOLUMPINThE
LEVSTE END

Marisol wrote and illustrated two stories—one about fall and one about playing dress-up. Notice how she tied the art together with the "bubble." This story says: **"The leaves fall from the trees. We get to jump in the leaves. The end."** These two logically related sentences are fully formed. Each has a prepositional phrase. Marisol accurately spelled twelve of the sixteen words on the page, indicating her knowledge of high-frequency words. She used a mixture of capital and lowercase letters, and we can also see that she is beginning to use spaces between her words.

MARISOL **2**

I PLAY DRES UP
MY DRESIZASPINC
AS SUNSEI I AM
A MIITRI HAV A BABE
THE CART

In this story, Marisol wrote about playing dress-up. The four sentences are well constructed and follow each other in a meaningful way: **"I play dress up. My dress is as pink as sunset. I am a mother. I have a baby [in] the cart."** Marisol already can compose stories that use simile (pink as sunset)! She used all capital letters but placed spaces between most words. Her picture reflected her precise meaning.

The Continuum of Literacy Learning, PreK

This section codifies six components of prekindergarten literacy instruction and describes how to use this information in the classroom. The continuum is part of a larger comprehensive document, *The Continuum of Literacy Learning, PreK–8: A Guide to Teaching* (Pinnell and Fountas 2011, 2008), which helps teachers establish a common vision for literacy achievement throughout elementary and middle school while adjusting expectations to fit their own environments.

Using the Prekindergarten Continuum to Plan for and Assess Teaching

This book describes life and learning in prekindergarten classrooms from the time children enter at about age three until they move on to kindergarten at age four or five. The prekindergarten continuum is a concise guide for selecting texts and learning goals for interactive read-aloud; shared and performance reading; writing about reading; writing; oral, visual, and technological communication; and phonics, spelling, and word study.

Purposes of the PreK Continuum

Some questions seem to come up all the time when teaching prekindergarteners:

- What do I look for when I choose books to read aloud?

- What kinds of responses can I expect from children when I read aloud? What should I teach them how to do?

- What kinds of books are appropriate for shared reading?

- To what degree can I expect children to attend to print in shared reading?

- To what extent should I expect independent reading of texts that have been used for shared reading?

- What can I expect children to be able to do as they handle books independently?

- What kinds of books should I have in the classroom library?

- How much writing can I expect children to be able to do?

- Should I expect children to write letters with standard formation?

- How many letters should they be able to name?

- Should they know a few words?

- How much should they know about letters and sounds?

- Should they be able to tell stories about their drawings?

- How elaborate should their stories and drawings be?

This continuum can help you address these questions.

At one time, we had almost no expectations for literacy learning prior to kindergarten. Children were thought to enter as "blank slates," ready to learn a lot but not knowing much. But times have changed because children's worlds have changed. These days, many children enter prekindergarten able to manipulate a computer or an electronic pad and understand a tremendous amount about literacy from observing the world around them.

We are not advocating the direct teaching of independent reading or writing in prekindergarten, but we do want to intentionally help children learn a great deal about the *nature* of reading and writing. Also, we are opposed to drilling children on isolated sounds and letters. All of the literacy activities described in this book are designed to present playful and joyful experiences and opportunities to nurture young readers and writers. The continuum is designed to help you pin down the specifics of your expectations for language and literacy learning in prekindergarten.

Using the PreK Continuum with Three-Year-Olds

As you look at the continuum, remember that you are looking at goals that children will be *moving toward* over a two-year period. Three-year-olds will vary widely on entry and will show paths of learning that are very much individual in nature. The continuum should be used to help you recognize progress—even in small steps, toward those goals. You will not expect three-year-olds to meet the goals, although some will surprise you with how rapidly they are learning. Having these goals in mind, however, will help you make the most of the rich literacy and play experiences you are providing.

Using the PreK Continuum with Four-Year-Olds

As children move toward the end of their fourth year, you will see evidence of a great many understandings. You can build on the strengths that emerge and help children expand knowledge of written language. Remember that *it is not necessary for a child to exhibit evidence of achieving every goal.* We are talking about a complex constellation of understandings that grow over time.

Organization of the PreK Continuum

The continuum for prekindergarten comprises six areas: Interactive Read-Aloud; Shared and Performance Reading; Writing About Reading; Writing; Oral, Visual, and Technological Communication; and Phonics, Spelling, and Word Study. We do not advocate formal guided reading lessons for prekindergarten children.

Interactive Read-Aloud and Shared and Performance Reading

The text-based reading areas (Interactive Read-Aloud and Shared and Performance Reading) include descriptions of texts appropriate for prekindergarteners, as well as the kind of evidence to look for (selecting goals)—thinking within, beyond, and about texts.

You will want to adjust your thinking to simpler levels for three-year-olds and for entering four-year-olds and build gradually. When selecting texts to read aloud and discuss, analyses of the following characteristics are applied: genres or forms, text structure, content, themes and ideas, language and literary features, sentence complexity, vocabulary, words (in shared and performance reading), illustrations, and book and print features.

Writing About Reading and Writing

The writing areas (Writing About Reading, and Writing) specify genres appropriate for prekindergarteners. Genres and forms for Writing About Reading are demonstrated through very simple interactive or shared writing and independent drawing and writing, including functional writing, narrative writing, and informational writing. Because Writing about Reading reveals so much about children's thinking, the goals include descriptions of evidence of thinking within, beyond, and about texts.

Most writing for preschool children is generated through very simple shared or interactive writing, or independent drawing and writing. Genres and forms for Writing include narrative, informational, poetic, and functional. The Writing category specifies expectations for craft, conventions, and writing process by the end of the second year of prekindergarten.

Oral, Visual, and Technological Communication

Even prekindergarteners are highly aware of technology. Children's use of websites and the games they play on technological devices must be supervised closely. The Oral, Visual, and Technological Communication area does not describe particular texts, because Internet texts vary and websites must be read in very different ways. The selected goals for this area include: listening and speaking, presentation, and technology.

Phonics, Spelling, and Word Study

The Phonics, Spelling, and Word Study area categorizes beginning awareness of the building blocks of language. Children may not be decoding words using letters and sounds or word parts, but they do have some basic understandings of words and the functions of letters. The expectations in the continuum reflect those understandings. The selected goals for this area include: early literacy concepts, phonological awareness, letter knowledge, letter-sound relationships, word meaning, spelling patterns, high-frequency words, word structure, and word-solving actions.

A Note About Guided Reading

We do not recommend formal guided reading instruction in prekindergarten; small-group reading instruction is not needed for this age group. However, if you sit down on the rug or at a table with a few children who have made the breakthrough to independent reading of simple texts, be sure to talk with them about the meaning of what they have read. We cannot overemphasize the importance of attention to comprehension from the very beginning of reading.

Using the PreK Continuum

Use the continuum to guide your teaching and reflect on children's learning within the contexts described. Scan the expectations to help you think of language to use or teaching points to make. Remember these are end goals, but they will not be reached without *work toward them* over the two-year period. We also suggest you use the continuum as the basis for brown-bag lunches or after-school sessions with your colleagues to discuss the range of opportunities for teaching and learning. Take one area at a time and talk about:

- What do we want our students to learn?
- What behaviors or evidence might we find of the kinds of learning we are looking for?

- How can we support literacy learning in a playful and joyful way?

There are many ways you can teach intentionally while engaging the interests of young children. For them, learning is an enjoyable, satisfying activity. It's more fun, of course, if it happens in an interesting way.

You can also use the continuum to help you prepare for conferences with children's families. Mine it for some ideas and language that you can introduce during your conversations. Showing concrete examples that demonstrate children's progress is a wonderful way to clarify for parents what their children are working on in school. (However, showing the continuum to parents is not a good idea; the information is too specialized and condensed. They may feel their children have to learn it all at once.)

Finally, give your children's kindergarten teachers a very specific description of what each child knows and is able to do with language and print. This is incredibly helpful and can make a huge difference in the level of informed support each child receives.

Key Understandings to Think About

* The purpose of the PreK Continuum is to guide teaching and reflect on behavioral evidence of learning.

* The PreK Continuum provides specific descriptions of the kinds of texts that are appropriate for each area of instruction.

* There are detailed lists of the behaviors and understandings that are appropriate instructional goals for kindergarteners as well as preschoolers.

* Another use for the PreK Continuum is as a base for conversations with colleagues to achieve a common vision for children's learning.

Notes

Interactive Read-Aloud and Literature Discussion

☐ **Selecting Texts:** *Characteristics of Texts for Reading Aloud and Discussion*

Genres/Forms

Genres

- Short poems, nursery rhymes, and songs
- Language and word play
- Traditional folktales
- Simple animal fantasy
- Realistic fiction
- Memoir
- Factual texts (simple and straightforward ABC books, label books, concept books, counting books, very simple informational books)

Forms

- Oral stories
- Picture books
- Wordless picture books
- Informational picture books
- Board books
- Books with texture, padding, pop-ups, pull-outs, sounds, or unusual features that promote interaction

Text Structure

- Informational texts that present a clear and simple sequence—one idea on each page spread
- Informational texts with simple description—one concept on each page spread
- Informational texts and stories with repeating patterns
- Many traditional tales with particular structures (cumulative tales, circular stories, and the use of "threes")
- Stories with simple narrative structure—beginning, series of episodes, and an ending
- Many books with repetition of episodes and refrains
- Texts with rhyme and rhythm

Content

- Language and word play (rhymes, nonsense, alliteration, and alphabet)
- Everyday actions familiar to young children (playing, making things, eating, getting dressed, bathing, cooking, shopping)
- Familiar topics (home, toys, pets, animals, food, playground, park, friends and family)
- A few topics related to the neighborhood or surrounding area (farm, zoo, park, woods, traffic, etc.)
- Themes and content that reflect a full range of cultures

Themes and Ideas

- Humor that is easy to grasp (silly characters, obvious jokes, funny situations)
- Obvious themes (friendship, family relationships, first responsibilities, growing, behavior)

Language and Literary Features

- Simple plots
- Easy-to-understand problems and solutions
- Memorable characters that are straightforward and uncomplicated
- Characters that change for obvious reasons (learn lessons, learn new things)
- Characters' actions that have clear consequences (reward for trying, etc.)
- Predictable character traits (sly, brave, silly)
- Stories with multiple characters, each easy to understand and predictable
- Some figurative language that will be familiar to most children
- Rhyme, rhythm, repetition
- Simple dialogue easily attributed to characters
- Some repetitive dialogue

Sentence Complexity

- Simple sentences, although more complex than children generally use in oral language
- Sentences that are easy for children to follow
- Some use of literary language (e.g. "once upon a time")

Vocabulary

- Many words that are in children's oral vocabulary
- Some memorable words that children can take on as language play
- Labels for familiar objects, animals, and activities
- A few interesting words that are new

Illustrations

- Large, clear, colorful illustrations in a variety of media
- Illustrations that add meaning to a story or informational text and offer high support for comprehension
- Very simple illustrations for informational texts—sometimes with labels
- Illustrations that sometimes move or have texture

Book and Print Features

- Some books with large print that children can see during read-aloud (labels, onomatopoeic words, simple phrases or sentences)
- Some special features in the illustrations and print that engage interest and make texts interactive (pop-up books, lift-the-flap books, see-through holes, sound effects)
- Title, author, and illustrator on cover and title page

The PreK Continuum

Interactive Read-Aloud and Literature Discussion

☐ **Selecting Goals:** *Behaviors and Understandings to Notice, Teach, and Support*

Thinking *within* the Text

- Notice and acquire understanding of new words from read-aloud context
- Use new words in discussion of a text
- Follow the events of a simple plot and remember them enough to discuss or reenact a story
- Understand simple problems and talk about them
- Talk about interesting information learned from a text
- Pick up important information while listening and use it in discussion
- As for and answer questions about key information in a nonfiction text
- Notice and use important information from the pictures
- Retell important parts of a story using the pictures after hearing several times
- Ask questions to clarify or deepen understanding of a text
- Join in on refrains or repeated sentences, phrases, and words after hearing a story several times
- Tell stories in response to pictures
- Play with words or language orally (for example, nonsense words or refrains from texts read aloud)
- Show awareness of a topic (content from a text) and make related comments or pose related questions)
- Mimic the teacher's expression and word stress when reenacting a text or joining in
- Use hand and body movements showing understanding that the pictures and words of a text convey meaning

Thinking *beyond* the Text

- Use background knowledge to understand settings, story problems, and characters
- Use background knowledge to understand the content of a text
- Acquire new content from listening to stories and informational texts
- Predict what will happen next in a story
- Talk about what a character is like, how a character feels, or what a character might do (inference)
- Make connections between new texts and those heard before
- Identify and repeat specific language that characters use in stories
- Make connections between texts and their own lives
- Interpret meaning from illustrations
- Understand that there can be different interpretations of the illustrations
- Use details from illustrations in discussion of a story or informational text
- Give reasons (either text-based or personal experience) to support thinking
- Discuss motivations of characters
- Discuss the problem in a story
- Discuss new information learned

Thinking *about* the Text

- Understand when texts are based on established sequences such as numbers, days of the week, or seasons
- Understand the meaning of some aspects of text structure (beginning, end, next)
- Understand that an author wrote the book
- Understand that an illustrator created the pictures in the book (or a photographer took photographs)
- Recognize that one author or illustrator might create several books
- Begin to form opinions about books and say why
- Share thinking about a story or topic
- Talk about how texts are similar and how they are different
- Understand that there can be different versions of the same story
- Identify favorite books and tell why
- Use specific vocabulary to talk about texts: *author, illustrator, cover, title, page, problem, beginning, ending*

Shared and Performance Reading

☐ **Selecting Texts:** *Characteristics of Texts for Sharing and Performing*

Genres/Forms

Genres

- Simple fantasy, most with talking animals or magic creatures
- Factual texts—ABC books, label books, concept books, counting books, very simple informational books
- Short poems, nursery rhymes, and songs
- Language and word play (including finger rhymes, hand rhymes, body movements)
- Traditional folktales
- Memoir
- Realistic fiction

Forms

- Enlarged poems, rhymes, and songs
- Enlarged picture storybooks and informational texts
- Texts produced through interactive and shared writing—lists, directions, sequences of actions, stories, poems, descriptions, dialogue from stories, menus

Text Structure

- Stories with simple plot structure (beginning, middle, ending)
- Stories with repeating patterns
- Many books with repetition of episodes and refrains
- Informational texts with very simple statements of description, simple chronological sequence, or simple naming
- Simple traditional tales that are familiar to many children

Content

- Stories with simple, easy-to-understand problems—beginning, events, and ending
- Language and word play—rhymes, alliteration
- ABC books, concepts such as colors, shapes, counting
- Familiar topics—animals, pets, families, food, neighborhood, friends, growing, weather such as rain or snow
- Informational texts about one simple, familiar topic
- Topics that may be in settings different from children's own but that have universal appeal

Themes and Ideas

- Obvious humor—silly situations and nonsense
- Familiar themes for children such as play, families, homes, and pre-school

Language and Literary Features

- Simple stories with beginning, middle (events of a plot), and ending
- Many texts with rhyme, rhythm, and repetition
- Some memorable characters
- Simple, understandable dialogue that is easily attributed to characters
- Characters' actions that have clear consequences (reward for trying, etc.)
- Predictable plots and stories
- Simple humor that appeals to young children

Sentence Complexity

- Sentences written in natural language
- Short, simple sentences that are easy for children to understand and remember (consider ELL)
- Sentences with a limited number of adjectives, adverbs, and clauses

Vocabulary

- A few content words (labels) related to concepts that children can understand
- Texts that contain mostly words that are in children's oral vocabularies
- A few words that are new to children but easy to understand in context
- Some words of high interest and novelty that will be memorable (for example, *huffed and puffed; roared; bam!*)

Words

- Simple plurals using *–s* or *–es*
- Some complex plurals that are in children's oral vocabulary (*children, sheep*)
- Some words with endings that are in children's oral vocabulary (*running, painting*) or that are easy to understand
- Words that have the same ending (rime—*it, bit, sit*)
- Many very simple high-frequency words that may over time become familiar enough to be visual signposts
- Alliterative sequences

Illustrations

- Bright, clear, colorful illustrations in a variety of media
- Details that add interest rather than overwhelm or distract
- Illustrations that provide high support for comprehending and language
- Poems or pieces of shared writing that have only small labels to cue language

Book and Print Features

- All texts on charts or in enlarged texts
- Print in a font big enough for the whole group (or a small group) to see clearly
- Clear spaces between words and between lines
- Limited number of lines on a page (usually 1 or 2 unless they are reading a well-known short poem or song)
- Simple punctuation (period, comma, question mark, exclamation mark, quotation marks)
- Title, author, and illustrator on cover and title page for books
- Page numbers
- Layout that supports phrasing by presenting word groups
- Words in bold or varying type sizes

The PreK Continuum

Shared and Performance Reading

☐ **Selecting Goals:** *Behaviors and Understandings to Notice, Teach, and Support*

Thinking *within* the Text

- Notice and use information from pictures to understand and remember text
- Follow the teacher's pointer in a coordinated way while reading text with group support
- Begin to notice aspects of print to help in tracking it during shared reading
- Understand the meaning of new words after reading them in a text and talking about them
- Engage in shared reading with fluency and expression
- Use expression in response to questions and exclamation marks
- Begin to recognize some simple punctuation
- Notice some letters in print
- Connect some letters in print with their names or with words they know
- Using phrasing, pausing, and word stress with the teacher's support
- Remember and use repeating language patterns
- Mimic the teacher's expression
- Talk about characters, problems, and events in a story
- Discuss how to read a text with the teacher and other children

Thinking *about* the Text

- Recognize and talk about the beginning and the ending of a story
- Understand that a book was written by a person and begin to use the term "author"
- Understand that a picture book was illustrated by a person and begin to use the term "illustrator"
- Talk about whether or not they liked a book and say why
- Talk about favorite parts of a story
- Recognize the same tale (traditional story) in different books
- Notice when a text is funny and say why
- Notice when the writer/illustrator has used special features of print such as very large print
- Notice and follow texts that are organized around a special feature such as numbers, days of the week, ABCs
- Notice when the writer has made the text rhyme

Thinking *beyond* the Text

- Make predictions as to what will happen in a story
- Anticipate exciting places or the ending of a story in discussion with the teacher
- Anticipate exciting places or the ending of a story by remembering it
- Express personal connections with the content of texts, characters, or events in a story
- Notice and talk about texts that are alike in some way
- Infer feelings of characters in stories

Writing About Reading

☐ **Selecting Genres and Forms:** *Most writing for preschool children is generated through very simple shared or interactive writing, and the genres and forms are likewise demonstrated through very simple interactive or shared writing. Often, teachers label pictures or children's drawings as a demonstration of writing. Preschool children's independent writing largely consists of drawing or painting accompanied by the use of whatever they have noticed about writing. They may write their names (or parts of them); they may use letter-like forms mixed with some known letters; they may use the letters they know over and over again in strings. It is helpful for teachers to invite children to talk about their drawings (stories or just labels). Teachers may write a simple sentence or two that the child dictates. Some children can remember and "read" this sentence.*

Functional Writing

- Drawings or paintings that reflect the subject of an informational book or something in a story
- Dictated labels or short sentences describing a drawing
- Lists of all kinds (things we like, things we are going to do, ingredients for cooking)
- Notes, messages, and simple letters
- Labels for photographs
- Directions showing a simple sentence

Informational Writing

- Drawings with labels showing information (what we learned) from a book
- Simple sentence telling an interesting fact (what we learned) from a book

Narrative Writing

- Drawings showing sequence of events in a story
- Speech bubbles showing dialogue (a word, phrase, or simple sentence)
- Simple sentence summarizing or telling the end of a story

A prekindergartener's writing about her brother

Writing About Reading

☐ **Selecting Goals:** *Behaviors and Understandings to Notice, Teach, and Support*

Thinking *within* the Text

- Use drawing (or other art media) to represent characters and actions from a story
- Use drawing (or other art media) to represent information from a book
- Label drawings (dictated, temporary spelling, or letter-like forms)
- Reenact or retell stories that have been heard
- Use some vocabulary from stories
- Reread (shared) to remember something from a story
- Find important details in illustrations
- Discuss the meaning of illustrations
- Use names of authors and illustrators

Thinking *beyond* the Text

- Draw to show how a character feels
- Label drawings to show what a character might be saying
- Dictate or use interactive writing to predict what might happen in a story
- Use interactive writing and drawing to show the events of a story in sequence (story map)
- Draw and sometimes label or dictate sentences about something in their lives prompted by characters or events in a story

Thinking *about* the Text

- Use some letter-like forms, letters, or temporary spellings to create texts that have some of the characteristics of published texts (cover, title, author, illustrations)
- Use interactive writing or temporary spellings to represent a funny or exciting part of a story
- Notice and remember some interesting language from a text, sometimes using it to dictate stories or talk about drawings

Writing

☐ **Selecting Purpose and Genre:** *Most writing for preschool children is generated through dictated writing or very simple shared or interactive writing. The teacher may guide children to tell about their own experiences or to retell something from a story. Sometimes teachers label pictures or children's drawings as a demonstration of writing. Preschool children's independent writing consists largely of drawing or painting accompanied by the use of whatever they have noticed about writing. They may write their names (or parts of them); they may use non-letter-like or letter-like forms mixed with some known letters; they may use the letters they know over and over in strings. Even if children are only pretending to write, we can tell a great deal about their growing knowledge of and interest in written language by observing how they use the space or create forms on the page. From their attempts we can observe that they are beginning to distinguish between pictures and print. You may want to invite children to talk about their drawings (stories or just labels). If the child requests it, you may write a simple sentence or two that the child dictates, but it is important not to write on the child's paper. If the child wants it, write on a stick-on note. Most children can remember and "read" their own sentences even if you cannot.*

Narrative: *(To tell a story)*

Memoir *(personal narrative, autobiography)*

Understanding the Genre
- Understand that you can talk, draw, and write about things that have happened to you
- Understand that when you talk about or write about something from your own life, you often use the words *I* or *we*
- Understand that you need to tell a story in the order in which things happened so your readers will understand them
- Understand that stories you tell should be interesting to your listeners or readers

Writing in the Genre
- Draw a picture and tell a story about it
- Draw a sequence of related pictures and tell about them
- Draw pictures in a simple book, sometimes including approximated writing, and tell a story in sequence about them
- Tell, draw, or approximate writing about stories they have heard or read
- Tell, draw, or approximate writing to tell about personal experiences
- Use some words orally that indicate passage of time (*then, again, after*)
- Talk about one's feelings while telling a story of an experience
- With teacher help, begin to use some features of narrative texts (drawings matching text, titles, page numbers, speech bubbles)

Informational: *(To explain or give facts about a topic)*

Literary Nonfiction

Understanding the Genre
- Understand that you can write to tell what you know about something
- Understand that a writer (and illustrator) wants to tell others information
- Begin to notice how the writers of nonfiction texts show facts (labeling, making clear drawings, showing pictures)

Writing in the Genre
- Make a drawing of an object or process and approximate writing or talking about it
- Make a series of drawings showing an object or process and approximate writing or talking about it
- Use a short book with related ideas to talk or approximate writing about a topic
- Show awareness of audience when drawing and approximating writing
- Begin to use (with teacher help) some features of informational text (page numbers, titles, labeled drawings)

Writing

☐ Selecting Purpose and Genre (cont.)

Poetic: *(To express feelings, sensory images, ideas, or stories)*

Poetry *(free verse, rhyme)*

Understanding the Genre

- Understand that a writer (or illustrator) can represent a song or rhyme
- Understand poetry (as well as songs and rhymes) as a pleasurable way to talk about feelings, tell stories, or tell how something looks or feels
- Notice interesting words (words for sounds, figurative words, unusual words) when reading poetry in a shared way
- Notice rhyming words when reading poetry in a shared way
- Begin to notice how space and lines are used in poems, songs, and rhymes
- Understand that a poem can be serious or funny

Writing in the Genre

- Actively participate in shared writing of a poem, song, or rhyme
- Illustrate poems with drawings
- Begin to intentionally use space in a way that represents poetry
- Talk about how something looks, smells, tastes, feels, or sounds
- Notice and enjoy rhyme and humor

Functional: *(To perform a practical task)*

Labels

Understanding the Genre

- Understand that a writer or illustrator can add labels to help readers understand drawings
- Understand that labels provide important information

Writing in the Genre

- Begin to label drawings in approximated writing
- Participate actively in suggesting labels during shared writing
- Create friendly letters in approximated form (notes, cards, invitations, email)

Friendly Letters

Understanding the Genre

- Understand that people use writing to communicate with each other
- Understand the different kinds of written communication people use (notes, letters, email)
- Understand that written communication can be used for different purposes (information, invitations, "thank you" letters)
- Understand that people include their names (and recipients' names) in written communications
- Understand that invitations must include specific information

Writing in the Genre

- Participate actively in writing notes, letters, invitations, etc., through shared and interactive writing
- Use shared or approximated writing to write to a known audience
- Actively participate in suggesting information to include in writing during shared/interactive writing
- Add illustrations to written messages

Lists and Procedures *(how-to)*

Understanding the Genre

- Understand the purpose of a list
- Understand that the form of a list is usually one item under another and it may be numbered
- Understand that captions can be written under pictures to give people more information
- Understand that a list of directions can help in knowing how to do something
- Understand that pictures will help readers understand information or how to do something

Writing in the Genre

- Actively participate in group writing of lists to help remember how to do something
- Suggest items for lists
- Actively participate in suggesting the order of items in a list
- Add drawings to lists
- Make a list for an authentic purpose

Writing About Reading *(all genres)*

(See the Writing About Reading continuum, on pages 237–238.)

Writing

☐ Selecting Goals: *Behaviors and Understandings to Notice, Teach, and Support*

Craft

Organization

Text Structure

- Express ideas related to a topic or a thematic study so that someone else can write them (dictation)
- Actively participate in shared or interactive writing around a topic or theme
- Tell stories for dictation that have a beginning, middle, and end
- Use approximated writing and pictures to make short books that tell a story or have information about a topic or theme
- Begin to write the title and author's name on the cover of a story

Beginnings, Endings, Titles

- Suggest titles for pieces of shared or interactive writing
- Suggest beginnings and endings for pieces of shared or interactive writing
- Use approximated writing to write either titles or endings of pieces of writing

Presentation of Ideas

- Tell about experiences or topics in a way that can be written by the teacher
- Present ideas in logical sequence
- Provide some supportive ideas for bigger ideas in talking about a topic or theme
- Suggest logically related ideas in group story or topic writing

Idea Development

- Provide details that support main topics or ideas during shared/interactive writing
- Explain points in dictated or shared/interactive writing

Language Use

- Understand that what you think you can say, and what you say you can write
- When talking about or retelling stories for dictation or shared/interactive writing, show evidence of awareness of the language of books

Word Choice

- Show awareness of new words encountered in interactive read-aloud or conversation
- Use new words when talking about drawings
- Use new words when telling stories or talking about an informational topic

Voice

- Begin to develop interesting ways of talking about personal experiences
- Begin to tell stories from a particular perspective
- Share thoughts about a theme or topic
- Add ideas and opinions about a theme or topic
- Participate actively in shared/interactive writing about what is known or remembered from a text

Conventions

Text Layout

- Begin to understand that print is laid out in certain ways and the lines and spaces are important
- Begin to understand that print is placed from top to bottom on a page
- Separate print (or approximated print) from pictures
- Begin to write words, letters, or approximated letters in clusters to show the look of words
- Show awareness of layout and use of space when copying print
- Show awareness of left-to-right directionality during shared/interactive writing
- Identify spaces between words in a piece of shared/interactive writing

Grammar

Sentence Structure *(note that English Language Learners may need more time and support)*

- Use simple but conventional sentence structure when suggesting ideas for interactive/shared writing
- Dictate simple but conventional sentences

Parts of Speech *(note that English language learners may need more time and support)*

- Use nouns and verbs in agreement most of the time when suggesting ideas for shared/interactive writing or producing language for dictation
- Use prepositional phrases when suggesting ideas for shared/interactive writing or producing language for dictation
- Use modifiers (*red* dress; ran *fast*)

Tense

- Use past tense in describing past events when suggesting ideas for shared/interactive writing or producing language for dictation
- Use present tense to describe something (*I like . . .*)
- Begin to use future tense (*I'm going to go. . .*)

Capitalization

- Understand that there are upper- and lowercase versions of letters
- Locate capital letters at the beginning of a sentence during shared/interactive writing or in a piece of dictated writing
- Write names with a capital letter at the beginning
- Show awareness of the first place of capital letters in words

Writing

☐ **Selecting Goals:** *Behaviors and Understandings to Notice, Teach, and Support* (cont.)

Punctuation

- Experiment with punctuation marks as signals
- Understand that there are punctuation marks in print
- Understand that punctuation marks are different from letters
- Understand that punctuation marks are related to the way text is read
- Sometimes use punctuation marks in approximated writing

Spelling

- Write in scribbles or random strings
- Repeat scribble shape over and over
- Mix in some letter-like symbols when writing in scribbles
- Write name conventionally (all capital letters or capital letter and lowercase)
- Use known letters from name to make repeated patterns on a page
- Understand that your name is a word
- Begin to be aware that a word is always spelled the same
- Use own knowledge of own speech to connect sounds to letters or words
- Write one or more words in approximated form (e.g., name, *lv (love), m (mom)*)

Handwriting/Word Processing

- Get hand to hold pencil and paper
- Hold pencil or marker with satisfactory grip
- Hold pencil or marker efficiently to begin to approximate writing or write a few letters
- Move pencil only in desired direction
- Begin to understand that writers make decisions about where to start
- Begin to understand that writers make decisions about the placement of pictures and print
- Write with a preferred hand
- Locate letters on a keyboard and understand how to press them to make them appear on a screen
- Use simple programs on the computer with adult help

Writing Process

Rehearsing/Planning

Purpose

- Draw and write for a specific purpose
- Plan drawing and writing for different purposes
- Begin to adjust drawing and dictated messages according to the purpose
- Choose paper for writing
- Choose topics to draw and write about (both as individuals and in groups)
- Write (or approximate writing) for a variety of purposes in particular environments (for example, restaurants, house, shops, doctor's office)
- Actively contribute to shared/interactive writing around a topic or theme
- Write name on drawing and writing

Audience

- Become aware of the people who will read the writing and what they will want to know
- Include important information that the audience needs to know

Oral Language

- Generate and expand ideas through talk with peers and the teacher
- Look for ideas and topics in personal experiences, shared through talk
- Use storytelling to generate and rehearse language (that may be written later)
- Tell stories in chronological order
- Retell stories in chronological order

The PreK Continuum

Writing

☐ **Selecting Goals:** *Behaviors and Understandings to Notice, Teach, and Support* (cont.)

Gathering Seeds/Resources/Experimenting with Writing

- Talk about ideas for writing and drawing
- Understand how writers get their ideas (telling about things that have happened or about what they know)
- Record information in drawing and approximated writing
- Use drawings as a source for ideas for writing

Content, Topic, Theme

- Understand a group of ideas related to an area of study or inquiry
- Observe objects in the environment (people, animals, etc.) as a source for group or individual writing
- Select topics or information for drawing and writing

Inquiry/Research

- Use drawings to tell a series of ideas learned through inquiry about a topic
- Use drawings to add information or revise thinking
- Ask questions about a topic
- Remember important information about a topic and contribute ideas to shared/interactive writing
- Remember important labels for drawings and dictate or write them approximately

Drafting/Revising

Understanding the Process

- Understand the role of a conference with the teacher to help in drawing and writing
- Understand that writers can share their writing with others
- Understand that writers can add to their drawings or approximated writings
- Actively participate in adding to or changing interactive/shared writing
- Understand that writers can create drawings or write like other writers and illustrators

Producing a Draft

- Convey a message in print
- Talk about, draw, and approximate writing to produce a piece
- Draw and approximate writing about a continuous message on a simple topic

Rereading

- Share drawing and writing with others
- Talk about, approximate the reading of, or read a message or story to the teacher
- Look carefully at drawings to see if details should be added

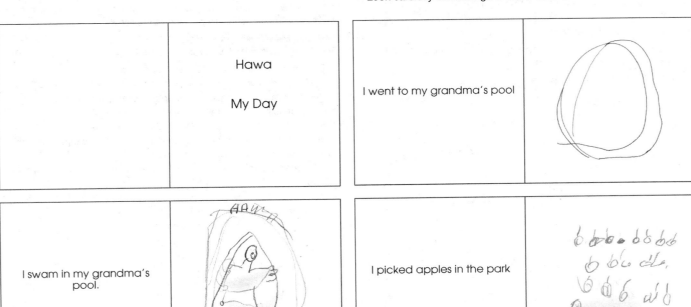

A prekindergartener's story about visiting her grandma

The PreK Continuum

Writing

☐ **Selecting Goals:** *Behaviors and Understandings to Notice, Teach, and Support* (cont.)

Adding Information

- Add details to drawings
- Add additional details in dictated or approximated writing to expand on a topic
- Add speech balloons to pictures to use dialogue

Deleting Information

- Delete or cover parts of drawings that do not fit

Reorganizing Information

- Understand that writers can change the way their writing is organized
- Give suggestions for moving sentences from one part to another to make the writing more interesting in group writing
- Give suggestions for adding words or sentences to provide more information in group writing
- Reorder drawings by cutting them apart and laying them out as pages

Changing Text

- Cross out to change a text
- Understand that writers can change text or drawings to make them clearer or more interesting to readers
- Participate in group decisions about changing text

Using Tools and Techniques

- Learn to use sticky notes to add information to drawings or writing
- Add pages to a book or booklet
- Cross out letters or words that are not needed

Editing and Proofreading

Understanding the Process

- Understand that writers try to make their writing and drawings interesting and informative
- Understand that making letters clearly and using space makes writing easier to read

Editing for Conventions

- Understand that the teacher is pointing out something in group writing that needs to be changed
- Notice as the teacher points out correct letter formation in group writing

Using Tools

- (Not applicable)

Publishing

- Create illustrations for a piece of group writing (shared/interactive)
- Share completed writing and drawing by talking about it to the class

Sketching and Drawing

- Use drawing as a way to plan for writing
- Use drawing and other art media to represent ideas and information
- Add or remove details to drawings to revise

Viewing Self as a Writer

- Take on approximated writing independently
- Understand how drawing and pictures are related
- Demonstrate confidence in attempts at drawing and writing
- Have ideas in mind to tell, write, draw about
- Select favorite drawings and writings from a collection
- Produce a quantity of drawing and approximated writing within the time available (for example, one per day)
- Keep working independently rather than waiting for the teacher to help
- Make attempts to solve problems
- Try out techniques that they see others using

Oral, Visual, and Technological Communication

☐ **Selecting Goals:** *Behaviors and Understandings to Notice, Teach, and Support*

Listening and Speaking

Listening and Understanding

- Listen with attention to texts that are read aloud
- Take a turn to speak
- Listen with attention and understanding to simple and clear directions
- Remember and follow directions that may have more than two steps
- Look at the person who is talking
- Listen actively to others as they read or talk
- Learn new words related to topics of inquiry in the classroom
- Show interest in words
- Show interest in listening to and talking about stories, poems, or informational texts
- Compare personal knowledge and experiences with what is heard
- Act out sentences in rhymes or stories

Social Interaction

- Speak in an audible voice
- Speak at appropriate volume for indoors
- Adjust volume as appropriate for different contexts
- Use polite terms such as *please* and *thank you*
- Engage in conversation during imaginary play
- Enter a conversation appropriately
- Sustain a conversation with others (teacher, family, peers)
- Engage in the turn-taking of conversation
- Engage in dramatic play
- Act out stories either with or without props
- Refrain from speaking while others are speaking

Extended Discussion

- Understand and use words related to familiar common experiences and topics (pets, body parts, food, clothes, transportation, classroom objects, home, family, and neighborhood)
- Follow the topic and add to the discussion
- Respond to and build on the statements of others
- Form clear questions to get information
- Participate actively in whole-class discussion or with a partner or in a small group
- Use some specific vocabulary (book, page, title, cover, author, illustrator)
- Learn new words related to topics of inquiry in the classroom
- Show interest in words and word play
- Act out stories with or without props
- Engage in dramatic play

Content

- Begin to verbalize reasons for problems, events, and actions
- Begin to discuss the concept of cause and effect
- Express opinions and explain reasoning (*because . . .*)
- Predict future events in a story
- Talk about what is already known about a topic
- Describe people and places in a story
- Report what is known or learned about an informational text
- Share knowledge of story structure by describing story parts or elements such as characters
- Talk about how people, places, or events are alike and different
- Talk about one's own feelings and those of others
- Recognize that others have feelings different from one's own
- Ask questions (demonstrate curiosity)

Oral, Visual, and Technological Communication

☐ **Selecting Goals:** *Behaviors and Understandings to Notice, Teach, and Support* (cont.)

Presentation

Voice

- Speak about a topic with enthusiasm
- Talk smoothly with little hesitation
- Tell stories in an interesting way
- Talk with confidence

Conventions

- Speak at appropriate volume to be heard, but not too loud
- Look at the audience (or other person) while talking
- Speak at an appropriate rate to be understood
- Enunciate words clearly

Organization

- Have a topic or response in mind before starting to speak
- Tell personal experiences in a logical sequence
- Show awareness of the audience when speaking
- Present information or ideas in an understandable way
- Speak to one topic and stay on topic

Word Choice

- Understand and use words related to familiar experiences and topics such as pets, body parts, food, clothes, transportation, classroom objects, home and family, neighborhood
- Use some language from stories when retelling them
- Use some words that describe (adjectives and adverbs)

Ideas and Content

- Recite songs and short poems
- Tell stories from personal experiences
- Retell stories from texts

Technology

General Communication

- Understand that the computer is a source of information (or entertainment)
- Find buttons and icons on the computer screen to use simple programs
- Know how to use the mouse
- Begin to understand the computer as a way to communicate

Gathering Information/Research

- Search for information with adult help
- Use simple websites with adult help

Phonics, Spelling, and Word Study

☐ **Selecting Goals:** *Behaviors and Understandings to Notice, Teach, and Support*

Early Literacy Concepts

- Notice and talk about photographs, pictures, drawings, and familiar written words (names, *Mom*)
- Note print in the environment and look for its meaning
- Understand that print conveys meaning
- Use print in a variety of ways—labels, signs, stories, books
- Notice the print in signs
- Distinguish between print and pictures
- Follow the print during shared reading (as cued by the pointer)
- Read a known text in unison with others
- Hold and handle books correctly (turning pages front to back, etc.)
- Understand the variety of purposes of print in reading
- Understand that a book has a title, author, and illustrator
- Understand that books are sources of information
- Recognize one's name
- Use letters in one's name to represent it or communicate other messages
- Understand the concept of *word, letter*
- Use left-to-right directionality and return to the left in shared reading of print and in group writing
- Understand the concept of *first* and *last* in written language
- Understand the concept of writing top to bottom

Phonological Awareness

Words

- Hear word boundaries
- Understand that words are made up of sounds

Rhyming Words

- Hear and say rhyming words
- Hear and connect rhyming words

Syllables

- Clap the syllables of words with teacher help

Onsets and Rimes

- Say the onsets and rimes of words with teacher help

Phonemes [PA]

- Say words slowly
- Be aware that words have sounds in them
- Play with the sounds of language
- Enjoy stories and poems that illustrate play with the sounds of language
- Recognize words that stand for sounds (*bang, pop*)

Letter Knowledge

Identifying Letters

- Notice that letters have different shapes
- Understand the concept of a letter
- Match letters that are alike by looking at their shapes
- Connect particular letters to their lives (names, names of family, environmental print)
- Distinguish letter forms by noticing particular parts (sticks, tails, dots, slants, circles, curves, tunnels, crosses)
- Categorize and connect letters by features (sticks, tails, dots, slants, circles, curves, tunnels, crosses)
- Produce some letter names
- Understand that letter orientation is important

Recognizing Letters in Words and Sentences

- Understand that words are made up of letters
- Locate some known letters in print

Forming Letters

- Use writing tools
- Use drawings to represent meaning
- Produce approximated writing
- Use approximated writing functionally (labels, lists, signs, names)
- Begin to use efficient and consistent motions to form letters
- Control direction in forming letters

Phonics, Spelling, and Word Study

☐ **Selecting Goals:** *Behaviors and Understandings to Notice, Teach, and Support* (cont.)

Letter-Sound Relationships

- Understand that there is a relationship between letters and the sounds in words
- Say words slowly as part of shared/interactive or independent writing
- Understand how to move from own language—sentences, words, letters—to approximate writing

Word Meaning

- Notice and use new and interesting words heard in texts read aloud and in conversation
- Notice new and interesting words in poems and other shared reading texts
- Use new words in conversation, in writing dictated to the teacher, and in shared/interactive writing
- Know the meaning of some concept words—simple colors, number words, shapes, days of the week, months of the year, holidays
- Learn the meaning of some words related to inquiry in the classroom

Spelling Patterns

- Recognize that there are patterns in words that you can hear and say

High-Frequency Words

- Understand that you look at the letters in a word to read it
- Recognize own name
- Recognize a few high-frequency words after experience in shared reading and interactive writing

Word Structure

Syllables

- Understand that words can have more than one part that you can hear
- Clap words to show awareness of syllables

Word-Solving Actions

- Recognize and locate own name
- Recognize and locate a few high-frequency words
- Make connections between own name and other words (same letters)
- Use own name and other known words as a resource in approximated writing

APPENDICES CONTENTS

A

Nursery Rhymes, Poetry, and Songs

TYPES OF POETRY

- **RHYMED VERSE:** Many poems for young children have lines that end with words that rhyme. These are often but not always rhyming couplets (each pair of lines rhyme).

- **WORD PLAY:** Some poems play with words by juxtaposing interesting word patterns in a humorous and playful way. Word play may include tongue twisters (poems with word arrangements that make them very difficult to recite without stumbling because the words are difficult to pronounce one after another).

- **HUMOROUS VERSE:** Humorous verse draws children's attention to absurdities as well as to the sounds and rhythms of language. Sometimes these humorous verses tell stories.

- **SONGS:** Songs are musical texts originally intended to be sung. You may recognize the traditional tunes of many songs, but if you don't, you can compose your own or simply have children chant them, enjoying the rhythm and rhyme.

- **ACTION SONGS AND POEMS:** Action songs and poems involve action along with rhythm and rhyme. This category includes fingerplays (simple actions and finger movements). There are also chants that accompany games or are simply enjoyable to say together. Chants, like songs, showcase rhythm and rhyme.

- **NURSERY RHYMES:** Traditional rhymes by anonymous poets have been passed down for generations. There are often many different versions. Originally serving as political satire for adults, they have been loved by children for generations. They usually rhyme in couplets or alternating lines and are highly rhythmic. The **Mother Goose rhymes**, which were published in the eighteenth century, are the best known, but equivalents exist around the world.

- **CONCEPT POEMS:** The poems in this category focus on concepts such as numbers, colors, ordinal words, seasons, animals, and any other similar categories of information. As children learn these verses, they start repeating the vocabulary that surrounds important concepts.

* Indicates additional verses not shown

TITLE	CATEGORY	WORDS/LYRICS	ACTIVITIES
A-Hunting We Will Go	Rhymed Verse, Song	Oh, a-hunting we will go, A-hunting we will go, We'll catch a fox and put him in a box, And then we'll let him go.	Listen for and identify the rhyming words. After children learn the song, substitute other animal names and objects that rhyme *(whale–pail, skunk–trunk, snail–jail, bear–chair)*
The Alphabet Song	Concept Song (alphabet)	A-B-C-D-E-F-G, H-I-J-K-L-M-N-O-P, Q-R-S, T-U-V, W-X, Y and Z. Now I've said my ABCs, Next time won't you sing with me?	Have children march around the room while they sing this song. Encourage them to chime in with gusto.
An Apple a Day	Rhymed Verse, Nursery Rhyme	An apple a day Sends the doctor away. Apple in the morning Doctor's warning. Roast apple at night Starves the doctor outright. Eat an apple going to bed Knock the doctor on the head. Three each day, seven days a week Ruddy apple, ruddy cheek.	Listen for and identify rhyming words. Have children clap or snap their fingers when they come to a rhyming word. You can substitute "Big red apple, fat red cheek" for the last line, or just tell children *ruddy* means *red*.
The Ants Go Marching	Song, Rhymed Verse, Nursery Rhyme, Concept Poem (insects, counting)	The ants go marching one by one, hurrah, hurrah The ants go marching one by one, hurrah, hurrah The ants go marching one by one, The little one stops to suck his thumb And they all go marching down, Into the ground, To get out of the rain. BOOM! BOOM! BOOM!*	Add new rhyming verses up to the number ten. The tune is the same as "When Johnny Comes Marching Home."

TITLE	CATEGORY	WORDS/LYRICS	ACTIVITIES
Apples and Bananas	Song, Word Play, Concept Song (eating, food)	I like to eat, eat, eat apples and bananas I like to eat, eat, eat apples and bananas I like to ate, ate, ate ay-ples and bay-nay-nays I like to ate, ate, ate ay-ples and bay-nay-nays*	Repeat the song changing the vowel sounds in *apples* and *bananas* to A, E, I, O U.
Apples, Peaches	Rhymed Verse, Concept Poem (months of the year)	Apples, peaches, Pears, plums, Tell me when your birthday comes.	Chant the rhyme repeatedly, followed by the name of each month of the year, in sequence. Have children raise their hands or stand up if their birthday occurs in the month that is said.
Apple Tree	Action Poem/Song, Concept Song (eating, food)	Way up high in an apple tree, Two little apples did I see. So I shook that tree as hard as I could. Down came the apples. Mmm, they were good!	Have children pantomime the actions of the song: • First line: Hold arms above head, fingers spread • Second line: Make fists • Third line: Wiggle entire body • Fourth line: Lower arms • Last line: Rub tummy
A-Tisket, A-Tasket	Action Song/ Poem, Rhymed Verse, Word Play	A-tisket a-tasket, A green and yellow basket. I wrote a letter to my love, And on the way I dropped it. I dropped it, I dropped it, And on the way I dropped it. A little boy [girl] picked it up, And put it in his [her] pocket.	Have children substitute a different rhyming sound and word for *A-tisket, A-tasket* and *basket*, and provide alternate lines for the rest of the song.
Baa, Baa, Black Sheep	Rhymed Verse, Mother Goose Rhyme, Concept Poem (animals, numbers)	Baa, baa, black sheep, Have you any wool? Yes sir, yes sir, three bags full. One for the master, And one for the dame, And one for the little boy Who lives down the lane.	Have one group sing or say the question, and a second group sing or say the response. Everyone may hold up one finger each time the word *one* is repeated.

* Indicates additional verses not shown

TITLE	CATEGORY	WORDS/LYRICS	ACTIVITIES
We're Going on a Bear Hunt	Action Poem	We're going on a bear hunt! We're gonna catch a big one! We're not scared. I see a wheat field. Can't go over it. Can't go under it! Let's go through it. We're going on a bear hunt! We're gonna catch a big one! We're not scared. I see a bridge. Can't go under it. Can't go around it. Let's go over it. (Repeat chorus) I see a lake. Can't go over it, can't go under it, let's swim!	Have children perform the following actions as they recite the poem, or create their own actions for these and any additional verses: • Line 5: clap hands and then move them back and forth in a swishing motion. • Line 10: stamp feet. • Last Line: arms swimming. When children know the sequence, you can end by pretending to see a bear and run back through the actions. (Use only 2 or 3 so they can remember.)
Bedtime	Rhymed Verse, Concept Poem (bedtime)	Down with the lambs, Up with the lark, Run to bed, children, Before it gets dark.	After they've learned the verse, have one group read the first line, a second group read the second line, and everyone read the last two lines.
Big and Small	Action Poem, Concept Poem (opposites)	I can make myself real big By standing up straight and tall. But when I'm tired of being big, I can make myself get small.	Children can make themselves "big," "tall," and "small" as they recite the poem.
Bingo	Action Song, Concept Song (letters)	There was a farmer, who had a dog, And Bingo was his name. Oh! B-I-N-G-O, B-I-N-G-O, B-I-N-G-O, And Bingo was his name. Oh!	Sing the entire song once, then repeat, leaving off the *B* and substituting a clap, a finger snap, or other short sound. Continue until all five letters have been replaced with claps, snaps, or sounds.

TITLE	CATEGORY	WORDS/LYRICS	ACTIVITIES
Boom Boom, Ain't It Great to Be Crazy?	Humorous Verse, Rhymed Verse	A horse and a flea and three blind mice sat on a curbstone shooting dice. The horse he slipped and fell on the flea, "Whoops," said the flea, "There's a horse on me!" Boom, boom, ain't it great to be crazy? Boom, boom, ain't it great to be crazy? Giddy and foolish the whole day through, Boom, boom, ain't it great to be crazy?*	Sing the song together. Identify the rhyming words (*mice/dice, flea/me*), and have children invent their own silly rhymes to add to the song.
Bought Me a Cat	Song, Humorous Verse, Word Play, Cumulative Verse	Bought me a cat and the cat pleased me, I fed my cat under yonder tree. Cat goes fiddle-i-fee. Bought me a hen and the hen pleased me, I fed my hen under yonder tree. Hen goes chimmy-chuck, chimmy-chuck, Cat goes fiddle-i-fee. Bought me a duck and the duck pleased me, I fed my duck under yonder tree. Duck goes quack, quack, Hen goes chimmy-chuck, chimmy-chuck, Cat goes fiddle-i-fee.*	Sing or recite the first four lines of the song. Have children invent and add more animals and animal sounds to the song. After you have several lines, organize the children into groups and have each group sing one line.

* Indicates additional verses not shown

TITLE	CATEGORY	WORDS/LYRICS	ACTIVITIES
Bumblebee Song	Action Song	I'm bringing home my baby bumblebee, Won't my mommy be so proud of me. I'm bringing home my baby bumble bee. Ouch! It stung me! I'm squashing up my baby bumblebee, Won't my mommy be so proud of me. I'm squashing up my baby bumblebee, EEEW! Yuck! I'm washing off my baby bumblebee, Won't my mommy be so proud of me. I'm washing off my baby bumblebee, Look! All gone!	Have children make up their own motions to the song as they sing. (Cup hands, squash bee, washing hands, holding up hands). You may want to try another version of the song: • We're bringing home a baby rhinoceros, Won't our mommies (vary with "daddies," "grannies," etc.) be so proud of us? We're bringing home a baby rhinoceros, Ooops! He swallowed us!
Clap Your Hands	Action Song	Clap, clap, clap your hands, Clap your hands with me. Clap them fast, Clap them slow, Clap your hands with me.	Have children clap their hands as they sing, then increase the speed of clapping when they sing fast, and slow down when they sing slow. Repeat with "stomp your feet" and "pat your knees."
Color Song	Concept Song (colors)	Red is the color for an apple to eat. Red is the color for cherries, too. Red is the color for strawberries. I like red, do you?	Using the same structure, create new verses for other colors, encouraging children to identify objects for each color, like blue sky, yellow sun, green leaves.
Diddle, Diddle, Dumpling	Rhymed Verse, Mother Goose Rhyme, Humorous Verse, Word Play	Diddle, diddle, dumpling, my son John, Went to bed with his trousers on. One shoe off and one shoe on, Diddle, diddle, dumpling, my son John.	Talk about the word *trousers* (meaning pants) and substitute other crazy things you could wear to bed. Substitute other nonsense words for *diddle, diddle, dumpling* as well.

TITLE	CATEGORY	WORDS/LYRICS	ACTIVITIES
Down by the Station	Song	Down by the station, Early in the morning, See the little puffer-bellies, All in a row. See the engine driver, Pull the little handle. Puff, puff! Toot, toot! Off we go.	Use simple instruments such as a bell and a tambourine to emphasize the words *puff* and *toot*. Have children scoot around the room to make a train.
Do Your Ears Hang Low?	Action Song, Rhymed Verse	Do your ears hang low? Do they wobble to and fro? Can you tie them in a knot? Can you tie them in a bow? Can you throw them o'er your shoulder Like a Continental Soldier? Do your ears hang low?*	Children will enjoy performing the actions for each line of the song. Invite them to add their own silly rhyming lines for ears, eyes, and nose.
One Little Elephant	Action Poem, Concept Poem (numbers, counting)	One little elephant went out to play On a spider's web one day. He had such enormous fun He called for another elephant to come.	Repeat with two, three, etc. and have each child join an elephant train.
The Farmer in the Dell	Nursery Rhyme, Action Song, Concept Poem, Cumulative Verse	The farmer in the dell, The farmer in the dell, Hi-ho, the derry-o, The farmer in the dell. The farmer takes a wife . . . The wife takes a child . . . The child takes a nurse . . . The nurse takes a cow . . . The cow takes a dog . . . The dog takes a cat . . . The cat takes a rat . . . The rat takes the cheese . . . The cheese stands alone.	Have the children join hands and form a circle around one child chosen as the farmer. As they sing, everyone walks in one direction. At the end of each verse, the chosen character chooses the next one to join them in the middle. When the cheese stands alone, all run back to their places in the circle and the cheese can become the next farmer.

* Indicates additional verses not shown

TITLE	CATEGORY	WORDS/LYRICS	ACTIVITIES
Fall	Action Poem, Concept Poem (seasons)	The leaves are green, the nuts are brown, They hang so high they will never fall down. Leave them alone till the bright fall weather, And then they will all come down together.	• First verse: raise arms sideward, wiggle fingers, make circles for nuts. • Second verse: stretch arms upward. • Third verse: move hands as if wind blows softly. • Final verse: bring arms down to side quickly.
Five Little Ants	Action Poem, Concept Poem (numbers, counting)	Five little ants in an ant hill, Busily working and never still. Do you think they are alive? See them come out . . . One, two, three, four, five.	• First verse: close fist, palm down. • Second verse: wiggle knuckles. • Final verse: bring fingers out one at a time.
Five Little Bunnies	Concept Poem (numbers, counting), Action Poem	Five little bunnies standing by the door, One hopped away, and then there were four. Four little bunnies sitting near a tree, One hopped away, and then there were three. Three little bunnies looking at you, One hopped away and then there were two. Two little bunnies enjoying the sun, One hopped away, and then there was one. One little bunny sitting all alone, He hopped away, and then there were none!	Hold up open hand and bend down one finger with each verse. Children can "hop" their bunny hands as they count down.

TITLE	CATEGORY	WORDS/LYRICS	ACTIVITIES
Five Little Ducks	Song, Nursery Rhyme, Concept Poem (numbers, counting)	Five little ducks went out to play Over the hill and far away. Daddy duck said "Quack, quack, quack." Four little ducks came waddling back.	Repeat: • Four little ducks, three little ducks, etc. • When you get to 0 ducks, end with "But when the Mama duck said 'QUACK, QUACK, QUACK,' five little ducks came waddling back!" • Children can act out the parts of Mama and Daddy duck and the five little ducks.
Five Little Pumpkins	Concept Poem (ordinal numbers), Action Poem/Song	Five little pumpkins sitting on a gate. First one said, "Oh my, it's getting late." Second one said, "There's a bat in the air." Third one said, "We don't care." Fourth one said, "Let's run, run, run." Fifth one said, "Let's have some fun." But whooo went the wind and out went the light, And five little pumpkins rolled out of sight.	Have children perform the rhyme as a fingerplay: hold up five fingers, wiggle one for each quote, cup mouth and blow for the wind, and roll one hand over the other for the last line.
Five Little Monkeys	Concept Poem/Song (numbers, counting), Action Poem/Song	Five little monkeys jumping on the bed. One fell off and bumped his head. So Momma called the doctor and the doctor said, No more monkeys jumping on the bed!	Repeat each verse, counting down to one. Act out the poem with five monkeys, the doctor, and Mama. Have one monkey leave the circle each time.
Five Little Speckled Frogs	Concept Poem/Song (counting, numbers)	Five little speckled frogs, Sitting on a hollow log Eating some most delicious bugs, Yum, yum. One jumped into the pool, Where it was nice and cool, Then there were four little speckled frogs.	Repeat: Four, three, two, one. Children will enjoy acting out the parts of the five frogs as they jump off the log.

* Indicates additional verses not shown

TITLE	CATEGORY	WORDS/LYRICS		ACTIVITIES
Five Little Monkeys in a Tree	Concept Poem (counting, numbers), Action Poem.	Five little monkeys Swinging in a tree, Teasing Mr. Crocodile, "You can't catch me!" Along comes Mr. Crocodile, Quiet as can be. Snap! Four little monkeys Swinging in a tree.		Repeat: four, three two, one. Act out the poem with five monkeys and the crocodile. Continue until all the monkeys have been snapped up.
Frosty Weather	Concept Poem (seasons)	Frosty weather, Snowy weather, When the wind blows, We all go together.		Invite children to imagine the sound of the wind. Ask some of them to supply wind sounds as the other children say the verse. They can also generate other words that go with *frosty* and *snowy*.
Fuzzy Wuzzy	Rhymed Verse, Word Play	Fuzzy Wuzzy was a bear. Fuzzy Wuzzy had no hair. Fuzzy Wuzzy wasn't fuzzy, Was he?		Discuss what Fuzzy Wuzzy looks like. Help children notice the subtle pronunciation difference between *wuzzy* and *was he,* as well as attend to the rising tone signaled by the question mark.
Georgy Porgy	Mother Goose Rhyme	Georgy Porgy, pudding and pie, Kissed the girls and made them cry. When the boys came out to play, Georgy Porgy ran away.		Have children clap twice on *Georgy* and twice on *Porgy* as they read or recite the poem.
Go to Bed	Rhymed Verse, Concept Poem (bedtime, opposites)	Go to bed late, Stay very small. Go to bed early, Grow very tall.		Recite the rhyme together, crouching down on the word *small*, and stretching up high when they say *tall*. Invite children to name other opposites.

TITLE	CATEGORY	WORDS/LYRICS	ACTIVITIES
Go to Bed Early	Rhymed Verse, Concept Poem (bedtime, opposites)	Go to bed early—wake up with joy, Go to bed late—tired girl or boy; Go to bed early—ready for play, Go to bed late—moping all day; Go to bed early—no pains or ills, Go to bed late—doctors and pills; Go to bed early—grow very tall, Go to bed late—stay very small.	After children are familiar with the words, have them create their own actions to accompany each line, or have two groups alternate reading the lines.
Good Morning to You	Rhymed Verse, Concept Song (morning)	Good morning to you! Good morning to you! We're all in our places With bright shining faces. Oh, this is the way to start a great day!*	Use as a gathering verse in the morning (additional verses can be used when returning from lunch and lining up to leave at end of day).
Great A	Rhymed Verse, Concept Song (uppercase and lowercase letters)	Great A, little a, bouncing B, The cat's in the cupboard And can't see me.	Select other uppercase and lowercase letters to insert into the form. You can change *great* to *big* or use the words *uppercase* and *lowercase*. Children can hold up large letter cards at appropriate points in the poem.
Head, Shoulders, Knees, and Toes	Action Song	Head, shoulders, knees, and toes, knees and toes. Head, shoulders, knees, and toes, knees and toes. Eyes and ears and mouth and nose. Head, shoulders, knees, and toes, knees and toes.	Touch head, shoulders, knees, toes, eyes, ears, mouth, and nose. Try going faster and faster each time, or omitting the words to each body part but still perform the motion.
Here Is a Bunny	Action Poem	Here is a bunny with ears so funny, And here is his hole in the ground. When a noise he hears, he pricks up his ears, And hops into his hole so round.	Curl fingers over thumb and "bounce fingers." Make a hole with thumb and forefinger of other hand. Hold "ears" up straight. Hop bunny over into the "hole."

* Indicates additional verses not shown

TITLE	CATEGORY	WORDS/LYRICS	ACTIVITIES
Hey, Diddle, Diddle	Mother Goose Rhyme, Rhymed Verse, Word Play	Hey, diddle, diddle, The cat and the fiddle, The cow jumped over the moon. The little dog laughed To see such sport, And the dish ran away with the spoon.	Create new verses by substituting different one-syllable animal names in place of *cow*.
Hickety, Pickety	Mother Goose Rhyme, Rhymed Verse	Hickety, pickety, my black hen. She lays eggs for gentlemen. Sometimes nine, And sometimes ten. Hickety, pickety, my black hen.	Children can use rhythm sticks to tap out the rhythm of the poem. Once the poem is learned, have the children tap one-, two-, and three-syllable words from the rhyme.
Hickory, Dickory, Dock!	Mother Goose Rhyme, Word Play	Hickory, dickory, dock! The mouse ran up the clock; The clock struck one, The mouse ran down. Hickory, dickory, dock!	Children can perform actions to accompany the poem (the motion of the pendulum, the mouse running up and down the clock, holding up one finger as the clock strikes one). You can also create additional versions using alternate rhyming words.
Hokey Pokey	Action Song	You put your right foot in, You put your right foot out, You put your right foot in And you shake it all about. You do the Hokey Pokey And you turn yourself around, That's what it's all about!*	Repeat with left foot, right hand, left hand, right shoulder, left shoulder, right hip, left hip, and whole self.
Hot Cross Buns	Nursery Rhyme, Song	Hot cross buns! Hot cross buns! One-a-penny, two-a-penny, Hot cross buns! If you have no daughters, Give them to your sons, One-a-penny, two-a-penny, Hot cross buns!	Have children clap three times every time they say *hot cross buns!*

TITLE	CATEGORY	WORDS/LYRICS	ACTIVITIES
Humpty Dumpty	Mother Goose Rhyme, Rhymed Verse, Humorous Verse	Humpty Dumpty sat on a wall, Humpty Dumpty had a great fall; All the king's horses and all the king's men Couldn't put Humpty together again.	Children may recite this poem in groups, one group saying the first two lines, the other group, the last two.
Hush, Little Baby	Rhymed Verse, Concept Poem/Song (bedtime)	Hush, little baby, don't say a word, Mama's going to buy you a mocking bird. If the mocking bird won't sing, Mama's going to buy you a diamond ring. If the diamond ring turns to brass, Mama's going to buy you a looking glass. If that looking glass gets broke, Mama's going to buy you a billy goat. If that billy goat runs away, Mama's going to buy you a bale of hay.*	Sing this song with the children. Some children may need help with the vocabulary *mocking bird, looking glass, billy goat,* and *bale of hay.* Have them help you create additional verses to this lullaby.
If You're Happy and You Know It	Action Song	If you're happy and you know it, Clap your hands! If you're happy and you know it, Clap your hands! If you're happy and you know it, Then your face will surely show it, If you're happy and you know it, Clap your hands!*	Have children clap hands twice after each line. Repeat with: • Stomp your feet • Shout "Hurray!" • Do all three
I'm a Little Teapot	Action Song/Poem	I'm a little teapot Short and stout, Here is my handle, Here is my spout. When I get all steamed up, I shout: "Tip me over and pour me out!"	Have children put one hand on hip to make a handle, hold out the other arm for a spout, then tip to one side as the tea pours out.

* Indicates additional verses not shown

TITLE	CATEGORY	WORDS/LYRICS	ACTIVITIES
It's Raining, It's Pouring	Nursery Rhyme, Rhymed Verse, Song	It's raining, it's pouring. The old man is snoring. Bumped his head And he went to bed And he couldn't get up in the morning. Rain, rain, go away, Come again another day, Little Johnny wants to play. Rain, rain, go away.	Have groups sing the song as a round, making rain sounds by tapping fingers on desks or other objects. Instead of "Little Johnny," you can just say the name of children with three syllable names, or you can use a child's first and last names.
The Itsy, Bitsy Spider	Nursery Rhyme, Action Song, Concept Poem (insects)	The itsy, bitsy spider Climbed up the waterspout. Down came the rain And washed the spider out. Out came the sun And dried up all the rain. And the itsy, bitsy spider Climbed up the spout again.	Touch the first finger of one hand to the opposite thumb, twist both hands, and then touch the first finger of the other hand to the other thumb, repeating the sequence as the spider makes its way up the waterspout. Children can create additional motions for the rest of the actions in the song.
Jack and Jill	Mother Goose Rhyme, Rhymed Verse	Jack and Jill Went up the hill To fetch a pail of water. Jack fell down And broke his crown And Jill came tumbling after.	Talk about the idea of a well, and discuss the meaning of *crown*. After children know the verse, have two children act out the parts as the rest of the class says it.
Jack, Be Nimble	Mother Goose Rhyme, Rhymed Verse	Jack, be nimble, Jack, be quick, Jack, jump over The candlestick.	Take turns jumping over a real or an imaginary candlestick, or a set of blocks or other low barrier.
Jack Sprat	Mother Goose Rhyme, Rhymed Verse, Humorous Verse	Jack Sprat could eat no fat. His wife could eat no lean. And so between them both, you see, They licked the platter clean.	Introduce the idea of opposites and help children think of some other examples (day/night, fast/slow, big/little)

TITLE	CATEGORY	WORDS/LYRICS	ACTIVITIES
Knick-Knack, Paddywhack	Nursery Rhyme, Word Play, Concept Poem (numbers)	This old man, he played one, He played knick-knack on his thumb, With a knick-knack, paddywhack, give your dog a bone; This old man came rolling home.*	Encourage children to think about number words and words that rhyme with them. Repeat with rhyming verses up to the number ten: • Two/shoe • Three/knee • Four/door • Five/hive • Six/sticks • Seven/pen • Eight/gate • Nine/spine • Ten/once again
Ladybug! Ladybug!	Nursery Rhyme, Rhymed Verse, Concept Poem (insects)	Ladybug! Ladybug! Fly away home. Your house is on fire And your children are gone. All except one, And that's little Ann, For she has crept under The frying pan.	Substitute other rhyming words for *Ann* and *frying pan* (For example: *Joan/telephone*)
Little Bo-Peep	Mother Goose Rhyme, Rhymed Verse, Concept Poem (animals)	Little Bo-Peep has lost her sheep, And doesn't know where to find them. Leave them alone and they'll come home, Wagging their tails behind them.	Recite the first two lines sadly, then be joyful when the sheep return wagging their tails.
Little Jack Horner	Mother Goose Rhyme, Rhymed Verse	Little Jack Horner Sat in a corner, Eating his holiday pie. He stuck in his thumb And pulled out a plum, And said, "What a good boy am I!"	Have children draw, dictate, and write their ideas about what holiday pie might be. Share these "recipes."

* Indicates additional verses not shown

TITLE	CATEGORY	WORDS/LYRICS	ACTIVITIES
Little Miss Muffet	Mother Goose Rhyme, Rhymed Verse, Concept Poem (insects)	Little Miss Muffet, Sat on a tuffet, Eating her curds and whey; Along came a spider, Who sat down beside her, And frightened Miss Muffet away!	Act out the story of the poem with children taking turns playing the parts of Miss Muffet and the spider.
Little Robin Redbreast	Mother Goose Rhyme, Rhymed Verse, Concept Poem (animals), Word Play	Little robin redbreast, Sat upon a rail. Niddle-noodle went his head, Wibble-wobble went his tail.	Have children invent other nonsense words like *niddle-noodle* and *wibble-wobble* that fit the actions of the verse.
London Bridge	Nursery Rhyme, Action Song	London Bridge is falling down, Falling down, falling down, London Bridge is falling down, My fair lady.*	Have children form a bridge by joining their hands, both arms stretched upward, while the other children march under, singing the song. On "My fair lady," the arch falls, capturing the child underneath who becomes an observer.
Mary Had a Little Lamb	Song, Nursery Rhyme, Rhymed Verse, Concept Poem (animals)	Mary had a little lamb, Its fleece was white as snow, And everywhere that Mary went, The lamb was sure to go. It followed her to school one day, Which was against the rule. It made the children laugh and play To see a lamb at school.	Have children draw, dictate, or write a story about Mary and her little lamb.
Mary, Mary, Quite Contrary	Nursery Rhyme, Rhymed Verse	Mary, Mary, quite contrary, How does your garden grow? With silver bells and cockleshells, And pretty maids all in a row.	Discuss what it means to be "contrary. Substitute class "members' names for *Mary*.

TITLE	CATEGORY	WORDS/LYRICS	ACTIVITIES
Old King Cole	Mother Goose Rhyme, Word Play	Old King Cole was a merry old soul, And a merry old soul was he. He called for his pipe, and he called for his bowl, And he called for his fiddlers three. Every fiddler had a fiddle fine, And a very fine fiddle had he, had he. Tweedle dum, tweedle dee, went the fiddlers three, Tweedle dum dee, dum dee deedle dee.	Have children invent other instruments to replace *fiddle*, and new nonsense words to replace *tweedle dum, tweedle dee* that represent the sounds of the new instruments.
One, Two, Buckle My Shoe	Mother Goose Rhyme, Rhymed Verse, Concept Poem (counting, numbers)	One, two, Buckle my shoe. Three, four, Shut the door. Five, six, Pick up sticks. Seven, eight, Lay them straight. Nine, ten, A big fat hen. Let's get up and count again!	Specific motions can be used to pantomime each pair of numbers. After children know the rhyme, write it on a chart using numerals in place of number words.
Pat-a-Cake	Mother Goose Rhyme, Action Poem/Song	Pat-a-cake, pat-a-cake, baker's man, Bake me a cake as fast as you can. Roll it, and prick it, and mark it with a B, And put it in the oven for Baby and me!	Recite in pairs. First two lines: pat hands on thighs, clap hands together at chest level, then put hands out, palms up, to pat partner's hands. Line 3: mime rolling, pricking, and writing a *B* in the air. Line 4: mime putting the cake in the oven, then pretend to cradle a baby.

* Indicates additional verses not shown

TITLE	CATEGORY	WORDS/LYRICS	ACTIVITIES
Pease Porridge Hot	Mother Goose Rhyme, Rhymed Verse	Pease porridge hot, Pease porridge cold, Pease porridge in the pot, Nine days old. Some like it hot, Some like it cold, Some like it in the pot, Nine days old.	Perform the actions of the poem, or divide into two groups and recite and perform alternate lines. Name other opposites like *hot* and *cold*.
Peter, Peter, Pumpkin-Eater	Nursery Rhyme, Mother Goose Rhyme	Peter, Peter, pumpkin-eater, Had a wife and couldn't keep her. He put her in a pumpkin shell, And there he kept her very well.	Ask children what it would be like to live in a pumpkin-shell house. Have them draw a picture and tell about it.
Pop! Goes the Weasel	Nursery Rhyme, Action Song	All around the cobbler's bench, The monkey chased the weasel; The monkey thought it was all in fun, Pop! goes the weasel. A penny for a spool of thread, A penny for a needle; That's the way the money goes, Pop! goes the weasel.	Act out the song with children popping up at the end. Discuss the meaning of *weasel* and *cobbler*.
Rain, Rain, Go Away	Song, Nursery Rhyme, Rhymed Verse	Rain, rain, go away, Come again another day. Little Johnny wants to play; Rain, rain, go away.	Substitute the names of other children in the class for "Johnny." Children can make gentle rain sounds by lightly tapping on desks or tables.
Ring Around the Rosie	Nursery Rhyme, Rhymed Verse, Action Poem/Song	Ring around the rosie, A pocket full of posies, Ashes! Ashes! We all fall down.	Have children join hands and walk in one direction as they say the words. Everyone falls down on the floor at the last line.

TITLE	CATEGORY	WORDS/LYRICS	ACTIVITIES
Row, Row, Row Your Boat	Nursery Rhyme, Rhymed Verse	Row, row, row your boat Gently down the stream; Merrily, merrily, merrily, merrily, Life is but a dream. Row, row, row your boat Down the jungle stream; If you see a crocodile, Don't forget to scream!	Sing the song while miming rowing. When children know the song well they can sing it as a round.
Six Little Ducks	Word Play, Humorous Verse, Concept Song (animals)	Six little ducks that I once knew, Fat ducks, pretty ducks they were too, But the one little duck with the feather on his back, He led the others with a quack-quack-quack. Down to the meadow they would go, Wiggle-wag, wiggle-wag, to and fro, But the one little duck with the feather on his back, He led the others with a quack-quack-quack.	Perform the duck sounds (quack-quack-quack) and actions (wiggle-wag) in the song. Have children substitute other actions for *fat* and *pretty*.
Teddy Bear, Teddy Bear	Nursery Rhyme, Action Poem, Concept Poem (bedtime)	Teddy bear, teddy bear, Turn around. Teddy bear, teddy bear, Touch the ground. Teddy bear, teddy bear, Touch your shoe. Teddy bear, teddy bear, Say howdy-do. Teddy bear, teddy bear, Turn out the light. Teddy bear, teddy bear, Say good night.	Have children perform the actions in the poem. Have children make up their own additional lines and verses.

* Indicates additional verses not shown

TITLE	CATEGORY	WORDS/LYRICS	ACTIVITIES
Three Blind Mice	Mother Goose Rhyme, Rhymed Verse, Concept Poem (animals), Song	Three blind mice, See how they run! They all ran after the farmer's wife, Who cut off their tails with a carving knife; Did you ever see such a sight in your life, As three blind mice?	Make flannelboard figures for the characters in the rhyme. Children can say the rhyme as they move figures around on the board.
Three Little Kittens	Nursery Rhyme, Rhymed Verse, Concept Poem (animals)	Three little kittens, They lost their mittens, And they began to cry, Oh, mother, dear, We sadly fear, Our mittens we have lost. What! Lost your mittens, You naughty kittens, Then you shall have no pie. Meow, meow, Then you shall have no pie.*	Have children make a story map with pictures, one for each verse.
Twinkle, Twinkle, Little Star	Song, Nursery Rhyme, Rhymed Verse	Twinkle, twinkle, little star, How I wonder what you are. Up above the world so high, Like a diamond in the sky. Twinkle, twinkle, little star, How I wonder what you are.	Have children recite the poem aloud, then substitute other words for *little star* and *diamond*, and illustrate the resulting poems with crayons.
To Market, to Market	Nursery Rhyme, Rhymed Verse	To market, to market, to buy a fat pig. Home again, home again, Jiggety jig.*	Have children draw and dictate or write how they might go to market and what they might buy.

TITLE	CATEGORY	WORDS/LYRICS	ACTIVITIES
Wheels on the Bus	Action Song	The wheels on the bus Go 'round and 'round, 'Round and 'round, 'Round and 'round, The wheels on the bus Go 'round and 'round, All around the town.*	Repeat with: wipers on the bus go swish, swish, swish; driver on the bus calls "Move on back!"; people on the bus get up and down; horn on the bus goes beep, beep, beep; baby on the bus cries "Wah, wah, wah"; parents on the bus go, "Shh, shh, shh." Have children perform all of the accompanying actions and sounds as they sing or recite each verse.
Where Is Thumbkin?	Nursery Rhyme, Action Song	Where is Thumbkin? Where is Thumbkin? Here I am, here I am. How are you today, sir? Very well, I thank you. Run away. Run away.*	Sing to the tune of "Are You Sleeping." Have children act out the lines, and then extend the rhyme by substituting all the other fingers, one at a time.

Text Sets

Organized by month and by topic, these sets of great books for preschoolers allow you to explore specific themes of interest to most PreK children.

Age 3

August/September

ANIMAL ALPHABET BOOKS

AUTHOR	TITLE	CITY	PUBLISHER	COPYRIGHT	ISBN
Beaton, Clare	Zoe and Her Zebra	Cambridge, MA	Barefoot Books	1999; 2000	1902283759; 9781902283753
Blackstone, Stella	Alligator Alphabet	Cambridge, MA	Barefoot Books	2005	1841484946; 9781841484945
Duke, Kate	The Guinea Pig ABC	New York	Dutton; Puffin	1983; 1993	0140547568; 9780140547566
Hague, Kathleen	Alphabears	New York	Holt, Rinehart, and Winston	1984	0805062084; 9780805062083
Polacco, Patricia	G Is for Goat	New York	Puffin	2006	0142405507; 9780142405505
Zuckerman, Andrew	Creature ABC	San Francisco	Chronicle Books	2009	0811869784; 9780811869782

GOING TO SCHOOL

Dewdney, Ann	Llama, Llama Misses Mama	New York	Viking	2009	0670061980; 9780670061983
Penn, Audrey	The Kissing Hand	Terre Haute, IN	Tanglewood Press	2007	1933718072; 9781933718071
Shannon, David	David Goes to School	New York	Blue Sky Press	1999	0590480871; 9780590480871
Wells, Rosemary	Timothy Goes to School	New York	Puffin	2000	0140567429; 9780140567427
Yolen, Jane	How Do Dinosaurs Go to School?	New York	Blue Sky Press	2007	0439020816; 9780439020817

WORDLESS BOOKS

Andreasen, Dan	The Treasure Bath	New York	Henry Holt	2009	0805086862; 9780805086867
dePaola, Tomie	The Hunter and the Animals	New York	Holiday House	1981	0823404285; 9780823404285
Hogrogian, Nonny	Cool Cat	New York	Roaring Brook Press (Macmillan)	2009	1596434295; 9781596434295

WORDLESS BOOKS, *CONT.*

Hutchins, Pat	Changes, Changes	New York	Aladdin	1987	0689711379; 9780689711374
Jay, Alison	Welcome to the Zoo	New York	Dial	2008	0803731779; 9780803731776

BEING BRAVE

Bergman, Mara	Snip Snap! What's That?	New York	Greenwillow	2005	0060777540; 9780060777548
Browne, Anthony	Silly Billy	London, UK	Walker Books	2007	1406305766; 9781406305760
Willems, Mo	Leonardo the Terrible Monster	New York	Hyperion	2005	0786852941; 9780786852949
Wilson, Karma	Bear Feels Scared	New York	Margaret K. McElderry	2008	0689859864; 9780689859861

October/November

BEING A FRIEND

Alborough, Jez	My Friend Bear	Cambridge, MA	Candlewick	1998	0590638300; 9780590638302
Browne, Anthony	Willy and Hugh	New York	Alfred A. Knopf; Red Fox	1991; 2000	0099407795; 9780099407799
Howe, James	Horace and Morris Join the Chorus (But What about Dolores?)	New York	Atheneum Books for Young Readers; Aladdin	2002; 2005	1416906169; 9781416906162
Hutchins, Pat	My Best Friend	New York	Greenwillow	1993	0688114857; 9780688114855
Raschka, Chris	Yo! Yes?	New York	Orchard Books; Scholastic	1993; 2007	0439921856; 9780439921855

MOTHER GOOSE AND RHYME BOOKS

Crews, Nina	The Neighborhood Mother Goose	New York	Greenwillow	2003	0060515732; 9780060515737
Elliot, David	On the Farm	New York	Candlewick	2008	0763633224; 9780763633226
Finch, Mary, and Clare Beaton	Playtime Rhymes for Little People	New York	Barefoot Books	2008	184686156X; 9781846861567
Ross, Tony	Three Little Kittens and Other Favorite Nursery Rhymes	New York	Henry Holt	2009	0805088857; 9780805088854

AUTUMN

Ehlert, Lois	Leaf Man	Orlando, FL	Harcourt Children's Books	2005	0152053042; 9780152053048
Rockwell, Anne	Apples and Pumpkins	New York	Macmillan; Aladdin	1989; 2005	1416908315; 9781416908319
Rylant, Cynthia	In November	New York	Sandpiper	2008	0152063420; 9780152063429
Rawlinson, Julia	Fletcher and the Falling Leaves	New York	Greenwillow	2008	00617573973; 9780061573972
Hubbell, Will	Pumpkin Jack	New York	Albert Whitman	2003	0807566667; 9780807566664

GRANDPARENTS

Bowen, Anna	I Loved You Before You Were Born	New York	HarperCollins	2001	0060287217; 9780060287214
dePaola, Tomie	Strega Nona	Englewood Cliffs, NJ	Prentice-Hall; Aladdin	1975; 1979	0671666061; 9780671666064
Dorros, Arthur	Abuela	New York	Puffin	1997	0140562257; 9780140562255
Greenfield, Eloise	Grandpa's Face	New York	Philomel; Putnam Juvenile	1988; 1996	0698113810; 9780698113817
Mayer, Mercer	Grandma, Grandpa, and Me	New York	HarperFestival	2007	0060539518; 9780060539511
Juster, Norton	The Hello, Goodbye Window	New York	Michael di Capua Books; Hyperion Books for Children	2005	0786809140; 9780786809141

THINGS THAT GO

AUTHOR	TITLE	CITY	PUBLISHER	COPYRIGHT	ISBN
Barton, Byron	My Car	New York	Greenwillow	2004	006058940X; 9780060589400
Crews, Donald	Freight Train	New York	Greenwillow	1993	0688129404; 9780688129408
Hubbell, Patricia	Trucks Whizz, Zoom, Rumble	Tarrytown, NY	Marshall Cavendish	2006	0761453288; 9780688158781
Lewis, Kevin	Chugga-Chugga Choo-Choo	New York	Hyperion	2001	0786807601; 9780786807604
London, Jonathan	A Truck Goes Rattley-Bumpa	New York	Henry Holt	2005	0805072330; 9780805072334
McMullan, Kate	I Stink!	New York	HarperCollins	2006	0064438368; 9780064438360
Willems, Mo	Don't Let the Pigeon Drive the Bus	New York	Hyperion	2003	078681988X; 9780078619881
Zelinsky, Paul	The Wheels on the Bus	New York	Dutton	1990	0525446443; 9780525446446

JOURNEYS

AUTHOR	TITLE	CITY	PUBLISHER	COPYRIGHT	ISBN
Degen, Bruce	Jamberry	New York	Harper and Row; HarperCollins	1983	0060214163; 9780060214166
Henkes, Kevin	Kitten's First Full Moon	New York	Greenwillow	2004	0060588284; 9780060588281
McCloskey, Robert	Make Way for Ducklings	New York	Viking; Live Oak Media	1941; 2004	1591127319; 9781591127314
Rosen, Michael	We're Going on a Bear Hunt	New York	Margaret K. McElderry Aladdin	1989; 2003	0689853491; 9780689853494
Van Allsburg, Chris	The Polar Express	Boston	Houghton Mifflin	1985	0395389496; 9780395389492
Williams, Sue	I Went Walking	San Diego	Harcourt Brace Jovanovich; Gulliver Books	1990	0152004718; 9780152004712

AUTHOR STUDY: LOIS EHLERT

AUTHOR	TITLE	CITY	PUBLISHER	COPYRIGHT	ISBN
Ehlert, Lois	Boo to You!	New York	Beach Lane Books (Simon and Schuster)	2009	1416986251; 9781416986256
Ehlert, Lois	Cuckoo/Cucú	San Diego	Harcourt Brace; Turtleback Books/ Sanval	1997; 2001	0613299175; 9780613299176
Ehlert, Lois	Feathers for Lunch	New York	Sandpiper	1996	0152009868; 9780152009861
Ehlert, Lois	Market Day	New York	Sandpiper	2002	0152168206; 9780152168209
Ehlert, Lois	Oodles of Animals	New York	Harcourt	2008	0152062742; 9780152062743
Ehlert, Lois	Wag a Tail	New York	Harcourt	2007	0152058435; 9780152058432

December/January

FUN WITH FOOD

AUTHOR	TITLE	CITY	PUBLISHER	COPYRIGHT	ISBN
Andreasen, Dan	The Baker's Dozen	New York	Henry Holt	2007	0805078096; 9780805078091
Carle, Eric	The Very Hungry Caterpillar	New York	Philomel	2009	0399250395; 9780399259392
Elffers, Joost	Fast Food	New York	Arthur Levine Books	2006	043911019X; 9780439110198
Fleming, Denise	Lunch	New York	Henry Holt	1996	0805046461; 9780805046465
Wells, Rosemary	Bunny Cakes	New York	Puffin	2000	0140566678; 9780140566673

BEING APART

Fleming, Denise	Buster Goes to Cowboy Camp	New York	Henry Holt	2008	0805078924; 9780805078923
Gorbachev, Valerie	The Missing Chick	Boston	Candlewick	2009	0763636762; 9780763636760
Lobel, Anita	Nini Here and There	New York	Greenwillow	2007	0060787678; 9780060787677
Tafuri, Nancy	Have You Seen My Duckling?	New York	Greenwillow	1984; 1991	0688109942; 9780688109943
Willems, Mo	Knuffle Bunny: A Cautionary Tale	New York	Hyperion Books for Children	2004	0786818700; 9780786818709

WINTER

Henkes, Kevin	Oh!	New York	Greenwillow	1999	0688170536; 9780688170530
Keets, Ezra Jack	The Snowy Day	New York	Viking; Puffin	1962; 1976	0140501827; 9780140501827
Shulevitz, Uri	Snow	New York	Farrar Straus Giroux	1998	0374370923; 9780374370923
Stringer, Lauren	Winter Is the Warmest Season	New York	Harcourt	2006	0152049673; 9780152049676

AUTHOR STUDY: LAURA VACCARO SEEGER

Vaccaro Seeger, Laura	Black? White! Day? Night!	New York	Roaring Brook Press (Macmillan)	2006	1596431857; 9781596431850
Vaccaro Seeger, Laura	Dog and Bear	New York	Roaring Brook Press (Macmillan)	2007	1596430532; 9781596430532
Vaccaro Seeger, Laura	First the Egg	New York	Roaring Brook Press (Macmillan)	2007	1596432721; 9781596432727
Vaccaro Seeger, Laura	The Hidden Alphabet	New York	Roaring Brook Press (Macmillan)	2003	0761319417; 9780761319412
Vaccaro Seeger, Laura	One Boy	New York	Roaring Book Press (Macmillan)	2008	1596432748; 9781596432741
Vaccaro Seeger, Laura	Walter Was Worried	New York	Roaring Brook Press (Macmillan)	2005; 2006	1596431962; 9781596431966

BEING YOURSELF

Beaumont, Karen	I Like Myself	New York	Harcourt	2004	0152020136; 9780152020132
Chodos-Irvine, Margaret	Ella Sarah Gets Dressed	San Diego	Harcourt	2003	0152164138; 9780152164133
Falconer, Ian	Olivia	New York	Atheneum	2000	0689829531; 9780689829536
Fleming, Denise	The Cow Who Clucked	New York	Henry Holt	2006	0805072659; 9780805072655
Howe, James	Horace and Morris Join the Chorus (But What about Dolores?)	New York	Atheneum Books for Young Readers; Aladdin	2002; 2005	1416906169; 9781416906162
Kraus, Robert	Leo the Late Bloomer	New York	HarperCollins	1994	006443348X; 9780064433488
Leaf, Munro	The Story of Ferdinand	New York	Viking	1936	0670674249; 9780670674244

RHYMING STORIES/POEMS

Scanlon, Elizabeth Garton	A Sock Is a Pocket for Your Toes: A Pocket Book	New York	HarperCollins	2004	0060295260; 9780060295264
Schertle, Alice	Button Up!	New York	HarperCollins		
Schertle, Alice	Teddy Bear, Teddy Bear	New York	HarperCollins	2003	1422355543; 9781422355541
Spinnelli, Eileen	Do You Have a Hat?	New York	Simon and Schuster	2004	0689862539; 9780689862533
Walton, Rick	The Bear Came Over to My House	New York	Puffin	2003	0698119886; 9780698119888

RHYMING STORIES/POEMS, *CONT.*

AUTHOR	TITLE	CITY	PUBLISHER	COPYRIGHT	ISBN
Weeks, Sarah	Mrs. McNosh Hangs Up Her Wash	New York	HarperCollins	2002	0060004798; 9780060004798
Yolen, Jane, and Andrew Fusek Peters	Here's a Little Poem	New York	Candlewick	2007	0763631418; 9780763631413

DANCE/MOVEMENT

AUTHOR	TITLE	CITY	PUBLISHER	COPYRIGHT	ISBN
Andreae, Giles	Giraffes Can't Dance	New York	Orchard Books	2001	0439287197; 9780439287197
Beaumont, Karen, and Jennifer Plecas	Baby Danced the Polka	New York	Dial Books for Young Readers	2004	0803725876; 9780803725874
Raffi	Shake My Sillies Out	New York	Crown; Crown Books for Young Readers	1987; 1988	0517566478; 9780517566473
Sis, Peter	Ballerina!	New York	Greenwillow	2001	0688179444; 9780688179441
Wilson, Karma	Hilda Must be Dancing	New York	Aladdin	2008	1416950834; 9781416950837

February/March/April

SIBLINGS

AUTHOR	TITLE	CITY	PUBLISHER	COPYRIGHT	ISBN
Winthrop, Elizabeth	Squashed in the Middle	New York	Henry Holt	2005	0805064974; 9780805064971
McPhail, David	Sisters	New York	Harcourt	2003	0152046593; 9780152046590
Wells, Rosemary	Morris's Disappearing Bag	New York	Puffin	2001	0142300047; 9780142300046
Reynolds, Peter	Ish	Cambridge, MA	Candlewick	2004	076362344X; 9780763623449
Henkes, Kevin	Sheila Rae, the Brave	New York	Greenwillow	1996	0688147380; 9780688147389
Banks, Kate	Max's Words	New York	Farrar Straus Giroux	2006	0374399492; 9780374399498
McBratney, Sam	You're All My Favorites	Cambridge, MA	Candlewick	2004	076362442X; 9780763624422
Polacco, Patricia	My Rotten Redheaded Older Brother	New York	Aladdin	1998	0689820364; 9780689820366

OUR COMMUNITY

AUTHOR	TITLE	CITY	PUBLISHER	COPYRIGHT	ISBN
Brett, Jan	The Town Mouse and the Country Mouse	New York	Putnam	2003	069811986X; 9780698119864
Burton, Virginia Lee	The Little House	Boston, MA	Houghton Mifflin	1978	0395181569; 9780395181560
Fleming, Denise	Alphabet Under Construction	New York	Henry Holt	2002; 2006	0805081127; 9780805081121
Hoban, Tana	I Read Signs	New York	Greenwillow; Scholastic	1983	0590486594; 9780590486590
Knudsen, Michelle	Library Lion	Cambridge, MA	Candlewick	2009	076363784X; 9780763637842
Lehman, Barbara	Museum Trip	Boston, MA	Houghton Mifflin	2006	0618581251; 9780618581252
Lobel, Arnold	On Market Street	New York	Greenwillow	1981; 1989	0688087450; 9780688087456

ANIMAL FOLKTALES/FABLES

AUTHOR	TITLE	CITY	PUBLISHER	COPYRIGHT	ISBN
Brett, Jan	Goldilocks and the Three Bears	New York	Dodd, Mead; Putnam Juvenile	1987; 1996	0698113586; 9780698113589
Galdone, Paul	The Little Red Hen	New York	Seabury Press; Sandpiper	1973; 1985	0899193498; 9780899193496
Pinkney, Jerry (adapted from Rudyard Kipling)	Rikki-Tikki-Tavi	New York	HarperCollins	2004	0060587857; 9780060587857

ANIMAL FOLKTALES/FABLES, *CONT.*

Pinkney, Jerry) (adapted from Hans Christian Andersen	The Ugly Duckling	New York	Morrow Junior Books; HarperCollins	1999	068815932X; 9780688159320
Young, Ed	Seven Blind Mice	New York	Philomel; Putnam Juvenile	1992; 2002	0698118952; 9780698118959

SPRING AND PLANTING

Bunting, Eve	Flower Garden	San Diego	Harcourt Brace Jovanovich; Sandpiper	1994; 2000	0152023720; 9780152023720
Carr, Jan	Splish, Splash, Spring	New York	Holiday House	2002	0823417544; 9780823417544
Ehlert, Lois	Growing Vegetable Soup	New York	Sandpiper	1990	0152325808; 9780152325800
Gomi, Taro	Spring is Here	San Francisco	Chronicle Books	1989; 1999	0811823318; 9780811823319
Krauss, Ruth	The Carrot Seed	New York	Harper and Brothers; HarperCollins	1945; 2004	0064432106; 9780064432108
Stevens, Janet	Tops and Bottoms	San Diego	Harcourt Brace	1995	0152928510; 9780152928513
Stewart, Sarah	The Gardener	New York	Farrar Straus Giroux; Square Fish	1997; 2007	031236749X; 9780312367497

AUTHOR STUDY: ROSEMARY WELLS

Wells, Rosemary	Max Cleans Up	New York	Puffin	2002	0142301337; 9780142301333
Wells, Rosemary	Bunny Party	New York	Puffin	2003	014250162X; 9780142501627
Wells, Rosemary	McDuff Moves In	New York	Hyperion	2005	0786856777; 9780786856770
Wells, Rosemary	Yoko's Paper Cranes	New York	Hyperion	2001	0786807377
Wells, Rosemary	Voyage to the Bunny Planet	New York	Viking	2008	0545094518; 9780670011032

ANIMAL COUNTING BOOKS

Baker, Keith	Big Fat Hen	San Diego	Harcourt Brace; Voyager Books	1994; 1999	0152019510; 9780152019518
Baker, Keith	Quack and Count	San Diego	Harcourt Brace; Voyager Books	1999; 2004	0152050256; 9780152050252
Beaton, Clare	One Moose, Twenty Mice	Cambridge, MA	Barefoot Books	2000	1841481297; 9781841481296
Christelow, Eileen	Five Little Monkeys Jumping on the Bed	New York	Clarion Books; Sandpiper	1989; 2006	0618836829; 9780618836826
Ives, Penny (illustrator)	Five Little Ducks	Swindon	Child's Play International	2007	1846431379; 9781846431371
Keats, Ezra Jack	Over in the Meadow	New York	Viking; Puffin	1999	0140565086; 9780140565089
Van Fleet, Mathew	One Yellow Lion	New York	Dial Books for Young Readers	1992	0803710992; 9780803710993

A BAD DAY

Bang, Molly	When Sophie Gets Angry, Really, Really Angry	New York	Blue Sky Press; Scholastic	1999	0439213193; 9780439213196
Carle, Eric	The Grouchy Ladybug	New York	T.Y. Crowel; HarperCollins	1977; 1996	0064434508; 9780064434508
Sendak, Maurice	Where the Wild Things Are	New York	Harper and Row; Harper Collins	1963; 1988	0060254920; 9780060254926
Shannon, David	No, David!	New York	Blue Sky Press	1998	0590930028; 9780590930024
Urban, Linda	Mouse Was Mad	Boston	Houghton Mifflin	2009	0152053379; 9780152053376
Wilson, Karma	Bear Feels Sick	New York	Margaret K. McElderry	2007	0689859856; 9780689859854

BEING CREATIVE/ART

AUTHOR	TITLE	CITY	PUBLISHER	COPYRIGHT	ISBN
Arnold, Katya	Elephants Can Paint Too	New York	Atheneum Books for Young Readers	2005	0689869851; 9780689869853
Beaumont, Karen	I Ain't Gonna Paint No More!	Orlando, FL	Harcourt Children's Books	2005	0152024883; 9780152024888
Johnson, Crockett	Harold and the Purple Crayon	New York	Harper and Row; HarperCollins	1955; 1998	0064430227; 9780064430227
McDonnell, Patrick	Art	Boston, MA	Little, Brown	2006	031611491X; 9780316114912
Reynolds, Peter	Ish	Cambridge, MA	Candlewick	2004	076362344X; 9780763623449
Reynolds, Peter	The Dot	Cambridge, MA	Candlewick	2003	0763619612; 9780763619619

BEDTIME

AUTHOR	TITLE	CITY	PUBLISHER	COPYRIGHT	ISBN
Asch, Frank	Barnyard Lullaby	New York	Aladdin	2001	0689842562; 9780689842566
Cousins, Lucy	Maisy's Bedtime	New York	Candlewick	1999	0763609080; 9780763609085
Fox, Mem	Time for Bed	New York	Red Wagon Books	1997	0152010661; 9780152010669
Rathman, Peggy	Goodnight, Gorilla	New York	Putnam	2000	0698116496; 9780698116498
Rothstein, Gloria L.	Sheep Asleep	New York	HarperColllins	2003	0060291052; 9780060291051
Shea, Bob	Dinosaur Vs. Bedtime!	New York	Hyperion	2008	1423113357; 9781423113355
Weeks, Sarah	Counting Ovejas	New York	Atheneum Books for Young Readers	2006	0689867506; 9780689867507
Wood, Audrey	Piggies	New York	Voyager Books	1995	0152002170; 9780152002176

AUTHOR STUDY: DONALD CREWS

AUTHOR	TITLE	CITY	PUBLISHER	COPYRIGHT	ISBN
Crews, Donald	Bigmama's	New York	Greenwillow	1991	0688158420; 9780688158422
Crews, Donald	Freight Train	New York	Greenwillow	1978; 1993	0688129404; 9780688129408
Crews, Donald	Sail Away	New York	Greenwillow	2000	0688175171; 9780688175177
Crews, Donald	Shortcut	New York	Greenwillow	1996	0688135765; 9780688135768
Crews, Donald	Ten Black Dots	New York	Scribner; Greenwillow	1968; 1995	0688135749
Crews, Donald	Truck	New York	Greenwillow	1991	0673816931; 9780688104818

May/June

MOMS AND DADS

AUTHOR	TITLE	CITY	PUBLISHER	COPYRIGHT	ISBN
Browne, Anthony	My Mom	New York	Farrar Straus Giroux	2009	0374400261; 9780374400262
Mayer, Mercer	Just Me and My Mom	New York	Random House	2001	030712584X; 9780307125842
Dorros, Arthur	Papá and Me	New York	HarperCollins; Rayo	2008	0060581565; 9780060581565
Kasza, Keiko	A Mother for Choco	New York	Putnam	1996	0698113640; 9780698113640
McBratney, Sam	Guess How Much I Love You	Cambridge, MA	Candlewick	1995; 2008	0763641758; 9780763641757
Simmons, Jane	Come Along, Daisy	Boston	Little, Brown	1998	0316797901; 9780316797900
Spinelli, Eileen	When Mama Comes Home Tonight	New York	Simon and Schuster	1998	0689810652
Williams, Vera B.	A Chair for My Mother	New York	Greenwillow	1984	0688040748; 9780688040741

YOUR BODY

Asim, Jabari	Whose Knees Are These?	New York	LB Kids	2006	0316735760; 9780316735766
Bang, Molly	A Book of Thanks (All of Me!)	New York	Blue Sky Press	2009	0545044243; 9780545044240
Kubler, Annie	Ten Little Fingers	Swindon	Child's Play International	2003	0859536106; 9780859536103
Raschka, Chris	Five for a Little One	New York	Atheneum	2006	069845995; 9780689845994

MOTHER NATURE

Ehlert, Lois	Waiting for Wings	San Diego	Harcourt Children's Books	2001	0152026088; 9780152026080
Fleming, Denise	In the Tall, Tall Grass	New York	Henry Holt	1991; 1995	0805039414; 9780805039412
Frasier, Debra	Out of the Ocean	New York	Harcourt	1998	0152163549; 9780152163549
Schaefer, Lola	This Is the Rain	New York	Greenwillow	2001	0688170390; 9780688170390
Vaccaro Seeger, Laura	First the Egg	New York	Roaring Brook Press	2007	1596432721; 9781596432727

COLORS

Carle, Eric	Brown Bear, Brown Bear, What Do You See?	New York	Henry Holt	1992; 2008	0805087184; 9780805087185
Ehlert, Lois	Color Farm	New York	Lippincott; HarperCollins	1990	0397324405; 9780397324408
Fox, Mem	Where Is the Green Sheep?	Orlando	Harcourt	2004	015204907X; 9780152049072
Gonzalez, Maya Christina	My Colors, My World	San Francisco, CA	Children's Book Press	2007	0892392215; 9780892392216
Hoban, Tana	Colors Everywhere	New York	Greenwillow	1995	0688127622; 9780688127626
Seeger, Laura Vaccaro	Lemons Are Not Red	Brookfield, CT	Roaring Brook Press	2004; 2006	1596431954; 9781596431959
Wood, Audrey and Bruce	The Deep Blue Sea: A Book of Colors	New York	Blue Sky Press	2005	0439753821; 9780439753821
Young, Ed	Seven Blind Mice	New York	Philomel; Putnam Juvenile	1992; 2002	0698118952; 9780698118959

AUTHOR STUDY: TANA HOBAN

Hoban, Tana	26 Letters and 99 Cents	New York	Greenwillow	1987; 1995	068814389X; 9780688143893
Hoban, Tana	Black & White	New York	HarperCollins	2007	0061172111; 9780061172113
Hoban, Tana	Exactly the Opposite	New York	Greenwillow	1997	0688154735; 9780688154738
Hoban, Tana	Is It Larger? Is It Smaller?	New York	Greenwillow	1997	0688152872; 9780688152871
Hoban, Tana	Is It Red? Is It Yellow? Is It Blue? An Adventure in Color	New York	Greenwillow	1978; 1987	0688070345; 9780688070342
Hoban, Tana	Over, Under &Through	New York	Aladdin	2008	1416975411; 9781416975410

MUSIC

Ackerman, Karen	Song and Dance Man	New York	Knopf Books for Young Readers	1988; 2003	0394893301; 9780394893303
Isadora, Rachel	Ben's Trumpet	New York	Greenwillow; Live Oak Media	1979; 1998	0874994330; 9780874994339
Moss, Lloyd	Zin! Zin! Zin! A Violin	New York	Simon and Schuster Books for Young Readers; Aladdin	1995; 2000	0689835248; 9780689835247
Twin, Michael	The Musical Life of Gustav Mole	Swinden, UK	Child's Play International	1990	0859533476; 9780859533478
Wheeler, Lisa	Jazz Baby	Orlando	Harcourt Children's Books	2007	0152025227; 9780152025229

Age 4

August/September

GOING TO SCHOOL

AUTHOR	TITLE	CITY	PUBLISHER	COPYRIGHT	ISBN
Kim, Joung Un, and Pak, Soyung	Sumi's First Day of School Ever	New York	Viking	2003	067003522X; 9780670035229
London, Jonathan	Froggy Goes to School	New York	Viking	1996	0670867268; 9780670867264
Reynolds, Peter	The Dot	Cambridge, MA	Candlewick	2003	0763619612; 9780763619619
Wells, Rosemary	Yoko	New York	Hyperion	2009	1423119835; 9781423119838
Wilson, Karma	Sweet Briar Goes to School	New York	Puffin	2005	0142402818; 9780142402818

WORDLESS BOOKS

AUTHOR	TITLE	CITY	PUBLISHER	COPYRIGHT	ISBN
Banyai, Istvan	Zoom	New York	Puffin	1998	0140557741; 9780140557749
Day, Alexandra	Good Dog, Carl	New York	Little Simon	1996	0689807481; 9780689807480
dePaola, Tomie	Pancakes for Breakfast	Boston, MA	Sandpiper (Houghton Mifflin)	1978	0156707683; 9780156707688
Jenkins, Steve	Looking Down	Boston, MA	Sandpiper (Houghton Mifflin)	2003	0618310983; 9780618310982
Lehman, Barbara	Trainstop	Boston, MA	Houghton Mifflin	2008	061875640X; 9780618756407
McDonnell, Patrick	South	Boston, MA	Little, Brown	2008	0316005096

AUTHOR STUDY: DENISE FLEMING

AUTHOR	TITLE	CITY	PUBLISHER	COPYRIGHT	ISBN
Fleming, Denise	Alphabet Under Construction	New York	Henry Holt	2002; 2006	0805081127; 9780805081121
Fleming, Denise	Buster Goes to Cowboy Camp	New York	Henry Holt	2008	0805078924; 9780805078923
Fleming, Denise	The Everything Book	New York	Henry Holt	2000; 2009	0805088695; 9780805088694
Fleming, Denise	In the Small, Small Pond	New York	Henry Holt	1993; 2007	0805081178; 9780805081176
Fleming, Denise	In the Tall, Tall Grass	New York	Henry Holt	1991; 1995	0805039414; 9780805039412

MOTHER GOOSE AND RHYME BOOKS

AUTHOR	TITLE	CITY	PUBLISHER	COPYRIGHT	ISBN
Lass, Bonnie, and Sturges, Philemon	Who Took the Cookies from the Cookie Jar?	Boston	Little, Brown	2000	0316820164; 9780316820165
Miranda, Anne	To Market, to Market	New York	Harcourt	2007	0152163980; 9780152163983
O'Connor, Jane	Ready, Set, Skip!	New York	Viking	2007	0142414239; 9780142414231
Schertle, Alice	Button Up!	New York	HarperCollins	2009	
Yolen, Jane, and Fusek Peters, Andrew	Here's a Little Poem	New York	Candlewick	2007	0763631418; 9780763631413

October/November

AUTUMN

AUTHOR	TITLE	CITY	PUBLISHER	COPYRIGHT	ISBN
Arnosky, Jim	Every Autumn Comes the Bear	New York	Putnam	1996	0698114051; 9780698114050
Rylant, Cynthia	In November	New York	Sandpiper	2008	0152063420; 9780152063429
Schnur, Steven	Autumn: An Alphabet Acrostic	New York	Clarion Books	1997	0395770432; 9780395770436
Spinelli, Eileen	I Know It's Autumn	New York	HarperCollins	2004	0060294221' 9780060294229

FOOD

Hoban, Russell	Bread and Jam for Frances	New York	HarperCollins	2008	0060838000; 9780060838003
Robart, Rose	The Cake that Mack Ate	Toronto	Kids Can Press; Little, Brown Books for Young Readers	1986; 1991	0316748919; 9780316748919
Rosenthal, Amy Krouse	Little Pea	San Francisco	Chronicle Books	2005	081184658X; 9780811846585
Steig, William	Pete's a Pizza	New York	HarperCollins	1998	0062051578; 9780062051578
Waber, Bernard	Fast Food! Gulp! Gulp!	Boston	Houghton Mifflin; Sandpiper	2001; 2005	0618555617; 9780618555611

ALPHABET BOOKS

Azzarian, Mary	A Farmer's Alphabet	Boston	David R. Godine	1981; 2005	087923394X; 9780879233945
Ehlert, Lois	Eating the Alphabet	San Diego	Harcourt Brace Jovanovich; Harcourt Big Books	1989; 1994	0152009027; 9780152009021
Ernst, Lisa Campbell	The Turn-Around, Upside-Down Alphabet Book	New York	Simon and Schuster Books for Young Readers	2004	0689856857; 9780689856853
Fleming, Denise	Alphabet Under Construction	New York	Henry Holt	2002; 2006	0805081127; 9780805081121
Johnson, Stephen	Alphabet City	New York	Viking; Puffin	1995; 1999	0140559043; 9780140559040
Lobel, Arnold	On Market Street	New York	Greenwillow	1981; 1989	0688087450; 9780688087456
Martin, Bill	Chicka, Chicka Boom Boom	New York	Simon and Schuster Books for Young Readers; Beach Lane Books	1989; 2009	1416990917; 9781416990918
Seeger, Laura Vaccaro	The Hidden Alphabet	Brookfield, CT	Roaring Brook Press	2003	0761319417; 9780761319412

YOUR BODY

Aliki	My Five Senses	New York	Harper Festival	1991	0060200502; 9780060200503
Barner, Bob	Dem Bones	San Francisco	Chronicle Books	1996	0811808270; 9780811808279
Carle, Eric	From Head to Toe	New York	HarperFestival	2007	0061119725; 9780061119729
Gershator, Phillis	Zzzing! Zzzing! Zzzing! A Yoruba Tale	New York	Orchard Books	1998	0531095231; 9780531095232
Martin, Bill Jr.	Here Are My Hands	New York	Henry Holt	2007	0805081194; 9780805081190

AUTHOR STUDY: PEGGY RATHMAN

Rathman, Peggy	10 Minutes Till Bedtime	New York	Puffin	2004	0142400246; 9780142400241
Rathman, Peggy	Goodnight, Gorilla	New York	Putnam	2000	0698116496; 9780698116498
Rathman, Peggy	Officer Buckle and Gloria	New York	Putnam Juvenile	1995	0399226168; 9780399226168
Rathman, Peggy	The Day the Babies Crawled Away	New York	Putnam Juvenile	2003	039923196X; 9780399231964

BEDTIME

Aliki	All By Myself!	New York	HarperColllins	2003	0064462536; 9780064462532
Dewdney, Anna	Llama Llama Red Pajama	New York	Viking	2005	0670059838; 9780670059836
Dunbar, Joyce	Tell Me Something Happy Before I Go to Sleep	New York	Harcourt	1998	015201795X; 9780152017958
Markes, Julie	Shhhh! Everybody's Sleeping	New York	HarperCollins	2005	0060537906; 9780060537906
Mayer, Mercer	Just Go to Bed!	New York	Random House	2001	0307119408; 9780307119407
Thomas, Shelly Moore	Good Night, Good Knight	New York	Dutton; Puffin	2000; 2002	0142302015; 9780142302019
Wood, Audrey	The Napping House	New York	Harcourt	1991	0152567119; 9780152567118

PARTNERS IN FRIENDSHIP

AUTHOR	TITLE	CITY	PUBLISHER	COPYRIGHT	ISBN
Browne, Anthony	Willy and Hugh	New York	Alfred A. Knopf; Red Fox	1991; 2000	0099407795; 9780099407799
Buck, Nola	Sid and Sam	New York	HarperCollins	1996; 1997	00644211X; 9780064442114
Dunrea, Olivier	Gossie and Gertie	Boston	Houghton Mifflin	2002	0618176764; 9780618176762
George, Jean Craighead	Goose and Duck	New York	Laura Geringer Books; HarperCollins	2008	0061170763; 9780061170768
Gutman, Anne	Gaspard and Lisa Friends Forever	New York	Alfred A. Knopf	2003	0375822534; 9780375822537
Hobbie, Holly	Toot and Puddle	Boston	Little, Brown	1997; 2007	0316167029; 9780316167024
Lobel, Arnold	Frog and Toad Are Friends	New York	Harper and Row	1970	0439655595; 9780439655590

December/January

WINTER

Bond, Rebecca	This Place in the Snow	New York	Dutton	2004	0525473084; 9780525473084
Gershator, Phillis	When It Starts to Snow	New York	Henry Holt	2001	0805067655; 9780805067651
Stewart, Melissa	Under the Snow	Atlanta, GA	Peachtree	2009	1561454931; 9781561454938
Tresselt, Alvin	White Snow, Bright Snow	New York	HarperCollins	1947	0688511619; 9780688511616
Yolen, Jane	Owl Moon	New York	Philomel	1987	0399214577; 9780399214578

BEING BRAVE

Browne, Anthony	Silly Billy	London, UK	Walker Books	2007	1406305766; 9781406305760
Emberley, Ed	Go Away Big Green Monster	Boston	Little, Brown	1992	0316236535; 9780316236539
Henkes, Kevin	Chrysanthemum	New York	Greenwillow	2007	061119741; 9780061119743
Nivola, Claire	The Forest	New York	Farrar Straus Giroux	2002	0374324522; 9780374324520
Waber, Bernard	Courage	Boston	Houghton Mifflin	2002	0618238557; 9780618238552

NUMBERS/COUNTING

Bang, Molly	Ten, Nine, Eight	New York	Greenwillow	1983; 1991	0688104800; 9780688104801
Crews, Donald	Ten Black Dots	New York	Scribner; Greenwillow	1968; 1995	0688135749
Ehlert, Lois	Fish Eyes: A Book You Can Count On	San Diego	Harcourt Brace Jovanovich; Voyager Books	1990; 1992	0152280510; 9780152280512
Falconer, Ian	Olivia Counts	New York	Atheneum Books for Young Readers; Simon and Schuster Children's Publishing	2002	0689836732; 9780689836732
Hoban, Tana	1, 2, 3	New York	Greenwillow	1985	068802579X; 9780688025793
Katz, Karen	Counting Kisses	New York	Margaret K. McElderry	2001	0689834705; 9780689834707
Kubler, Annie	Ten Little Fingers	Swindon	Child's Play International	2003	0859536106; 9780859536103
Seeger, Laura Vaccaro	One Boy	New York	Roaring Book Press	2008	1596432748; 9781596432741

SEPARATION

Coffelt, Nancy	Fred Stays With Me!	New York	Little, Brown	2007	0316882690; 9780316882699
Taback, Sims	I Miss You Every Day	New York	Viking	2007	0670061921; 9780670061921

SEPARATION, *CONT.*

| Van Laan, Nancy | Little Fish, Lost | New York | Atheneum Books for Young Readers | 1998 | 0689843720; 9780689843723 |
| Waber, Bernard | Ira Sleeps Over | Boston | Houghton Mifflin | 1972; 1973 | 0395138930; 9780395138939 |

ANIMAL FOLKTALES/FABLES

Brett, Jan	The Three Snow Bears	New York	Putnam	2007	0399247920; 9780399247927
Galdone, Paul	The Old Woman and Her Pig		McGraw-Hill	1960	0070227217; 9780070227217
Marshall, James	The Three Little Pigs	New York	Dial Books for Young Readers	1989	0803705913; 9780803705913
McDermott, Gerald	Raven: A Trickster Tale from the Pacific Northwest	San Diego	Harcourt Brace Jovanovich; Sandpiper	1993; 2001	0152024492; 9780152024499
Pinkney, Jerry	The Lion and the Mouse	New York	Little, Brown	2007	0316013560; 9780316013567

AUTHOR STUDY: JERRY PINKNEY

Pinkney, Jerry	Little Red Riding Hood	New York	Little, Brown	2007	0316013552; 9780316013550
Pinkney, Jerry	The Lion and the Mouse	New York	Little, Brown	2007	0316013560; 9780316013567
Pinkney, Jerry (adapted from Rudyard Kipling)	Rikki-Tikki-Tavi	New York	HarperCollins	2004	0060587857; 9780060587857
Pinkney, Jerry	Three Little Kittens	New York	Dial	2010	0803735332; 9780803735330
Pinkney, Jerry (adapted from Hans Christian Andersen)	The Ugly Duckling	New York	Morrow Junior Books; HarperCollins	1999	068815932X; 9780688159320

COLORS

Barry, Francis	Duckie's Rainbow	Cambridge, MA	Candlewick; Walker Books	2003; 2004	0744596467; 9780744596465
Ehlert, Lois	Color Zoo	New York	Lippincott; HarperCollins	1989	0397322593; 9780397322596
Feeney, Stephanie	Hawaii Is a Rainbow	Honolulu	University of Hawaii Press	1985	0824810074; 9780824810078
Katz, Karen	The Color of Us	New York	Henry Holt	1999; 2007	0805081186; 9780805081183
Larios, Julie	Yellow Elephant	Orlando	Harcourt	2006	0152054227; 9780152054229
Lionni, Leo	A Color of His Own	New York	Pantheon Books; Knopf Books for Young Readers	1975; 2006	0375836977; 9780375836978
Mockford, Caroline	Cleo's Color Book	Cambridge, MA	Barefoot Books	2006	1905236301; 9781905236305

ANIMALS IN THE WILD

Arnosky, Jim	Raccoon on His Own	New York	Puffin	2003	0142500712; 9780142500712
Butler, John	Can You Growl Like a Bear?	Atlanta	Peachtree	2007	156145396X; 9781561453962
Henkes, Kevin	Old Bear	New York	Greenwillow	2008	0061552054; 9780061552052
Jenkins, Steve, and Page, Robin	Move!	New York	Houghton Mifflin	2006	061864637X; 9780618646371
Jenkins, Steve	What Do You Do With a Tail Like This?	Boston	Houghton Mifflin	2003	0618256288; 9780618256280
Lunde, Darrin	Hello, Bumblebee Bat	Watertown, MA	Charlesbridge	2007	1570913749; 9781570913747
Tafuri, Nancy	The Busy Little Squirrel	New York	Simon and Schuster	2007	0689873417; 9780689873416

February/March/April

IMAGINATION

AUTHOR	TITLE	CITY	PUBLISHER	COPYRIGHT	ISBN
Grey, Mini	Traction Man Is Here!	New York	Alfred A. Knopf	2005	0375831916; 9780375831911
Johnson, Crockett	Harold and the Purple Crayon	New York	Harper and Row; HarperCollins	1955; 1998	0064430227; 9780064430227
Lehman, Barbara	The Red Book	Boston	Houghton Mifflin	2004	0618428585; 9780618428588
Sendak, Maurice	In the Night Kitchen	New York	Harper Collins	1996	0060266686; 9780060266684
Wiesner, David	Flotsam	New York	Clarion Books	2006	0618194576; 9780618194575
Wright, Joanna	The Secret Circus	New York	Roaring Brook Press	2009	1596434031; 9781596434035

CUMULATIVE STORIES

AUTHOR	TITLE	CITY	PUBLISHER	COPYRIGHT	ISBN
Bond, Felicia	Tumble Bumble	Asheville, NC; New York	Front Street; Harper Collins	1996; 2000	0064435857; 9780064435857
Burningham, John	Mr. Gumpy's Outing	New York	Holt, Rinehart and Winston; Henry Holt	1970; 1995	080503854X; 9780805038545
Emberley, Barbara	Drummer Hoff	Englewood Cliffs, NJ	Prentice-Hall; Aladdin	1967; 1972	067166249X; 9780671662493
Low, Joseph	Mice Twice	New York	Atheneum; Aladdin	1980; 1986	0689710607; 9780689710605
Swanson, Susan Marie	The House in the Night	Boston	Houghton Mifflin	2008	0618862447; 9780618862443
Taback, Simms	This Is the House that Jack Built	New York	G.P. Putnam's Sons; Puffin	2002; 2004	0142402001; 9780142402009

MOTHER NATURE

AUTHOR	TITLE	CITY	PUBLISHER	COPYRIGHT	ISBN
Allen, Marjorie N.	Changes	New York	Macmillan	1991	0021790698; 9780021790692
James, Simon	The Wild Woods	Cambridge, MA	Candlewick	1993	1406308455; 9781406308457
Tresselt, Alvin	Rain Drop Splash	New York	Lothrop, Lee and Shepard; HarperCollins	1946; 1990	0688093523; 9780688093525
Udry, Janice May	A Tree Is Nice	New York	Harper; HarperCollins	1956; 1987	0064431479; 9780064431477
Zolotow, Charlotte	The Storm Book	New York	HarperCollins	1952; 1989	0064431940; 9780064431941

AUTHOR STUDY: MO WILLEMS

AUTHOR	TITLE	CITY	PUBLISHER	COPYRIGHT	ISBN
Willems, Mo	Don't Let the Pigeon Drive the Bus	New York	Hyperion Books for Children	2003	078681988X; 9780786819881
Willems, Mo	The Pigeon Finds a Hot Dog	New York	Hyperion Books for Children	2004	0786818697; 9780786818693
Willems, Mo	Knuffle Bunny: A Cautionary Tale	New York	Hyperion Books for Children	2004	0786818700; 9780786818709
Willems, Mo	Knuffle Bunny Too: A Case of Mistaken Identity	New York	Hyperion Books for Children	2007	1423102991; 9781423102991
Willems, Mo	Leonardo the Terrible Monster	New York	Hyperion	2005	0786852941; 9780786852949

FAMILIES

AUTHOR	TITLE	CITY	PUBLISHER	COPYRIGHT	ISBN
Chodos-Irvine, Margaret	Ella Sarah Gets Dressed	San Diego	Harcourt	2003	0152164138; 9780152164133
Coffelt, Nancy	Fred Stays With Me!	New York	Little, Brown	2007	0316882690; 9780316882699
Crews, Donald	Bigmama's	New York	Greenwillow	1991	0688158420; 9780688158422

FAMILIES, *CONT.*

Rylant, Cynthia	The Relatives Came	New York	Bradbury Press; Live Oak Media	1985; 2005	0874995329; 9780874995329
Williams, Vera B.	"More More More," Said the Baby	New York	Greenwillow	1990; 1996	0688147364; 9780688147365

RHYMING STORIES

Low, Alice	Aunt Lucy Went to Buy a Hat	New York	HarperCollins	2004	0060089717; 9780060089719
Marzollo, Jean	Pretend You're a Cat	New York	Dial	1990	0140559930; 9780140559934
Scanlon, Elizabeth Garton	A Sock Is a Pocket for Your Toes: A Pocket Book	New York	HarperCollins	2004	0060295260; 9780060295264
Schertle, Alice	Teddy Bear, Teddy Bear	New York	HarperCollins	2003	1422355543; 9781422355541
Spinnelli, Eileen	Do You Have a Hat?	New York	Simon and Schuster	2004	0689862539; 9780689862533
Walton, Rick	The Bear Came Over to My House	New York	Puffin	2003	0698119886; 9780698119888
Weeks, Sarah	Mrs. McNosh Hangs Up Her Wash	New York	HarperCollins	2002	0060004798; 9780060004798

MOODS

Curtis, Jamie Lee	Today I Feel Silly and Other Moods That Make My Day	New York	HarperCollins	1998	0060245603; 9780060245603
Dannenberg, Julie	First Day Jitters	Watertown, MA	Charlesbridge	2000	158089061X; 9781580890618
Numeroff, Laura	Beatrice Doesn't Want To	New York; Cambridge, MA	F. Watts; Candlewick	1981; 2008	0763638439; 9780763638436
Shoshan, Beth	That's When I'm Happy	New York	Parragon	2007	1405495383; 9781405495387
Urban, Linda	Mouse Was Mad	Boston	Houghton Mifflin	2009	0152053379; 9780152053376

AUTHOR STUDY: LEO LIONNI

Lionni, Leo	A Busy Year	New York	Alfred A. Knopf; David McKay	1992; 2004	0679824642; 9780679824640
Lionni, Leo	A Color of His Own	New York	Pantheon Books; Knopf Books for Young Readers	1975; 2006	0375836977; 9780375836978
Lionni, Leo	Frederick	New York	Pantheon	1967	378769577X; 9783787695775
Lionni, Leo	It's Mine!	New York	Alfred A. Knopf; Dragonfly Books	1986; 1996	0679880844; 9780679880844
Lionni, Leo	Swimmy	New York	Pantheon; Dragonfly Books	1963; 1973	0394826205; 9780394826202

CLASSIC STORIES

Bemelmans, Ludwig	Madeline	New York	Simon and Schuster; Viking	1939; 1967	0670445800; 9780670445806
Milne, A. A.	The Complete Tales of Winnie the Pooh	New York	Dutton Children's Books	1994; 1996	0525457232; 9780525457237
Eastman, P.D.	Are You My Mother?	New York	Beginner Books; Random House Books for Young Readers	1960; 1966	0394900189; 9780394900186
Gag, Wanda	Millions of Cats	New York	Coward-McCann; Puffin	1928; 2006	0142407089; 9780142407080
Potter, Beatrix	The Tale of Peter Rabbit	Springfield, MA	McLoughlin Brothers; Frederick Warne	1928; 2002	0723247706; 9780723247708
Rey, H.A.	Curious George	Boston	Houghton Mifflin	1941; 1998	0395922720; 9780395922729
Slobodkina, Esphyr	Caps for Sale	New York	W. R. Scott; HarperFestival	1940; 2008	0061474533; 9780061474538

CLASSIC STORIES, *CONT.*

AUTHOR	TITLE	CITY	PUBLISHER	COPYRIGHT	ISBN
Dr. Seuss	The Cat in the Hat	New York	Random House; Random House Books for Young Readers	1957; 1966	0394900014; 9780394900018
Wise Brown, Margaret	The Runaway Bunny	New York and London	Harper; HarperCollins	1942; 2005	0060775823; 9780060775827

May/June

AUTHOR STUDY: MERCER MAYER

AUTHOR	TITLE	CITY	PUBLISHER	COPYRIGHT	ISBN
Mayer, Mercer	Just for You	New York	Random House	1998	030711838X; 9780307118387
Mayer, Mercer	There's an Alligator Under My Bed	New York	Dial	1987	0803703740; 9780803703742
Mayer, Mercer	A Boy, a Dog, and a Frog	New York	Dial	2003	0803728808; 9780803728806
Mayer, Mercer	The Bravest Knight	New York	Dial	2007	0803732066; 9780803732063
Mayer, Mercer	There's Something in My Attic	New York	Puffin	1992	0140548130; 9780140548136

OCEAN LIFE

AUTHOR	TITLE	CITY	PUBLISHER	COPYRIGHT	ISBN
Baker, Jeannie	Where the Forest Meets the Sea	New York	Greenwillow	1987; 1988	0688063632; 9780688063634
Frasier, Debra	Out of the Ocean	New York	Harcourt	1998	0152163549; 9780152163549
Lee, Suzy	Wave	San Francisco	Chronicle Books	2008	081185924X; 9780811859240
Lionni, Leo	Swimmy	New York	Pantheon; Dragonfly Books	1963; 1973	0394826205; 9780394826202
Pfister, Marcus	The Rainbow Fish	New York	North-South Books	1992; 1995	1558584412; 9781558584419
Van Laan, Nancy	Little Fish, Lost	New York	Atheneum Books for Young Readers	1998	0689843720; 9780689843723
Wiesner, David	Flotsam	New York	Clarion Books	2006	0618194576; 9780618194575

SIDEKICKS

AUTHOR	TITLE	CITY	PUBLISHER	COPYRIGHT	ISBN
Bianco, Margery Williams	The Velveteen Rabbit	New York	George H. Doran; HCI	1922; 2005	0757303331; 9780757303333
Burton, Virginia Lee	Mike Mulligan and His Steam Shovel	Boston	Houghton Mifflin	1939; 1993	0395259398; 9780395259399
de Regniers, Beatrice Schenk	May I Bring a Friend?	New York	Atheneum; Aladdin	1964; 1989	0689713533; 9780689713538
Freeman, Don	Corduroy	New York	Viking	1968; 2008	0670063363; 9780670063369
Omerod, Jan	Miss Mouse's Day	New York	HarperCollins	2001	0688163334; 9780688163334
Rathmann, Peggy	Officer Buckle and Gloria	New York	Putnam Juvenile	1995	0399226168; 9780399226168

FOLKTALES/FABLES

AUTHOR	TITLE	CITY	PUBLISHER	COPYRIGHT	ISBN
Brett, Jan	The Gingerbread Baby	New York	Putnam	1999	0399234446; 9780399234446
Dayrell, Elphinstone	Why the Sun and the Moon Live in the Sky	Boston	Houghton Mifflin; Sandpiper	1968; 1990	0395539637; 9780395539637
dePaola, Tomie	The Legend of the Bluebonnet	New York	Putnam	1983; 1996	0698113594; 9780698113596
Ehlert, Lois	Moon Rope	San Diego	Harcourt Brace Jovanovich; Voyager Books	1992; 2003	015201702X; 9780152017026

FOLKTALES/FABLES, *CONT.*

Gilman, Phoebe	Something from Nothing	New York	Scholastic	1992	0590472801; 9780590472807
Haley, Gail	A Story, A Story	New York	Atheneum	1970	0689205112; 9780689205118
Sedgwick, Marcus (adapted from Hans Christian Andersen)	The Emperor's New Clothes	San Francisco	Chronicle Books	2004	0811845699; 9780811845694
Shulevitz, Uri	The Treasure	New York	Farrar Straus Giroux	1978; 1979	0374377405; 9780374377403
Taback, Simms	There Was an Old Lady Who Swallowed a Fly	New York	Viking	1997	0670869392; 9780670869398

PETS

Bauer, Marion Dane	If You Were Born a Kitten	New York	Aladdin	2001	0689842120; 9780689842122
Broach, Elise	Wet Dog!	New York	Dial	2005	0142408557; 9780142408551
Harper, Dan	Sit, Truman!	New York	Sandpiper	2004	015205068X; 9780152050689
Harper, Isabelle	My Cats Nick and Nora	New York	Blue Sky Press	2002	0590476351; 9780590476355
LaRochelle, David	The Best Pet of All	New York	Puffin	2009	0142412724; 9780142412725
Lee, Hector Viveros	I Had a Hippopotamus	New York	Lee and Low Books	1998	1880000628; 9781880000625
McCarty, Peter	Hondo and Fabian	New York	Henry Holt; Square Fish	2002; 2007	0312367473; 9780312367473
Roth, Susan	Great Big Guinea Pigs	London	Bloomsbury	2006	1582347247; 9781582347240

AUTHOR STUDY: BARBARA LEHMAN

Lehman, Barbara	Museum Trip	Boston, MA	Houghton Mifflin	2006	0618581251; 9780618581252
Lehman, Barbara	Rainstorm	Boston, MA	Houghton Mifflin	2007	0618756396; 9780618756391
Lehman, Barbara	The Red Book	Boston	Houghton Mifflin	2004	0618428585; 9780618428588
Lehman, Barbara	Trainstop	Boston, MA	Houghton Mifflin	2008	061875640X; 9780618756407

Inquiry Projects

In this section you will find twelve inquiry projects, selected because they will probably be of interest to three- and four-year olds. Each project is designed to take several days, but you may decide to take more time, spreading the activities out a bit.

These projects, and the activities described within them, are presented for your choice. You may not want to do all of them, and you may choose to modify any of them to meet the learning and developmental needs of your children.

As you select and plan projects and activities, always keep the needs of your specific children in mind. Think about their age and level of independence. Some of the activities may not be appropriate for three-year-olds who are just entering prekindergarten and learning the basic routines of school, but will be fine for more experienced four-year-olds.

You will also want to consider the size of the group. You need enough children for a good conversation, but in general, the larger the group, the more difficult it will be to conduct the activity with only one adult. For some of the messier activities and also for the field trips, we suggest that you enlist parents or other adults so that children can work or walk in small groups. Use your own judgment regarding group sizes and readiness.

Here are some suggestions for making the most of these inquiry projects:

- Be open to discovery! You will have in mind some things you want the children to learn, but they may take the inquiry in new or unexpected directions, and make new discoveries. You may want to have an occasional "discovery sharing" conversation so that they can express new learning.

- Organize materials well in advance of the project so you can move through the days smoothly.

- Save materials that lend themselves to being used over several years (puppets, games, items for the play corner). Store them in plastic containers on high shelves or in another area so that they do not clutter up the room.

- Some of the book collections can be stored to use each year (with perhaps a new addition or two). Or, you can use the Internet to access your public library. If you have a book list handy (with titles, authors, and ISBN numbers), you can order the books when needed.

- If children have learned and enjoyed an activity, don't be afraid to repeat it or provide it as a "choice" on future days.

- If you do not like an activity, skip or modify it. You can also substitute other activities. (See the chapters in this book for suggestions.)

- Be aware that some children will always need more help and support than others. Keep an eye out for them.

- If you enlist other adults, share your goals with them. Talk about what you expect children to learn and how you hope the activity will go.

- Keep the pace moving quickly. Activities or sharing times should not drag on unnecessarily.

- Share what children are learning with their families, through newsletters or a website that they can access. (It is also a good way to enlist extra help and materials.)

- All of the books listed for these projects can be found in Appendix E, and songs and lyrics in Appendix A.

Colors

Day 1

✳ **COUNTING COLORS** Prompt children to notice the variety of colors worn by their classmates each day. Have children sit in a circle. Ask: *How many different colors do we see just in this circle?* Have children name all of the colors represented by their clothing. Hold up a posterboard chart showing common colors (red, blue, green, yellow, orange, purple, pink, white, brown, black) along with the printed label. Ask: *How many of us are wearing red today? How many are wearing blue?* (Include each color on the chart.) As children name and count colors, put a tally mark for each on the chart. Or, glue a colored dot or square on the line to match the color. This provides a strong visual signal that makes it easy to identify the most popular colors without having to count to higher numbers. Ask: *Can you tell which color is the most popular color being worn today?* Extend the activity by asking children to choose a favorite color and then count the number of objects that are that color in their bedroom at home (they may need help from an adult). Have them record (or dictate) the total and share it at school the next day.

Planting seeds

✳ **MUSICAL COLORS** Have children work with partners. Assign each pair a different color (you may give them each a colored square of construction paper as a reminder). Say: *We're going to hunt for different colors. What colors do you think we'll find in this room?* Give children time to look around the room and name colors. Say: *I'm going to play some music. When the music stops, you have to find your color and stand next to it.* Have children walk in a circle around the perimeter of the room. Play the music and stop it at regular intervals, as in musical chairs. You may need to check the room ahead of time to be sure there is fair representation of all colors.

Day 2

❋ **PLANTING A RAINBOW** Read the book *Planting a Rainbow*, by Lois Ehlert. Ask: *Why do you think this book is called* Planting a Rainbow? *What are some of the colors and flowers we read about in this book?* Provide children with colored tissue paper, white construction paper, crayons, scissors, and glue. Have them use the materials to create their own garden of flowers, or just one flower. As an extension, help children plant seeds for flowers of their own. (Be sure you use hardy flowers, like marigolds, that will grow well in an indoor environment.) Provide them with plastic cups filled with soil, seeds, and water. Label each cup with the child's name.

❋ **NATURE'S AMAZING COLORS** Show children photographs of a variety of colors in nature. You may bring in photos from magazines or share pictures from photography books, calendars, and other sources. If possible, bring in colorful fruits, vegetables, and flowers. Try to show as much variety of color as possible. Pass the photos around or display them on a table where children can see them easily. Ask: *What are some of the colors you see in these pictures/objects? How would you describe these colors?* Have children use art materials such as colored tissue paper, paints, colored pencils, pastel crayons, old magazines, and colored construction paper to create their own illustrations of color in nature. They may want to focus on one object, or a scene.

Day 3

❋ **TASTING COLORS** Bring in a variety of different-colored fruits and vegetables (prewashed) and display them on paper plates, cut in pieces small enough to eat. Invite children to taste the different foods (be aware of any food allergies). Ask: *Are the colors on the insides of these foods the same as the colors on the outside? Can you tell how something is going to taste by its color?*

❋ **DESCRIBING COLORS** Share with children different pictures of colored objects. You may use the same photographs you used on Day 2 and/or add additional photographs or objects. Invite children to describe the colors they see. Encourage them to use their imagination and all of their senses when describing colors. For example, a child might describe the green of the grass as "sweet" or "cool" or "soft." Ask: *Do some colors make you feel happy? sad? cold? warm? When we're sad, sometimes we say we feel blue. Why do you think that is?*

Day 4

✳ **"MARY HAD A LITTLE LAMB"** Sing or recite this poem with children. Ask: *How does this poem describe the lamb's fleece? Is that a good way to describe a lamb's fleece? Why?* Have children think of other color descriptions for animals. Guide them by giving them a sentence to complete, such as: The flamingo's feathers were as pink as _____." For younger children, use something they can see ("as pink as Rosie's shirt").

✳ **BROWN BEAR, BROWN BEAR** Read the book *Brown Bear, Brown Bear, What Do You See?* by Bill Martin and Eric Carle. Prepare puppets made from craft sticks and paper cutouts; each puppet should represent a different-colored animal from the book. (You may want to make additional animals/colors.) Have children sit in a circle. Give each child a puppet. The whole group says, "Brown Bear, Brown Bear, what do you see?" The child sitting next to the child whose turn it is holds up his puppet (for example, a red bird). The child whose turn it is says, "I see a red bird looking at me." Go around the circle, each child taking a turn. You can repeat this activity with other colors/puppets. These puppets can be used over and over.

✳ **TIE-DYE T-SHIRTS** Have each child bring in a plain white t-shirt from home, or provide them for the class. Ask: *What makes our clothes the colors they are? How do you think people used to color their clothes? Where did the colors come from?* Demonstrate how to tie-dye a t-shirt. (Use the proper precautions when using the dye: only adults should handle the dye and dye mixture.) Mix the dye with water per the directions on the packet. You may want to choose several different colors and surprise students with the results, or have them choose colors. Have students wrap rubber bands tightly around their t-shirts (provide assistance as needed, or do this ahead of time). Place each t-shirt in the dye for 15 or 20 minutes per the directions. Rinse with water and ring out. Hang to dry. This project will require lots of adult support—you may want to invite volunteers into your classroom on this day! Alternatively, you can have children make nontoxic play dough and dye it using food coloring.

Songs

- Color Song
- "Mary Had a Little Lamb"

Books

- Ehlert, Lois: *Color Farm*
- Ehlert, Lois: *Color Zoo*
- Feeney, Stephanie: *Hawaii Is a Rainbow*
- Fleming, Denise: *The Everything Book*
- Fox, Mem: *Where Is the Green Sheep?*
- Gonzalez, Maya Christina: *My Colors, My World*
- Hoban, Tana: *Colors Everywhere*
- Hoban, Tana: *Is It Red? Is It Yellow? Is It Blue? An Adventure in Color*
- Katz, Karen: *The Color of Us*
- Larios, Julie: *Yellow Elephant*
- Lehman, Barbara: *The Red Book*
- Lionni, Leo: *A Color of His Own*
- Martin, Bill and Carle, Eric: *Brown Bear, Brown Bear, What do you See?*
- Mockford, Caroline: *Cleo's Color Book*
- Rogers, Alan: *Red Rhino*
- Serfozo, Mary: *Who Said Red?*
- Seeger, Laura Vaccaro: *Lemons Are Not Red*
- Shahan, Sherry: *Spicy Hot Colors/Colores Picantes*
- Shannon, George: *White Is for Blueberry*
- Van Fleet, Mathew: *Fuzzy Yellow Ducklings*
- Walsh, Ellen Stohl: *Mouse Paint*
- Wood, Audrey and Bruce: *The Deep Blue Sea: A Book of Colors*

Shapes

Day 1

✳ **SHAPE ART** Hand out colorful circles made from construction paper (children can cut out the circle shapes themselves if they are able). Ask: *What shape is this? Can you find anything in this room that is the same shape?* Then hand out smaller triangle shapes. Ask: *What shape is this? How is it different from the circle shape? Can you find anything in this room that is the same shape?* Hand out square shapes. Ask: *What shape is this? How is it different from the circle shape and the triangle shape? Can you find anything in this room that is the same shape?* Invite children to make animals, buildings, vehicles or some other object of their choosing using their circle shapes, triangle shapes, square shapes, glue, markers or crayons, and any other decorative materials you have on hand. (Some suggestions: caterpillars, mice, birds, cats, houses or buildings, cars, trains).

Making shapes with dough

✳ **MAKING SHAPES WITH DOUGH** Make play dough with children (you can find recipes on the internet, or try this simple recipe: mix ½ cup salt, ½ cup water, 1 cup flour, food coloring). Give each child a small ball of the dough to work with. Have them roll it flat and then use cookie cutters to create different shapes. Allow the dough to dry and then have children paint their shapes using different colors. Ask: *What are some of the different shapes you made? How would you describe that shape?* Alternatively, bring in the ingredients for cookies and allow the children to help roll the dough and cut out the cookies. Bake the cookies and have children decorate them.

Day 2

✳ **SHAPES GUESSING GAME**   Have children sit on the floor in a circle. Say: *We're going to play the game I Spy with things we see in this room.* Each child takes a turn choosing an object within sight of the whole group. The child whose turn it is describes the shape and one or two other attributes of that object, such as, "I spy something round with numbers on it" (clock), or, "I spy something square with words inside" (book). Have each child take a turn while the others try to guess the object. Alternatively, you can give each child a piece of paper with a drawing of a common object on it—a box, a ball, the roof of a house, etc.—and have each child describe the attributes of their object, including the shape, while others try to guess what it is.

Day 3

✳ **SHAPES TREASURE HUNT**   Gather children for a shapes treasure hunt. Say: *Today we're going to hunt for shapes that are all around us. As we walk, keep your eyes open for the shapes you see on your list.* Give each child a pencil and a list with pictures of common shapes, such as square, circle, octagon, triangle, rectangle, oval, and star. Say: *Can anyone guess where we might see some of these shapes?* If possible, lead children on a short walk through the neighborhood, pausing to point out shapes in signs, buildings, vehicles, and other objects in the community. Have children put a mark next to each shape each time they find it. When you return to the classroom, ask: *Did you find all of the shapes? Which shape did you see the most often?* If you're unable to take the children outside, set up a shape treasure hunt inside by replicating some of the signs and other objects children might see in the community.

Books

- Blackstone, Stella: *Bear in a Square*
- Emberley, Rebecca: *My Shapes/Mis Formas*
- Hoban, Tana: *I Read Signs*
- Hoban, Tana: *Shapes, Shapes, Shapes*
- Gravett, Emily: *Orange Pear Apple Bear*

All About Me

Day 1

✳ **THUMBPRINT ART** Point out to children that no two thumbprints, snowflakes, or children are alike! Although we share many common attributes, we are each different in our own way. Ask: *In what ways are we all the*

Playing the mirror game

same? What are some of the ways that we are different? These differences are what make us special. Give each child a piece of heavy white paper or card stock, and place inkpads on each table (two or more children can share an inkpad). Help children press their thumbs on the inkpad, and then on the paper. Let them observe their thumbprints with a magnifying glass and compare them. Ask: *What do you notice?* After children have made their thumbprints, have them use markers and crayons or colored pencils to give their thumbprints legs, eyes, hair, or any kind of decoration.

✳ **THE MIRROR GAME** Begin the activity by focusing children on their individual abilities. Ask: *How high can you jump? How long can you balance on one foot?* (Suggest other movements and have children try each.) Play a game of Simon Says and then tell children that they are going to play a game similar to Simon Says called the mirror game. Have children stand or sit facing a partner. Children take turns being the leader, slowly performing movements like crossing their arms, standing on one foot, etc., while the other player imitates the leader's movements as closely as possible, as if they're looking in a mirror. Make the game more specific to the child's individual routines. Ask questions like: *What kinds of things do you do to get ready for school each day? Do you eat a bowl of cereal? Brush your teeth?* Encourage them to act out their morning routines.

✳ **MUSICAL INSTRUMENTS**   Share with children a collection of musical instruments like bells, tambourines, harmonicas, drums, and maracas. (Include any instruments you have on hand that children can use easily.) Demonstrate how to use each instrument. Ask: *What does this sound remind you of? How would you describe this sound?* Have children take turns experimenting with each instrument. Then ask them to choose an instrument that they like best or help them say how they feel on that day. Ask questions like: *Which instrument makes a happy sound? Which makes a playful sound?* Encourage the children to explain why they chose a particular instrument to represent their personality or mood.

Day 2

✳ **INSIDE/OUTSIDE SELF-PORTRAITS**   Remind children of the thumbprint activity from the previous day. Ask: *What are some of the things we talked about that make us different from everyone else? Are those things on your inside or your outside?* Allow children time to identify and share different characteristics. Explain that today they are going to explore some things on the outside, like hair and skin, and also things on the inside, like kindness and curiosity. Have children lie on their backs on a piece of newsprint paper. Trace and cut out an outline of each child. Children can decorate their figures using a variety of material (try to have a wide variety of colors, textures, and materials available and encourage children to choose the colors and styles they want). Children can decorate their outlines using everything they know about themselves. They can draw or glue pictures of things they love to place inside the outline, or can represent their inner qualities using symbols (for example, a heart to show kindness). They may draw pictures of family members. Or, they may select more concrete things such as foods or games they like. You may need additional time for this activity and can return to it on subsequent days. When figures are complete, have the children "introduce" their figure to the rest of the class and tell important things about themselves.

✳ **POPSICLE-STICK PUPPETS**   As an extension of, or alternative to the self-portrait activity, use the same materials and invite children to make smaller versions of themselves to use as puppets. Provide them with precut paper figures about the size of a hand, mounted on a stiff cardboard backing. If you are building on the self-portrait activity, children can create their puppets based on the earlier discussion. If you have not made the full-size self-portraits, initiate the same discussion about internal and external qualities that make us unique. When finished, glue each figure to a popsicle stick. Invite children to use their figures to perform a puppet show about themselves alone or with a partner, or to play with other children's figures.

✳ **DANCE MOVES**   Ask: *What are some of the ways that we express ourselves? When we paint, do our paintings look the same? Do we sound the same when we sing? Do we look the same when we dance?* Invite the class, working together, to create one dance made up of moves created by each individual child. Begin by dividing the class into small groups of three or four. Have each child within the group create a unique movement, such as hopping on one foot three times or spinning around twice. Have each group choose a song they like and perform the moves, each member has created, in sequence, for the rest of the class.

Day 3

✳ **MY FAVORITE THINGS**   Lead a discussion about favorite things. You may want to write down and display categories of favorites where children can see them, with a visual representation of each (categories might include favorite animals, seasons, colors, foods, people, sports, etc.). Say: *We're going to talk about our favorite things.* Ask questions like: *What is your favorite food? What is your favorite holiday?* Encourage children to share the reasons for their choices. After the discussion, have children make books about their favorites using paper, fabric scraps, crayons and markers, magazine photos, glue, and any other appropriate supplies. (Cut paper and staple pages together so that each child has a blank book of several pages in length, or use ready-made blank books.) Encourage children to write labels for or brief descriptions of their illustrations if they are able. They can add to their books throughout the year. The book-making activity will work best in small groups with lots of adult support. (See also "Me Boxes" in Appendix D, Lesson 16, and "Bookmaking," Lesson 11.)

✳ **PATTERN CHANT**   Say: *We're going to continue exploring our favorite things, but in a different way.* Sit on the floor with the children in a circle. Slap your thighs and clap your hands or snap your fingers in a simple pattern. Have the children repeat the pattern with you, and then add the words "I like . . . ," filling in names of things you like from a specific category, like "fruits I like," or "animals I like." Going around the circle, each child names something he or she likes from the category. Once each child has had a turn, choose a new category and start again.

✳ **MY FAVORITE PLACES**   Ask: *What are some of your favorite places to be? Are your favorite places far away or nearby?* Name some favorite places and talk about what makes them special. Then have children draw a picture of a favorite place and/or, if able, write (or make marks like writing) a label and brief description of a favorite place. If children have a favorite place in the classroom, schoolyard, or neighborhood, you may want to take a walking trip to visit some of those places, allowing children to share what they like about them.

Day 4

✳ **SHARING OUR TALENTS**   Begin by discussing what it means to be good at something, focusing on the fact that we all have many talents, both big and small. Ask: *What is one small thing you are good at? What is one big thing?* For example, you may be good at something simple, like doing somersaults, and you may be good at something more complicated, like caring for a pet or being a good friend. Discuss what it takes to be good at something and how it feels when someone compliments you on your talents. Have children choose one thing they are good at. Hand out pre-cut shapes that children can decorate (using markers, glitter, stars, etc.) to create award certificates or trophies. Label each award with the talent the child has chosen. (Children can write their own names and talents if they are able.) Display the awards in the classroom. Then invite children to share with others by teaching them their unique talent.

Songs

- Have children sing new words to a familiar tune; for example, they can make up their own "song about myself" using a favorite tune like "Mary Had a Little Lamb" but substituting a different favorite pet and their own name.
- Have children sing "I Love Apples and Bananas," substituting favorite fruits or foods.
- Have children sing "Boom Boom Ain't It Great to Be Crazy" and make up their own crazy moves to accompany the song.

Books

- Beaumont, Karen: *I Like Myself*
- Chodos-Irvine, Margaret: *Ella Sarah Gets Dressed*
- Falconer, Ian: *Olivia*
- Fleming, Denise: *The Cow Who Clucked*
- Howe, James: *Horace and Morris Join the Chorus (But What About Dolores?)*
- Kraus, Robert: *Leo the Late Bloomer*
- Leaf, Munro: *The Story of Ferdinand*

INQUIRY PROJECT

My Body

Day 1

✳ **"HEAD, SHOULDERS, KNEES, AND TOES"** Have children stand in a circle. Begin singing the song "Head, Shoulders, Knees, and Toes" slowly so children can follow as you demonstrate the words and movements. Use both hands as you touch each of the body parts while singing (see Appendix A for song lyrics). After you have performed the song a few times, invite children to sit. Ask: *What body parts can you name? What do you use those body parts for?*

✳ **USING OUR BODIES** Have children sit in a circle. Pass around a basket containing slips of paper on which are written the names of body parts along with corresponding pictures. (Some suggestions are feet, hands, eyes, ears, mouth, nose, tongue, fingers, knees, back, elbows, arms, legs, neck, and head.) Have each child choose a slip of paper from the basket. Then choose a slip yourself and demonstrate carrying out an activity featuring that body part (for example, say, *I use my feet to stomp*, while stomping on the floor). Then have each child take a turn. Encourage children to be as creative as possible.

Singing "Head, Shoulders, Knees, and Toes"

Day 2

✳ **OBSTACLE COURSE** Set up a small obstacle course using cones, chairs, pillows, and/or any other objects that children can safely walk and run around, jump or climb over, crawl through, etc. You can set up your obstacle course inside or, if weather permits, outside in a play area (you can incorporate playground equipment if available). Give children a specific route to follow, demonstrate what you would like them to do, and then allow each child to go through the course at least twice. Afterward, sit in a circle. Ask: *What body parts did you use when we did the obstacle course? What did you use them for?*

✳ **HAND/FOOTPRINTS** Arrange trays filled with different-colored washable paints on a central table. Divide the class into small groups. Give each child a piece of plain white construction paper. Invite children to choose a paint color, dip the palm of their hand in the paint tray, then press it firmly on the paper to make a handprint. Ask: *What do you notice about your handprint? How are the fingers different?* Next, roll out butcher paper and give children a shallow tray of water. (This activity can be done outside on pavement in a safe area.) Have them dip their feet in the water tray and then step firmly on the butcher paper. Encourage them to walk and run on the paper, leaving "tracks." Ask: *What do you notice about your footprints? How do they change when you run?*

✳ **DO THE "HOKEY POKEY"** Invite children to sing and dance the "Hokey Pokey." Because they may not be ready to discern left from right yet, you can substitute the words "one hand" or "one foot" for left hand and right hand, etc. Include as many body parts as you can.

Day 3

(These sensory activities can be spread out over three days rather than done all at once.)

✳ **MYSTERY OBJECTS** Children can expand their inquiry by exploring the five senses: sight, sound, smell, touch, and taste. Have children sit in a circle on the floor. Hold up an apple. Ask: *What is this? How do you know?* Encourage children to talk about the color, shape, and size of the fruit. Ask: *Did you use your ears to tell what this object is? What did you use?* Have children close their eyes. Pass a banana around the circle. Say: *I'm passing something around. Try to guess what it is without using your eyes.* Wait while each child has a turn holding the banana. Put it away and then ask: *Can you tell me what that was? How do you know?* Encourage children to talk about the texture of the banana, the shape, the size, and the smell. Repeat the activity with other familiar fruits or objects (soap, flowers, leaves, etc.)

✳ **MYSTERY SOUNDS**   Have children sit in a circle on the floor. Say: *Close your eyes and listen. I'm going to make a sound. Try to guess what made the sound.* Use different objects to make sounds that will be familiar to most children—a book closing (close it firmly), a chair scraping on the floor, biting into an apple, scissors cutting paper, a door opening or closing, etc. After each sound ask: *What sound did you hear? What made that sound? How do you know?* Encourage children to talk about how they use their sense of hearing to help them every day.

✳ **MYSTERY FOODS**   Determine whether any children in the class have food allergies before doing this activity. (Some children might prefer to use only their sense of smell and touch to identify the foods.) Set up a long table with a variety of foods arranged separately on paper plates. Try to include familiar foods that have a variety of tastes, smells, and textures (orange or apple slices, marshmallows, grapes, popcorn or crackers, carrot or celery sticks). Blindfold the children or have them close their eyes. Have them take turns trying to identify each food by using their sense of taste, touch, and smell.

Day 4

✳ **MEASURE YOURSELF**   Children can measure their height using nonstandard units of measure. Ask: *About how tall do you think you are? Are you taller than this chair? Are you shorter than the doorway?* Encourage them to compare their size to objects in the room or to other children. Ask: *Who do you think is taller? How do you know?* Children may want to measure themselves against each other, standing back-to-back. Next, have each child lie flat on a piece of butcher paper with their heels lined up at the bottom of the paper. Mark each child's height, then write their name next to the line (children can write their own names if they are able). When finished, hang the butcher paper on the wall.

✳ **"BIG AND SMALL"**   Children will enjoy singing this song, stretching themselves to stand up tall, then crouching down low to make themselves small. After they have performed the song a few times, discuss things that they see each day that are big and small, or short and tall. Ask: *What things in this room are short? What things are tall?*

Day 5

✳ **INSIDE BODY PARTS** Have children sit in a circle. Say: *We've talked about some of the parts of our body that we use every day, like our hands and feet.* Ask: *What are some important parts that are* inside *our bodies?* (children may name things like bones, muscles, heart, etc.) Have children stand up. Say: *Show me what would happen to you if you had no bones in your body!* Encourage children to experiment with being "boneless." Ask: *What parts of your body can you bend? Show me what would happen if you couldn't bend your elbows, knees, or hips!*

✳ **KID OLYMPICS** Invite children to participate in their own silly "Kid Olympics." Events might include jumping, hopping on one foot, running or walking backward, turning somersaults, and skipping. (The event can be held indoors or out.) After the event, have children gather in a circle. Ask: *Can you tell me again what some of the things are that your legs help you do? What about your hands? Your eyes?* Review other useful body parts. Have each child draw a picture (if able, they can write a word or sentence as well) that shows them doing a physical activity they love.

Songs

- "Head, Shoulders, Knees, and Toes"
- "The Hokey Pokey"
- "Big and Small"
- "Do Your Ears Hang Low?" (good for naming body parts)
- "Going on a Bear Hunt" (good for acting out physical movement)

Books

- Aliki: *My Five Senses*
- Asim, Jabari: *Whose Knees Are These?*
- Bang, Molly: *A Book of Thanks (All of Me!)*
- Barner, Bob: *Dem Bones*
- Gershator, Phillis: *Zzzing! Zzzing! Zzzing! A Yoruba Tale*
- Kubler, Annie: *Ten Little Fingers*
- Martin, Bill Jr.: *Here Are My Hands*
- Raschka, Chris: *Five for a Little One*

Moods and Feelings

Day 1

✳ **FEELING HAPPY** Sing the song "If You're Happy and You Know It" with children while standing. Encourage them to make up their own movements to accompany the song, or introduce simple percussion instruments for children to use to express happiness (ring a bell, beat a drum, shake a tambourine, etc.). After the song discuss some things that children can do if they're not happy. Say: *Think about all of the ways we just showed our happiness—clapping our hands, stomping our feet, shouting hooray! What are some things we can do if we're feeling angry? What are some things we can do if we're feeling sad?*

Talking about feelings

✳ **UNDERSTANDING FEELINGS** Ask: *What kinds of things make you feel happy? What kinds of things make you feel sad?* (You can repeat the question for any number of emotions: anger, frustration, loneliness, etc.) Give each child two paper circles and crayons or markers. Demonstrate how to draw a happy face on one, a sad face on another. Read a story, describe an event, or act out a scenario using puppets. Ask: *How do you think these characters feel?* Ask children to hold up the happy face or sad face.

✳ **SUNSHINE AND CLOUDS** Ask each child to take a turn sharing one thing from the day that was their "sunshine," and one thing that was their "cloud." Or, if you don't want children to see clouds as negative, just have them name one happy thing and maybe something that made them feel sad or sorry. Encourage children to be as general or as specific as they want; for example, a child might say her sunshine was her family, or she might say her sunshine was seeing a bird in the window.

Day 2

✳ **EXPRESSING FEELINGS** Remind children that there are many ways to express our moods and feelings. Ask children to sit quietly and listen while you play different selections of music. Choose music that is clearly happy, sad, angry, etc. You might do this by paying particular attention to the pace and volume of the music, as well as the instruments used. After you play each piece ask: *How did this music sound to you? If you had to choose a mood or feeling for this music, what would it be?* Extend the activity by having children draw or paint while they listen to each piece of music. Encourage them to express the mood of the music through their use of color and pattern. Or, have them move the way the music makes them feel.

✳ **EXPRESSING FEELINGS THROUGH MOVEMENT** Divide children into groups of three or four. Ask them to choose a mood, such as happy, sad, or angry and then choose the music they think reflects that mood

Expressing feelings

(use the same music you chose for the activity above). Invite them to create a dance or to perform creative movements that express that mood. You may want to demonstrate first by showing how you can make an angry face, clench your fists, and stomp your feet to show anger. Invite each group to share their movements with the remaining class members and see whether they can guess what the emotion or mood is. Extend the activity by inviting the class to participate in a Happy Parade, Scared Parade, Sad Parade, or Silly Parade, etc. Allow them to decide on a theme and then use their bodies and facial expressions to illustrate the emotion. If your class is large, you may want to involve parents and make this a small-group activity.

Day 3

❋ **ROLE-PLAYING WITH PUPPETS** Gather children in a group. (Remind them of the role playing they did with puppets earlier in the week, if you chose to do that activity.) Say: *Let's think again about some of the things that make us feel happy.* Have children identify different situations in which they feel happy, sad, scared, worried, or angry. Invite them to take turns role-playing different scenarios with puppets. When they've finished, have them return to their seats and complete and illustrate the following sentence: "When [blank] happens, I feel [blank]." (Children that are able can write a descriptive word or sentence to accompany their picture.) You may want to do this with a small group or when you have extra adult support.

Songs

These songs, with their different tempos and rhythms, lend themselves well to expressing different moods:

- "Boom, Boom, Ain't It Great to Be Crazy?"
- "Bought Me a Cat"
- "Bumblebee Song"
- "Good Morning to You"
- "It's Raining, It's Pouring"
- "Pop Goes the Weasel"
- "Rain, Rain Go Away"

Books

- Bang, Molly: *When Sophie Gets Angry, Really, Really Angry*
- Carle, Eric: *The Grouchy Ladybug*
- Curtis, Jamie Lee: *Today I Feel Silly and Other Moods That Make My Day*
- Dannenberg, Julie: *First Day Jitters*
- Numeroff, Laura: *Beatrice Doesn't Want To*
- Shoshan, Beth: *That's When I'm Happy*
- Urban, Linda: *Mouse Was Mad*
- Willems, Mo: *Knuffle Bunny: A Cautionary Tale*
- Wilson, Karma: *Bear Feels Scared*

Friends and Friendship

Day 1

✳ **SING A FRIENDSHIP SONG** Gather children and introduce the song "If You're Friendly and You Know It" (to be sung to the tune of "If You're Happy and You Know It"). Ask: *What words or actions can we substitute for* clap hands, stomp feet, *etc., that show our friendliness?* (For example, children might sing "If you're friendly and you know it give a hug [shake hands] [say hello].") Have children sing the song and turn to the person next to them to perform each gesture. Invent as many verses as time allows.

Riding the friendship train

✳ **MAKE A FRIENDSHIP GARDEN** Gather children in a circle. Ask: *What are some things that friends do for each other? How do we show our friends and families that we care about them?* Go around the circle and give each child a turn sharing something that a friend does or something they do to show they care for a friend or family member. Tell children that each act of kindness we do is like a flower blooming in a garden. Hand out pre-cut pieces of colored construction paper in the shape of flowers, and materials for decorating them, such as tissue paper, crayons, markers, stickers, glitter, and glue. Point out a bulletin board or other display space with a green "garden" background. Say: *Each time a friend does something kind for you, decorate one of these flowers and plant it in our Friendship Garden.* At the end of the day, ask children to share some of the acts of kindness that prompted them to "plant" flowers.

Day 2

✳ **RIDE THE FRIENDSHIP TRAIN** Have children line up single-file and put their hands on the hips or shoulders of the person in front of them. Say: *We're going to ride the friendship train. The object of this game is to follow the person in front of you without letting go and without tugging.* Put on some lively music and direct the children to follow you on a path through the classroom or outside on the playground. Let children take turns leading the train, and encourage them to speed up, slow down, and try different routes. Afterward, ask: *Was it hard to stay together? What made it easier?*

✳ **BEING WITH FRIENDS** Ask: *What are some of your favorite things to do by yourself? What are some of your favorite things to do with your friends?* Have children share some of the things they do alone and with friends. Then give them coloring or painting materials and have them create a picture of themselves doing a favorite activity alone and another picture of them doing a favorite activity with a friend (of any age) (children who are able can write a few words or a brief descriptive sentence). Invite them to display their pictures and share with the rest of the class what they drew.

Day 3

✳ **MAKING UP** Role-play with children different ways to make up with a friend after you've hurt each other's feelings. Ask: *Can you think of a time when a friend has hurt your feelings? What happened? How did you feel?* Have children work with a partner or in small groups and act out different scenarios for making up. (For example, one child might feel left out of a game, and the other children might apologize and invite the child to join the game.) Alternatively, or as an extension of the activity, choose a small group of children to act out a scenario showing a dispute between friends. Stop the performance before there is a resolution. Ask: *What do you think the friends should do? How can they fix this problem and feel better?* Invite the class to offer solutions, and guide them to an agreement. Have the performers act out the most popular resolution. Alternatively, read a story aloud about a dispute among friends and let children come up with their own ending. Have them illustrate (and/or write if they are able) their ending to the story.

✳ **MAKING NEW FRIENDS** Share with children the words and music for the song "Make New Friends, But Keep the Old." You can recite the poem if you don't know the tune. Discuss with them what the words mean. Ask: *What is special about making new friends? What is special about friends we've had for a long time? Why is it important to have both?* Discuss with children the difference between old friends and new. Sing the song together.

Being with friends

Songs

- "Make New Friends, But Keep the Old"

     Make new friends,

     But keep the old.

     One is Silver,

     And the other is gold.

- Have children sing new words to a familiar tune. For example, they can make up their own "song about friendship" using a favorite tune but substituting a friend's name, or they can substitute a word like *friendly* in the song "If You're Happy and You Know It."

Books

- Alborough, Jez: *My Friend Bear*
- Browne, Anthony: *Willy and Hugh*
- Buck, Nola: *Sid and Sam*
- Dunrea, Olivier: *Gossie and Gertie*
- George, Craighead Jean: *Goose and Duck*
- Gutman, Anne: *Gaspard and Lisa: Friends Forever*
- Hobbie, Holly: *Toot and Puddle*
- Hutchins, Pat: *My Best Friend*
- Lobel, Arnold: *Frog and Toad Are Friends*
- Raschka, Chris: *Yo! Yes?*

Pets

Day 1

✳ **FAVORITE PET SURVEY** Invite children to name different kinds of common pets. (Select this option with sensitivity to cultural diversity. In some cultures, pets are not acceptable.) Ask: *What is a pet? What are some types of pets that you know?* Write the kinds of pets children mention across the top of a large piece of paper mounted on the wall. Put a picture of each kind of pet next to the label. Say: *We're going to see which type of pet is the most popular. Raise your hand if the pet I name is your favorite.* Read each kind of pet out loud and have children raise a hand to indicate a favorite. Put a symbol or check mark next to the label. When everyone has voted, have children count with you to add up the total and see which pet is most popular.

Caring for pets

✳ **POUNCE LIKE A CAT** Ask: *Do all animals move the same way? How would you describe the way a cat moves? How about a dog?* Elicit descriptions about the movements of other common pets. Say: *Let's pounce like a cat. Let's hop like a bunny.* Divide the class into small groups. Assign each group a pet identity such as dogs, cats, frogs, fish, and bunnies. Have each group practice their animal movements, and then invite them to perform for the rest of the class. Alternatively, you may play a game in which one player acts like a certain pet and the rest of the group has to guess what animal the player is imitating.

✳ **"THE ANTS GO MARCHING"** Invite children to sing this song (see page 252) while marching in a circle, around the room, or in an outdoor play area. Extend the activity by substituting other animals for "ants" and other movements for each animal; for example, you might sing "The frogs go hopping," or "The cats go prowling." Encourage children to use some of the pets and movements they used in the previous activity.

Day 2

✳ **CARING FOR PETS** Have each child bring in a stuffed animal from home, or provide one for them if necessary. Ask: *What are some of the wild animals we see or know about that live where we live?* (Children may mention birds, squirrels, rabbits, skunks, raccoons, fish, deer, or other animals common in their community.) *How are pets different from these wild animals? What are some of the things you would need to do every day to care for a pet?* After the discussion, make a brief list together of some of the important ways we care for pets (lists may include providing food and water, taking them to the vet, and grooming and exercising them). Explain that they are going to be responsible for their "pet" (stuffed animal) for the rest of the day (extend the activity for several days if you wish) and must make sure they're being cared for properly. Invite children to pretend to care for their pets. At the end of the activity ask: *What is the most challenging part of caring for a pet?*

✳ **"TEDDY BEAR, TEDDY BEAR"** Invite children to sing this song and perform the related movements (see page 269). After they know the words and movements they can make up their own additional verses or substitute verses and movements.

Day 3

❋ **TRIP TO AN ANIMAL SHELTER** If you're able, arrange to take the class on a trip to a local animal shelter. (Children will benefit more from seeing an animal shelter than a pet store, and learning about the importance of caring for and finding homes for all animals.) If possible, arrange for someone at the animal shelter to take the class on a tour and explain how the animals are cared for. Alternatively, or as an extension, arrange for the class to visit a veterinary clinic and/or invite a veterinarian to speak to the class about caring for pets.

❋ **CREATE YOUR OWN PET COLLAGE** Even if children don't own a pet, they can create a pet collage. Have children choose a favorite kind of pet and create a collage using materials such as magazine clippings, paint, paper, fabric, glue, and similar materials you are able to provide. The collage should tell a story about the pet—what type of pet and the pet's appearance, how it is cared for (food, sleeping area or pet house, grooming accessories, exercise routines, etc.). If they are able, children can write their pet's name (or dictate it) and write or dictate a brief descriptive sentence about the pet. Invite children to display their collages and tell about them.

❋ **PLAY "THE CLAPPING GAME"** Sit on the floor with the children in a circle. Slap your thighs and clap your hands or snap your fingers in a simple pattern. Say: *We're going to play a clapping game. We all take turns naming something, like types of animals. Listen to me: "Clapping game. Names of animals. Such as dog."* (Say the words in time to the pattern you are clapping.) Have the children repeat the pattern with you, naming a different pet each time. Continue playing using different categories for as long as time allows, for example, foods, things you wear, places, children's names. Along with listening to and duplicating a pattern, children can internalize categories of things that are connected.

Songs

- "The Ants Go Marching"
- "Baa Baa Black Sheep"
- "Bingo"
- "Bought Me a Cat"
- "Five Little Bunnies"
- "Five Little Speckled Frogs"
- "Here Is a Bunny"
- "Mary Had a Little Lamb"
- "Teddy Bear, Teddy Bear"
- "Three Little Kittens"

Books

- Bauer, Marion Dane: *If You Were Born a Kitten*
- Broach, Elise: *Wet Dog!*
- Harper, Dan: *Sit, Truman!*
- Harper, Isabelle: *My Cats Nick and Nora*
- Harper, Isabelle: *My Dog Rosie*
- Harper, Isabelle: *Our New Puppy*
- LaRochelle, David: *The Best Pet of All*
- Lee, Hector Viveros: *I Had a Hippopotamus*
- McCarty, Peter: *Hondo and Fabian*
- Roth, Susan: *Great Big Guinea Pigs*

Community

Day 1

✳ **THE PEOPLE IN YOUR NEIGHBORHOOD** Gather children in a group. Ask: *Who are some of the people you see in your neighborhood each day? What are some of the jobs that people in your neighborhood do?* Have children work in small groups or with partners. Have them role-play or use puppets to act out different neighborhood scenarios. (For example, going to the market to buy milk.)

Building a city

✳ **BUILD A TOWN/CITY** Provide building materials such as Legos, blocks, empty shoeboxes, empty containers. Ask: *What does your neighborhood [community, town, city] look like? Are there tall buildings? houses? parks? playgrounds?* Encourage children to use the building materials to create towns or neighborhoods. You may also want to provide toy people/dolls for them to play with once their towns are built. Encourage them to interact with one another as they play. While they are playing, ask questions such as: *What is happening in this building? What is this person's job?* Alternatively, you may have children draw or paint a picture of their neighborhood, town, or city. This works best as a small-group activity.

Day 2

✳ **EXPLORING THE NEIGHBORHOOD** Take children on a preplanned walking route around the neighborhood. If this is not an option, consider walking around the school or playground. First, give each child a copy of a simple hand-drawn map that shows the route you will take along with some of the places and landmarks you will pass along the way. Ask: *Do you* *recognize any of the things on this map?* Encourage children to look at their maps as you walk and note the landmarks along the way. For example, say: *Here is the tall tree shown on the map next to the post office.* As you come to each of the places on the map, stop and notice where you are. Talk about what the place is and what its purpose is. Back in the classroom, ask: *What are some of the places we saw today on our walk?* Encourage children to mention places and things not shown on the map as well.

✳ **DRAW A NEIGHBORHOOD** Have children draw a picture of something they saw on their walk. Have them write or dictate a sentence describing what they saw. Ask: *What do you like best about our school neighborhood? What do you like best about your neighborhood at home?*

Day 3

✳ **MARKET SCAVENGER HUNT** Arrange ahead of time to visit a local market. (Organize extra adult support so you have a 1 to 4 or 1 to 5 ratio.) If possible, have the store owner or manager introduce herself or himself to the children and explain something about how the store is organized. Have children work in pairs or in small groups. Give each group a pre-made list with two or three items written on it (with an accompanying picture representation), such as apples, oranges, milk, and bread. Try to choose items that will require them to visit different aisles/areas. Have children collect all the items on their list. Return to school and make a healthy snack with the items purchased. Ask: *Why are markets an important part of our community?*

✳ **PLAY MARKET** Have children recall what they saw and did at the market. Ask: *How did you find what you were looking for in the store? Who helped you?* Have children organize their own pretend market in the classroom (they can do so in the play corner if you have one). Provide them with items to purchase (use old milk and juice cartons, cans, empty cereal boxes, and other packaging that has been thoroughly cleaned and has no sharp edges). Provide play money, and move furniture to approximate a checkout counter and areas to display food. Encourage them to take turns being customers and store personnel.

Day 4

❋ **VISIT THE POST OFFICE**   Have children come to school with their address written down by a family member. They can dictate or write a brief message to themselves or someone in their family who resides at the same address. Pass around stamps, paper, and envelopes to each child. Explain why a stamp is necessary and where to place it on the envelope. Children can write or dictate their message (or draw) to family members and then put their "letters" in the envelopes provided. Visit the local post office. Arrange to have someone give children a tour of the facility and explain what happens when mail comes in and goes out. Talk about what a mail carrier does. Direct children to mail their letters in the proper mailbox at the post office. Remind them to note how long it takes for them to receive their letters in the mail.

❋ **PLAY POST OFFICE**   Set up a class mailbox made from an old shoebox or some other empty box or container. Give each child an empty box to decorate and use as their own mailbox, and have them write their names on the side if they are able. Invite children to make letters, drawings, or cards for one another and post them in the class mailbox. Then have them take turns playing the part of the mail carrier and collecting and delivering the mail to each individual mailbox. Be sure that everyone gets mail.

Day 5

❋ **VISIT THE LIBRARY**   Ask: *How many of you have been to the local library? Do you know what a library is for?* Arrange ahead of time to have someone give the children a tour of the library, focusing on the children's room, the organization/location of books, bathrooms, drinking fountains, and other important areas, and the rules for borrowing books and obtaining a library card. Give children time to explore the library and look at books. Back at school, ask: *What kinds of books did you see at the library? What did you notice about how the books were organized? Why are libraries an important part of our community?*

❋ **PLAY LIBRARY**   Have children create their own library card—a pre-cut card they can decorate and write their name on. When children are done decorating, laminate the cards if possible. Turn your existing play corner into a library or arrange a portion of the classroom to simulate a library that includes a checkout desk and a box for returned books. Allow children to decide which books to include in their library and how to organize them. Limit the play library to books children know well—not too many. (Visit your local library to learn how books are checked out and set children up to use the same method.) Have children take turns playing the librarian and the patrons.

Day 6

❋ **VISIT A FIRE STATION** Arrange ahead of time to visit your local fire station (alternatively, you can arrange to have a firefighter visit the classroom to speak to the children about fire safety). Have the children tour the station and learn about what the firefighters do and what the vehicles and other equipment are used for. Ask: *Why are firefighters such an important part of our community? How do they help to keep us safe?*

❋ **PLAY FIRE STATION** In your existing play corner or another area of the classroom set up a pretend fire station by providing fire hats, coats, and short lengths of rope that children can use as hoses. *Ask: What are some of the things we learned about the firefighters do to help people?* Have children take turns acting out fire or first aid rescues.

Day 7

❋ **FOLLOWING SIGNS** Put music on and have children line up single file. Have them follow a route through the classroom or on the playground that includes various signs with words, colors, and symbols on them (arrows, hands, red, yellow, green, etc.) telling children to stop, go, slow down, turn left, turn right, do not enter. Children can also take turns pretending to be cars and pedestrians while one child directs traffic. Ask: *Why is it important for everyone to pay attention to signs and do what they say?*

Books

- Brett, Jan: *The Town Mouse and the Country Mouse*
- Burton, Virginia Lee: *The Little House*
- Fleming, Denise: *Alphabet Under Construction*
- Hoban, Tana: *I Read Signs*
- Knudsen, Michelle: *Library Lion*
- Lehman, Barbara: *Museum Trip*
- Lobel, Arnold: *On Market Street*

Journeys

Day 1

❋ **GETTING AROUND** Ask: *What are some of the ways we get from one place to another? What are some of the ways we can get to places that are very far away?* Encourage children to name ways to get around, including walking, biking, riding in a car or bus, taking a train or an airplane or a boat. Then ask: *How do you get to school each morning?* Write the types of transportation that children mention across the top of a large piece of paper mounted on the wall. Put a picture of each type of transportation next to the label. Say: *We're going to see which way most of you get to school.* Read each type of transportation (for example, car, bus, walk) out loud and have children raise their hands to indicate the method they use. Put a symbol or check mark next to the label for each hand raised. Have children count with you to add up the total and see which method of transportation is used most often.

Packing for a trip

❋ **IMAGINARY JOURNEYS** Ask: *Who has taken a trip somewhere close by or far away? Where did you go? How did you get there?* Have children lie down in comfortable spots on the floor. Dim the lights and put on quiet, relaxing music. Say: *Another word for* trip *is* journey. *We're going to take an imaginary journey. Close your eyes and listen: We're riding on a train. Can you feel the train rocking? Can you hear the clackety-clack of the wheels on the rails? Now the train is stopping. We're getting off. I see a beautiful beach with white sand. I can feel how soft the sand is under my feet. What else do we see on this beach? What do we hear? What do we smell?* Invite children to offer their own sights, sounds, and smells and to volunteer other destinations, such as a snowy mountain or a busy city street.

✳ **MAKE A POSTCARD** Hand out postcard-size cardstock. Share different postcard images that show a variety of destinations. Say: *When you take a trip somewhere, you can send a postcard to someone that shows them where you've been.* Have children draw a picture of one of the places they visited on their imaginary journey or of another place they've been or would like to visit. Have them write (or dictate) a short message to someone that says what they'll do while they're there.

Day 2

✳ **GO ON A BEAR HUNT** Read the book *We're Going on a Bear Hunt* by Michael Rosen with children. After you've read it through once, have children help create movements to go with each new line, or have them stand and act out the words with their own movements. Ask: *Where did the family in this story begin their journey? Where did they end their journey? What do you like best about going on a journey? What do you like best about coming home?*

✳ **PACKING FOR A TRIP** Ask: *What do you need to take with you when you go on an overnight trip? What if it's hot where you're going? What if it's cold?* Ask questions to elicit responses about appropriate clothing for different types of weather and different types of activities. Provide children with a variety of dress-up clothes (coats, boots, scarves, mittens, shorts, swimsuits, etc.) and suitcases, backpacks, and duffel bags in the play corner, and invite them to pack for an imaginary trip. You may also have some books so they can pack a book for the trip. Extend the activity by having them act out flying in an airplane or taking a train or other form of transportation to their destination. Alternatively, have children use old magazines to cut out pictures of things they would want to pack for a trip. (If children cannot cut easily, the pictures could be pre-cut.) Have them glue the pictures on to a drawing of an open bag. If they wish, they can make a packing list with pictures or words. Ask: *Where are you going? What kinds of things will you do when you get there?*

Day 3

✳ **READ THE YOKO BOOKS** Read the books *Yoko*, *Yoko's Paper Cranes*, and *Yoko Writes Her Name*, by Rosemary Wells. (You may spread this activity out over three days.) Discuss the books with the children. Ask: *What are some of the problems Yoko had in these stories? Why do you think she had those problems? What happens in the end of each story?* Explain that Yoko was from another country, Japan. Ask: *What are some of the things that Yoko did differently from the other children in her class?* Read *Yoko's Paper Cranes*. Help children find Japan and the United States on a map. Show them the route that Yoko's letters to her grandparents had to travel from the United States to Japan. Ask: *How do you think Yoko felt being so far away from her grandparents and other familiar things?*

✳ **CHOOSE A YOKO ACTIVITY** As a follow-up activity to reading the Yoko books, invite children to take part in an International Food Day like the one in *Yoko*, or help children create simple origami animals like the ones in *Yoko's Paper Cranes*. Children can also "draw" some of the Japanese-like characters from *Yoko Writes Her Name* using brushes and paint.

Day 4

✳ **BOOK JOURNEYS** Organize a collection of fiction and nonfiction books in the classroom that have a travel theme and that feature information about other places and cultures. Arrange the books in a specific area of the classroom; you may want to include a small rug on the floor and explain to children that it is a "magic" carpet that can take them to faraway places. Ask: *How can books help us travel to other places? What can we learn by traveling to new places and trying new things?*

Songs

- "Wheels on the Bus "
- "Down by the Station"
- "Five Little Ducks"
- "Row, Row, Row Your Boat"

Books

- Barton, Byron: *My Car*
- Crews, Donald: *Freight Train*
- Degen, Bruce: *Jamberry*
- Henkes, Kevin: *Kitten's First Full Moon*
- Lewis, Kevin: *Chugga-Chugga Choo-Choo*
- McCloskey, Robert: *Make Way for Ducklings*
- Rosen, Michael: *We're Going on a Bear Hunt*
- Sendak, Maurice: *Where the Wild Things Are*
- Van Allsburg, Chris: *The Polar Express*
- Wells, Rosemary: *Yoko*
- Wells, Rosemary: *Yoko's Paper Cranes*
- Wells, Rosemary: *Yoko Writes Her Name*
- Williams, Sue: *I Went Walking*
- Zelinsky, Paul: *The Wheels on the Bus*

INQUIRY PROJECT

Food

Day 1

✴ **PLAY THE CLAPPING GAME** Sit on the floor with the children in a circle. Slap your thighs and clap your hands or snap your fingers in a simple pattern. Say: *We're going to play a clapping game. We all take turns naming something, like types of foods. Listen to me: "Clapping Game. Names of fruits. Banana."* (Say the words in time to the pattern you are clapping.) Have the children repeat the pattern with you, naming a different fruit (or other food) each time. Continue playing using different categories for as long as time allows. Alternatively, everyone says the name of the fruit and then say it clapping for each part: *"banana"*; *"ba-nan-a"* (clap, clap, clap).

✴ **FAVORITE FOODS SURVEY** Talk about favorite foods with the children. Ask: *What is your favorite fruit to eat? What vegetables do you like? What is your favorite snack?* Continue to discuss food favorites. Choose a food category and take a survey to see which food is most popular. Write the names of fruits, vegetables, snacks, breakfast foods, or other foods across the top of a large piece of paper mounted on the wall. Put a picture of each type of food next to the name. Say each type of food out loud and have children raise their hand if that food is their favorite. Put a symbol or check mark next to the name to represent each child's vote. When everyone has voted, have children count with you to add up the total and see which food is most popular. For younger children, just glue or draw a dot or square for each vote. If these are uniform size, children can quickly estimate which is the favorite. This can be confirmed by counting.

Playing restaurant

Day 2

✳ **TASTE TEST** Invite children to do a taste test blindfolded, beginning with simple foods and gradually working up to testing foods with multiple ingredients. (You may want to enlist extra adult help for this activity and be aware of any food allergies ahead of time.) Have them begin by wearing a blindfold and tasting a small amount of food from a paper cup or a dish. Choose foods that most children will be familiar with—orange or apple slices, crackers, carrot sticks, pretzels, etc. (Be sure to check for food allergies.) Gradually include complex food tastes with different flavors and spices, such as gingerbread or pumpkin muffins. Ask: *Can you tell what food this is? Can you tell what some of the ingredients are? Which tastes did you like best?* Discuss the differences between sweet foods and spicy or salty foods.

✳ **PLAY RESTAURANT** Ask: *Have you ever been to a restaurant to eat? What kind of food did you eat? Where did you sit? Who cooked the food? Did someone bring the food to your table?* Discuss things like menus, cooks, and waitstaff with children. Then say: *We're going to make our own restaurant with our own menus. What kind of restaurant should we have? What kinds of foods should we serve?* Working together, create a menu and a name for the restaurant. (Limit menu items to five or six choices.) Children can write the items (if they are able) or draw pictures and then decorate the menus. Set up a pretend restaurant in the play corner or other area of the classroom by placing smaller tables together. Allow children to take turns being customers and restaurant staff.

Day 3

✳ **EAT HEALTHY**   Read the book *Growing Vegetable Soup*, by Lois Ehlert. Ask: *What are some of the healthy foods you read about in this book? Where do many healthy foods like these come from? What are some other healthy foods you eat? What are some foods that aren't healthy for our bodies?* Discuss healthy foods and unhealthy foods. Talk about where fruits and vegetables come from. Introduce children to terms like *junk food* and *fast food*. Invite children to look through magazines and other printed papers to find pictures of healthy and unhealthy foods. Have them, in small groups, cut out examples of each and make a collage that shows healthy food and junk food. Ask: *Why is it important to eat healthy foods each day?*

Waiting to order

Songs

- "An Apple a Day"
- "Apples and Bananas"
- "Apples, Peaches"
- "Apple Tree"
- "Hot Cross Buns"
- "Jack Sprat"
- "Little Miss Muffet"
- "Pat-a-Cake"
- "Pease Porridge Hot"

Books

- Andreasen, Dan: *The Baker's Dozen*
- Carle, Eric: *The Very Hungry Caterpillar*
- Ehlert, Lois: *Growing Vegetable Soup*
- Elffers, Joost: *Fast Food*
- Fleming, Denise: *Lunch*
- Hoban, Russell: *Bread and Jam for Frances*
- Robart, Rose: *The Cake that Mack Ate*
- Rosenthal, Amy Krouse: *Little Pea*
- Steig, William: *Pete's a Pizza*
- Waber, Bernard: *Fast Food! Gulp! Gulp!*
- Wells, Rosemary: *Bunny Cakes*

Water

Day 1

(and ongoing)

✳ **EXPLORE WHERE WATER COMES FROM** Ask: *What are some of the places in your house where you get water? What do you use the water for?* Have children suggest as many uses for water as they can think of, including drinking, washing dishes, bathing, watering plants, and caring for pets. Ask: *Where are some of the places in nature where you can find water? Where does the rain come from?* Allow children to speculate about where they think rainwater comes from and to name as many natural sources of water as they can.

Materials for water play

Observe the weather for a week (or more) and have children notice when it is cloudy and when it is sunny. When it rains, put buckets or pails outside and collect rainwater. (Be sure they understand that they should not taste rain water.) Have children notice what happens to the ground after it rains (muddy, puddles, etc.). It's not necessary for children to draw the correct conclusions as long as they are observing and noting what happens. Ask: *Did we collect a lot of water when it rained? What could we use that water for? Why is the rain important to the plants and animals that live outdoors?*

✳ **WATER PLAY** This works best as a small-group activity. Provide a variety of plastic containers. Have each child fill his container with water (from the water table, a large water bucket, or the classroom sink) and then place it on a table set aside for this activity. The container should be full enough that objects can be dropped in but water still has space to rise. Place bowls, pebbles, marbles, and other small objects on the table. Have children gradually add one kind of object to their container of water and note what happens (water will be displaced and will eventually overflow). Have them repeat the experiment using different objects and noting the results for each. Ask: *What happens when we add objects to the water? Has this ever happened to you at home?* Children might mention that water gets higher (water displacement) when they get in a full bathtub or when they put dishes in a full sink.

Day 2

✳ **WHAT FLOATS?**   Have children, in small groups, explore what floats in water and what sinks. Give them various objects of different weights and densities that will float or sink in the classroom water table or individual water containers. Have them experiment with each object and observe which floats best. Ask: *Which object floated best? Which sank fast? Which sank slowly? Why do you think that happened?*

✳ **WATER MUSIC**   This works best as a small-group activity. Invite children to sit on the floor in front of a low table. Line up several glasses of the same size in a row. Use a pitcher to pour varying amounts of water into each glass, increasing the water level so that the last glass contains the most water. Using a spoon, gently tap each glass so that children can hear the higher and lower notes created. Invite each child to take a turn tapping the glasses, and encourage them to create their own melodies.

Songs

- "It's Raining, It's Pouring"
- "Rain, Rain, Go Away"
- "The Itsy Bitsy Spider"
- "Jack and Jill"
- "Row, Row, Row Your Boat"

Books

- Fleming, Denise: *In the Small, Small Pond*
- Frasier, Debra: *Out of the Ocean*
- Lee, Suzy: *Wave*
- Schaefer, Lola: *This Is the Rain*
- Tresselt, Alvin: *Rain Drop Splash*
- Wiesner, David: *Flotsam*

Animal Babies

Day 1

✳ **BEING A BABY** Ask: *What is something that you can do that a baby can't do?* Invite children to demonstrate some of the things they can do—walk, run, jump, talk, write, etc. Ask: *What are some of the ways we take care of babies until they can do things for themselves?* Talk about ways we care for babies. Invite children, using dolls, to role-play scenarios that involve caring for a baby, such as feeding a baby a bottle, rocking it to sleep, carrying, or pushing in a stroller.

Making a nest

✳ **EXPLORING DIFFERENCES** Help children explore the differences between animal babies and human babies. Read the books *Animal Babies*, by Harry McNaught, and *Baby Animal Families*, by Gyo Fujikawa, or books that describe baby animals in the wild. Hand out books and magazines with pictures of baby animals. Ask: *What are some of the ways that animals take care of their babies? When you were a baby, do you think you could do the same things that baby animals can do?* Invite children to make a picture showing a human parent caring for a baby and a picture showing an animal caring for its baby. Talk about the ways they are different.

✳ **FIVE LITTLE ANIMALS** Have children choose one or more of the "Five Little . . ." songs/rhymes included in Appendix A and act out the movements. For example, a group of five children may choose "Five Little Monkeys" and act out the movements while the remaining class members recite the rhyme out loud.

Day 2

✽ **BUILDING A NEST** Ask: *Where did you sleep when you were a baby? Where do you think baby animals sleep?* Talk about familiar animals, like birds, squirrels, and rabbits, and invite children to speculate about where they might sleep and why (for example, children might guess that baby birds sleep in a nest, or that baby squirrels sleep in a tree). Read books about birds, such as *About Birds*, by Cathryn Sill, or show children pictures of different birds' nests. (If possible, bring children outdoors and show them birds' nests, or bring an empty nest into the classroom for children to observe.) Ask: *What do you think birds use to make their nests? Where do they find the things they need?* Provide small groups of children with a variety of materials to use to make nests of their own, such as yarn, straw, raffia, twigs or small branches, pipe cleaners, and clay or play dough. Have them display their nests in the classroom.

Day 3

✽ **TAKE A FIELD TRIP** Take a field trip to a place in your town or city where children might observe live baby animals, such as a zoo, science museum, animal shelter, or natural history museum. If possible, arrange ahead of time for a tour of the exhibit space and for someone to speak to the children about the baby animals and how they are cared for.

✽ **PLAY ANIMALS** Have children bring in a stuffed or plastic animal from home (provide animals for children who need them). Have children create their own pretend animal play area. Encourage them to demonstrate what they know about how animal parents care for their young and how animal babies behave.

Songs

- "Elephant"
- "Five Little Ants"
- "Five Little Bunnies"
- "Five Little Ducks"
- "Five Little Monkeys"
- "Five Little Speckled Frogs"
- "Here Is a Bunny"
- "Six Little Ducks"
- "Three Little Kittens"

Books

- Bauer, Marion Dane: *If You Were Born a Kitten*
- Carle, Eric: *Eric Carle's Animals, Animals*
- Franco, Betsy: *Birdsongs*
- Fujikawa, Gyo: *Baby Animal Families*
- Henkes, Kevin: *Kitten's First Full Moon*
- McNaught, Harry: *Animal Babies*
- Sill, Cathryn: *About Birds*
- Simmons, Jane: *Come Along, Daisy!*
- Tafuri, Nancy: *The Busy Little Squirrel*
- Vaccaro Seeger, Laura: *First the Egg*
- Waddell, Martin: *Owl Babies*

Literacy and Language Lessons

These thirty-five lessons introduce prekindergarteners to the world of literacy in joyful and engaging ways. Some require additional support or are more appropriate for older preK children. Because there is a wide range of developmental abilities within most prekindergarten classrooms, use the lessons that meet the individual and changing needs of your students. Some lessons describe a specific set of steps for a particular activity, while others are generative frameworks you can use with a variety of activities or materials, in different ways, again and again.

Shared Reading

This lesson can be used again and again, with a variety of books or poems. As texts, choose your favorite songs, poems, and rhymes. If you create charts, include some simple pictures to support the text, either drawing them yourself or using clip art or photographs.

RATIONALE Young children love joining you in "reading" or approximating a simple text on a chart or in a big book, and doing so helps them develop print awareness. Though the children may not be "reading the print" they will internalize the language and follow along as you point to each word (left to right, returning to the left side).

YOU NEED

- A simple large-print big book, or simple poems, songs, or rhymes written in large print on chart paper accompanied by drawings or art (see Appendix A for poems, songs, and rhymes)
- Highlighter tape

Teach

- Gather in the meeting area and make sure everyone can see the text, read the poem, rhyme, or story or sing the song in a clear, expressive voice one or two times as the children listen.

- Discuss the meaning of the text.

- Invite the children to join you on the refrain, the repeated language, or the whole text, as appropriate.

- In subsequent lessons, invite a child or two to locate a letter they recognize (often from their names). Have the child mark the letter with highlighter tape. It's best to have just one or two children come up so that the lesson remains short, well-paced, and focused. Choose children based on teaching points within their learning zone—one child might be asked to highlight the first letter in his name, while another might be asked to highlight a familiar word. (Keep a checklist of children who've had a turn.)

Link

Help the children connect the book, poem, rhyme, or song to others with the same topic, author, or illustrator.

Expand

- As children's awareness of print and facility with shared reading develop, choose other elements of the text for children to come up and highlight.

- Some children may enjoy "reading" favorite shared reading texts at a center or at other times during the day. Make sure these texts are accessible to children to read and reread.

- If the text lends itself to it, have children act out the words as they say them.

LESSON 2

Interactive Read-Aloud

YOU NEED

- Beautiful, clearly written, age-appropriate picture books (see Appendix B and Appendix E for recommended books)

This lesson is meant to be a framework and can be used again and again.

RATIONALE   Reading and discussing a variety of high-quality texts with interesting content, language, and vocabulary creates a rich literacy foundation. Consider children's interests, other texts you have read and can build on, and the variety of types of texts recommended in the *PreK Continuum.*

Teach

- Plan your introduction, and place sticky notes at places within the text reminding you to stop and demonstrate responding to the text, or invite the children to share their thinking.
- Position the class so that everyone can see the book and begin reading.
- Link the text to other books or topics the children are learning about.
- Vary your intonation and speed to interpret the author's meaning (read with expression).
- Invite the children to share their spontaneous thinking.
- Invite children's responses to your comments or questions about the text or illustrations. Consider having them turn and talk in pairs about questions you pose.
- Discuss the text with the children so it becomes memorable.
- Perhaps list the title or put a photocopy of the cover on a chart so children have a visual reminder of all the books they've shared.

Link

Select related books in Appendix B or Appendix E or in the text sets in Chapter 11 and use them to develop in-depth knowledge of topics, authors, illustrators, or genres.

Expand

Have the children paint, make collages, draw, make puppets, role-play, or participate in other activities that help them understand the text. (See Chapter 11.)

READING   **LESSON 3**

Recipes

YOU NEED

- Large-print chart with a recipe, along with illustrations of each item and of the final product. Use very simple recipes such as making a sandwich or fruit salad
- Ingredients for the recipe
- Cooking utensils

This lesson works best as a small-group activity with adult support. It is meant to be a framework and can be used again and again.

RATIONALE   Following recipes is authentic reading in action. It's fun to make something together and eat what you've made!

Teach

- Read the recipe, holding up each ingredient and pointing to the corresponding picture on the chart. (The recipe may be a product of interactive writing.)
- Remind students that it is important to follow what the recipe says exactly when measuring. (This is a good link to math!)
- Have individual children help you complete each step of the recipe sequence while others watch. Children love to pour, mix, and spread.
- Eat the results of your work!

Link

- Remind children that they can use recipes at home with their families, too. Perhaps send a letter home explaining the benefits of cooking and using recipes with children (or include this information in a regular newsletter).
- Announce that the children can "read" the recipe again in the play corner.

Expand

- Begin a class recipe book by punching holes in the top of the recipe chart and adding rings and a cover.
- Send a printed copy of the recipe home for families to try, or make a class recipe book as a family gift.
- Use interactive writing to create a few sentences about the experience.
- Read aloud books about recipes and cooking, such as *Cook-a-Doodle-Do*, by Janet Stevens and Susan Stevens Crummel; *Peanut Butter and Jelly*, by Nadine Bernard Westcott; or *The Little Red Hen (Makes a Pizza)*, by Philemon Sturges.

Story Sequencing

YOU NEED

- Blank chart paper or big book pages
- A dark-color marker
- Art materials as appropriate

This lesson is meant to be a framework and can be used again and again. This can be a whole-group or small-group lesson. Three-year-olds will need adult support to do this, probably as a whole-class activity. Four-year-olds also may need support at first but as they become more practiced, they will enjoy retelling and sequencing picture cards independently with a partner.

RATIONALE Looking at and retelling books you have read to the children helps them internalize story structure and language. After you have read and reread some simple, familiar stories, have children retell the story to each other and then practice story sequencing with picture cards.

Teach

- Reread a simple, familiar story, such as *The Very Hungry Caterpillar* by Eric Carle.

- Show your students a set of picture cards that represent characters and events in the story. Have the children help you put the cards in sequential order (you could use a pocket chart), and then retell the story in simple language as you look at the cards together.

- Divide the whole group (or small group) into pairs. (If this is a whole-class activity, keep the partnerships in a circle on the rug so you can walk easily from one to the next.) Give each pair a set of picture cards. Ask the children to arrange the cards in order to show the action of the story from beginning to end.

- Support children in retelling the story to their partner using the picture cards.

Link

Have children talk about how the story would change if the events of the story were in a different sequence. Invite them to talk about why they arranged each card as they did, and encourage them to use the language from the story.

Expand

Invite children to make picture cards of their own, using a simple story they are familiar with. Talk about the sequence of events in the story before they begin making their cards. Laminate the cards and have children share them with one another.

WRITING　　　　**LESSON 5**

Interactive Writing

YOU NEED

- Blank chart paper or big book pages
- A dark-color marker
- Art materials as appropriate

This lesson is meant to be a framework that can be used again and again. The activity can be done with your whole class, a small group, or a single child.

RATIONALE　 In interactive writing, you and the children create a text together for a particular purpose and audience. You write most of the text, but carefully choose several places to invite students to "share the pen" (at first, have them write a letter or a part of their name, for example). This written text can be read over and over.

Teach

- Talk with the children about an experience, thereby grounding the writing you are about to do (e.g., a letter to a zookeeper, a recipe for making peanut butter sandwiches, a shopping list) in an authentic purpose. The richness of the written text develops from the richness of the talk.

- Use the conversation to guide what you write; for example, ask, *How will we say that?*

- Write one word at a time, repeating the whole sentence as you add each word so the children learn language structure. Invite a child to write a letter (or her or his name) at selected points as appropriate. You may use a verbal description to help the child form the letter (see Appendix H, Verbal Path). In some cases you may want to guide the child's hand.

- Reread the text several times when completed.

- You may want to have children, at their tables, draw pictures that you later cut out and add to the chart.

Link

Remind children about what they know how to do (e.g., write the first letter of their name, say a word slowly) and ask them to use this knowledge when they write independently.

Expand

- Provide more rich opportunities to write with real purpose.

- Have the children help you create more texts for reading lessons.

WRITING   **LESSON 6**

Interactive Drawing

This lesson can be used again and again. You may continue the drawing over several sessions, especially if you have chosen a complex subject. (As children become more proficient you'll highlight more sophisticated drawing techniques and choose more complex subjects.) At first, choose something simple and familiar that can be completed in one session—an object or a person, not an experience. Help children notice the details.

RATIONALE   Children's drawings represent their thinking. When you ask a child to talk about her earliest primitive drawings, you hear her thinking. (Very often children talk to themselves while drawing.) You can help young children learn how to create images that represent their thinking by demonstrating ways to draw and enabling them to see objects and people more precisely as you work on a class drawing together. When children first begin to draw, they play with making marks on a page and do not distinguish drawing from writing. As children become more aware of print, some of the marks they make begin to look more letterlike.

Teach

- Tell the children that artists and writers can use drawings to show their thinking on paper.

- Briefly show them some examples of different types of drawings in books. Ask them what they notice about the drawings. You may have them turn and talk to each other about what they notice, and then share two or three children's examples with the whole group. This should take only a moment or two.

- Tell them that just like the authors and artists in the books they love, they can show their thinking on paper too.

- Tell them that today you will be making a picture of whatever object you have chosen (for example, a vase of flowers). Tell them that the first thing artists do is look very carefully at the thing they are drawing. Have students look very carefully at the object and talk about what they notice.

- Begin your drawing, "thinking aloud" for the children as you go.

- Ask what is missing from the drawing (for example, you could leave out the flower stems).

YOU NEED

- Chart paper or large blank paper for drawing

- Markers or other drawing implements that will be easy for children to use and whose marks will be easy for children to see

- Picture books with examples of different kinds of drawings

- A predetermined subject for your drawing (the first time you present the lesson)

- Invite one child to come to the front and add the thing that is missing from the drawing. Discuss what shape that thing is, where it should be located on the picture, etc.

- Repeat this process with two or three more students, highlighting whatever aspects of drawing you are focusing on.

Link

As you read stories aloud, stop to help the children notice details in objects and people. Remind them that they can include such details when they are drawing.

Expand

- Start a drawing of a particular object or scene. Add to the scene each day, putting in more details, highlighting new things about drawing (different shapes, different styles etc).

- Use interactive drawing to create a class big book about a shared experience (see Lesson 12).

Verbal Path

YOU NEED

- Dark-color, washable or erasable markers
- Large chart paper or individual writing books
- Verbal path directions (Appendix H)

RATIONALE Young children need numerous opportunities to explore using different writing implements to create a variety of forms (drawings). When they are beginning to learn to write letters, learning the specific motor movements for writing letters will help them make efficient, legible letter forms. Pairing the verbal path descriptions with motor movements helps children form letters efficiently. Eventually, they will internalize the language, and the actions will become automatic. You will not be doing specific handwriting lessons but rather embedding the verbal path language in other writing contexts.

Teach

- When you invite a child to contribute a letter during interactive writing or when you want to support letter formation in independent writing or any other activity involving writing letters, demonstrate making the letter while saying the language that supports it.

- Be careful not to overdo these prompts when children are just learning to make marks on paper. They first need opportunities to explore making marks on the page without constraints.

- When you think the children are ready to proceed without the prompts, discontinue the language support.

Link

Be sure to use the same language each time you support letter formation. Consistency is key. Since teaching children to write their name is a priority, teach the correct formation of those letters.

Expand

Help the children notice the letters they formed well.

Alphabet Book Making

YOU NEED

- A blank big book (large sheets of paper stapled together) with twenty-six pages, one for each letter of the alphabet
- A large collection of pictures (cut them out of magazines or draw them yourself)
- Markers for writing the letters and making drawings

In this lesson, you begin creating a whole-class alphabet book that you'll add to together in the next few days. Read many alphabet books with your children before beginning this work. (See Appendix E and Chapter 19.)

RATIONALE Young children are beginning to understand that there are twenty-six different letters in the alphabet and that these letters are put together to form words. They are beginning to learn that each letter has a form, a name, and represents a sound. When you read or make alphabet books with them, they have the opportunity to read and reread the letter or the picture many times, which helps them internalize this awareness.

Teach

- Remind children about the alphabet books they have read and how each book shows all twenty-six letters along with a picture and/or word representing something that starts with that letter. You may want to have several examples on hand to jog their memories.

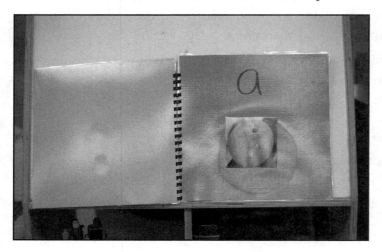

- Tell your students that you will be creating an alphabet book together, starting with the letter *a*. Write the letter *a* on the first page of the blank book you have prepared as your students watch. Then ask a child (or several, if you have multiple pictures to add) to come up and add a picture of something that begins with *a* to the page.

- On the following day review the letter *a* and associated pictures on the completed page. Then create the next page with the letter *b*.

- Repeat until all pages of the big book are filled. Place the book in the reading area so children can look at it independently.

Link

Invite the children to find more pictures from magazines or newspapers at home to glue on each page.

Expand

Give each child a small, twenty-six-page 8-½-by-11-inch stapled book with a letter on each page. Invite them to take the books home and make their own alphabet books with their family members.

My Book

This lesson explains how to launch the My Book project; children make one page today and the other pages on following days. This activity works best with a small group.

YOU NEED

- Blank copies of the first My Book page for each student (My Book by _____) See Appendix J for template

- A sample My Book that you have made about yourself

- Colored pencils, markers, crayons, or other drawing implements

RATIONALE Children in preschool are beginning to connect the marks they see written on paper with meaning. They are experimenting with writing for their own enjoyment, but they are also aware that writing has many real-life purposes, and they enjoy "playing" at purposeful writing, just as they enjoy playing at other things. This activity lets children practice writing and drawing about what they know about themselves.

Teach

- First, talk with the children about the purpose of the writing they are about to do, which is to share what they know about themselves—their names, ages, birthdays, what they enjoy doing with family and friends, and what some of their "favorites" are (their favorite color, for example). Be judicious about which pages to include. If the children don't yet know their birthdays, for example, leave that page out.

- Read each page of your sample My Book to your students. Then show them the blank page they will be working on today. Tell them that they will be drawing a picture of themselves on that page. You might talk about trying to make their pictures look like them—choosing colors that match colors they are wearing, etc. Three-year-olds will most likely need a lot of adult support with this (you may even want to have some small plastic mirrors for children to use as they draw).

- Send the children to their seats to begin working. As they work, support those children who need help writing their name, and remind them to add as many details as they can to their pictures.

Link

Tell your students that they will be making the other pages of the book on other days.

Expand

- As children share their books with others, encourage them to tell more about each page— telling the names of family members or describing activities they enjoy doing and why, for example.

- Display the books for the children to see and "read" for themselves.

- Invite the children to add to their My Book over time. Make additional pages that describe other important activities, people, and experiences in children's lives. (Also refer to the inquiry project "All About Me," in Appendix C).

BOOKS　　　　**LESSON 10**

Class Big Book: Songs and Poems

This lesson is meant to be a framework and can be used again and again.

RATIONALE When children say rhymes or sing songs aloud they develop their knowledge of the sounds of language. They also learn new vocabulary, language structures, and content. They come to love the poems and songs you read together during shared reading and love looking through them again and again when they are put together into a big book. This lesson introduces the class big book to the class; you will add new poems and songs to it throughout the year.

YOU NEED

- A tablet of blank chart paper or some other kind of large blank book
- Large-print copy of poem or song

Mary had a little lamb.
Its fleece
was white as snow.
And everywhere
that Mary went
the lamb
was sure to go.

Teach

- Explain that you will be collecting all the poems and songs the children learn during the year in the blank book you have prepared.
- Read a poem or song (one the children have previously worked with) several times, and then glue it into the book as the children watch.
- Tell them they will be adding drawings to match the characters or objects in the poem or song, and send them off to draw at their tables.
- Collect the students' drawings and, later, cut them out and glue them on the page with the poem or song. Revisit the page after you have added their pictures. (Perhaps ask children to guess which poem it is based on the pictures they see.)

Link

Before introducing a new poem or song to say or sing, invite the children to choose an old favorite from your book.

Expand

Have each child create art around a small-print version of a very short and memorable poem or song. Photocopy it and give children a copy to take home. Alternatively, each child can glue the poem or song in a personal blank notebook. (An example might be "Happy Birthday to You" with the child's name inserted.)

BOOKS   **LESSON 11**

Bookmaking

Bookmaking works best as a small-group activity during choice time. It can be done in a specified bookmaking area/table, or in the writing center/area. This lesson is an introduction you might present to the whole class.

RATIONALE   Young children are natural writers. Their drawings and marks on the page represent their thinking, and they can tell you all about the meaning they are trying to convey. They love to tell their stories and share the thinking behind their scribbles and drawings. When they make books, they view themselves as writers who have something to say to others.

Teach

- Tell the children they can create books, just like the authors and illustrators they know. Show them a few picture books that are examples of different ways authors/illustrators put pictures and words on paper to tell their stories or give information. (Show only a few examples of books you have read aloud in the past as it's important to keep this part short and to the point so children stay focused.) Don't read the stories; just show a couple of representative pages. Use label books, wordless books, alphabet books, and information picture books, as well as picture storybooks so they see that books can be about so many different topics.

- Tell the children they will be making books in the bookmaking area. Show them one of the blank books you have made, as well as some of the papers they can use later for covers. Tell them they can use pictures and words to tell stories—stories about things that really happened, made-up stories, or stories that teach people things.

- Direct children to their choice time activities. It's best to have an adult working in the bookmaking area at first until all the children have been introduced to it, both to help children manage the materials and to teach them about bookmaking (choosing an idea, representing your idea on paper, making the book before making the cover, etc.).

- After choice time activities have been completed, have the children who made books share them with the class as a celebration.

Link

Tell your students to keep thinking about ideas for books to make, and remind them that bookmaking will be an option during choice time (or other times you choose).

Expand

- List the titles of the books the children have made on a poster headed "Books by Our Authors." Next to each title write the child's name.

- Explore different ways to make books. Use a variety of bindings (e.g., tape, sewn, stapled, bound) and other materials. Share books of different sizes and design styles as models.

LESSON 12

Original Class Big Book

YOU NEED

- Chart paper or other large blank paper stapled together into a big booklet
- Markers or other drawing implements that produce marks that are easy to see
- A shared experience that lends itself to being turned into a sequential story

This project will take several sessions to complete. You should probably finish the book within two weeks in order to maintain interest and focus.

RATIONALE   This lesson combines several skills children have been practicing separately—interactive drawing, interactive writing, and shared reading. Creating an original class big book about a shared experience is an excellent way to scaffold skills you hope children will eventually be able to perform independently. It's also a wonderful community-building experience. Children are extremely motivated to retell a favorite shared experience and will be equally motivated to read and reread the book when it is finished. Creating a big book together is an opportunity to highlight any number of skills—story sequencing, drawing, phonemic awareness, writing, etc.—depending on your children's ages and needs. Three-year-olds can practice sequentially retelling a shared experience and drawing. Four-year-olds can do these same things and also practice sharing the pen to write letters representing sounds they hear in words and even some simple words they know on sight.

Teach

- Tell the children that together you will make a book about a shared experience.

- Ask children to think together about how the story should start. You may have children turn and talk together and then share two or three ideas.

- When you have decided how the story should begin, ask children what you should draw to show that part of the story. Again, you may have children turn and talk or just solicit several ideas.

- If appropriate for your class, use interactive drawing (see Lesson 6) and interactive writing (see Lesson 5) to create the first page of your book, including simple text children will be able to practice "reading" when the book is finished. Highlight whatever aspects of drawing and writing you are working on as you ask individuals to come up and share the pen. For example, you might have a three-year-old come up and add the sun in a story of a walk through the neighborhood, then have an almost four-year-old add the *S* for *sun.*

- Work on one page of the story each day. Continue until the book is finished. You can use the book for shared reading. Also make it available for students to look at during other times in the day.

Link

Remind students that they can use these same skills (be specific) when they are making their own books. When students are writing independently, remind them of things they've practiced when making the class big book.

Expand

- Write a nonfiction book together collecting information students have learned through an inquiry project.

- Write a big book together as a thank you for a class volunteer or visitor.

　　　　LESSON 13

Book Boxes

YOU NEED

- Cards for book titles
- Shoeboxes or other boxes and baskets
- Recycled materials
- Glue, markers, colored papers
- Sample box celebrating your own favorite book to use as an example

This activity needs the support of children's family members. Before you begin, send a letter home explaining the project and asking family members to collect shoeboxes and recycled art materials and help their child choose objects from home that are related to their favorite book.

RATIONALE Children enjoy rereading and revisiting many of their favorite books and are eager to look at and retell stories you have read to them. Help deepen their connection with books by inviting them to create book boxes—simple shoeboxes or other boxes or baskets that they decorate and fill with small objects that are related to a favorite book. The box might contain pictures or objects that the book makes them think about or that they can use to tell the story. When they've completed their box they can talk about and share it with others. Some teachers have all children share on the same day; others give each child a special day on which to share their book and objects.

Teach

- Explain to the children that they are going to collect, in special book boxes, items related to a book they love. Show them your example, and tell them that today they will be working on decorating their boxes. Show them the available materials.

- Have the children decorate their boxes. They can look through a favorite book for ideas.

- Have them glue a large book title card on the box to identify it (they can dictate the title as you write it on the card).

- Children may then put objects in the boxes as they think of them. (Many will not want to leave favorite items at school and will bring them on the day they are scheduled to share.)

- Each week (or month) have a special day when one child or several children share their favorite book and their book box. Read the book aloud, then have the children share what each object tells about the book and why they chose it.

Link

- List the objects in each box on the inside of the box cover.
- After you read aloud stories, ask the children what objects they think they might include in a book box related to that story.

Expand

Use interactive writing to write a letter home to families explaining what the children are doing with their book boxes.

LETTERS, SOUNDS, AND WORDS   **LESSON 14**

Oral Games and Phonemes

YOU NEED

• A variety of poems and songs (see Appendix A)

This lesson can be used again and again with different sounds and words to develop strong sensitivity to the sounds of language.

RATIONALE A goal of early learning is to develop a love for language. One aspect of learning language is becoming sensitive to the units of sound that make up the language. prekindergarteners can learn to hear rhymes or syllables (word parts) and beginning/ending sounds (individual sounds or phonemes). Songs and games are means by which children use language in joyful ways and at the same time become sensitive to the sounds of language (see Chapter 8). If you sing songs and say poems with your children often, they have a repertoire of known songs and poems you can use to highlight rhymes, syllable, beginning and ending sounds, etc.

Teach

• Sing a song or say a poem together.

• Point out the rhyming words and ask students to think of other words they know that sound the same.

• Ask children to respond to questions related to units of sound. ("I'm thinking of a word that rhymes with *Jill*. What do you think it is?" "I'm thinking of a word that sounds like *Janessa* at the beginning.")

Link

Use songs, poems, or oral games while children are cleaning up, getting their jackets, traveling to the rest room, etc.

Expand

Invite children to suggest innovations for the songs or poems you teach (substituting new rhyming words, for example). Appendix A has a variety of suggestions for activities related to specific songs, rhymes, and poems.

Picture Sort

You can do this activity for a brief time with your whole class or for longer periods with small groups.

RATIONALE prekindergarteners are developing a sensitivity and attentiveness to the sounds they hear in language. When you invite them to join you in singing songs or reciting poems, you give them opportunities to develop their awareness of rhymes in words. Activities like singing and reciting are best because they allow children to attend only to the sounds they hear. Picture cards representing words that rhyme (with some non-rhyming pictures/words included) help children develop their awareness of rhyme.

YOU NEED

- Familiar poems
  (see Appendix A)

- Picture cards representing words that rhyme. (Available in many school materials including Phonics Lessons, Pinnell and Fountas, Heinemann 2003)

- Pocket chart

Teach

- Explain that as you and the children say poems together out loud the ends of some words sound the same. Read a poem that is very familiar to your class and ask the children to notice the rhyming words in that poem. You may want to highlight the rhyming words (*dock* and *clock* in "Hickory Dickory Dock," for example).

- Tell the children that there are lots of words that sound the same as the rhyming words in the poem. For "Hickory Dickory Dock," for example, show them a picture card whose label rhymes with *clock*, like *sock*. Say the word clearly and place the picture card in a pocket chart. Tell your students that together you will look through the picture cards to find other words that rhyme with *sock* and *clock*—that sound the same at the end. Then show them another picture card that rhymes (e.g., *block*), say the word it represents out loud, and place the card next to the first card.

- Hold up pairs of picture cards and ask children whether they rhyme. Place the rhyming cards in the pocket chart.

- Review the pairs of rhyming words by having the children say them aloud.

Link

Tell your students to keep their ears open and listen for rhyming words in other poems or songs they know.

Expand

- As you read poems, place highlighter tape on the rhyming words and have the children say those words louder.

- In an adult-supported activity, have children spread picture cards on a table and match the ones that rhyme.

- Repeat this lesson with picture cards that represent things that start with the same sound (e.g., *sun, star*). Have the children listen for the sound as you exaggerate or emphasize it.

"Me" Boxes

YOU NEED

- Name cards
- Shoeboxes, baskets, or similar containers
- Recycled materials
- Glue, markers, colored papers
- Pictures of small objects for children who aren't able to bring things from home

Carry out this activity over several months. Store the boxes along a window sill (if you have one) or on shelves. Many teachers find this project works best as a small-group choice time activity with adult support. You can also ask family members to help their child collect objects to bring in for the "Me" Box.

RATIONALE A major goal of early learning is developing oral language. Young children love to talk about themselves, and sharing items that represent important memories can be a wonderful way to stimulate conversation. "Me" Boxes are simple shoeboxes, baskets, or similar containers which the children decorate and in which they place small objects that are special to them. They then talk about and share them with others.

Teach

- Create your own "Me" Box of special items (for example, a shell because you love the beach) and share it with the class to stir their enthusiasm.
- Explain that as a project activity, each child will create a "Me" Box to fill with special items.
- Have three or four students at a time come to a special table or area where you have materials set up and support them as they decorate their boxes. (A teacher's aide or volunteer can do this for you.)
- After students are finished decorating their "Me" Boxes, have them glue a large name card on the box to identify it.
- Each week have a special day on which the children who have made "Me" Boxes can add items to their boxes and share what the contents tell about them. These items may also become topics for drawing and writing in bookmaking.

Link

- List the objects in each child's box on the inside of the box cover.

- After you read stories aloud, ask the children what objects they think a character from that book might put in her or his "Me" Box.

Expand

Use interactive writing to write a letter to family members explaining what children are doing with their "Me" Boxes.

Text Innovations

YOU NEED

- A poem, song, rhyming book, or other text that has repetitive language

Do this activity as a whole class in your meeting area or as the students are moving from place to place.

RATIONALE When young children become familiar with the language or structure of a poem, song, or book, they internalize it and make it their own. They enjoy experiencing the same text over and over until it becomes an old favorite. This is an ideal time to "innovate" a text by substituting names, other rhyming words, even silly words. For example, you can substitute children's names for the animals in Eric Carle's *Brown Bear, Brown Bear*: "Michael, Michael, what do you see? I see Paulo looking at me."

Teach

- Reread a text that has become an old favorite.

- Model leaving out a word in the text and "innovating" by substituting a word or phrase. For example, in "Hickory Dickory Dock," you might substitute the word *sock, dock,* or *block* for *clock.*

- As you read the text again, pause before the word you're going to replace and invite the children to say the new word with you.

- Ask the students to come up with ideas for other words they could substitute. In "Hickory Dickory Dock" you might prompt them to come up with *rock* or *block.*

Link

Repeat the process with rhyming books such as *Green as a Bean, Who Took the Cookies From the Cookie Jar?, We're Going on a Bear Hunt, The Bear Came Over to My House,* and *Ready, Set, Skip!* Actions and words in songs such as "The Wheels on the Bus" can be adapted as well. (See Appendix A).

Expand

Create a big book that includes the children's innovations and have the children contribute the art. They will enjoy reading the book over and over again. Children especially enjoy books that use their own names or friends' names.

LANGUAGE

LESSON 18

Storytelling

- Favorite picture books (unless the students will be telling their own stories)

This lesson can be used again and again. Provide plenty of support, especially for three-year-olds (you can share the storytelling).

RATIONALE When children hear stories, they learn how language represents thinking or ideas. When they tell their own stories, or retell stories of others, they practice expressing thoughts and ideas with language. Numerous opportunities to tell and retell favorite stories expand children's thinking, language skills, and vocabulary, and support their ability to move from telling stories to writing them.

Teach

This lesson can be taught in different ways. Here are some options:

- When you read aloud, stop at a few points to give the children opportunities to turn and talk about something specific to the story.

- After reading several related books (e.g., several versions of the story of Goldilocks and the Three Bears, or several books about seasons) have pairs of children share a book, look at the pictures, and tell the stories to each other.

- Tell important stories from your own experience on topics you know about and care about or assign a topic such as a story about your grandparents or a special birthday.

- Invite pairs of children to tell each other a story. Be sure each child tells you the topic of his or her story beforehand. Give them enough time, and change partners regularly.

Link

Keep a list of topics the children have told stories about so they can see that everyone has stories to tell and are aware of the kinds of topics others are telling stories about. Read the list prior to storytelling time.

Expand

As you read aloud picture books by various authors, talk about where the authors likely got their ideas for their stories. Help children learn that authors tell stories about what is important to them or what they know about.

LANGUAGE   **LESSON 19**

Puppet Making

YOU NEED

- Glue, popsicle sticks or tongue depressors, brown paper bags, colored paper, tissue paper, cardboard
- Buttons, fabric scraps, and other recycled materials

RATIONALE Children love making and playing with puppets. When children play with puppets they assume many different roles (animals, characters from stories, members of their community) and tell stories or share information through dialogue that enriches their oral language development.

Teach

- Talk with the children about characters from the stories you have read.
- Have each child make a puppet representing their favorite character. (Alternatively, everyone can make the same character.)
- Show the children the materials they can use to make the puppet.
- Vary the kinds of puppets (sock puppets, stick puppets, paper bag puppets).
- Circulate, helping children execute their unique creations.
- Invite children to make their puppets "talk."

Link

Invite the children to take their finished puppets to the play corner and put on a puppet show. They might also enjoy more casual play with a partner or in small groups, letting their puppets "talk" to each other or play together.

Expand

Read aloud books with just a few favorite, memorable characters that lend themselves to simple puppet shows, like *Goldilocks and the Three Bears* or *The Three Little Pigs*.

LESSON 20

Play Corner

This lesson, which introduces children to a new environment in the play corner, can be used again and again.

RATIONALE   Play is essential to help children develop imagination, language, vocabulary, literacy, and life skills. You can create many authentic play environments—a restaurant, a market, a veterinarian's office—complete with all the print and nonprint artifacts that support learning.

YOU NEED

- Props related to the environment (see Chapter 4, Figure 4.21)

- Books, writing materials, and other print materials appropriate to the environment (see Chapter 4, Figure 4.21)

Teach

- Read aloud a variety of books to build children's knowledge about and pique their interest in the new play corner environment.

- Tell the children that there will be new things to play with in the play corner. Remind them about the books they have been reading, and ask them to guess what kinds of things they might find in the play corner. (You may want to show them some of these objects.)

- Remind the children that everyone will get a turn in the play corner! Use whatever system works to ensure fairness and prevent overcrowding.

Link

Ask students for suggestions about things that could be added to the play corner. You could make a list and arrange it together.

Expand

- Use interactive writing and shared reading to create artifacts related to the environment (recipes or menus for the restaurant or an appointment book for the veterinarian, for example).

- Read aloud a variety of texts related to the play corner theme. (See the list of books in Appendix E.)

　　　LESSON 21

Recognizing Signs and Symbols

YOU NEED

- *I Read Symbols,* by Tana Hoban
- Cards with familiar symbols (These are available commercially in school supply stores or on the Internet; you can also take digital photos of familiar signs or symbols and print them from your computer)

RATIONALE　Prekindergarteners will often notice familiar words and symbols in their larger world—a stop sign or the name of a favorite restaurant, for example. Children naturally want to read and understand these signs and symbols, and they can use this awareness that print is meaningful to learn new words and understandings.

Teach

- Read *I Read Symbols* by Tana Hoban aloud.
- Talk with the children about the different symbols in the book, which ones they recognize, and what they mean.
- If possible, walk around the neighborhood and point out signs and symbols from the book. Alternatively, reproduce appropriately sized and colored symbols and display them in your classroom. (You may want to do this in addition to going outside.)
- Hold up pictures of a variety of signs and symbols and ask the children to identify them. Talk about what to do when you see a particular sign or symbol (stop at a stop sign, for example).

Link

Point out signs and symbols in the school. Discuss what they mean.

Expand

- Set up a route through the classroom or on the playground that includes many signs and symbols. Have children walk from sign to sign and talk about what each one means.
- Keep a class list of signs and symbols that the children see on their way to school or in other places. Have them draw a picture of each symbol and then share what they think it means.

　　LESSON 22

Descriptive Words

This lesson can be used again and again to stimulate children's curiosity about words and develop their vocabulary.

RATIONALE　Vocabulary contributes significantly to reading comprehension, and children's ability to express themselves is closely related to the words they understand. You can encourage them to use new words as they investigate a topic, listen to and discuss stories that you read aloud, and participate in the shared reading of poems, songs, and rhymes.

YOU NEED

- Engaging books and stories (see Appendix E)
- Poems, rhymes, and songs (see Appendix A)
- Baskets or boxes for word categories and cards for labels

Teach

- Keep a list of descriptive vocabulary words as you share stories, poems, and rhymes with the children.

- Bring in a collection of everyday objects (stuffed animals, kitchen utensils, food items, clothing) you can use to revisit the descriptive vocabulary words from your reading. Pass the objects around one at a time and give each child a chance to look at and touch the objects.

- Discuss each object. Remind children of descriptive vocabulary words they are familiar with from their reading. (For example, if children have read the poem "Twinkle, Twinkle, Little Star," you might repeat the poem and then describe an object as *twinkly* or *sparkly*.)

- Classify each object by color, size, texture, or any other criteria you choose. For example, place all soft objects in one basket and all shiny objects in another. Try classifying the same objects according to several different criteria, always eliciting as much descriptive language from the children as possible.

Link

Point out and describe other objects in the room and categorize them using descriptive words.

Expand

Keep small baskets or boxes in the classroom, labeled with a descriptive word, that contain representative objects (or pictures of those objects). Encourage children to add objects to the baskets. Change the labels to new words from time to time.

LESSON 23

Alphabet Hunt

YOU NEED

- Photos (or drawings) of letters in the environment

- Stapled chart paper or a blank big book, one letter (in alphabetical order) written on each page

- Markers

RATIONALE As children become more and more familiar with what letters look like, they begin to notice them everywhere! For example, if they know the letter *W*, they may notice it on a cereal box (*Wheaties*) or on a store front (*Walgreens* or *Wendy's*). Children can learn a lot about print by paying attention to their everyday environment both inside and outside the classroom.

Teach

- If possible, lead a walk around the neighborhood looking for names of familiar businesses that begin with the letters of the alphabet (popular chain restaurants and stores, for example). Take photos or make drawings of these names.

- Paste the photographs or drawings on the appropriate page of the stapled chart paper or big book.

- For two or three weeks, add examples to the chart. Reread the alphabet book frequently as you are creating it, and when it is finished, keep it in your classroom for children to reread.

Link

- Make a small photocopied version of the book for each child to reread and take home.

- Give the children a blank alphabet book so they can make the same type of book with their families.

Expand

- Have children hunt for letters in the print in your classroom.

- Read aloud Mary Hill's books *Signs on the Road*, *Signs at the Store*, and *Signs at the Park*; Tana Hoban's *I Read Signs*; and/or *City Signs*, by Zoran Milich.

LESSON 24

Alphabet Nature Walk

YOU NEED

- A shoebox for collecting objects
- Stapled construction paper or a blank big book
- Markers

With three-year-olds, this activity will be much more about the walk and the collecting than about generating letters/sounds. You'll simply expose them to the idea by mentioning the initial letters/sounds of the objects they find. Many four-year-olds will begin thinking of letters/sounds on their own.

RATIONALE In searching for natural objects and talking with you and each other about the initial letters and sounds in the objects' labels, children encounter the idea that we think about letters in meaningful contexts every day.

Teach

- Walk around the playground or neighborhood pointing out and collecting natural objects whose labels begin with different letters. For example, you might collect an acorn, a daffodil, a blade of grass, a leaf, a pinecone, a rose, a stick, and a twig. If this "nature walk" isn't possible, bring in photographs of these same objects (or you can cut them out of magazines). Simple, colorful drawings are also okay.

- Place the objects (or the representations of them) in the shoebox. Discuss the objects, including colors and textures.

- Glue each object (or photograph of the object) to a piece of paper and write the corresponding initial letter (e.g., leaf, *L*).

- Add to the book over time. Reread it as a class. You may create a complete, sequential alphabet book, containing an object from the natural world to represent each letter, but this is not necessary.

Link

Remind children that everything they see in nature has a name that starts with a letter. Encourage them to think and talk about this with their family members when they are outdoors.

Expand

- Give each child a blank book from which to made his or her own alphabet book of natural objects.

- Read aloud alphabet books that use natural objects, such as *The Flower Alphabet Book*, by Jerry Pallotta, and *A B Cedar: An Alphabet of Trees*, by George Lyon.

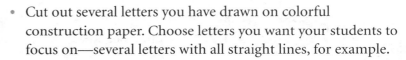

Alphabet Hide-and-Seek

This lesson can be used again and again to develop children's familiarity with the letters.

RATIONALE   Children need to think about the distinctive features of letters—what makes each letter different from every other letter. In addition to the important work of noticing and using letters that are embedded within meaningful text, young children also enjoy exploring the individual features of the letters.

YOU NEED

- Colored construction paper, scissors
- Stapled chart paper or a blank big book
- Markers

Teach

- Cut out several letters you have drawn on colorful construction paper. Choose letters you want your students to focus on—several letters with all straight lines, for example.

- Hide the letters somewhere in the classroom where children will be able to find them easily.

- Tell the children you have a mystery for them to solve—some letters have disappeared and they must find them. Show them pictures of the letters and ask children to describe their attributes.

- Invite the children to search for the letters. After they find them all, collect the letters and reassemble as a group. Examine the letters together and have the children talk about how they could tell which letter was which based on its attributes.

- Repeat the activity with other letters.

Link

Collect the letters in a basket as children find them until you've collected the whole alphabet. Invite children to put the letters in order or to hide them again.

Expand

Invite children to point out letters in classroom print that correspond to the hidden letters.

Alphabet Linking Chart

YOU NEED

- A pointer
- An enlarged version of an alphabet linking chart (see Appendix G)

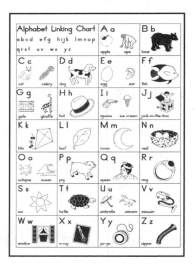

RATIONALE Prekindergarteners are becoming aware of the print symbols that represent meaning in books. They also begin to notice the distinctive shapes of some letters and their individual sounds. They may associate the sounds and the letters with the label a picture represents.

Teach

- Explain that you are going to show them a chart with letters that will be fun to read together.
- Read, chant, or sing (to the tune of "The Alphabet Song") the chart aloud several times, varying the way you read it and pointing to each letter.
- Invite the children to say or sing the chart with you. (The pictures will support them.)

Link

When children are ready to begin writing letters to represent the sounds they hear in words, remind them about this chart. ("You want to write *car*? Look at the chart. It starts like in *cat*.")

Expand

- Cut up a large alphabet chart into squares, one letter on each square. Give the children a set of colored plastic magnet letters to match with the letters in the boxes.
- Give the children a small copy of the alphabet linking chart and a chopstick, and have them sing or read the letters to a partner using the pictures as clues.

LESSON 27

Letter Exploration

YOU NEED

- Buckets of letters of a variety of sizes and materials (foam, plastic, multicolored)

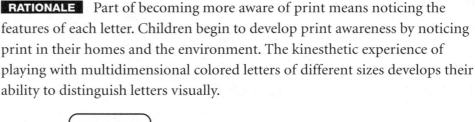

RATIONALE Part of becoming more aware of print means noticing the features of each letter. Children begin to develop print awareness by noticing print in their homes and the environment. The kinesthetic experience of playing with multidimensional colored letters of different sizes develops their ability to distinguish letters visually.

Teach

- Invite the children to tell what the objects in the buckets are called, or explain to them that all the items in the buckets are called letters.
- Tell them they may have seen some of the letters before in school, at home, or in the neighborhood.
- Explain that they can empty the bucket and play with the letters on the table or put them on their whiteboard.
- Give the children time to explore the letters in whatever way they wish.
- Observe what they do with the letters and what they say about them.

Link

Tell your students that the letters will be available for them to explore again and again (during choice time, for example).

Expand

- Read a number of alphabet books, review the alphabet linking chart, have the children trace sandpaper letters, or have them sort letters with similar features into piles. Help them learn the word *letters*.
- Have children find any letters in their name in other classroom print. (They can use a name card as support.)
- Have children find two letters that look the same.

Letter Sort

YOU NEED

- A large magnetic board
- Individual whiteboards (preferably magnetic)
- Buckets of colorful plastic letters
- Plastic bowls or cups for children to sort letters into
- "Ways to Sort Letters" (Appendix I)

This lesson is most successful when working with a small group of children in a center activity, so that everyone can see and touch the letters as you introduce the concept of sorting.

RATIONALE To learn and read English young children need to distinguish between the symbols that make up the English alphabet. Sorting letters helps children develop their ability to notice the distinguishing features of each letter. Noticing the ways children put together a pile of letters and what they say about them will help you understand what they are learning about print.

Teach

- Explain to the children that they can play with letters. Tell them they may notice some letters that they have seen before.
- Spread a pile of letters on the table. Demonstrate several ways to sort them (refer to "Ways to Sort Letters," Appendix I, for ideas—for example, by color, matching pairs, letters with circles).
- Ask the children to sort the letters into piles or into the plastic bowls you've provided. Let them can decide how.
- Give the children time to play with and sort letters.

Link

Tell the children that the letters and cups will be available for playing with and sorting again (during choice time, for example).

Expand

- Show children how the colorful plastic letters are the same shapes as the letters in a simple alphabet book.
- Include letters made of different materials (foam, rubber, etc.) and letters of different sizes in the sorting buckets. Demonstrate some new ways to sort— letters with tails, letters with no tails, for example.

LANGUAGE

LESSON 29

Making Letters Using Play Dough (or Ready-Made Clay)

YOU NEED

- Large letter cards for models
- A recipe for play dough or quantities of ready-made clay (You can find recipes on the Internet, or try this simple recipe: mix ½ cup salt, ½ cup water, 1 cup flour, food coloring)
- Paper trays or paper plates

RATIONALE Children need to learn what makes one letter different from another. This means more than looking at letters—it also includes touching them. Offering students many kinds of kinesthetic experiences helps them notice and learn the features of letters.

Teach

- Ideally, first create the play dough recipe using interactive writing. Then post the recipe where children can see it.

- Make the play dough with the children. (Alternatively, use ready-made clay.)

- Hold up a large letter card and use the play dough (or clay) to make the letter on a paper plate.

- Explain that the children should choose a letter card and make that letter using their hands to mold the play dough (or clay). (You might suggest they choose the first letter in their name.)

Link

Look for opportunities to connect the letter each child made with a page in an alphabet book you read aloud so they understand that the letter can be any size or color and can be seen in many places.

Expand

Have the children find each letter on the alphabet linking chart or select it from a magnetic cookie sheet displaying magnet letters.

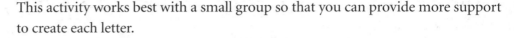

NAMES   **LESSON 30**

Tissue Paper Names

This activity works best with a small group so that you can provide more support to create each letter.

RATIONALE Working with letters kinesthetically supports young children's print awareness or ability to look at print. This activity helps the children attend to the distinctive features of each letter in their name.

YOU NEED

- Individual children's names written in black on a strip of card stock
- Your name written in black on card stock
- White glue in shallow cups
- Large sheets of drawing paper
- Baskets of individual squares of many colors of tissue paper for each table

Teach

- Hold up the card on which you've written your name and explain that these are the letters in your name.

  - Show children how to take a small piece of tissue paper, bunch it up, dip it in glue and paste it over the line representing the first letter on the card.

  - Repeat the process with a few more letters in your name until the children understand what to do.

  - Give the children their name cards and have them work at tables.

  - When they complete their name cards, you might have them glue the card to the bottom of a sheet of drawing paper and make a self-portrait.

  - Display the portraits on the walls of the classroom.

Link

Include children's names wherever you can in the classroom—on cubbies, above coat hooks, on a birthday list, etc.

Expand

Give children name cards (name written in black on card stock) and a box of colored or metallic gummed stars. Have them affix the stars along the lines that form the letters of their name, so their name is spelled out in stars. Then have them glue the name card at the bottom of a sheet of paper and draw a self-portrait.

NAMES   **LESSON 31**

Name Chart

YOU NEED

- A large name card for each child
- A pocket chart

RATIONALE   Young children are learning how to look at print. Some have noticed print in the environment and can name familiar signs or symbols. Their name is important to them, and they are beginning to recognize it (or letters and letter sequences in it). (Four-year-olds may begin to recognize their classmates' names as well.) Activities centered on children's names encourage this recognition.

Chan	Jaliezah
Dillon	Jerry
Elizabeth	Jok
Esther	Kenyang
Ethan	Manuel
Hawa	Owen
Hussein	Rachel

Teach

- Explain to children that they are going to do some special work with their names.
- Show the children the stack of cards you've made—each child's name in large, black print (in alphabetical order).
- Hold up the first child's name and read it. Ask the children to say it.
- Have the child come up and put her name in the first slot on the pocket chart (point to it). ("This is Aleeta's name. Aleeta begins with *A*. Say Aleeta. Aleeta, put your name in this pocket of the chart.")
- Repeat with each child's name, filling in the slots so the names appear vertically in alphabetical order.
- Read the complete name chart with the children.

Link

Create a permanent name chart and post it in the classroom.

Expand

- Refer to the chart often when children are writing letters to represent sounds in words ("Oh, you're writing *dog*? That's *d*, like in Damian's name on the chart here!").
- Give each of the children a large name card to decorate with favorite or significant colors and images. Invite them to display their name cards in class.

LESSON 32

Name Poems

RATIONALE Working with names is a powerful way for children to develop print and sound awareness. Once the children have learned songs and poems that use names, they can substitute their names for those in the songs or poems.

YOU NEED

- A chart displaying the words to a familiar poem or song that includes proper name(s) (see Appendix A), with a piece of Velcro in place of the name(s)
- Names of children on word cards backed with Velcro

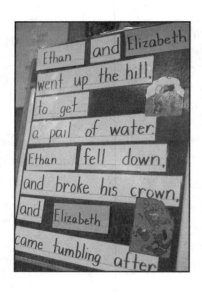

Teach

- Recite the poem or sing the song two or three times. Have the children join you in the reciting or singing when appropriate.

- Tell your students that you're going to change the poem or song a little bit by substituting the names of children in the class. At first, don't work with print at all; just say the poem or sing the song with the substituted name.

- As children become familiar with the process, place children's name cards in the blank spaces on the written version of the poem or song as you substitute the names.

Link

Substitute the names of children in the class as you read books with names, such as *No, David!* by David Shannon and *Knuffle Bunny* by Mo Willems.

Expand

Have the children suggest other names they know to substitute in the poems or songs. You might select a particular letter and substitute names with that first letter.

NAMES   **LESSON 33**

Name Puzzles

This activity works best with a small group, so you can give students lots of support both with the letters and with managing the materials.

RATIONALE Children learn about letters by using their own name as an example. Once you have created a name chart for the classroom, children can use their individual name puzzle to help them learn how to look at the letters in their name in sequence.

YOU NEED

- Name puzzle for each child (name strip cut into squares with letters). Each letter square should have a dot at the bottom to indicate the correct orientation

- Name puzzle folder with name envelope inside to hold letters. Each folder and envelope should have the child's name written on it clearly

- Crayons or unsharpened pencils for children to use as pointers (alternatively, they can just point with their finger)

Teach

- Explain that you are going to help the children learn how to use a name puzzle.

- Lay a name puzzle envelope on a desk or table so all the children can see the name on it.

- Take the letters out of the envelope and match them with the letters in the name written on the envelope. Using a pointer (or your finger), demonstrate how to check letter by letter.

- Now tell the children to take out their envelopes and lay them flat so they can see their names.

- Have them take out the letters, face up, and mix them up.

- Have them put their names together two times, mixing up the letters afterward each time.

- Demonstrate how to put the puzzle away in the envelope and store the folder in a tub with the name on the folder facing up.

Link

Have the children use these puzzles at the letter and word area or at other appropriate times.

Expand

If children become very skilled at putting their own names together, they can try each other's names.

LESSON 34

YOU NEED

- Individual children's names written in black on a strip of card stock
- Magnetic letters
- Salt and/or sand spread out on a flat surface or in a tray
- A drop cloth to spread below your table to catch the sand/salt that falls
- Blank paper and dark-color markers

Making Names Using Tactile Materials

This works best as a small-group, supervised lesson (at a center perhaps), so you can help children manage materials.

RATIONALE   It is important for young children to explore the unique features of letters using tactile materials. Children can find and draw the first letter of their name and eventually make their name using magnetic letters and other tactile materials like sand and salt.

Teach

- Show children individual name cards and explain to the children that the letters in their name are written in black on the card.
- Show children how to trace the letters of their name in the layer of sand or salt that you have spread on a flat surface. Alternatively or additionally, invite children to make their names using the magnetic letters.
- After the children have used the tactile materials to make their name, have them write the letters with a marker on paper if they are ready for this kind of work.

Link

Encourage children to experiment with forming letters from other tactile materials. For example, they could trace their name in the dirt or in sand at the beach or on a cement surface with chalk.

Expand

Give children name cards (name written in black on card stock) and a variety of small tactile materials such as beans, pom-poms, beads, and dried elbow pasta. Have them trace the letters of their name with a glue stick, and then decorate each letter by gluing different materials to it.

INQUIRY | **LESSON 35**

Inquiry

YOU NEED

- See Appendix C for sample inquiry projects. Materials depend on the topic but will most likely include a variety of art materials, props to be used in the play corner, musical instruments, familiar foods, books, songs and poems, and writing materials

This is not a lesson completed in a day; it's meant to be used as a framework for beginning an inquiry project with the children.

RATIONALE Preschoolers' natural curiosity lends itself to the kind of focused play in which children investigate something they're interested in— you guide them, but they do the thinking. If the topic is pets, they might read related books or explore pets through art and music. They might visit an animal shelter or veterinarian's office and meet and talk to people who know about pets. They might engage in interactive writing activities and dramatic play in the play corner. Inquiry projects always involve talking, listening, discovering, touching, experimenting, and finding out. They may involve cooking, building, looking closely at things, drawing, painting, writing, and reading. As children seek information, their growing understanding will take them down new paths of inquiry and discovery.

Teach

- Identify a real question, problem, or topic of interest.

- Plan how your students will investigate the question, problem, or topic.

- Gather resources or introduce experiences that will help children learn more about the question, problem, or topic.

- Help students analyze, summarize, and perhaps record the information (talk, write, draw).

- Draw conclusions and share findings.

Link

Encourage children to use language to explain, describe, and seek information as often as possible throughout the school day.

Expand

Inquiry projects may take no longer than ten minutes, or they may continue over the course of several days, weeks, or months, depending on the topic. Encourage children to investigate a particular topic outside school hours as well.

APPENDIX
E

Recommended Books
for Preschool Children

Counting/Numbers

AUTHOR	TITLE	CITY	PUBLISHER	COPYRIGHT	ISBN
Anno, Mitsumasa	Anno's Counting Book	New York	Crowell; HarperFestival	1975; 1992	0064433153; 9780064433150
Baker, Keith	Big Fat Hen	San Diego	Harcourt Brace; Voyager Books	1994; 1999	0152019510; 9780152019518
Baker, Keith	Quack and Count	San Diego	Harcourt Brace; Voyager Books	1999; 2004	0152050256; 9780152050252
Bang, Molly	Ten, Nine, Eight	New York	Greenwillow Books	1983; 1991	0688104800; 9780688104801
Beaton, Clare	One Moose, Twenty Mice	Cambridge, MA	Barefoot Books	2000	1841481297; 9781841481296
Blackstone, Stella and Corr, Christopher	My Granny Went to Market: A Round-the-World Counting Rhyme	Cambridge, MA	Barefoot Books	1995; 2006	190523662X; 9781905236626
Crews, Donald	Ten Black Dots	New York	Scribner; Greenwillow Books	1968; 1995	0688135749
Christelow, Eileen	Five Little Monkeys Jumping on the Bed	New York	Clarion Books; Sandpiper	1989; 2006	0618836829; 9780618836826
Christelow, Eileen	Five Little Monkeys Sitting in a Tree	New York	Clarion Books; Sandpiper	1991; 2007	0618852840; 9780618852840
Cousins, Lucy	Maisy's Big Flap Book	Cambridge, MA	Candlewick Press; Walker Books Ltd	2001; 2007	1406306886; 9781406306880
Ehlert, Lois	Fish Eyes: A Book You Can Count On	San Diego	Harcourt Brace Jovanovich; Voyager Books	1990; 1992	0152280510; 9780152280512
Falconer, Ian	Olivia Counts	New York	Atheneum Books for Young Readers; Simon & Schuster Children's	2002	0689836732; 9780689836732
Falwell, Cathryn	Feast for 10	New York	Clarion Books	1993	0395620376; 9780395620373
Falwell, Cathryn	Turtle Splash: Countdown at the Pond	New York	Greenwillow Books	2001; 2008	0061429279; 9780061429279
Feelings, Muriel	Moja Means One: Swahili Counting Book	New York	Dial Press; Puffin	1971; 1992	0140546626; 9780140546620
Fleming, Denise	The Everything Book	New York	Henry Holt	2000; 2009	0805088695; 9780805088694
Hoban, Tana	1, 2, 3	New York	Greenwillow Books	1985	068802579X; 9780688025793
Hoban, Tana	26 Letters and 99 Cents	New York	Greenwillow Books	1987; 1995	068814389X; 9780688143893
Hughes, Shirley	Alfie's 1 2 3	New York	Lothrop, Lee, & Shepard Books	2000	0688177050; 9780688177058

Ives, Penny (illustrator)	Five Little Ducks	Swindon	Childs Play Intl Ltd	2007	1846431379; 9781846431371
Jay, Alison	1-2-3: A Child's First Counting Book	New York	Dutton Children's Books	2007	0525478361; 9780525478362
Johnson, Stephen	City by Numbers	New York	Viking; Puffin	1998; 2003	0140566368; 9780140566369
Katz, Karen	Counting Kisses	New York	Margaret K. McElderry Books	2001	0689834705; 9780689834707
Keats, Ezra Jack	Over in the Meadow	New York	Viking; Puffin	1999	0140565086; 9780140565089
Kubler, Annie	Ten Little Fingers	Swindon	Child's Play Intl Ltd	2003	0859536106; 9780859536103
Lewis, Kevin	My Truck is Stuck!	New York	Hyperion Books for Children	2002; 2006	078683739X; 9780786837397
Martin, Bill (et al.)	Chicka, Chicka 1-2-3	New York	Simon & Schuster Books for Young Readers	2004; 2009	1416996117; 9781416996118
Mora, Pat	Uno, Dos, Tres: One, Two, Three	New York	Clarion Books; Sandpiper	1996; 2000	0618054685; 9780618054688
Raffi	Five Little Ducks	New York	Crown	1989; 1992	0517583607; 9780517583609
Root, Phyllis	One Duck Stuck	Cambridge, MA	Candlewick Press	1998; 2003	0763615668; 9780763615666
Roth, Susan	My Love for You	New York	Scholastic	2000	0439114993; 9780439114998
Runnells, Treesha	Ten Wishing Stars	Santa Monica, CA	Piggy Toes Press; Intervisual Books	2003	1581171870; 9781581171877
Seeger, Laura Vaccaro	One Boy	New York	Roaring Book Press	2008	1596432748; 9781596432741
Tudor, Tasha	1 is One	New York	Oxford University Press; Simon & Schuster Books for Young Readers	1956; 2000	0689828438; 9780689828430
Van Fleet, Mathew	One Yellow Lion	New York	Dial Books for Young Readers	1992	0803710992; 9780803710993
Walton, Rick	So Many Bunnies: A Bedtime ABC and Counting Book	New York	Lothrop, Lee & Shepard/ Morrow; Harper Collins	1998	0688136567; 9780688136567

Letters/Alphabet

AUTHOR	TITLE	CITY	PUBLISHER	COPYRIGHT	ISBN
Anno, Mitsumasa	Anno's Alphabet	New York	Crowell; HarperTrophy	1974; 1988	0064431908; 9780064431903
Azzarian, Mary	A Farmer's Alphabet	Boston	David .R. Godine;	1981; 2005	087923394X; 9780879233945
Beaton, Clare	Zoe and Her Zebra	Cambridge, MA	Barefoot Books	1999; 2000	1902283759; 9781902283753
Blackstone, Stella	Alligator Alphabet	Cambridge, MA	Barefoot Books	2005	1841484946; 9781841484945
Bruchac, Joseph	Many Nations: An Alphabet of Native America	Mahwah, NJ	Bridgewater Books; Scholastic	1997; 2004	043963590X; 9780439635905
Cronin, Doreen and Lewin, Betsy	Click, Clack, Quackity-Quack	New York	Atheneum Books for Young Readers	2005	0689877153; 9780689877155
Doodler, Todd	The Zoo I Drew	New York	Random House	2009	0375852018; 9780375852015
Doyle, Charlotte	The Bouncing, Dancing, Galloping ABC	New York	G. P. Putnam	2006	039923778X; 9780399237782
Duke, Kate	The Guinea Pig ABC	New York	Dutton; Puffin	1983; 1993	0140547568; 9780140547566
Ehlert, Lois	Eating the Alphabet	San Diego	Harcourt Brace Jovanovich; Harcourt Big Books	1989; 1994	0152009027; 9780152009021
Ernst, Lisa Campbell	The Turn-Around, Upside-Down Alphabet Book	New York	Simon & Schuster Books for Young Readers	2004	0689856857; 9780689856853
Falwell, Cathryn	Word Wizard	New York	Clarion Books; Sandpiper	1998; 2006	0618689249; 9780618689248

Feelings, Muriel	Jambo Means Hello: A Swahili Alphabet Book	New York	Puffin	1992	0140546529; 9780140546521
Feeney, Stephanie	A is for Aloha	Honolulu	University of Hawaii Press	1980	0824807227; 9780824807221
Fleming, Denise	Alphabet Under Construction	New York	Henry Holt	2002; 2006	0805081127; 9780805081121
Fleming, Denise	The Everything Book	New York	Henry Holt	2000; 2009	0805088695; 9780805088694
Floca, Brian	The Racecar Alphabet	New York	Atheneum Books for Young Readers	2003	0689850913; 9780689850912
Got, Yves	Sam's Big Book of Words	San Francisco	Chronicle Books	2001	0811830888; 9780811830881
Hague, Kathleen	Alphabears	New York	Holt, Rinehart, and Winston	1984	0805062084; 9780805062083
Hill, Susan and Moore, Margie	Ruby Bakes a Cake	New York	HarperCollins Publishers; Zonderkidz	2004; 2010	0310720222; 9780310720225
Hoban, Tana	26 Letters and 99 Cents	New York	Greenwillow Books	1987; 1995	068814389X; 9780688143893
Hoban, Tana	I Read Signs	New York	Greenwillow Books; Scholastic Inc	1983	0590486594; 9780590486590
Jay, Alison	A B C: A Child's First Alphabet Book	New York	Dutton Children's Books	2003; 2005	0525475249; 9780525475248
Jay, Alison	Picture This…	Dorking, Surrey	Templar Publishing	1999; 2000	184011049X; 9781840110494
Johnson, Stephen	Alphabet City	New York	Viking; Puffin	1995; 1999	0140559043; 9780140559040
Lionni, Leo	The Alphabet Tree	New York	Knopf/Random House	2004	0394810163; 9780394810164
Lobel, Arnold	On Market Street	New York	Greenwillow Books	1981; 1989	0688087450; 9780688087456
MacDonald, Suse	Alphabatics	New York	Aladdin Books	1992	0689716257; 9780689716256
Martin, Bill	Chicka, Chicka Boom Boom	New York	Simon & Schuster Books for Young Readers; Beach Lane Books	1989; 2009	1416990917; 9781416990918
Mallat, Kathy	Trouble on the Tracks	New York	Walker & Company	2001	0802787711; 9780802787712
Mockford, Caroline	Cleo's Alphabet Book	Cambridge, MA	Barefoot Books	2003; 2007	1841481653; 9781841481654
Munari, Bruno	Bruno Munari's ABC	San Francisco	Chronicle Books	2006	0811854639; 9780811854634
Pearle, Ida	A Child's Day: An Alphabet of Play	New York	Harcourt	2008	0152065520; 9780152065522
Polacco, Patricia	G is for Goat	New York	Puffin	2006	0142405507; 9780142405505
Seeger, Laura Vaccaro	The Hidden Alphabet	Brookfield, CT	Roaring Brook Press	2003	0761319417; 9780761319412
Van Allsburg, Chris	The Z Was Zapped	Boston, MA	Houghton Mifflin	1987	0395446120; 9780395446126
Walton, Rick	So Many Bunnies: A Bedtime ABC and Counting Book	New York	Lothrop, Lee & Shepard/ Morrow; Harper Collins	1998	0688136567; 9780688136567
Wood, Audrey	Alphabet Adventure	New York	Blue Sky Press	2001	043908069X; 9780439080699
Zuckerman, Andrew	Creature ABC	San Francisco	Chronicle Books	2009	0811869784; 9780811869782

Wordless Books

AUTHOR	TITLE	CITY	PUBLISHER	COPYRIGHT	ISBN
Andreasen, Dan	The Treasure Bath	New York	Henry Holt and Co.	2009	0805086862; 9780805086867
Bang, Molly	The Grey Lady and the Strawberry Snatcher	New York	Aladdin	1996	0689803818; 9780689803819
Banyai, Istvan	Zoom	New York	Puffin	1998	0140557741; 9780140557749
Day, Alexandra	Good Dog, Carl	New York	Little Simon	1996	0689807481; 9780689807480
dePaola, Tomie	Pancakes for Breakfast	Boston, MA	Sandpiper (Houghton Mifflin)	1978	0156707683; 9780156707688

dePaola, Tomie	The Hunter and the Animals	New York	Holiday House	1981	0823404285; 9780823404285
Franson, Scott	Un-Brella	New York	Roaring Brook Press (Macmillan)	2007	1596431792; 9781596431799
Geisert, Arthur	Oops	Boston, MA	Houghton Mifflin	2006	0618609040; 9780618609048
Hoban, Tana	Black & White	New York	HarperCollins	2007	0061172111; 9780061172113
Hogrogian, Nonny	Cool Cat	New York	Roaring Brook Press (Macmillan)	2009	1596434295; 9781596434295
Hutchins, Pat	Changes, Changes	New York	Aladdin	1987	0689711379; 9780689711374
Jay, Alison	Welcome to the Zoo	New York	Dial	2008	0803731779; 9780803731776
Jenkins, Steve	Looking Down	Boston, MA	Sandpiper (Houghton Mifflin)	2003	0618310983; 9780618310982
Lehman, Barbara	Museum Trip	Boston, MA	Houghton Mifflin	2006	0618581251; 9780618581252
Lehman, Barbara	Rainstorm	Boston, MA	Houghton Mifflin	2007	0618756396; 9780618756391
Lehman, Barbara	Trainstop	Boston, MA	Houghton Mifflin	2008	061875640X; 9780618756407
Mayer, Mercer	Frog on His Own	New York	Dial	2003	0803728832; 9780803728837
McDonnell, Patrick	South	Boston, MA	Little, Brown	2008	0316005096
Newgarden, Mark	Bow-Wow Bugs a Bug	New York	Harcourt	2007	0152058133; 9780152058135
Schories, Pat	Breakfast for Jack	Brooklyn, NY	Handprint Books	2004	1932425160; 9781932425161
Thomson, Bill	Chalk	Tarrytown, NY	Marshall Cavendish	2010	0761455264; 9780761455264
Weisner, David	Tuesday	Boston, MA	Sandpiper (Houghton Mifflin)	1997	0395870828; 9780395870822

Colors/Shapes

AUTHOR	TITLE	CITY	PUBLISHER	COPYRIGHT	ISBN
Allen, Marjorie N. and Rotner, Shelley	Changes	New York	Macmillan Pub. Co.; Atheneum	1991	0027002527; 9780027002522
Barry, Francis	Duckie's Rainbow	Cambridge, MA	Candlewick Press; Walker Books Ltd	2003; 2004	0744596467; 9780744596465
Blackstone, Stella	Bear in a Square	Cambridge, MA	Barefoot Books	2002; 2006	1846860555; 9781846860553
Carle, Eric	Brown Bear, Brown Bear, What do you See?	New York	Henry Holt	1992; 2008	0805087184; 9780805087185
Chodos-Irvine, Margaret	Ella Sarah Gets Dressed	San Diego	Harcourt	2003	0152164138; 9780152164133
Crews, Donald	Freight Train	New York	Greenwillow Books	1978; 1993	0688129404; 9780688129408
Ehlert, Lois	Color Farm	New York	Lippincott; HarperCollins	1990	0397324405; 9780397324408
Ehlert, Lois	Color Zoo	New York	Lippincott; HarperCollins	1989	0397322593; 9780397322596
Emberley, Rebecca	My Shapes/Mis Formas	Boston	Little, Brown & Co.	2000	0316233552; 9780316233552
Feeney, Stephanie	Hawaii is a Rainbow	Honolulu	University of Hawaii Press	1985	0824810074; 9780824810078
Fleming, Denise	The Everything Book	New York	Henry Holt	2000; 2009	0805088695; 9780805088694
Fox, Mem	Where is the Green Sheep?	Orlando	Harcourt	2004	015204907X; 9780152049072
Gonzalez, Maya Christina	My Colors, My World	San Francisco, CA	Children's Book Press	2007	0892392215; 9780892392216
Gravett, Emily	Orange Pear Apple Bear	New York	Simon & Schuster Books for Young Readers	2007	1416939997; 9781416939993

Guy, Ginger Foglesong	Siesta	New York	Greenwillow Books	2005	0060560614; 9780060560614
Hoban, Tana	Colors Everywhere	New York	Greenwillow Books	1995	0688127622; 9780688127626
Hoban, Tana	I Read Signs	New York	Greenwillow Books	1983	0688023177; 9780688023171
Hoban, Tana	Is It Red? Is It Yellow? Is It Blue? An Adventure in Color	New York	Greenwillow Books	1978; 1987	0688070345; 9780688070342
Hoban, Tana	Shapes, Shapes, Shapes	New York	Greenwillow Books	1986; 1996	0688147402; 9780688147402
Katz, Karen	The Color of Us	New York	Henry Holt & Co.	1999; 2007	0805081186; 9780805081183
Larios, Julie	Yellow Elephant	Orlando	Harcourt	2006	0152054227; 9780152054229
Lehman, Barbara	The Red Book	Boston	Houghton Mifflin	2004	0618428585; 9780618428588
Lionni, Leo	A Color of His Own	New York	Pantheon Books; Knopf Books for Young Readers	1975; 2006	0375836977; 9780375836978
Mockford, Caroline	Cleo's Color Book	Cambridge, MA	Barefoot Books	2006	1905236301; 9781905236305
Rogers, Alan	Red Rhino	Milwaukee	G. Stevens Children's Books; Two-Can Publishing, Inc	1990; 1997	1587281546; 9781587281549
Serfozo, Mary	Who Said Red?	New York	M.K. McElderry Books;	1988; 1992	0689716516; 9780689716515
Seeger, Laura Vaccaro	Lemons Are Not Red	Brookfield, CT	Roaring Brook Press	2004; 2006	1596431954; 9781596431959
Shahan, Sherry	Spicy Hot Colors/Colores Picantes	Little Rock, AR	August House LittleFolk	2004; 2007	0874838150; 9780874838152
Shannon, George	White is for Blueberry	New York	Greenwillow Books	2005	006029275X; 9780060292751
Van Fleet, Mathew	Fuzzy Yellow Ducklings	New York	Dial Books for Young Readers	1995	0803717598; 9780803717596
Van Fleet, Mathew	One Yellow Lion	New York	Dial Books for Young Readers	1992	0803710992; 9780803710993
Walsh, Ellen Stohl	Mouse Paint	San Diego	Harcourt Brace Jovanovich; Voyager Books	1989; 1995	0152001182; 9780152001186
Winthrop, Elizabeth	Shoes	New York	Harper & Row	1986	0060265914; 9780060265915
Wood, Audrey and Bruce	The Deep Blue Sea: A Book of Colors	New York	Blue Sky Press	2005	0439753821; 9780439753821
Yolen, Jane	How Do Dinosaurs Learn Their Colors?	New York	Blue Sky Press	2006	0439856531; 9780439856539
Young, Ed	Seven Blind Mice	New York	Philomel Books;	1992; 2002	0698118952; 9780698118959

Bedtime

AUTHOR	TITLE	CITY	PUBLISHER	COPYRIGHT	ISBN
Aliki	All By Myself!	New York	HarperColllins Publishers	2003	0064462536; 9780064462532
Asch, Frank	Barnyard Lullaby	New York	Aladdin	2001	0689842562; 9780689842566
Boynton, Sandra	The Going-to-Bed Book	New York	Little Simon	1982	0671449028; 9780671449025
Cousins, Lucy	Maisy's Bedtime	New York	Candlewick	1999	0763609080; 9780763609085
Dewdney, Anna	Llama Llama Red Pajama	New York	Viking	2005	0670059838; 9780670059836
Dunbar, Joyce	Tell Me Something Happy Before I Go to Sleep	New York	Harcourt	1998	015201795X; 9780152017958
Fox, Mem	Time for Bed	New York	Red Wagon Books	1997	0152010661; 9780152010669
Markes, Julie	Shhhh! Everybody's Sleeping	New York	HarperCollins	2005	0060537906; 9780060537906
Mayer, Mercer	Just Go to Bed!	New York	Random House	2001	0307119408; 9780307119407

Rathman, Peggy	10 Minutes Till Bedtime	New York	Puffin	2004	0142400246; 9780142400241
Rathman, Peggy	Goodnight, Gorilla	New York	Putnam	2000	0698116496; 9780698116498
Rothstein, Gloria L.	Sheep Asleep	New York	HarperColllins Publishers	2003	0060291052; 9780060291051
Ryder, Joanna	Won't You Be My Kissaroo?	New York	Harcourt	2004	015202641X; 9780152026417
Shea, Bob	Dinosaur Vs. Bedtime!	New York	Hyperion	2008	1423113357; 9781423113355
Spinelli, Eileen	When Mama Comes Home Tonight	New York	Simon and Schuster	1998	0689810652
Thomas, Shelly Moore	Good Night, Good Knight	New York	Dutton; Puffin	2000; 2002	0142302015; 9780142302019
Weeks, Sarah	Counting Ovejas	New York	Atheneum Books for Young Readers	2006	0689867506; 9780689867507
Wood, Audrey	The Napping House	New York	Harcourt	1991	0152567119; 9780152567118
Wood, Audrey	Piggies	New York	Voyager Books	1995	0152002170; 9780152002176
Yolen, Jane, and Stemple, Heidi	Sleep, Black Bear, Sleep	New York	HarperCollins	2007	0060815604; 9780060815608

Animals

AUTHOR	TITLE	CITY	PUBLISHER	COPYRIGHT	ISBN
Arnosky, Jim	Raccoon on His Own	New York	Puffin	2003	0142500712; 9780142500712
Bauer, Marion Dane	If You Were Born a Kitten	New York	Aladdin	2001	0689842120; 9780689842122
Broach, Elise	Wet Dog!	New York	Dial Books	2005	0142408557; 9780142408551
Butler, John	Can You Growl Like a Bear?	Atlanta	Peachtree	2007	156145396X; 9781561453962
Carle, Eric	The Very Hungry Caterpillar	New York	Collins Publishers; Philomel	1979; 1994	0399226907; 9780399226908
Cronin, Doreen	Click, Clack, Moo: Cows That Type	New York	Simon and Schuster	2000	0689832133; 9781416903482
Harper, Dan	Sit, Truman!	New York	Sandpiper	2004	015205068X; 9780152050689
Harper, Isabelle	My Cats Nick and Nora	New York	Blue Sky Press	2002	0590476351; 9780590476355
Harper, Isabelle	My Dog Rosie	New York	Scholastic	1994	059047619X; 9780590476195
Harper, Isabelle	Our New Puppy	New York	Scholastic	2001	043919993X; 9780439199933
Henkes, Kevin	A Good Day	New York	HarperCollins	2007	006114018X; 9780061140181
Henkes, Kevin	Kitten's First Full Moon	New York	Greenwillow Books	2004	0060588284; 9780060588281
Henkes, Kevin	Old Bear	New York	Greenwillow Books	2008	0061552054; 9780061552052
Jenkins, Steve, and Page, Robin	Move!	New York	Houghton Mifflin	2006	061864637X; 9780618646371
Jenkins, Steve	What Do You Do With a Tail Like This?	Boston	Houghton Mifflin	2003	0618256288; 9780618256280
Knudsen, Michelle	Library Lion	Cambridge, MA	Candlewick Press	2009	076363784X; 9780763637842
LaRochelle, David	The Best Pet of All	New York	Puffin	2009	0142412724; 9780142412725
Lee, Hector Viveros	I Had a Hippopotamus	New York	Lee and Low Books	1998	1880000628; 9781880000625
Martin, Bill Jr.	Brown Bear, Brown Bear, What do you See?	New York	Henry Holt	1992; 2008	0805087184; 9780805087185
Martin, Bill Jr.	Panda Bear, Panda Bear, What Do You See?	New York	Henry Holt	2007	080508102X; 9780805081022
McCarty, Peter	Hondo and Fabian	New York	Henry Holt; Square Fish	2002; 2007	0312367473; 9780312367473
Roth, Susan	Great Big Guinea Pigs	London	Bloomsbury	2006	1582347247; 9781582347240

Simmons, Jane	Come Along, Daisy!	Boston	Little, Brown	1998; 2003	0316168785; 9780316168786
Tafuri, Nancy	The Busy Little Squirrel	New York	Simon and Schuster	2007	0689873417; 9780689873416
Van Laan, Nancy	Little Fish, Lost	New York	Atheneum Books for Young Readers	1998	0689843720; 9780689843723
Wilson, Karma	Moose Tracks	New York	Margaret McElderry	2006	0689834373; 9780689834370
Wise Brown, Margaret	Big Red Barn	New York	HarperFestival	1995	0694006246; 9780694006243

Rhyming/Poetry/Mother Goose

AUTHOR	TITLE	CITY	PUBLISHER	COPYRIGHT	ISBN
Beaumont, Karen	Duck, Duck, Goose! A Coyote's on the Loose	New York	HarperCollins	2004	006050827; 9780060508029
Carle, Eric	Eric Carle's Animals, Animals	New York	Putnam	1999	0698118553; 9780698118553
Crews, Nina	The Neighborhood Mother Goose	New York	Greenwillow	2003	0060515732; 9780060515737
Degan, Bruce	Jamberry	New York	HarperFestival	1995	0694006513; 9780694006519
dePaola, Tomie	Tomie's Little Book of Poems	New York	Putnam	2004	0399242708; 9780399242700
Elliot, David	On the Farm	New York	Candlewick	2008	0763633224; 9780763633226
Finch, Mary, and Beaton, Clare	Playtime Rhymes for Little People	New York	Barefoot Books	2008	184686156X; 9781846861567
Fox, Mem	The Magic Hat	New York	Voyager	2006	0152057153; 9780152057153
Kuskin, Karla	Green as a Bean	New York	HarperCollins	2007	0060753323; 9780060753320
Lass, Bonnie, and Sturges, Philemon	Who Took the Cookies from the Cookie Jar?	Boston	Little, Brown	2000	0316820164; 9780316820165
Lewis, Kevin	My Truck is Stuck!	New York	Hyperion	2002	078680534X
Loomis, Christine	Rush Hour	Boston	Houghton Mifflin	1996	039569129X; 9780395691298
Low, Alice	Aunt Lucy Went to Buy a Hat	New York	HarperCollins	2004	0060089717; 9780060089719
Martin, Bill Jr.	The Bill Martin Jr. Big Book of Poetry	New York	Simon and Schuster	2008	1416939717; 9781416939719
Marzollo, Jean	Pretend You're a Cat	New York	Dial Books	1990	0140559930; 9780140559934
Miranda, Anne	To Market, to Market	New York	Harcourt	2007	0152163980; 9780152163983
O'Connor, Jane	Ready, Set, Skip!	New York	Viking	2007	0142414239; 9780142414231
Opie, Iona	My Very First Mother Goose	New York	Candlewick	1996	1564026205; 9781564026200
Rosen, Michael	We're Going on a Bear Hunt	New York	Margaret K. McElderry Books/Aladdin	1989; 2003	0689853491; 9780689853494
Ross, Tony	Three Little Kittens and Other Favorite Nursery Rhymes	New York	Henry Holt and Co.	2009	0805088857; 9780805088854
Scanlon, Elizabeth Garton	A Sock is a Pocket for Your Toes: A Pocket Book	New York	HarperCollins	2004	0060295260; 9780060295264
Schertle, Alice	Button Up!	New York	HarperCollins		
Schertle, Alice	Teddy Bear, Teddy Bear	New York	HarperCollins	2003	1422355543; 9781422355541
Spinnelli, Eileen	Do You Have a Hat?	New York	Simon and Schuster	2004	0689862539; 9780689862533
Walton, Rick	The Bear Came Over to My House	New York	Puffin	2003	0698119886; 9780698119888
Weeks, Sarah	Mrs. McNosh Hangs Up Her Wash	New York	HarperCollins	2002	0060004798; 9780060004798
Yolen, Jane, and Fusek Peters, Andrew	Here's a Little Poem	New York	Candlewick	2007	0763631418; 9780763631413

Friendship/Family

AUTHOR	TITLE	CITY	PUBLISHER	COPYRIGHT	ISBN
Alborough, Jez	My Friend Bear	Cambridge, MA	Candlewick Press	1998	0590638300; 9780590638302
Aliki	We Are Best Friends	New York	Greenwillow Books	1982; 1987	068807037X; 9780688070373
Becker, Bonny	A Visitor for Bear	Cambridge, MA	Candlewick Press	2008	0763628077; 9780763628079
Bloom, Suzanne	A Splendid Friend, Indeed	Honesdale, PA	Boyds Mills Press	2005; 2009	159078488X; 9781590784884
Browne, Anthony	My Mom	New York	Farrar, Straus and Giroux	2009	0374400261; 9780374400262
Browne, Anthony	Willy and Hugh	New York	A.A. Knopf; Red Fox	1991; 2000	0099407795; 9780099407799
Buck, Nola	Sid and Sam	New York	HarperCollins Publishers	1996; 1997	00644211X; 9780064442114
Carle, Eric	Do You Want to be My Friend?	New York	Crowell; Philomel	1971; 1988	0399215980; 9780399215988
Carle, Eric and Iwamura, Kazuo	Where are you Going? To See My Friend!	New York	Orchard Books	2003	0439416590; 9780439416597
Chodos-Irvine, Margaret	Best, Best Friends	Orlando	Harcourt	2006	0152056947; 9780152056940
Chodos-Irvine, Margaret	Ella Sarah Gets Dressed	San Diego	Harcourt	2003	0152164138; 9780152164133
Coffelt, Nancy	Fred Stays With Me!	New York	Little Brown	2007	0316882690; 9780316882699
Cousins, Lucy	Where are Maisy's Friends?	Somerville, MA	Candlewick Press; Walker Books Ltd	2000; 2010	074457532X; 9780744575323
Creech, Sharon	A Fine, Fine School	New York	Joanna Cotler Books; Harper Collins Pub	2001; 2003	0060007281; 9780060007287
Crews, Donald	Bigmama's	New York	Greenwillow Books	1991	0688158420; 9780688158422
DeBear, Kristen	Be Quiet, Marina!	New York	Star Bright Books	2001	1887734791; 9781887734790
dePaola, Tomie	Strega Nona	Englewood Cliffs, NJ	Prentice-Hall; Aladdin	1975; 1979	0671666061; 9780671666064
Dorros, Arthur	Papá and Me	New York	HarperCollins Publishers; Rayo	2008	0060581565; 9780060581565
Dunrea, Olivier	Gossie and Gertie	Boston	Houghton Mifflin Company	2002	0618176764; 9780618176762
Falconer, Ian	Olivia	New York	Atheneum Books for Young Readers	2000	0689829531; 9780689829536
Foley, Greg	Thank You Bear	New York	Viking	2007	0670061654; 9780670061655
Fox, Mem	Tough Boris	New York	Voyager Books	1998	0152018913; 9780152018917
George, Craighead Jean	Goose and Duck	New York	Laura Geringer Books; HarperCollins	2008	0061170763; 9780061170768
Greenfield, Eloise	Grandpa's Face	New York	Philomel Books; Putnam Juvenile	1988; 1996	0698113810; 9780698113817
Gutman, Anne	Gaspard and Lisa Friends Forever	New York	Knopf	2003	0375822534; 9780375822537
Henkes, Kevin	A Weekend with Wendell	New York	Greenwillow Books	1986; 1995	0688140246; 9780688140243
Henkes, Kevin	Jessica	New York	Greenwillow Books	1989; 1998	0688158471; 9780688158477
Henkes, Kevin	Wemberly Worried	New York	Greenwillow Books	2000; 2010	0061857769; 9780061857768
Hobbie, Holly	Toot and Puddle	Boston	Little, Brown	1997; 2007	0316167029; 9780316167024
Howe, James	Horace and Morris Join the Chorus (But What about Dolores?)	New York	Atheneum Books for Young Readers; Aladdin	2002; 2005	1416906169; 9781416906162
Hutchins, Pat	My Best Friend	New York	Greenwillow Books	1993	0688114857; 9780688114855

Hutchins, Pat	Titch	New York	Macmillan; Aladdin	1971; 1993	0689716885; 9780689716881
Jarrell, Randall	The Gingerbread Rabbit	New York	Macmillan; HarperCollins	1964; 2004	0060533021; 9780060533021
Joyce, William	A Day with Wilbur Robinson	New York	Harper & Row; Laura Geringer Books	1990; 2006	0060890983; 9780060890988
Keller, Holly	Farfallina and Marcel	New York	Greenwillow Books	2002; 2005	0064438724; 9780064438728
Lerman, Rory S.	Charlie's Checklist	New York	Orchard books; Scholastic Inc.	1997; 2000	0531071731; 9780531071731
Lionni, Leo	Frederick	New York	Pantheon	1967	378769577X; 9783787695775
Lobel, Anita	Nini Here and There	New York	Greenwillow	2007	0060787678; 9780060787677
Lobel, Arnold	Frog and Toad are Friends	New York	Harper and Row	1970	0439655595; 9780439655590
McPhail, David	Sisters	New York	Harcourt	2003	0152046593; 9780152046590
Ormerod, Jan	Miss Mouse's Day	New York	HarperCollins	2001	0688163335; 9780688163334
Polacco, Patricia	Emma Kate	New York	Puffin	2008	0142411965; 9780142411964
Pfister, Marcus	The Rainbow Fish	New York	North-South Books	1992; 1995	1558584412; 9781558584419
Raschka, Chris	Yo! Yes?	New York	Orchard books; Scholastic	1993; 2007	0439921856; 9780439921855
Rathman, Peggy	Officer Buckle and Gloria	New York	Putnam Juvenile	1995	0399226168; 9780399226168
Rogers, Fred	Making Friends	New York	Putnam Juvenile	1987; 1996	0698114094; 9780698114098
Rylant, Cynthia	The Relatives Came	New York	Bradbury Press; Live Oak Media	1985; 2005	0874995329; 9780874995329
Say, Allen	Grandfather's Journey	Boston	Houghton Mifflin; Sandpiper	1993; 2008	0547076800; 9780547076805
Schenk de Regniers, Beatrice	May I Bring a Friend?	New York	Atheneum; Aladdin	1964; 1989	0689713533; 9780689713538
Shannon, George	Dance Away	New York	Greenwillow Books	1982; 1991	0688104835; 9780688104832
Simmons, Jane	Come Along, Daisy	Boston	Little, Brown	1998	0316797901; 9780316797900
Tafuri, Nancy	Have You Seen My Duckling?	New York	Greenwillow Books	1984; 1991	0688109942; 9780688109943
Williams, Vera B.	"More More More," Said the Baby	New York	Greenwillow Books	1990; 1996	0688147364; 9780688147365
Winthrop, Elizabeth	Squashed in the Middle	New York	Henry Holt	2005	0805064974; 9780805064971

Feelings

AUTHOR	TITLE	CITY	PUBLISHER	COPYRIGHT	ISBN
Alborough, Jez	Hug	Cambridge, MA	Candlewick Press	2000; 2009	0763645109; 9780763645106
Aliki	Feelings	New York	Greenwillow Books	1984; 1986	068806518X; 9780688065188
Bang, Molly	When Sophie Gets Angry, Really, Really Angry	New York	Blue Sky Press; Scholastic	1999	0439213193; 9780439213196
Beaumont, Karen	I Like Myself	New York	Harcourt	2004	0152020136; 9780152020132
Browne, Anthony	Willy and Hugh	New York	A.A. Knopf; Red Fox	1991; 2000	0099407795; 9780099407799
Carle, Eric	The Grouchy Ladybug	New York	T.Y. Crowell Co; HarperCollins	1977; 1996	0064434508; 9780064434508
Curtis, Jamie Lee	Today I Feel Silly and Other Moods That Make My Day	New York	HarperCollins Publishers	1998	0060245603; 9780060245603
Dannenberg, Julie	First Day Jitters	Watertown, MA	Charlesbridge Publishing	2000	158089061X; 9781580890618
Fleming, Denise	Buster Goes to Cowboy Camp	New York	Henry Holt & Co	2008	0805078924; 9780805078923
Henkes, Kevin	A Good Day	New York	Greenwillow Books	2007	006114018X; 9780061140181
Henkes, Kevin	Owen	New York	Greenwillow Books	1993	0688114490; 9780688114497

Keller, Holly	Brave Horace	New York	Greenwillow Books	1998	0688154077; 9780688154073
Lionni, Leo	It's Mine!	New York	Knopf; Dragonfly Books	1986; 1996	0679880844; 9780679880844
Lionni, Leo	Swimmy	New York	Pantheon; Dragonfly Books	1963; 1973	0394826205; 9780394826202
McBratney, Sam	Guess How Much I Love You	Cambridge, MA	Candlewick Press	1995; 2008	0763641758; 9780763641757
Murphy, Mary	How Kind	Cambridge, MA	Candlewick Press; Walker Books Ltd	2002; 2004	1844284662; 9781844284665
Numeroff, Laura	Beatrice Doesn't Want To	New York; Cambridge, MA	F. Watts; Candlewick Press	1981; 2008	0763638439; 9780763638436
Omerod, Jan	Miss Mouse's Day	New York	HarperCollins	2001	0688163334; 9780688163334
Seeger, Laura Vaccaro	Walter Was Worried	Brookfield, CT	Roaring Brook Press	2005; 2006	1596431962; 9781596431966
Shannon, David	No, David!	New York	Blue Sky Press	1998	0590930028; 9780590930024
Shoshan, Beth	That's When I'm Happy	New York	Parragon Inc	2007	1405495383; 9781405495387
Urban, Linda	Mouse Was Mad	Boston	Houghton Mifflin	2009	0152053379; 9780152053376
Van Leeuwen, Jean	Wait for Me! Said Maggie McGee	New York	Dial	2001	0803723571; 9780803723573
Waber, Bernard	Courage	Boston	Houghton Mifflin Co	2002	0618238557; 9780618238552
Waber, Bernard	Ira Sleeps Over	Boston	Houghton Mifflin Co	1972; 1973	0395138930; 9780395138939
Wells, Rosemary	Shy Charles	New York	Dial Books for Young Readers; Puffin	1988; 2001	0140568433; 9780140568431
Wells, Rosemary	Noisy Nora	New York	Dial Press; Puffin	1973; 2000	0140567283; 9780140567281
Willems, Mo	Knuffle Bunny: A Cautionary Tale	New York	Hyperion Books for Children	2004	0786818700; 9780786818709
Willis, Jeanne	Never Too Little to Love	Cambridge, MA	Candlewick Press; Walker Books Ltd	2005	0744596505; 9780744596502
Wilson, Karma	Bear Feels Sick	New York	M.K. McElderry Books	2007	0689859856; 9780689859854

Folktales/Fables

AUTHOR	TITLE	CITY	PUBLISHER	COPYRIGHT	ISBN
Brett, Jan	Goldilocks and the Three Bears	New York	Dodd, Mead; Putnam Juvenile	1987; 1996	0698113586; 9780698113589
Brett, Jan	The Gingerbread Baby	New York	Putnam	1999	0399234446; 9780399234446
Brett, Jan	The Mitten	New York	Putnam	2009	0399252967; 9780399252969
Brett, Jan	The Three Snow Bears	New York	Putnam	2007	0399247920; 9780399247927
Brett, Jan	The Town Mouse and the Country Mouse	New York	Putnam	2003	069811986X; 9780698119864
Dayrell, Elphinstone	Why the Sun and the Moon Live in the Sky	Boston	Houghton Mifflin; Sandpiper	1968; 1990	0395539637; 9780395539637
dePaola, Tomie	The Legend of the Bluebonnet	New York	Putnam	1983; 1996	0698113594; 9780698113596
Ehlert, Lois	Cuckoo/Cucú	San Diego	Harcourt Brace; Turtleback Books/Sanval	1997; 2001	0613299175; 9780613299176
Ehlert, Lois	Moon Rope	San Diego	Harcourt Brace Jovanovich; Voyager Books	1992; 2003	015201702X; 9780152017026
Emberly, Rebecca	Chicken Little	Brookfield, CT	Roaring Book Press	2009	1596434634; 9781596434646
Galdone, Paul	The Little Red Hen	New York	Seabury Press; Sandpiper	1973; 1985	0899193498; 9780899193496
Galdone, Paul	The Old Woman and Her Pig		McGraw-Hill Book Co.	1960	0070227217; 9780070227217
Gilman, Phoebe	Something from Nothing	New York	Scholastic	1992	0590472801; 9780590472807

Haley, Gail	A Story, A Story	New York	Atheneum	1970	0689205112; 9780689205118
Hyman, Trina Schart	Little Red Riding Hood	New York	Holiday House	1983; 1987	0823406539; 9780823406531
Knutson, Barbara	Love and Roast Chicken: A Trickster Tale from the Andes Mountains	Minneapolis	Carolrhoda Books	2004	1575056577; 9781575056579
Lamarche, Jim (adapted from Jacob Grimm)	The Elves and the Shoemaker	San Francisco	Chronicle Books		0811834778; 9780811834773
Marshall, James	The Three Little Pigs	New York	Dial Books for Young Readers	1989	0803705913; 9780803705913
Marshall, James	Goldilocks and the Three Bears	New York	Dial Books for Young Readers; Puffin	1988; 1998	0140563660; 9780140563665
McDermott, Gerald	Anansi the Spider: A Tale from the Ashanti	New York	Holt, Rinehart and Winston; Henry Holt and Company	1972; 1987	0805003118; 9780805003116
McDermott, Gerald	Raven: A Trickster Tale from the Pacific Northwest	San Diego	Harcourt Brace Jovanovich; Sandpiper	1993; 2001	0152024492; 9780152024499
Montes, Marisa	Juan Bobo Goes to Work	New York	Harper Collins Publishers; Rayo	2000	0688162339; 9780688162337
Morales, Yuyi	Little Night	New Milford, CT	Roaring Brook Press	2007	1596430885; 9781596430884
Pinkney, Jerry	Little Red Riding Hood	New York	Little, Brown	2007	0316013552; 9780316013550
Pinkney, Jerry	The Lion and the Mouse	New York	Little, Brown	2007	0316013560; 9780316013567
Pinkney, Jerry (adapted from Rudyard Kipling)	Rikki-Tikki-Tavi	New York	HarperCollins	2004	0060587857; 9780060587857
Pinkney, Jerry (adapted from Hans Christian Andersen)	The Ugly Duckling	New York	Morrow Junior Books; HarperCollins	1999	068815932X; 9780688159320
Sedgwick, Marcus (adapted from Hans Christian Andersen)	The Emperor's New Clothes	San Francisco	Chronicle Books	2004	0811845699; 9780811845694
Shulevitz, Uri	The Treasure	New York	Farrar, Straus, Giroux	1978; 1979	0374377405; 9780374377403
Stevens, Janet	Tops and Bottoms	San Diego	Harcourt Brace	1995	0152928510; 9780152928513
Steptoe, John	Mufaro's Beautiful Daughters	New York	Lothrop, Lee & Shepard Books; HarperFestival	1987; 1993	0688129358; 9780688129354
Taback, Simms	Joseph Had a Little Overcoat	New York	Random House; Live Oak Media	1977; 2001	0874997836; 9780874997835
Taback, Simms	There was an Old Lady Who Swallowed a Fly	New York	Viking	1997	0670869392; 9780670869398
Willey, Margaret	Clever Beatrice	New York	Antheneum Books for Young Readers; Aladdin	2001; 2004	068987068X; 9780689870682
Young, Ed	Seven Blind Mice	New York	Philomel Books; Putnam Juvenile	1992; 2002	0698118952; 9780698118959

Food

AUTHOR	TITLE	CITY	PUBLISHER	COPYRIGHT	ISBN
Andreasen, Dan	The Baker's Dozen	New York	Henry Holt and Co.	2007	0805078096; 9780805078091
Carle, Eric	The Very Hungry Caterpillar	New York	Collins Publishers; Philomel	1979; 1994	0399226907; 9780399226908
Degen, Bruce	Jamberry	New York	Harper & Row; HarperCollins	1983	0060214163; 9780060214166

AUTHOR	TITLE	CITY	PUBLISHER	COPYRIGHT	ISBN
Durant, Alan	Burger Boy		Clarion Books	2006	0618714669; 9780618714667
Ehlert, Lois	Growing Vegetable Soup		Sandpiper	1990	0152325808; 9780152325800
Elffers, Joost	Fast Food	New York	Arthur Levine Books	2006	043911019X; 9780439110198
Hoban, Russell	Bread and Jam for Frances	New York	HarperCollins	2008	0060838000; 9780060838003
Robart, Rose	The Cake that Mack Ate	Toronto	Kids Can Press; Little, Brown Books for Young Readers	1986; 1991	0316748919; 9780316748919
Rosenthal, Amy Krouse	Little Pea	San Francisco	Chronicle Books	2005	081184658X; 9780811846585
Steig, William	Pete's a Pizza	New York	HarperCollins	1998	0062051578; 9780062051578
Waber, Bernard	Fast Food! Gulp! Gulp!	Boston	Houghton Mifflin Co; Sandpiper	2001; 2005	0618555617; 9780618555611

Your Body

AUTHOR	TITLE	CITY	PUBLISHER	COPYRIGHT	ISBN
Aliki	My Five Senses	New York	Harper Festival	1991	0060200502; 9780060200503
Asim, Jabari	Whose Knees Are These?	New York	LB Kids	2006	0316735760; 9780316735766
Bang, Molly	A Book of Thanks (All of Me!)	New York	Blue Sky Press	2009	0545044243; 9780545044240
Barner, Bob	Dem Bones	San Francisco	Chronicle Books	1996	0811808270; 9780811808279
Gershator, Phillis	Zzzing! Zzzing! Zzzing! A Yoruba Tale	New York	Orchard Books	1998	0531095231; 9780531095232
Kubler, Annie	Ten Little Fingers	Swindon	Child's Play Intl Ltd	2003	0859536106; 9780859536103
Martin, Bill Jr.	Here Are My Hands	New York	Henry Holt and Co.	2007	0805081194; 9780805081190
Raschka, Chris	Five for a Little One	New York	Atheneum	2006	069845995; 9780689845994

Cumulative Stories/Rhymes

AUTHOR	TITLE	CITY	PUBLISHER	COPYRIGHT	ISBN
Aardema, Verna	Bringing the Rain to Kapiti Plain	New York	Dial Press; Puffin	1981; 1992	0140546162; 9780140546163
Allen, Jonathan	Chicken Licken	San Diego	Corgi Childrens; Harcourt	1997; 1999	0552143383; 9780552143387
Bell, Babs	The Bridge Is Up!	New York	HarperCollins Pub; Hmh School	2004; 2006	0153650893; 9780153650895
Beaumont, Karen	Move Over, Rover!	Orlando	Harcourt	2006	0152019790; 9780152019792
Bond, Felicia	Tumble Bumble	Arden, NC; New York	Front Street; Harper Collins	1996; 2000	0064435857; 9780064435857
Burningham, John	Mr. Gumpy's Outing	New York	Holt, Rinehart and Winston; Henry Holt and Co.	1970; 1995	080503854X; 9780805038545
Emberley, Barbara	Drummer Hoff	Englewood Cliffs, NJ	Prentice-Hall; Aladdin	1967; 1972	067166249X; 9780671662493
Hutchins, Pat	Good-Night Owl!	New York	Macmillan; Aladdin	1972; 1990	0689713711; 9780689713712
Low, Joseph	Mice Twice	New York	Atheneum; Aladdin	1980; 1986	0689710607; 9780689710605
Robart, Rose	The Cake that Mack Ate	Toronto	Kids Can Press; Little, Brown Books for Young Readers	1986; 1991	0316748919; 9780316748919

Shulman, Lisa	Old MacDonald Had a Woodshop	New York	Puffin	2004	0399235965; 9780399235962
Swanson, Susan Marie	The House in the Night	Boston	Houghton Mifflin Co	2008	0618862447; 9780618862443
Taback, Simms	This is the House that Jack Built	New York	G.P. Putnam's Sons; Puffin	2002; 2004	0142402001; 9780142402009
Von Buhler, Cynthia	The Cat Who Wouldn't Come Inside	Boston	Houghton Mifflin	2006	0618563148; 9780618563142
Williams, Sue	I Went Walking	San Diego	Harcourt Brace Jovanovich; Gulliver Books	1990	0152004718; 9780152004712
Williams, Sue	Let's Go Visiting	San Diego	Harcourt Brace; Voyager Books	1998; 2000	0152024107; 9780152024109
Winter, Jeanette	The House that Jack Built	New York	Dial Books for Young Readers; Puffin	2000; 2003	0142301264; 9780142301265
Wood, Audrey	Silly Sally	New York	Red Wagon Books	1999	0152059024; 9780152059026

Nature/Seasons

AUTHOR	TITLE	CITY	PUBLISHER	COPYRIGHT	ISBN
Allen, Marjorie N.	Changes	New York	Macmillan	1991	0021790698; 9780021790692
Baker, Jeannie	Where the Forest Meets the Sea	New York	Greenwillow Books	1987; 1988	0688063632; 9780688063634
Bond. Rebecca	This Place in the Snow	New York	Dutton	2004	0525473084; 9780525473084
Bunting, Eve	Flower Garden	San Diego	Harcourt Brace Jovanovich; Sandpiper	1994; 2000	0152023720; 9780152023720
Carr, Jan	Splish, Splash, Spring	New York	Holiday House	2002	0823417544; 9780823417544
Ehlert, Lois	Leaf Man	Orlando, FL	Harcourt Children's Books	2005	0152053042; 9780152053048
Ehlert, Lois	Planting a Rainbow	San Diego	Harcourt Brace Jovanovich; Voyager Books	1988; 1992	0152626107; 9780152626105
Ehlert, Lois	Waiting for Wings	San Diego	Harcourt Children's Books	2001	0152026088; 9780152026080
Fleming, Denise	In the Small, Small Pond	New York	Henry Holt and Co.	1993; 2007	0805081178; 9780805081176
Fleming, Denise	In the Tall, Tall Grass	New York	Henry Holt and Co.	1991; 1995	0805039414; 9780805039412
Franco, Betsy	Birdsongs	New York	Margaret McElderry Books	2007	0689877773; 9780689877773
Frasier, Debra	Out of the Ocean	New York	Harcourt	1998	0152163549; 9780152163549
Gershator, Phillis	Listen, Listen	Cambridge, MA	Barefoot Books	2007	1846860849; 9781846860843
Gershator, Phillis	When It Starts to Snow	New York	Henry Holt	2001	0805067655; 9780805067651
Gomi, Taro	Spring is Here	San Francisco	Chronicle Books	1989; 1999	0811823318; 9780811823319
Henkes, Kevin	Oh!	New York	Greenwillow Books	1999	0688170536; 9780688170530
James, Simon	The Wild Woods	Cambridge, MA	Candlewick Press	1993	1406308455; 9781406308457
Lee, Suzy	Wave	San Francisco	Chronicle Books	2008	081185924X; 9780811859240
Lionni, Leo	A Busy Year	New York	Alfred A. Knopf; David McKay Company	1992; 2004	0679824642; 9780679824640
Lunde, Darrin	Hello, Bumblebee Bat	Watertown, MA	Charlesbridge	2007	1570913749; 9781570913747
Rockwell, Anne	Apples and Pumpkins	New York	Macmillan; Aladdin	1989; 2005	1416908315; 9781416908319
Rylant, Cynthia	In November	New York	Sandpiper	2008	0152063420; 9780152063429
Schaefer, Lola	This is the Rain	New York	Greenwillow	2001	0688170390; 9780688170390
Shulevitz, Uri	Snow	New York	Farrar Straus Giroux	1998	0374370923; 9780374370923

Siddals, Mary McKenna	Tell Me a Season	New York	Clarion	1997	0618130586; 9780618130580
Sill, Cathryn	About Birds	Atlanta	Peachtree	1997	1561451479; 9781561451470
Stewart, Sarah	The Gardener	New York	Farrar Straus Giroux; Square Fish	1997; 2007	031236749X; 9780312367497
Stringer, Lauren	Winter is the Warmest Season	New York	Harcourt	2006	0152049673; 9780152049676
Tresselt, Alvin	Rain Drop Splash	New York	Lothrop, Lee & Shepard Co; HarperCollins	1946; 1990	0688093523; 9780688093525
Udry, Janice May	A Tree is Nice	New York	Harper; HarperCollins	1956; 1987	0064431479; 9780064431477
Vaccaro Seeger, Laura	First the Egg	New York	Roaring Brook Press	2007	1596432721; 9781596432727
Wiesner, David	Flotsam	New York	Clarion Books	2006	0618194576; 9780618194575
Williams, Vera B.	Cherries and Cherry Pits	New York	Greenwillow Books	1986	0688104789; 9780688104788
Yolen, Jane	Owl Moon	New York	Philomel Books	1987	0399214577; 9780399214578
Zolotow, Charlotte	The Storm Book	New York	HarperCollins	1952; 1989	0064431940; 9780064431941

Music and Arts

AUTHOR	TITLE	CITY	PUBLISHER	COPYRIGHT	ISBN
Ackerman, Karen	Song and Dance Man	New York	Knopf Books for Young Readers	1988; 2003	0394893301; 9780394893303
Andreae, Giles	Giraffes Can't Dance	New York	Orchard Books	2001	0439287197; 9780439287197
Arnold, Katya	Elephants Can Paint Too	New York	Atheneum Books for Young Readers	2005	0689869851; 9780689869853
Barner, Bob	Dem Bones	San Francisco	Chronicle Books	1996	0811808270; 9780811808279
Beaumont, Karen, and Plecas, Jennifer	Baby Danced the Polka	New York	Dial Books for Young Readers	2004	0803725876; 9780803725874
Beaumont, Karen	I Ain't Gonna Paint No More!	Orlando, FL	Harcourt Childrens Books	2005	0152024883; 9780152024888
Briggs Martin, Jacqueline	Snowflake Bentley	Boston	Houghton Mifflin; Sandpiper	1998; 2009	0547248296; 9780547248295
Bryan, Ashley	Let It Shine; Three Favorite Spirituals	New York	Atheneum	2007	0689847327; 9780689847325
Halpern, Sheri	What Shall We Do When We All Go Out?	New York	Houghton Mifflin	1996	0395752477; 9780395752470
Ho, Minfong	Hush! A Thai Lullaby	New York	Orchard Books; Scholastic	1996; 2000	0531071669; 9780531071663
Hurd, Thatcher	Mama Don't Allow	New York	Harper & Row; HarperCollins	1984; 1985	0064430782; 9780064430784
Isadora, Rachel	Ben's Trumpet	New York	Greenwillow Books; Live Oak Media	1979; 1998	0874994330; 9780874994339
Johnson, Crockett	Harold and the Purple Crayon	New York	Harper & Row; HarperCollins	1955; 1998	0064430227; 9780064430227
Kuskin, Karla	The Philharmonic Gets Dressed	New York	HarperCollins	1986	006443124X; 9780064431248
McDonnell, Patrick	Art	Boston, MA	Little, Brown	2006	031611491X; 9780316114912
Moss, Lloyd	Zin! Zin! Zin! A Violin	New York	Simon & Schuster Books for Young Readers; Aladdin	1995; 2000	0689835248; 9780689835247
Paxton, Tom	The Marvelous Toy	New York	HarperCollins	1996	0688138790; 9780688138790

Raffi	Shake My Sillies Out	New York	Crown Publishers; Crown Books for Young Readers	1987; 1988	0517566478; 9780517566473
Reynolds, Peter	Ish	Cambridge, MA	Candlewick Press	2004	076362344X; 9780763623449
Reynolds, Peter	The Dot	Cambridge, MA	Candlewick Press	2003	0763619612; 9780763619619
Seder, Rufus Butler	Gallop! A Scanimation Picture Book	New York	Workman Publishing Company	2007	0761147632; 9780761147633
Sis, Peter	Ballerina!	New York	Greenwillow Books	2001	0688179444; 9780688179441
Sis, Peter	Play Mozart, Play!	New York	Greenwillow Books	2006	0061121819; 9780061121814
Twin, Michael	The Musical Life of Gustav Mole	Swinden, UK	Child's Play International	1990	0859533476; 9780859533478
Weatherford, Carole	Before John Was a Jazz Giant	New York	Henry Holt	2008	0805079947; 9780805079944
Wheeler, Lisa	Jazz Baby	Orlando	Harcourt Children's Books	2007	0152025227; 9780152025229
Wiesner, David	Sector 7	New York	Clarion Books	1999	0395746566; 9780395746561
Zelinsky, Paul	Knick-Knack Paddywhack	New York	Dutton	2002	0525469087; 9780525469087

Vehicles

AUTHOR	TITLE	CITY	PUBLISHER	COPYRIGHT	ISBN
Alborough, Jez	Duck in the Truck	San Diego	Kane/Miller	2000	1933605766; 9781933605760
Rex, Michael	Truck Duck	New York	G.P. Putnam's Sons	2004	0399250921; 9780399250927
Timmers, Leo	Who Is Driving?	New York	Bloomsbury	2007	1599900211; 9781599900216
Barton, Byron	My Car	New York	Greenwillow	2004	006058940X; 9780060589400
Barton, Byron	Trains	New York	HarperFestival	1998	0694011673; 9780694011674
Crews, Donald	Freight Train	New York	Greenwillow	1993	0688129404; 9780688129408
Crews, Donald	Truck	New York	Greenwillow	1991	0673816931; 9780688104818
Hubbell, Patricia	Trucks Whizz, Zoom, Rumble	Tarrytown, NY	Marshall Cavendish	2006	0761453288; 9780688158781
Lewis, Kevin	Chugga-Chugga Choo-Choo	New York	Hyperion	2001	0786807601; 9780786807604
Lewis, Kevin	My Truck is Stuck	New York	Hyperion	2002	078680534X; 9780786805341
London, Jonathan	A Truck Goes Rattley-Bumpa	New York	Henry Holt	2005	0805072330; 9780805072334
Shaw, Nancy	Sheep in a Jeep	New York	HMH Books	2009	0547237758; 9780547237756
Sis, Peter	Fire Truck	Greenwillow	New York	1998	0688158781; 9780688158781
Stoeke, Janet Morgan	Minerva Louise and the Red Truck	New York	Dutton	2002	0525469095; 9780525469094
Willems, Mo	Don't Let the Pigeon Drive the Bus	New York	Hyperion	2003	078681988X; 9780078619881
Zelinsky, Paul	The Wheels on the Bus	New York	Dutton	1990	0525446443; 9780525446446

Caldecott Award Winners

AUTHOR	TITLE	CITY	PUBLISHER	COPYRIGHT	ISBN
Aardema, Verna	Why Mosquitoes Buzz in People's Ears	New York	Dial Press; Puffin	1975; 2004	0140549056; 9780140549058
Ackerman, Karen	Song and Dance Man	New York	Knopf Books for Young Readers	1988; 2003	0394893301; 9780394893303
Bemelmans, Ludwig	Madeline's Rescue	New York	Viking Press	1953; 2000	0140566511; 9780140566512

Brown, Marcia	Once a Mouse	New York	Scribner; Aladdin	1961; 1989	0689713436; 9780689713439
Brown, Margaret Wise	The Little Island	New York	Doubleday Book for Young Readers	1946; 2003	0385746407; 9780385746403
Burton, Virginia Lee	The Little House	Boston	Houghton Mifflin	1942; 2009	0547131046; 9780547131047
de Regniers, Beatrice Schenk	May I Bring a Friend?	New York	Atheneum; Aladdin	1964; 1989	0689713533; 9780689713538
Emberley, Barbara	Drummer Hoff	Englewood Cliffs, NJ	Prentice-Hall; Aladdin	1967; 1972	067166249X; 9780671662493
Hader, Berta & Elmer	The Big Snow	New York	Macmillan Co.	1948; 1993	0689717571; 9780689717574
Haley, Gail E.	A Story, A Story	New York	Atheneum	1970	0689205112; 9780689205118
Hall, Donald	Ox-Cart Man	New York	Viking Press; Puffin	1979; 1983	0140504419; 9780140504415
Henkes, Kevin	Kitten's First Full Moon	New York	Greenwillow Books	2004	0060588284; 9780060588281
Juster, Norton	The Hello, Goodbye Window	New York	Michael di Capua Books; Hyperion Books for Children	2005	0786809140; 9780786809141
Keats, Ezra Jack	The Snowy Day	New York	Viking Press; Puffin	1962; 1976	0140501827; 9780140501827
Langstaff, John	Frog Went A-Courtin'	New York	Harcourt Brace; Sandpiper	1955; 1972	0156339005; 9780156339001
Lipkind, William	Finders Keepers	New York	Harcourt, Brace; Sandpiper	1951; 1989	0156309505; 9780156309509
Martin, Jacqueline Briggs	Snowflake Bentley	Boston	Houghton Mifflin; Sandpiper	1998; 2009	0547248296; 9780547248295
McCloskey, Robert	Make Way for Ducklings	New York	Viking Press; Live Oak Media	1941; 2004	1591127319; 9781591127314
McCloskey, Robert	Time of Wonder	New York	Viking Press; Puffin	1957	0140502017; 9780140502015
Ness, Evaline	Sam, Bangs & Moonshine	New York	Holt, Rinehart and Winston; Henry Holt and Co	1966; 1971	0805003150; 9780805003154
Petersham, Maud & Miska	The Rooster Crows	New York	The Macmillan Company; Aladdin	1945; 1987	0689711530; 9780689711534
Rathmann, Peggy	Officer Buckle and Gloria	New York	Putnam Juvenile	1995	0399226168; 9780399226168
Robbins, Ruth	Baboushka and the Three Kings	Berkeley, CA	Parnassus Press; Sandpiper	1960; 1986	0395426472; 9780395426470
Rohmann, Eric	My Friend Rabbit	Brookfield, CT	Roaring Brook Press; Square Fish	2002; 2007	031236752X; 9780312367527
Sendak, Maurice	Where the Wild Things Are	New York	Harper & Row; Harper Collins	1963; 1988	0060254920; 9780060254926
Spier, Peter	Noah's Ark	Garden City, NY	Doubleday; Dragonfly Books	1977; 1992	0440406935; 9780440406938
Swanson, Susan Marie	The House in the Night	Boston	Houghton Mifflin Co	2008	1618862447; 9780618862443
Taback, Simms	Joseph Had a Little Overcoat	New York	Random House; Live Oak Media	1977; 2001	0874997836; 9780874997835
Tresselt, Alvin	White Snow, Bright Snow	New York	Lothrop, Lee & Shepard Co.; HarperCollins	1947; 1988	0688082947; 9780688082949
Udry, Janice May	A Tree Is Nice	New York	Harper; HarperCollins	1956; 1987	0064431479; 9780064431477
Van Allsburg, Chris	Jumanji	Boston	Houghton Mifflin Co.	1981	0395304482; 9780395304488
Van Allsburg, Chris	The Polar Express	Boston	Houghton Mifflin	1985	0395389496; 9780395389492
Yolen, Jane	Owl Moon	New York	Philomel Books	1987	0399214577; 9780399214578
Yorinks, Arthur	Hey, Al	New York	Farrar, Straus and Giroux	1986; 1989	0374429855; 9780374429850
Young, Ed	Lon Po Po: A Red-Riding Hood Story from China	New York	Philomel Books; Putnam Juvenile	1989; 1996	0698113829; 9780698113824

Horn Book Winners

AUTHOR	TITLE	CITY	PUBLISHER	COPYRIGHT	ISBN
Anno, Mitsumasa	Anno's Alphabet	New York	Crowell; HarperTrophy	1974; 1988	0064431908; 9780064431903
Anno, Mitsumasa	Anno's Journey	Cleveland	Collins-World; Putnam Juvenile	1977; 1997	1698114337; 9780698114333
Bang, Molly	The Paper Crane	New York	Greenwillow Books	1985; 1987	0688073336; 9780688073336
Banks, Kate	And If the Moon Could Talk	New York	Frances Foster Books; Farrar, Straus and Giroux	1998; 2005	0374435588; 9780374435585
Bean, Jonathan	At Night	New York	Farrar, Straus Giroux	2007	0374304467; 9780374304461
Briggs, Raymond	The Snowman	New York	Random House; Puffin Books	1978; 1998	0241139384; 9780241139387
Burningham, John	Mr. Gumpy's Outing	New York	Holt, Rinehart and Winston; Henry Holt and Co.	1970; 1995	080503854X; 9780805038545
Cowley, Joy	Red-Eyed Tree Frog	New York	Scholastic Press	1999; 2006	043978221X; 9780439782210
Ehlert, Lois	Leaf Man	Orlando, FL	Harcourt Children's Books	2005	0152053042; 9780152053048
Graham, Bob	"Let's Get a Pup!" Said Kate	Cambridge, MA	Candlewick Press	2001; 2003	0763621935; 9780763625368
Grey, Mini	Traction Man Is Here!	New York	Alfred A. Knopf	2005	0375831916; 9780375831911
Hest, Amy	In the Rain with Baby Duck	Cambridge, MA	Candlewick Press	1995; 1999	0763606979; 9780763606978
Hoban, Tana	1, 2, 3	New York	Greenwillow Books	1985	068802579X; 9780688025793
Hurd, Thacher	Mama Don't Allow	New York	Harper & Row; HarperCollins	1984; 1985	0064430782; 9780064430784
Keats, Ezra Jack	Hi, Cat!	New York	Macmillan; Viking Juvenile	1970; 1999	0670885460; 9780670885466
Mahy, Margaret	Bubble Trouble	New York	Clarion Books	2009	0547074212; 9780547074214
Mosel, Arlene	Tikki Tikki Tembo	New York	Rinehart and Winston; Square Fish	1968; 2007	0312367481; 9780312367480
Pinkney, Brian	The Adventures of Sparrowboy	New York	Simon & Schuster Books for Young Readers; Aladdin	1997; 2000	0689835345; 9780689835346
Root, Phyllis	Big Momma Makes the World	Cambridge, MA	Candlewick Press; Walker Books Ltd	2002	0744573823; 9780744573824
Seeger, Laura Vaccaro	Dog and Bear: Two Friends, Three Stories	New Milford, CT	Roaring Brook Press	2007	1596430532; 9781596430532
Steptoe, John	Mufaro's Beautiful Daughters	New York	Lothrop, Lee & Shepard Books; HarperFestival	1987; 1993	0688129358; 9780688129354
Van Allsburg, Chris	The Garden of Abdul Gasazi	Boston	Houghton Mifflin	1979	039527804X; 9780395278048
Wells, Rosemary	Shy Charles	New York	Dial Books for Young Readers; Puffin	1988; 2001	0140568433; 9780140568431
Young, Ed	Lon Po Po: A Red-Riding Hood Story from China	New York	Philomel Books; Putnam Juvenile	1989; 1996	0698113829; 9780698113824
Young, Ed	Seven Blind Mice	New York	Philomel Books; Putnam Juvenile	1992; 2002	0698118952; 9780698118959

Older Classics

AUTHOR	TITLE	CITY	PUBLISHER	COPYRIGHT	ISBN
Archambault, John	Chicka Chicka Boom Boom	New York	Simon & Schuster Books for Young Readers; Beach Lane Books	1989; 2009	1416990917; 9781416990918

Bemelmans, Ludwig	Madeline	New York	Simon and Schuster; Viking Press	1939; 1967	0670445800; 9780670445806
Bianco, Margery Williams	The Velveteen Rabbit	New York	George H. Doran Company; HCI	1922; 2005	0757303331; 9780757303333
Brown, Margaret Wise	The Little Island	New York	Doubleday Book for Young Readers	1946; 2003	0385746407; 9780385746403
Burton, Virginia Lee	Mike Mulligan and His Steam Shovel	Boston	Houghton Mifflin	1939; 1993	0395259398; 9780395259399
Carle, Eric	The Very Hungry Caterpillar	New York	Collins Publishers; Philomel	1979; 1994	0399226907; 9780399226908
Degen, Bruce	Jamberry	New York	Harper & Row; HarperCollins	1983	0060214163; 9780060214166
Eastman, P.D.	Are You My Mother?	New York	Beginner Books; Random House Books for Young Readers	1960; 1966	0394900189; 9780394900186
Freeman, Don	Corduroy	New York	Viking Press	1968; 2008	0670063363; 9780670063369
Gag, Wanda	Millions of Cats	New York	Coward-McCann, Inc.; Puffin	1928; 2006	0142407089; 9780142407080
Johnson, Crockett	Harold and the Purple Crayon	New York	Harper & Row; HarperCollins	1955; 1998	0064430227; 9780064430227
Keets, Ezra Jack	The Snowy Day	New York	Viking Press; Puffin	1962; 1976	0140501827; 9780140501827
Krauss, Ruth	The Carrot Seed	New York	Harper & Brothers; HarperCollins	1945; 2004	0064432106; 9780064432108
Leaf, Munro	The Story of Ferdinand	New York	The Viking Press	1936	0670674249; 9780670674244
McBratney, Sam	Guess How Much I Love You	Cambridge, MA	Candlewick Press	1995; 2008	0763641758; 9780763641757
McCloskey, Robert	Blueberries for Sal	New York	Viking Press	1948	0670175919; 9780670175918
Milne, A. A.	The Complete Tales of Winnie the Pooh	New York	Dutton Children's Books	1994; 1996	0525457232; 9780525457237
Mosel, Arlene	Tikki Tikki Tembo	New York	Rinehart and Winston; Square Fish	1968; 2007	0312367481; 9780312367480
Potter, Beatrix	The Tale of Peter Rabbit	Springfield, MA	McLoughlin Bros.; Warne	1928; 2002	0723247706; 9780723247708
Rey, H.A.	Curious George	Boston	Houghton Mifflin Company	1941; 1998	0395922720; 9780395922729
Rosen, Michael	We're Going on a Bear Hunt	New York	Margaret K. McElderry Books/Aladdin	1989; 2003	0689853491; 9780689853494
Sendak, Maurice	Where the Wild Things Are	New York	Harper & Row; Harper Collins	1963; 1988	0060254920; 9780060254926
Slobodkina, Esphyr	Caps for Sale	New York	W. R. Scott, Inc.; HarperFestival	1940; 2008	0061474533; 9780061474538
Steptoe, John	Stevie	New York	Harper & Row; HarperCollins	1969; 1986	0064431223; 9780064431224
Dr. Seuss	Green Eggs and Ham	New York	Beginner Books; Random House Books for Young Readers	1960	0545002850; 9780583324205
Dr. Seuss	Horton Hatches the Egg	New York	Random House; Random House Books for Young Readers	1940; 2004	039480077X; 9780394800776
Dr. Seuss	The Cat in the Hat	New York	Random House; Random House Books for Young Readers	1957; 1966	0394900014; 9780394900018
Wise Brown, Margaret	The Runaway Bunny	New York and London	Harper; HarperCollins	1942; 2005	0060775823; 9780060775827
Zion, Gene	Harry the Dirty Dog	New York	Harper; HarperCollins	1956; 1976	006443009X; 9780064430098

Preschool Developmental Information Chart

	By 3 years old (36 months)	By 4 years old (48 months)	By 5 years old (60 months)
Cognitive Development (child's ability to learn and solve problems)	• Sorts objects into categories (e.g., shape, color) • Matches pictures to objects • Plays make believe and represents familiar experiences using dolls, animals, and people in play • Understands beginning number concepts (e.g., "two") • Assembles puzzles with 3 or 4 pieces • Comprehends simple time concepts (e.g., "now," "soon," and "later") • Beginning awareness of cause-and-effect relationships • Learns by doing and through senses • Able to copy a circle	• Names some colors • May know some numbers and understands the concept of counting • Thinking is literal • Pretend play becomes more complex and may incorporate fantasy • Understands "same" and "different" • Beginning to have a sense of time (e.g, past, present, and future) but does not yet understand the duration of time • Draws a figure with 2-4 body parts • Writes some capital letters • Comprehends more complex number and spatial concepts (e.g., more, less, bigger, behind, next to) • Starts to recognize shared characteristics of objects (e.g., round, soft, animals) and can sort objects into categories • Continues to learn by doing and through the senses • Begins to understand that symbols and images can represent real objects	• Counts 10 or more objects • Recognizes and names at least 4 colors • Generates stories based on imagination • Can tell the difference between fantasy and reality most of the time • Better understanding of time and sequential order • Begins to be able to arrange objects in order from smallest to largest • Copies shapes including a triangle • Comprehends and names opposites • Lacks adult logic, thinking is simple • Familiar with things used every day in their homes and lives (e.g., food, money) • Identifies "left" and right" • Constructs complex puzzle

	By 3 years old (36 months)	By 4 years old (48 months)	By 5 years old (60 months)
Social and Emotional Development (child's ability to interact with others and to appropriately control his/her emotions)	• Follows simple directions; enjoys helping with tasks around the house (e.g., setting the table for meals, laundry) • Begins to ask for help when needed • Engages in solitary play but will play near other children • Not able to play cooperatively or share • Understands concept of "mine" and "not mine" • Copies adults and peers • Can choose between two things • Beginning awareness of the moods/feelings of others • Expresses a range of feelings • Expresses positive feelings toward friends • Prefers routines and may protest changes in routines • Able to separate from parents	• Able to play cooperatively (e.g., takes turns, shares) • Works out conflicts and solves problems • Able to communicate anger with words instead of physical actions • Capable of feeling envy • Comprehends the concept of lying and may lie to protect self • Creative and pretend play continues to expand • Pretends to be "mom" or "dad" • Fantasy play becomes increasingly creative and child occasionally has trouble telling the difference between fantasy and reality • Imagines that unfamiliar images may be "monsters" • Enjoys novel experiences • Increasingly more independent • Able to dress and undress self • Views self as whole person with body, thoughts, and emotions	• Understands right versus wrong and follows rules • Copies adults and motivated to receive positive feedback • Understands the difference between being honest and dishonest • Values friends and wants to play with others rather than be alone • Wants to please friends • Understands the concept of gender • Prefers to play with children of the same sex • Wants to be like peers and may put down those who are different • More independent; wants to accomplish things without adult help • Enjoys make-believe play involving dress up • Likes to perform (e.g., sing, dance, and act) • Variable; can be demanding and also can be cooperative
Speech and Language Development (child's ability to understand and use language)	• Able to understand most of what is said and 75 percent of speech is intelligible • Speaks in short, complete sentences (3-5 words) • Can answer simple questions • Follows 2 part commands • States own name, age, and gender • Uses pronouns (e.g., I, you, me, we), and some plurals • Understands simple spatial concepts (e.g., in, on, over, under) • Able to identify common objects and pictures	• 1,500-word vocabulary • Speech is able to be understood by strangers • Speaks in more complex sentences of (5-6 words) • Able to use words to explain the use of common objects • Uses verbs with "ing" endings and uses some irregular past tenses (e.g., "ran," "fell") • Follows some basic grammar rules • Comprehends words that relate two ideas to one another (e.g., if, why, when) • Relates simple stories	• Speech is fluent; correctly uses plurals, pronouns, tenses • Language is more complex; sentences are composed of 5 words or more • Says full name and address • Tells stories that are longer and recalls parts of stories • Comprehends rhyming • Curious about many things and seeks knowledge

	By 3 years old (36 months)	By 4 years old (48 months)	By 5 years old (60 months)
Fine Motor Development (child's ability to use small muscles, specifically hands and fingers, to manipulate objects)	• Constructs simple puzzles • Controls writing utensil enough to make up-and-down, side-to-side, and circular lines • Can reproduce simple shapes (e.g., circle) • Manipulates art materials (e.g., clay, finger paints) and other small objects • Can turn the pages of a book • Builds a tower of at least 6 blocks	• Can reproduce a cross and square • Can copy some capital letters • Draws figure with 2-4 body parts • Able to cut along a line with scissors • Self care skills are developing-can brush teeth, comb hair, wash, and dress with minimal help • Comfortable using fork and spoon on own	• Hand preference is established • Holds pencil with mature grip • Draws figure with body • Able to produce some letters and copy shapes (e.g., triangle) • Controls crayon/marker and colors within lines • Can cut and paste simple shapes • Usually cares for own personal needs (e.g., dresses and undresses self, brushes own teeth, feeds self with fork and spoon, and uses toilet independently) • Able to lace shoes but does not tie yet
Gross Motor Development (child's ability to use large muscles)	• Walks easily, in almost adult-like manner • Runs, navigating around objects without difficulty • Kicks, throws overhead, and catches balls • Independently climbs ladders and uses slides • Pedals and rides a tricycle on own • Climbs stairs alternating feet (up and down)	• More controlled when running. • Moves backward and forward with skill, and gallops • Catches, throws, and bounces a ball easily most of the time • Can balance on one foot for at least 5 seconds and can hop on one foot • Able to do somersault	• Runs like an adult, skips • Walks on tiptoe, and on a balance beam • Can balance on one foot for at least 10 seconds • Skates, swings, and jumps rope • May learn to swim or ride a bike

Sources: Shelov, Steven and Hannermann, Robert. *Caring for Your Baby and Young Child: Birth to Age Five.* 2004. New York: American Academy of Pediatrics/Bantam Books; "Learn the Signs - Milestones." 2010. Centers for Disease Control and Prevention. <http:www.cdc.gov/actearly>; "Mayo Clinic Child Development Chart: Preschool Milestones by Mayo Clinic Staff." 2010. MayoClinic.com <http://MayoClinic.com >; Destefanis, Joyce and Firchow, Nancy. "Developmental Milestones: Ages 3 Through 5." 2010. GreatSchools.org <http://GreatSchools.org>.

Alphabet Linking Chart

a b c d e f g h i j k l m n o p

q r s t u v w x y z

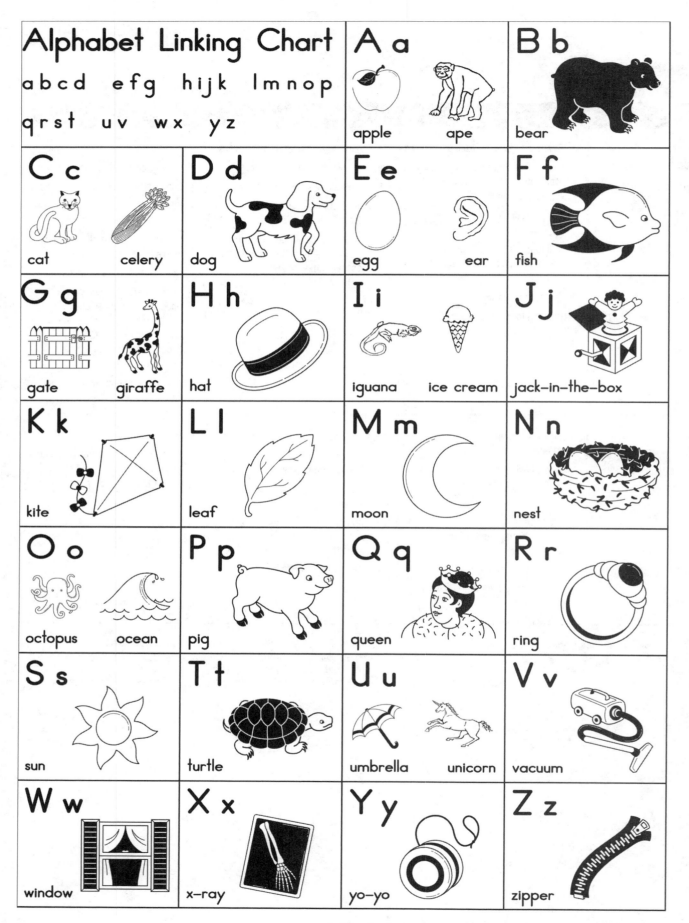

A a apple ape

B b bear

C c cat celery

D d dog

E e egg ear

F f fish

G g gate giraffe

H h hat

I i iguana ice cream

J j jack-in-the-box

K k kite

L l leaf

M m moon

N n nest

O o octopus ocean

P p pig

Q q queen

R r ring

S s sun

T t turtle

U u umbrella unicorn

V v vacuum

W w window

X x x-ray

Y y yo-yo

Z z zipper

APPENDIX

H

Verbal Path

Sometimes it helps children to say aloud the directions for "making" a letter. This "verbal path" helps them to understand the directional movement that is essential. In addition, it gives the teacher and child a language to talk through the letter and its features. Here, we suggest language for creating a verbal path to the distinctive features of letters.

Lowercase Letter Formation

a — pull back, around, up, and down

b — pull down, up, around

c — pull back and around

d — pull back, around, up, and down

e — pull across, back, and around

f — pull back, down, and cross

g — pull back, around, up, down, and under

h — pull down, up, over, and down

i — pull down, dot

j — pull down, curve around, dot

k — pull down, pull in, pull out

l — pull down

m — pull down, up, over, down and up, over and down

n — pull down, up, over, and down

o — pull back and around

p — pull down, up, and around

q — pull back, around, up, and down

r — pull down, up, and over

s — pull back, in, around, and back around

t — pull down and cross

u — pull down, around, up and down

v — slant down, up

w — slant down, up, down, up

x — slant down, slant down

y — slant in, slant and down

z — across, slant down, across

Uppercase Letter Formation

A — slant down, slant down, across

B — pull down, up, around and in, back and around

C — pull back and around

D — pull down, up, around

E — pull down, across, across, and across

F — pull down, across, across

G — pull back, around, across

H — pull down, pull down, across

I — pull down, across, across

J — pull down, curve around, across

K — pull down, slant in, slant out

L — pull down, across

M — pull down, slant down, slant up, pull down

N — pull down, slant down, pull up

O — pull back and around

P — pull down, up, and around

Q — pull back and around and cross

R — pull down, up, around, in, and slant down

S — pull back, in, around, down, and back around

T — pull down, across

U — pull down, around, up, and down

V — slant down, slant up

W — slant down up, down up

X — slant down, slant down

Y — slant in, slant, and down

Z — across, slant down, across

by color

| blue letters | red letters | yellow letters | green letters |

by consonants/vowels

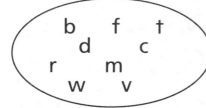

by slant/straight lines

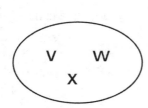

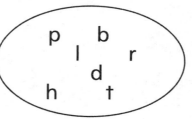

by upper/lower case

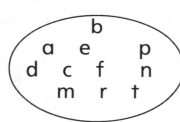

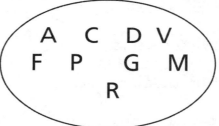

by tails/no tails

by circles/no circles

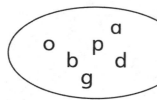

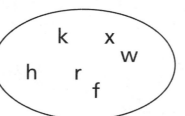

by tunnels/no tunnels

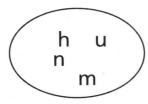

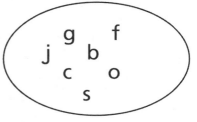

by long sticks/short sticks

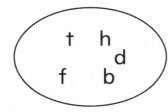

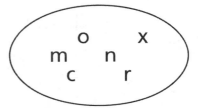

by tall/short

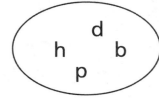

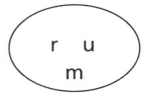

by dots/no dots

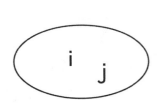

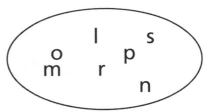

by same lowercase/uppercase match

x w p o c s u v z

X W P O C S U V Z

by different lowercase/uppercase match

a b d e f g h i j k l m n q r t y

A B D E F G H I J K L M N Q R T Y

My Book

by _____

My name is _____.

My birthday is _____ .

I am _____ years old.

I live at _____ .

My phone number is _____ .

My favorite color is _____.

Here is my family.

Here are my friends.

We like to _____ .

We read books at school.

I love school!

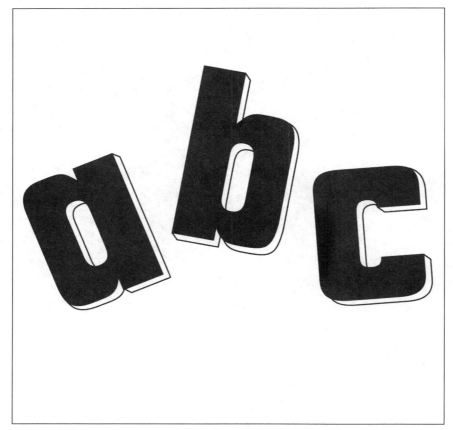

Letter Work

Art

Book Activities

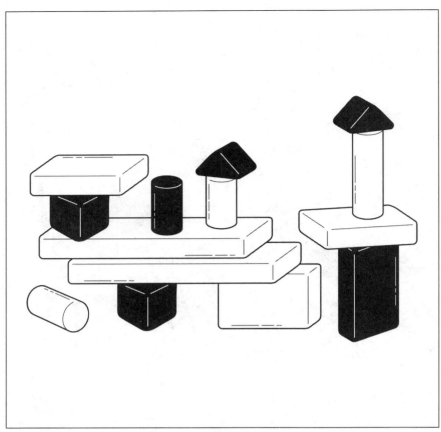

Blocks

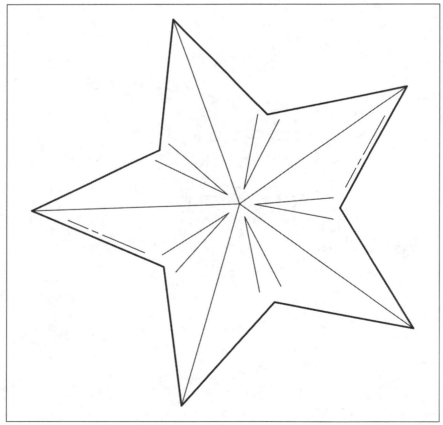

Choice

Computer

Cooking

Inquiry

Library

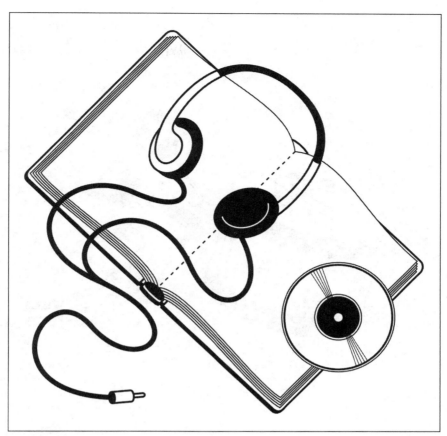

Listening Area

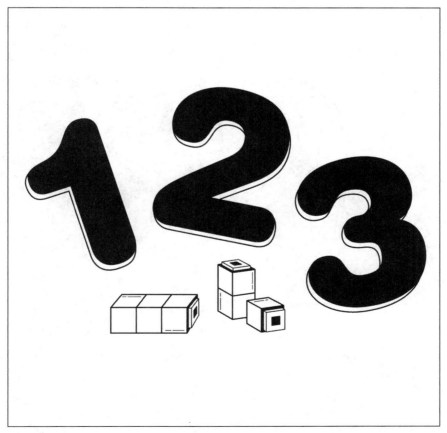

Math

Music

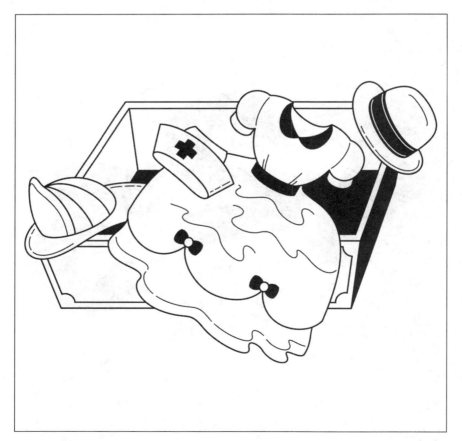

Play Corner

Puzzles/Games

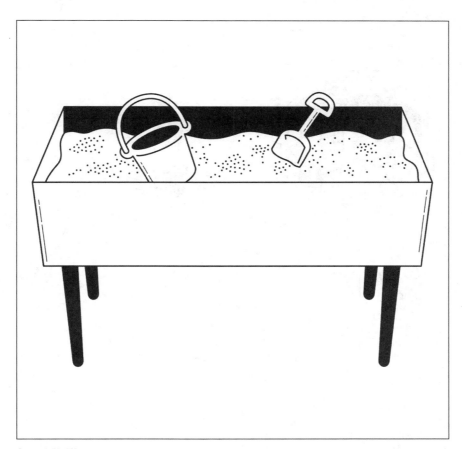

Sand Table

Science

Social Studies

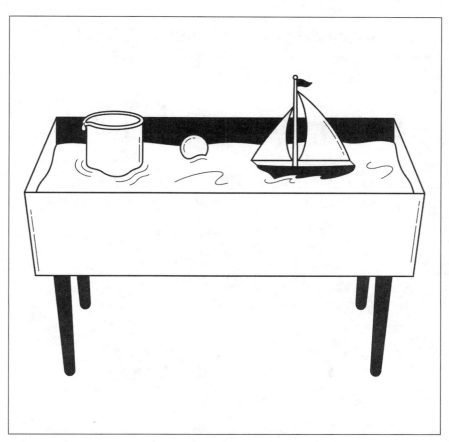

Water Table

Writing/Bookmaking

Uppercase Letter Recognition Sheet

H	E	M	T
I	P	V	U
O	C	W	B
X	Q	J	S
G	N	Y	K
Z	R	A	F
L	D		

Lowercase Letter Recognition Sheet

h	e	m	t
i	p	v	u
o	c	w	b
x	q	j	s
g	n	y	k
z	r	a	f
l	d		

APPENDIX N: *Rhyming Cards*

APPENDIX O

Master List of Materials

Classroom Materials

- Weather Chart Icons/Pictures
- Job Chart Icons/Pictures
- Choice Time Chart Icons/Pictures
- Environmental signs
- Pointer
- Easel(s)
- Low chair(s), rocking chair
- Large-format Poems, Songs
- Big Books
- Name Cards
- Letter Books
- Large Magnetic Board
- Whiteboard(s)
- Bulletin Board(s)
- Pocket Chart(s)
- Chart Paper/Flip Chart
- Carpet Squares or Small Mats
- Picture Cards (Picture Set)
- Parent Newsletter
- Verbal Path Directions

Suggested Bulletin Boards/ Charts

- Attendance Chart (Who is Here Today?)
- Name Chart(s)
- Alphabet Chart(s)

- Weather Chart (daily)
- Calendar (Monthly/daily)
- Job Chart (daily)
- Schedule (daily, weekly)
- Birthday List or Calendar
- Choice Time Chart (daily)
- Classroom Rules or Guidelines
- Parent Board
- Children's Board (children choose what to display)
- Things That Start With…(letter c, etc.)
- Word Wall(s)

Teacher Materials

- Variety of paper, including chart paper (white or cream)
- Variety of writing tools, including dark markers
- Index cards
- Sticky notes
- Laminating machine
- Clothespins or clips for charts
- Velcro or other reusable adhesive for charts
- Colorful stickers
- Masking tape, clear tape, highlighter tape
- Storage: Plastic bins, boxes, tubs, and baskets, clear plastic containers, milk crates, small buckets
- Furniture: low shelving (child height), child-size tables and chairs, oversize pillows or beanbag chairs, rugs/carpets, lamps, low tables for work areas

Alphabet/Letter-Related Materials

- Magnetic and foam letters
- Letter cards
- Picture cards
- Letter Books
- Cut-up sentences
- Name puzzles
- Blank books
- Tactile materials for forming letters (shaving cream, sand/salt, sandpaper, play dough, tissue paper)

Art/Writing Materials

- Variety of writing tools: crayons, markers, colored pencils, paints, pastel crayons, paintbrushes
- Containers for water
- Easels
- Clips
- Variety of paper (white and colored construction paper, newsprint, colored tissue paper, oak tag, poster board, card stock, butcher paper)
- Recycled materials (empty cardboard and plastic bottles and containers, newspapers, magazines, cardboard, empty paper towel and toilet paper rolls, empty cans, shoeboxes, etc.)
- Glue, glue sticks, tape
- Fabric scraps, ribbon, string, yarn, raffia, cotton balls
- Glitter, stickers
- Buttons, shells, beads, interlocking beads
- Popsicle/craft sticks
- Brown paper bags
- Sand, shaving cream (for tracing letters)
- Correction tape, sticky notes
- Envelopes, folders
- Paper plates

Materials for Games

- Card Stock
- Letter Cards
- Picture Cards
- Word Cards
- Dot and/or Numeral Cards or dice
- Plastic chips or other markers
- Picture Lotto
- Labeled plastic bags or boxes for storage
- Laminating (or other protective covering

Materials for Assessment

- Enlarged Published Texts, Poems, or Texts from Interactive/Shared Writing
- Trade Books
- Paper/index cards, clipboard (for recording observations)
- Writing materials (teacher and child)
- Folder of collected samples of children's drawings and writings, samples of children's bookmaking efforts
- Magnetic (and other) letters for sorting
- Letter cards
- Alphabet Linking Chart
- Name Chart
- Uppercase and Lowercase Letter Recognition Sheets
- Initial Sounds Picture Cards
- Rhyming Cards
- Sentence Strips

Materials for Classroom Learning Areas

- **MEETING AREA** carpet, carpet squares/circles, teacher's chair, books display, calendar, magnetic easel

- **LIBRARY** picture books, colorful plastic tubs and/or baskets for storage, large pillows, book-related toys and stuffed animals, book stands

- **LISTENING AREA** books, chairs (2), small table, CDs and tapes, CD and/or tape player, headphones (at least 2 sets)

- **PLAY CORNER** theme-related books and writing tools, play artifacts (often theme-related; see Chapter 4, Figure 4.21) such as stove, sink, refrigerator, tables, cupboard, doll bed, dishes, food, telephone, puppets, dress-up clothes

- **ART** recycled materials, crayons, washable paints and markers, pencils, colored and textured paper, paintbrushes, containers for water, magazines and newspapers, safety scissors, ink pads and stamps, clay or play dough, cookie cutters, stencils, glue or glue sticks, tape

- **WRITING** blank books, pencils, crayons, washable markers, colored and textured papers, white correction tape, scissors, glue or glue sticks, letters stamps and ink pads, letter tiles, letter sponges, whiteboards, notebooks, traceable letters, sandpaper letters, stencils, alphabet chart, sticky notes

- **BOOKMAKING** Pens, pencils, washable markers, crayons, blank books (pre-stapled) or paper for making books, chart paper (for shared/interactive writing), alphabet chart, name chart, familiar books

- **BLOCKS** wooden blocks of varying shapes and sizes, toy signs, vehicles, furnished dollhouse and people, Legos and/or other connecting building toys, cardboard blocks, small basket with paper, writing materials, and tape for making labels and signs

- **PUZZLES AND GAMES** variety of simple puzzles, including letter and word puzzles, magnetic letters, pattern blocks, Unifix cubes, and manipulatives such as beads and buttons

- **SAND TABLE** Sand or rice, cups and containers of various shapes and sizes, clear and opaque containers, spoons, shovels, or other digging tools, plastic funnels, plastic figures such as animals, dinosaurs, or people

- **WATER TABLE** water, cups and containers of various shapes and sizes, clear and opaque containers, plastic funnels, plastic figures such as sea creatures and boats

- **MUSIC** simple musical instruments, child-made instruments, music player and headsets, music CDs and/or tapes

- **SCIENCE** magnifying glasses, natural materials (pinecones, rocks and stones, leaves, branches, seashells), soil/seeds for planting, plastic containers for planting, writing tools, paper, nonfiction picture books

- **SOCIAL STUDIES** Familiar signs and symbols, theme-related community artifacts such as letters and postage stamps, theme-related nonfiction books on subjects such as foods, families, and community workers

- **MATH** Manipulatives for counting and comparing, pattern blocks, rods, coins, Legos, counting bears, Unifix cubes, colored plastic disks, number cards, rulers, math games

- **COMPUTER** simple computers and printers, a variety of computer games that support literacy and math learning

Materials for Inquiry Projects

- **ALL ABOUT ME** plain white paper or card stock, ink pads, variety of musical instruments, newsprint, craft sticks, paints, pencils, crayons, markers, yarn, fabric scraps, glitter, white and colored construction paper, glue, scissors, cardboard, magazines, blank books, pre-cut paper award trophies and/or medals

- **ANIMAL BABIES** dolls, doll accessories, yarn, straw, raffia, twigs or small branches, pipe cleaners, clay or play dough, stuffed animals, pictures of, or books about birds, drawing materials

- **COLORS** poster board, white and colored construction paper, music CDs or tapes, colored tissue paper, scissors, glue, paints, crayons, colored pencils and markers, old magazines, books with color photos of natural objects, paper plates, craft sticks, play dough, plastic cups, flower seeds, soil, water, fruits, vegetables, flowers (or pictures of each), colored dyes, white t-shirts

- **COMMUNITY** Puppets, building materials (empty shoeboxes, plastic and cardboard containers, Legos, blocks, etc.), simple, hand-drawn maps of your neighborhood, writing and drawing tools, plain white paper, pre-made shopping lists, pretend play props for market (empty juice and milk containers, cans, cereal boxes, play money etc.), postage stamps, envelopes, empty shoeboxes, pre-made, laminated cards (for library play), fire station pretend play props, familiar signs and symbols

- **FOOD** Chart paper, familiar foods, writing and drawing materials, magazines, collage materials

- **FRIENDS AND FRIENDSHIP** pre-cut colored construction paper flowers, white and colored construction paper, paints, tissue paper, crayons, markers, stickers, glitter, glue

- **JOURNEYS** Chart paper, drawing and writing materials, music CDs or tapes, dress-up clothes, suitcases or other "luggage," small carpet square

- **MOODS AND FEELINGS** simple percussion instruments, pre-cut paper circles, markers, crayons, music CDs or tapes, puppets

- **MY BODY** white and colored construction paper, butcher paper, washable paint, shallow trays, water, fruits/foods with variety of textures/smells

- **PETS** Chart paper, stuffed animals, writing paper and tools, magazines, fabric scraps, glue, scissors, various papers for collage

- **SHAPES** Colored construction paper, scissors, glue, markers, crayons, play dough, basic shapes cookie cutters, cookie dough, trays for baking

- **WATER** water, water table or sink, buckets, pails, variety of plastic containers, pebbles, marbles (or other small objects), water glasses of varying size, spoons

Glossary of Terms

alphabet book (ABC book): A book that helps children develop the concept and sequence of the alphabet by pairing labels beginning with each letter with pictures of people, animals, or objects the labels represent.

alphabet linking chart: A chart containing upper- and lowercase letters of the alphabet paired with pictures representing words beginning with each letter (*a, apple*, for example).

alphabetic principle: The concept that there is a relationship between the spoken sounds in oral language and the graphic forms in written language.

analyze (as a strategic action): To examine the elements of a text in order to know more about how it is constructed and notice aspects of the writer's craft.

assessment: A means for gathering information or data that reveals what learners control, partially control, or do not yet control consistently.

assisted performance: The level at which a child can perform well in cooperation with the teacher (the upper boundary of the zone of proximal development).

behaviors: Observable actions.

blend (in the context of phonological awareness): To combine sounds or word parts.

book and print features (as text characteristics): The physical attributes of a text.

centers (in the classroom): Specific work areas designated for specific activities.

circle games: Participating in language play, singing action songs, and sharing while sitting in a circle.

constructive learning: Building knowledge through experiences.

cognitive development: A child's ability to learn and solve problems.

content (as a text characteristic): The subject matter of a text.

contrastive principle: Establishing opposites in early writing behavior.

core literacy activities: Activities that support children's literacy learning, such as shared reading and interactive writing.

critique (as a strategic action): To evaluate a text based on the reader's personal, world, or text knowledge and think critically about the ideas expressed.

directionality: The orientation of print (in the English language, from left to right).

directional principle: The convention of writing in English that requires that words be written left to write across each line and from the top to the bottom of the page.

distinctive letter features: Visual features that make each letter of the alphabet different from every other letter.

early literacy concepts: Very early understandings related to how written language or print is organized and used—how it works.

emergent reader: A learner who is beginning to develop phonemic awareness and concepts of print.

emergent writer: A learner who is beginning to understand that she or he can communicate using writing in a variety of ways.

English language learners (ELLs): People who are learning English as a language in addition to their native language.

environmental print: Any print that children encounter in the world around them.

fiction: An invented story, usually a narrative.

fine motor development: A child's ability to use small muscles, specifically hands and fingers, to manipulate objects.

fluency (in reading): To read continuous text with appropriate momentum, phrasing, pauses, intonation, and stress.

fluency (in word solving): Speed, accuracy, and flexibility in decoding words.

functional genres: Text categories in which the purpose is to accomplish a practical task.

genre: A category of written text that is characterized by a particular style, form, or content.

gross motor development: A child's ability to use large muscles.

high-frequency words: Words that occur often in spoken and written language (*the*, for example).

independent level: The level at which a child is able to work alone (the lower boundary of the zone of proximal development).

infer (as a strategic action): To go beyond the literal meaning of a text and to think about what is not stated but implied by the writer.

informational genres: Text categories in which the purpose is to inform or to give facts about a topic.

inquiry: The kind of focused activity one performs when pursuing a topic of interest.

interactive drawing: An instructional context in which the teacher and students cooperatively plan and compose a drawing.

interactive read-aloud: An instructional context in which children actively listen and respond to the teacher's oral reading of a text.

interactive writing: An instructional context in which the teacher and students cooperatively plan, compose, and write a group text.

intonation: The rise and fall in vocal pitch used to convey meaning.

inventory principle: The principle that children organize of take stock of what they know about letters and words.

language and literary features (as text characteristics): Characteristics of written language that are qualitatively different from those of spoken language.

language awareness: Familiarity with what words are, what they mean, and how they are used.

learning zone: The level at which it is most productive to aim one's teaching for each student (the zone of proximal development).

letter knowledge: The ability to recognize and label the graphic symbols of language.

letter-sound correspondence: Recognizing the corresponding sound of a specific letter when that letter is seen or recognizing the graphic symbol of a specific letter when that letter is heard.

letter-sound relationships: See *letter-sound correspondence.*

literary nonfiction: Engaging factual texts that present information on a topic in interesting ways.

memoir: An account of an important or formative event, usually part of a person's life.

mentor texts: Books or other texts used as examples of excellent writing.

narrative talk: The talk that children engage in when telling stories.

narrative genres: Text categories in which the purpose is to tell a story.

nonfiction: A text based on fact.

nursery rhyme: A short rhyme for children, usually telling a story.

onset (in a syllable): The part (consonant, consonant cluster, or consonant digraph) that comes before the vowel.

onset-rime segmentation: The identification and separation of onsets (first part) and rimes (last part, containing the vowel) in words.

phoneme: The smallest unit of sound in spoken language.

phonetic principle: A predictable sound-spelling generalization or relationship.

phonics: The knowledge of letter-sound relationships and how they are used in reading and writing.

phonological awareness: Familiarity with words, rhyming words, onsets and rimes, syllables, and individual sounds (phonemes).

phonemic awareness: The ability to hear individual sounds in words and to identify particular sounds.

play corner: An area in the classroom designated for imaginative play and discovery.

poetic genres: Text categories in which the purpose is to use poetic form to explain feelings, sensory images, ideas, or stories.

print awareness: Familiarity with basic information about how print works.

realistic fiction: An invented story that could happen.

recurring principle (in drawing and writing): The idea that children repeat what they know over and over.

return sweep (in reading): Going back to the right margin to read the next line.

rhyme: The ending part (rime) of a word that sounds like the ending part (rime) of another word.

rime: The ending part of a word containing the vowel.

segment (verb): To divide (a word) into parts.

shared reading: An instructional technique in which the teacher leads a group of students in reading a big book in order to introduce aspects of literacy.

shared writing: An instructional technique in which the teacher leads a group of students in composing a coherent text together.

story awareness: Familiarity with the ways stories are organized.

strategic action: Any one of many simultaneous, coordinated thinking activities that go on in a reader's head.

stress (in oral reading): The emphasis given to some syllables or words.

syllable: A minimal unit of sequential speech sounds composed of a vowel sound or a consonant-vowel combination.

syntax: The study of how sentences are formed and of the grammatical rules that govern their formation.

synthesize (as a strategic action): To combine new information or ideas gained by reading text with existing knowledge to create new understandings.

text structure: The overall architecture or organization of a piece of writing.

theme: The central idea or concept in a story or the message the author is conveying.

thinking within, beyond, and about the text: Three ways of thinking about a text while reading. Thinking within the text, readers efficiently and effectively understand what is on the page, the author's literal message. Thinking beyond the text, readers make inferences and put text ideas together in different ways to construct the text's meaning. Thinking about the text, readers analyze and critique the author's craft.

verbal path: Language prompts paired with motor movements to help children learn to form letters correctly.

vocabulary: Words and their meanings.

working vocabulary: The words a person knows and uses in conversation.

zone of proximal development: The difference between a child's independent ability level and his or her ability level with adult support.

Children's Book References

Andreasen, Dan. 2009. *The Treasure Bath*. New York: Henry Holt and Company, Christy Ottaviano Books.

Askani, Tanja. 2009. *A Friend Like You*. New York: Scholastic.

Aylesworth, Jim. 2009. Il. *Our Abe Lincoln: An Old tune with New Lyrics*. New York: Scholastic.

Aylesworth, Jim. 1998. *The Gingerbread Man*. New York: Scholastic Press.

Baddrel, Ivor. 2007. *Cock-A-Doodle Quack Quack*. Oxford, UK: David Fickling Books.

Baker, Keith. 2009. *Just How Long Can a Long String Be?!* New York: Arthur A. Levine Books, An Imprint of Scholastic.

Brown, Marcia. 2010. *Stone Soup* (reprint). New York: Atheneum.

Bunting, Eve. 2007. Il. Jeff Mack. *Hurry! Hurry!* Boston, MA: Houghton Mifflin Harcourt.

Burningham, John. 2009. *It's a Secret!* Somerville, MA: Candlewick Press.

Carle, Eric. 2007. *Eric Carle's Opposites*. New York: Grosset & Dunlap

Carle, Eric. 1994. *The Very Hungry Caterpillar*. New York: Philomel.

Carle, Eric. 1990. *The Very Quiet Cricket*. New York: Philomel.

Crews, Donald. 1993. *Freight Train*. New York: Greenwillow.

Crews, Donald. 1995. *Ten Black Dots*. New York: Greenwillow.

Cuyler, Margery. 2007. *The Biggest, Best Snowman*. New York: Scholastic.

Day, Alexandra. 2010. *Good Dog Carl*. New York: Simon and Schuster.

Doodler, Todd H. 2009. *The Zoo I Drew*. New York: Random House.

Doyle, Charlotte. 2006. Il. Julia Gorton. *The Bouncing, Dancing, Galloping ABC*. New York: G.P. Putnam's Sons.

Ehlert, Lois. 1991. *Growing Vegetable Soup*. New York: Sandpiper (Houghton Mifflin).

Ehlert, Lois. 1994. *Eating the Alphabet*. New York: Harcourt.

Ehlert, Lois. 2008. *Planting a Rainbow*. New York: HMH Books

Emberley, Ed. 2007. *Bye-Bye, Big Bad Bullybug!* New York: LB Kids.

Emberley, Rebecca, & Emberley, Ed. 2009. *Chicken Little*. New York: Roaring Brook Press, A Neal Porter Book.

Falconer, Ian. 2000. *Olivia*. New York: Atheneum/Simon and Schuster.

Fleming, Denise. 2007. *In the Small, Small Pond*. New York: Henry Holt.

Fleming, Denise. 1995. *In the Tall, Tall Grass*. New York: Henry Holt.

Fox, Mem. 1997. Ill. Jane Dyer. *Time for Bed*. New York: Sandpiper (Houghton Mifflin).

Fox, Mem. 2004. Il. Judy Horacek. *Where Is the Green Sheep?* Boston, MA: Houghton Mifflin Harcourt.

Freeman, Don. 2008. *Corduroy* (Anniversary Edition). New York: Viking.

Fujikawa, Gyo. 2008. *Baby Animal Families*. New York: Sterling

Gibbons, Gail. 2007. *The Vegetables We Eat*. New York: Holiday House.

Hall, Zoe. 1999. *Its Pumpkin Time*. New York: Scholastic Paperbacks

Harper, Jessica. 2006. Il. G. Brian Karas *A Place Called Kindergarten*. New York: G. P. Putnam's Sons.

Henkes, Kevin. 2004. *Kitten's First Full Moon*. New York: Greenwillow.

Henkes, Kevin. 1996. *Lily's Purple Plastic Purse*. New York: Greenwillow.

Henkes, Kevin. 2007. *A Good Day*. New York: Greenwillow, An Imprint of HarperCollins Publishers.

Hill, Eric. 1980. *Where's Spot?* New York: Putnam Juvenile.

Hoberman, Mary Ann, & Westcott, Nadine Bernard. 2003. *Miss Mary Mack: A Hand Clapping Rhyme*. New York: Little, Brown, and Company.

Hutchins, Pat. 1994. *The Doorbell Rang*. New York: Greenwillow Books (HarperCollins).

Jay, Alison. 2008. *Welcome to the Zoo*. New York: Dial Books for Young Readers, a Division of Penguin Young Readers Group.

Kerly, Barbara. 2002. *A Cool Drink of Water*. Washington, D.C.: National Geographic Society.

Kingsley, Emily Perl. 1980. Il. Richard Brown. *I Can Do It Myself*. A Sesame Street Golden Press Book published by Western Publishing Company, Inc. in conjunction with Children's Television Workshop.

Krauss, Ruth. 2004. *The Carrot Seed*. New York: HarperCollins.

Lee, Spike, & Lee, Tonya Lewis. 2002. *Please, Baby, Please*. New York: Simon & Schuster Books for Young Readers.

Lee, Suzy. 2008. *Wave*. San Francisco, CA: Chronicle Books.

Lehman, Barbara. 2008. *Trainstop*. Boston, MA: Houghton Mifflin Company.

Lester, Helen. 1988. Il. Lynn Munsinger. *Tacky the Penguin*. Boston, MA: Houghton Mifflin Harcourt.

Lewis, Kevin. 2002. Il. Daniel Kirk. *My Truck Is Stuck*. Hyperion.

Lithgow, John. 2008. Il. Robert Neubecker. *I Got Two Dogs*. New York: Simon & Schuster Books for Young Readers.

London, Jonathan. 2005. Il. Deninse Roche. *Truck Goes Rattley-Bumpa*. New York: Henry Holt.

Lyon, George Ella. 1996 *ABCedar: An Alphabet of Trees*. London UK: Orchard Books.

Maestro, Betsy. 1994. *Why Do Leaves Change Color?* New York: HarperCollins

Manushkin, Fran. 2009. Il. Tracy Dockray. *The Tushy Book*. New York: Feiwel and Friends.

Martin, Bill Jr. 2008. *Big Book of Poetry*. New York: Simon & Schuster Books for Young Readers.

Martin, Bill. 2008. *Brown Bear, Brown Bear, What Do You See?* Il. Eric Carle. New York: Henry Holt and Co.

Martin, Bill. 2006. *Chicka Chicka Boom Boom*. New York: Little, Simon.

Mayo, Margaret. 2002. *Dig Dig Digging*. New York: Henry Holt.

Miranda, Anne. 2001. *To Market To Market*. Il. Janet Stevens. New York: Sandpiper (Houghton Mifflin)

McCloskey, Robert. 1976. *Blueberries for Sal*. New York: Picture Puffins (Puffin Books)

McDonnell, Patrick. 2008. *South*. New York: Little, Brown, and Company.

McNaught, Harry. 1977. *Animal Babies*. New York: Random House.

Morris, Ann. 1993. *Bread, Bread, Bread*. New York: HarperCollins (Around the World Series)

Morris, Ann. 1993. *Hats, Hats, Hats*. New York: HarperCollins. (Around the World Series)

Munari, Bruno. 1960. *Bruno Munari's ABC*. San Francisco, CA: Chronicle Books.

Munsch, Robert L. 1995. *Love You Forever*. Il. Sheila McGraw. New York: Firefly Books.

Nayar, Nandini. 2006, 2009. Il. Prioti Roy. *What Should I Make?* Berkely, CA: Tricycle Press.

Newgarden, Mark, & Cash, Megan Montague. 2009. *Bow-Wow: 12 Months Running*. Boston, MA: Houghton Mifflin Harcourt.

Newgarden, Mark, & Cash, Megan Montague. 2009. *Bow-Wow's Colorful Life.* Boston, MA: Houghton Mifflin Harcourt.

Numeroff, Laura. 1985. *If You Give a Mouse a Cookie.* New York: HarperCollins.

Numeroff, Laura. 1994. *If You Give a Moose a Muffin.* New York: HarperCollins.

Pallotta, Jerry. 1989. *The Flower Alphabet Book.* Watertown, MA: Charlsbridge.

Pearle, Ida. 2008. *A Child's Day: An Alphabet of Play.* New York: Harcourt.

Pinckney, Jerry. 2009. *The Lion and the Mouse.* New York: Little, Brown, and Company.

Portis, Antoinette. 2008. *A Penguin Story.* New York: Harper Collins.

Rand, Ann & Paul. 1956, 2009. *I Know a Lot of Things.* San Francisco, CA: Chronicle Books.

Rey, H.A. 2006. *Curious George Rides a Bike.* New York: HMH Books.

Rockwell, Anne. 2005. *Apples and Pumpkins.* New York: Aladdin (Simon and Schuster)

Rockwell, Anne. 2008. *My Preschool.* New York: Henry Holt and Company.

Rosen, Michael. 2009, Anniversary Edition. Il. Helen Oxenbury. *We're Going on a Bear Hunt.* New York: Margaret K. McElderry

Rosenthal, Amy Krouse, & Lichtenheld, Tom. 2009. *Duck! Rabbit!* San Francisco, CA: Chronicle Books LLC.

Schertle, Alice. 2008. Il. Jill McElmurry. *Little Blue Truck.* Boston, MA: Houghton Mifflin Harcourt.

Schuette, Sarah L. 2003. *An Alphabet Salad: Fruits and Vegetables from A to Z.* Mankato, MN: Capstone Press.

Shannon, David. 1998. *No, David!* New York: Scholastic.

Sill, Cathryn. 1997. *About Birds.* Atlanta: Peachtree Publishers.

Silverstein, Shel. 1964. *The Giving Tree.* New York: Harper and Row.

Singer, Marilyn. 2009. Il. Evan Polenghi. *I'm Your Bus.* New York: Scholastic Press.

Singer, Marilyn. 2009. Il. David Milgrim. *I'm Getting a Checkup.* Boston, MA: Clarion Books, Houghton Mifflin Harcourt.

Thomas, Jan. 2009. *Here Comes the Big, Mean Dust Bunny!* New York: Beach Lane Books.

Tofts, Hannah. 2007. Il. Rupert Horrox. *I Eat Fruit.* Chicago, IL: Zero to Ten.

Waddell, Martin. 1996. Il. Patrick Benson. *Owl Babies.* Somerville, MA: Candlewick

Ward, Cindy. 1997. *Cookie's Week.* New York: Putnam Juvenile.

Wells, Rosemary. 1998. *Yoko.* New York: Hyperion.

Wells, Rosemary. 2008. *Yoko Writes Her Name.* New York: Hyperion.

Wells, Rosemary. 2009. *Yoko's Paper Cranes.* New York: Hyperion.

Wells, Rosemary. 2000. *Noisy Nora.* New York: Viking Juvenile.

Westcott, Nadine Bernard. 1992. *Peanut Butter and Jelly: A Play Rhyme.* New York: Puffin Books

Whitford, Rebecca, & Selway, Martina. *Little Yoga: A Toddler's First Book of Yoga.* New York: Henry Holt and Company.

Willems, Mo. 2004. *Knuffle Bunny.* New York: Scholastic.

Williams, Sue. 1990. *I Went Walking.* New York: Harcourt.

Wise Brown, Margaret. 2005. Ill. Clement Hurd. *Goodnight Moon.* New York: HarperCollins.

Wise Brown, Margaret. 2003. Ill. Garth Williams. *Little Fur Family.* New York: HarperFestival.

Zuckerman, Andrew. 2009. *Creature abc.* San Francisco, CA: Chronicle Books.

APPENDIX
R

Professional References

Barnes, D. & Todd, F. 1977. Communication and Learning in Small Groups. London: Routledge and Kegan Paul.

Barnes, Douglas. 1976. From Communication to Curriculum. Harmondsworth: Penguin Books.

Bell, Donna, and Jarvis, Donna. 2002. Letting Go of "Letter of the Week." *Primary Voices K–6, 11,* 2, October, 2002, 10–24.

Bodrova, Elena, and Leong, Deborah. 1999. *Tools of the Mind: A Vygotskian Approach to Early Childhood Education.* Upper Saddle0 River, NJ: Prentice Hall.

Burns, S. B., Griffin, P. & Snow, C. E., Eds. 1999. *Starting Out Right: A Guide to Promoting Children's Reading Success.* Committee on the Prevention of Reading Difficulties in Young Children, Commission on Behavioral and Social Sciences and Education. Washington, DC: National Academy Press.

Chenfield, Mimi Brodsky. 2002. *Creative Experiences for Young Children.* Portsmouth, NH: Heinemann.

Clay, M. M. 1991. *Becoming Literate: The Construction of Inner Control.* Portsmouth, NH: Heinemann.

Clay, M. M. 1998. *By Different Paths to Common Outcomes.* Portland, ME: Stenhouse Publishers.

Clay, M. M. 2001. *Change Over Time in Children's Literacy Development.* Portsmouth, NH: Heinemann.

Clay, M. M. 2005. *The Observation Survey of Early Literacy Achievement.* Chicago, IL: Heinemann Library.

Clay, M. M. 1975. *What Did I Write?* Portsmouth, NH: Heinemann.

Dooley, C. M., & Matthews, M. 2009. Emergent Comprehension: Understanding Comprehension Development Among Young Literacy Learners. *Journal of Early Childhood Literacy,* 9; 269. DOI: 10.1177/146879840935110. http://ecl.sagepub.com/cgi/contentabsgtract/9/3/269 Published by SAGE http://www.sagepublications.com

Fisher, B. 1996. Moving Beyond "Letter of the Week." *Teaching Pre K–8.* Jan.

Fountas, I. C., & Pinnell, G. S. 1996 *Guided Reading: Good First Teaching for All Students.* Portsmouth, NH: Heinemann.

Fountas, I. C., & Pinnell, G. S. 2007. *Benchmark Assessment System 1: Grades K–2, Levels A–N.* Portsmouth, NH: Heinemann. [Optional Assessments for Alphabet Knowledge and Phonemic Awareness.]

Glover, Matt. 2009. *Engaging Young Writers.* Portsmouth, NH: Heinemann.

Hart, B., & Risley. T 1995. *Meaningful Differences in the Everyday Experience of Young American Children.* Baltimore: Brookes.

Horn, M., & Giacobbe, M. E. 2007. *Talking, Drawing, Writing: Lessons for Our Youngest Writers.* Portland, ME: Stenhouse.

Kaye, E. L. 2008. "Second Graders' Reading Behaviors: A Study of Variety, Complexity, and Change." *Literacy Teaching and Learning* 10 (2): 51–75.

Kempton, Susan L. 2007. *The Literacy Kindergarten: Where Wonder and Discovery Thrive.* Portsmouth, NH: Heinemann.

Kirk, E.W., & Clark, P. 2005. Beginning with Names: Using Children's Names to Facilitate Early Literacy Learning. *Childhood Education,* Spring, 2005. http://finarticles.com/p/articles 10/1 2009

Kirkland, L., Aldreidge, J., & Kuby, P. 2007. *Integrating Environmental Print, Across the Curriculum, PreK–3: Making Literacy Instruction Meaningful.* Thousand Oaks, CA: Corwin Press.

Knoff, Howard. 2001. "The Stop and Think Social Skills Program." Longmont, CO: Sopris West.

Lindfors, J. W. 1999. *Children's Inquiry: Using Language to Make Sense of the World (Language and Literacy Series, Teachers College Press).* New York: Teachers College Press.

McCarrier, A., I. C. Fountas, and Pinnell, G. S. 1999. *Interactive Writing: How Language and Literacy Come Together.* Portsmouth, NH: Heinemann.

McGee, Lea M. 2007. *Transforming Literacy Practices in Prekindergarten: Research-Based Practices That Give All Children the Opportunity to Reach Their Potential as Learners.* New York: Scholastic.

Mercer, Neil. 2008. Talk and the Development of Reasoning and Understanding. *Human Development,* 2008: 51:90–100. DOI: 10.1159/000113158.

Miller, Edward, & Almon, Joan. March, 2009. *Crisis in the Kindergarten: Why Children Need to Play in School.* Summary and Recommendations, A Report from the Alliance for Childhood.

National Association for the Education of Young Children. 1998. Learning to Read and Write: Developmentally Appropriate Practices for Young Children: *A joint position statement of the* International Reading Association *and the* National Association for the Education of Young Children. In *Young Children,* July 1998, 53 (4): 30–46.

Neuman, Susan B, and Dwyer, J. 2009. Missing in Action: Vocabulary Instruction in Pre-K. *The Reading Teacher,* 62(5), 384–392. DOI:10.1598/RT.62.5.2.

Owocki, Gretchen. 2007. *Literate Days: Reading and Writing with Prekindergarten and Primary Children: Teacher's Guide.* Portsmouth, NH: Heinemann Firsthand.

Paley, Vivian Gussin. 1987. *Wally's Stories.* Cambridge, MA: Harvard University Press.

Pink, Daniel. 2006. *A Whole New Mind.* New York: Riverhead Books.

Pinnell, G. S., & Fountas, I. C. 2008. *Leveled Literacy Intervention.* Portsmouth, NH: Heinemann.

Pinnell, G. S., & Fountas, I. C. 2006. *Phonics Lessons with CD-ROM, Grades K, 1, and 2.* Portsmouth, NH: Heinemann

Pinnell, G. S., & Fountas, I. C. 2006. *Word Study Lessons.* Portsmouth, NH: Heinemann.

Pinnell, G. S., & Fountas, I. C. 2004. *Sing a Song of Poetry, K: A Teaching Resource for Phonics, Word Study, and Fluency.* Portsmouth, NH: Heinemann.

Ray, Katie Wood, and Glover, Matt. 2008. *Already Ready: Nurturing Writers in Prekindergarten and Kindergarten.* Portsmouth, NH: Heinemann.

Reninger, Kristen Bourdage, and Wilkinson, Ian A.G. 2010. "Using Discussions to Promote Striving Readers' High-level Comprehension of Literary Texts." *Building Struggling Students' Higher Level Literacy.* Interventional Reading Association.

Resnick, Lauren B., & Snow, Catherine E. 2009. *Speaking and Listening for Preschool Through Third Grade.* Revised Edition. University of Pittsburgh and The National Center on Education and the Economy. Published under license. The New Standards® trademark is owned by the University of Pittsburgh and The National Center on Education and the Economy at 555 13th Street NW, Suite 500 West, Washington, D.C. 20004, USA.

Scarborough, H. 1998. Early Identification of Children at Risk for Reading Disabilities: Phonological Awareness and Some Other Promising Predictors. In B., Shapiro, P. Accerdo, & A. Capute (Eds.). *Specific Reading Disability: A View of the Spectrum* (pp. 75–119). Timonium, MD: York Press.

Sénéchal, M., Ouellette, G., & Rodney, D. 2006. The Misunderstood Giant: On the Predictive Role of Early Vocabulary to Future Reading. In D. Dickinson & S.B. Neuman (Eds.), *Handbook of Early Literacy Research* (Vol. 2, pp. 173–182). New York: Guilford.

Vygotsky, L.S. 1978. *Mind in Society: The Development of Higher Psychological Processes.* Cambridge, MA: Harvard University Press.

Vygotsky, L.S. 1986. *Thought and Language.* Cambridge, MA: MIT Press.

Weir, Ruth. 1962. *Language in the Crib.* Palo Alto, CA: Stanford University.

Wells, G. 1999. Dialogic Inquiry: Toward a Sociocultural Practice and Theory of Education. Cambridge: Cambridge University Press.

Wertsch, J.V. 1979. From Social Interaction to Higher Psychological Processes: A Clarification and Application of Vygotsky's Theory. *Human Development, 22,* 1–22.

Wilkinson, Ian A.G., Soter, Anna O., and Murphy, P. Karen. 2010. Developing a Model of Quality Talk about Literary Text. In M.G. McKeown and L. Kucan (Eds.), *Bringing Reading Researchers to Life: Essays in Honor of Isabel l. Beck.* New York: Guilford Press.

INDEX